Excerpts taken from:

Health Skills for Wellness, Third Edition
by B.E. (Buzz) Pruitt, Ed.D, Kathy Teer Crumpler, M.P.H., and Deborah Prothrow-Smith, M.D.
Copyright © 2001 by Prentice Hall, Inc.
A Pearson Education Company
Upper Saddle River, New Jersey 07458

The Career Fitness Program: Exercising Your Options, Sixth Edition
by Diane Sukiennik, William Bendat, and Lisa Raufman
Copyright © 2001, 1998, 1995, 1992, 1989, 1986 by Prentice Hall, Inc.

World Geography: Building a Global Perspective
by Thomas J. Baerwald and Celeste Fraser
Copyright © 2002 by Prentice Hall, Inc.

**Pearson
Custom Publishing**
is a division of

PEARSON

www.pearsonhighered.com

ISBN 10: 0-536-48245-4
ISBN 13: 978-0-536-48245-7

D1266453

INTRODUCTION TO THE
NAVY
JUNIOR RESERVE OFFICER TRAINING CORPS

Excerpts taken from:

Health Skills for Wellness, Third Edition
by B.E. (Buzz) Pruitt, Kathy Teer Crumpler, and Deborah Prothrow-Smith

The Career Fitness Program: Exercising Your Options, Sixth Edition
by Diane Sukiennik, William Bendat, and Lisa Raufman

World Geography: Building a Global Perspective
by Thomas J. Baerwald and Celeste Fraser

Custom Publishing

New York   Boston   San Francisco
London   Toronto   Sydney   Tokyo   Singapore   Madrid
Mexico City   Munich   Paris   Cape Town   Hong Kong   Montreal

To

The Cadets, Instructors, and Staff
of the
Navy Junior ROTC
Past, Present, and Future—
Those Who
Learn to Lead
Choose to Succeed

Contents

Unit III   Citizenship and American Government   101

Contents

NJROTC
and Your Future

Chapter 1

Introduction to the Navy Junior Reserve Officers Training Corps Program

- **certified**
- **color guard**
- **marksmanship**
- **instill**
- **orderliness**
- **precision**
- **honor**
- **courage**
- **commitment**
- **apathy**
- **ignorance**
- **curriculum**
- **maritime**
- **buoyancy**
- **seamanship**
- **protocol**
- **meticulous**

What You Will Learn to Do

This chapter will introduce you to the Navy Junior Reserve Officers Training Corps—its background, mission, curriculum, and activities, as well as its benefits to cadets.

Skills and Knowledge You Will Gain Along the Way

✔ Explain the history and background of the NJROTC

✔ Describe the NJROTC's mission, goals, and policies

✔ Describe the Navy Core Values

✔ Describe the Naval Science curriculum

✔ Describe NJROTC unit activities

✔ Explain the NJROTC program's benefits

History and Background of the NJROTC Program

Congratulations! You have chosen to take part in one of the most diverse and interesting programs a high school student can participate in, joining more than half a million other students across the United States. The Junior Reserve Officer Training Corps, or JROTC, program currently enrolls students in more than 3,000 programs ranging from Alaska, Hawaii, and the continental United States to Japan, Italy, and Spain.

The JROTC program was the brainchild of Army inspector Lt Edgar R. Stevens, who in 1911 began teaching high school students the values and discipline of a military life in the hopes of molding these students into better citizens. From this idea came the formation of the JROTC program with the signing of the National Defense Act of 1916 and the establishment of the first JROTC at Leavenworth High School in Kansas in 1917.

After World Wars I and II, the JROTC program saw little to no growth because of limited funding and personnel. This lack of growth prompted Congress to pass the JROTC Vitalization Act of 1964, which allowed the other service branches to offer JROTC as well. The first Navy Junior Reserve Officers Training Corps (NJROTC) programs began in 1966. Today there are 620 NJROTC programs.

The JROTC Vitalization Act charges the Secretary of the Navy with the maintenance and continued support of the NJROTC program. To this end, the Naval Service Training Command (NSTC), was established in Great Lakes, Illinois, to manage funding as well as the personnel and materials the NJROTC programs use. The program's office is in Pensacola, Florida. Directly beneath NSTC are area managers, who control the NJRTOC's areas of operation and are responsible for maintaining the integrity of the programs in their areas through annual inspections. Beneath the area managers are program managers, or NJROTC instructors.

Students like you participate in more than 620 NJROTC programs in the United States, Italy, Japan, and Spain.

Key Terms

certified—
officially approved

color guard—
the ceremonial escort for the flag

marksmanship—
skill in shooting at a target

Key Term

instill—
to introduce by gradual persistent efforts

Meeting here in the US Capitol, Congress created the NJROTC program to instill in students the values of citizenship and service to the country.
Courtesy of Eyewire/Getty Images

NJROTC instructors must be certified by the Navy. They are retired Navy, Marine Corps, and Coast Guard officers and enlisted personnel. Senior Naval Science Instructors (SNSI) are retired officers in charge of the individual programs, while Naval Science Instructors (NSI) are retired officers or senior petty officers who assist the SNSIs. The Naval Service Training Command certifies instructors on the basis of their active-duty records in positions of responsibility, meaning that most instructors have extensive experience in leadership and management positions. Some instructors also have experience as teachers and counselors.

The Navy provides textbooks, computers, audio-visual equipment, and other materials for the Naval Science classroom, as well as uniforms for students to wear while they are in the program. Each unit also receives equipment for extracurricular activities like color guard, drill team, and marksmanship, as well as funding for orientation trips to military bases and other sites of importance to unit members.

The NJROTC program is a joint effort of the US Navy and local school systems to enhance the education of students who join. But the instructors work for the principals of their schools, just as any other teacher does. Local educators are responsible for administering the NJROTC program at their schools and for assisting the program as needed.

The NJROTC's Mission, Goals, and Policies

The JROTC program's mission is stated in the National Defense Act of 1916: The purpose of JROTC is "to instill in students the value of citizenship, service to the United States, personal responsibility, and a sense of accomplishment."

To this end, the NSTC has established specific goals for the NJROTC program. These goals are as follows:

- **Promote patriotism.** This means love of country, respect for the flag, and pride in the government and the American way of life.
- **Develop informed and responsible citizens.** NJROTC should make students aware of their responsibilities, duties, and rights.
- **Promote habits of orderliness and precision.** Experience shows that such habits help people succeed in life.
- **Develop a high degree of personal honor, self-reliance, self-discipline, and leadership.** These qualities are embodied by the Navy's Core Values of Honor, Courage, and Commitment.
- **Promote an understanding of the basic elements and requirements for national security.** Students should understand the need for armed forces and their relationship to a democratic government.
- **Develop respect for and an understanding of the need for constituted authority in a democratic society.** Students should understand why we have laws and governments.
- **Provide incentives to live healthy and drug-free lives.** Students should know how drug use and other harmful actions affect both themselves and others.
- **Develop leadership potential.** The NJROTC program provides students with a wide range of opportunities to test themselves in leadership roles such as leading a drill team and performing a staff job.
- **Promote high school completion.** Students should know the value of their education.
- **Provide information on the military services as a possible career.**

A Focus on You

The focus of the NJROTC program is on *you*. The opportunities provided by the instructors, the school, the area manager, the NSTC, the Secretary of the Navy, and the Congress itself are designed to assist you in improving yourself and your fellow cadets. These opportunities are provided in the hope that you will learn through the NJROTC program the Core Values of honor, courage, and commitment, as well as qualities such as self-discipline, cooperation, and teamwork. Mastering the military skills that your instructors will teach you will give you confidence in yourself and those around you, as well as the pride of a job well done. Moreover, your actions through community service will allow you to play a role in the development and betterment of your community and to discover what it really means to be a citizen.

Another advantage of the NJROTC program is the opportunity to lead and to teach your fellow cadets what you have learned during your time in the program. Many cadet graduates of these programs say these opportunities were the most lasting benefit of NJROTC. They say that these opportunities provided them with connections and friendships that lasted long after they graduated from high school.

Key Terms

orderliness—
neatness; freedom from disorder

precision—
exactness

The focus of the NJROTC program is on you, the cadet.

NJROTC, however, is still a military-sponsored program and as such has requirements for your continued participation. These requirements mean that a cadet must:

- Be enrolled as a regular student in Grades 9 through 12 at the school hosting the unit
- Be a citizen or legal permanent resident of the United States
- Be sufficiently fit to participate in the school's physical education program
- Be selected by the NJROTC instructor with the approval of the school principal
- Have acceptable grades in school
- Maintain acceptable standards of conduct
- Meet NJROTC personal-grooming standards.

NJROTC is responsible for maintaining its standards of enrollment. Unfortunately, some individuals cannot meet these standards. When a cadet chooses to leave the program or fails to live up to its standards, he or she is *disenrolled*. Standards for disenrollment include the following:

- Failure to maintain academic standards
- Poor behavior or lack of aptitude
- Leaving school (dropping out or moving)
- Cadet's own request
- Physical conditions, such as injury or inability to meet fitness standards.

Navy Core Values

A goal of the NJROTC program is to teach and instill the value of citizenship. Through the Core Values of the Navy—honor, courage, and commitment—you will learn to become a better citizen, regardless of whether you chose to continue on into the Navy or another of the armed forces.

Values are your most deeply held ideals, beliefs, or principles. You learn values all your life, often without realizing it, from

- family
- faith community or spiritual tradition
- school
- friends
- community
- country.

These values affect your thoughts, feelings, and behavior. They are the basis on which you make many of the difficult decisions that you face throughout your life. People who have compromised or lost touch with their values may engage in lawless or unethical behavior, which can lead to unfortunate consequences. The Navy's Core Values are heavily emphasized during your involvement with the NJROTC program, in the hopes that you will learn from them and avoid the traps that apathy or ignorance can create.

Key Terms

honor—
a keen sense of ethical conduct

courage—
mental or moral strength to venture, persevere, and withstand danger, fear, or difficulty

commitment—
a state of being bound, emotionally or intellectually, to a course of action, or to a person or persons

apathy—
a lack of feeling or emotion; a lack of interest or concern

ignorance—
lack of knowledge, education, or awareness

Definition of Navy Core Values

As a member of the NJROTC program, you have chosen to dedicate yourself to the Core Values of honor, courage, and commitment. These build a foundation of trust and leadership upon which your NJROTC unit is based. These values are the principles that will give you strength and guide you in your daily activities throughout your stay in the program. Your duty as a cadet is to be faithful to these Core Values and to exemplify their true worth through your words and actions:

- *Honor*—I am accountable for my professional and personal behavior. I will be mindful of the privilege I have to serve my fellow Americans.
- *Courage*—Courage is the value that gives me the moral and mental strength to do what is right, with confidence and resolution, even in the face of temptation or adversity.
- *Commitment*—the day-to-day duty of every man and woman in the NJROTC program is to join together as a team to improve the quality of their unit, their fellow cadets and classmates, and themselves.

Behaviors That Detract From Navy Core Values

Four patterns of behavior detract from the Navy Core Values: *hazing, discrimination, sexual harassment*, and *fraternization*.

Hazing is any conduct that causes another person to suffer to be exposed to an activity that is:

- cruel
- abusive
- humiliating
- oppressive
- demeaning
- harmful.

Many people think of hazing as only something college fraternities do, but it can take place in any kind of organization, including NJROTC. Hazing can be especially damaging to people in high school. In their vulnerable teenage years, young people long for friendship, approval, and acceptance. This leaves them open to peer pressure, which can lead them to do foolish or even dangerous things they would otherwise avoid.

Discrimination is any act that denies equal treatment to individuals because of their race, gender, ethnicity, religion, or other differences.

Sexual harassment is a particular form of gender discrimination. It involves unwanted sexual advances, direct or indirect requests for sexual favors, verbal or physical conduct of a sexual nature, or the creation of an atmosphere of fear and distrust. For instance, if you hang a suggestive photo in your locker, that may be a form of sexual harassment because it may cause someone else who sees it discomfort or embarrassment. You'll read more about discrimination and sexual harassment in Unit II, Chapter 4.

Fraternization is an inappropriate relationship between a superior and a subordinate—between a boss and an employee, or a teacher and a student, for instance—that could result in favoritism or discipline problems on the job. The rules on this are not as strict in NJROTC as in the Navy itself. Nevertheless, cadet officers should avoid dating their subordinates. In fact, they should avoid any friendships that could create, or even be perceived as, unfair or favoritism.

These four behaviors—hazing, discrimination, sexual harassment, and fraternization—violate the Navy Core Values. Sticking to the Core Values will help you avoid these four behaviors. If you value your sense of honor, you won't want to haze or harass anyone. If you have the courage to resist peer pressure, you will be able to avoid misbehavior and even talk others out of it. If you are committed to respect for other people, these behaviors will simply lose their appeal.

Practicing the Navy Core Values

Mastering the Core Values is not a matter of instinct. It is something that you must learn through conscious effort. After time, you will act instinctively on these values. The acronym *LATAR* is one tool that can help you master the Core Values:

- **L**earn
- **A**dopt
- **T**hink
- **A**ct
- **R**eevaluate.

Learn: Know the Core Values and how they contribute to the Navy's readiness.

Adopt: Adopt the values as your own and live them 24/7—at home, at school, everywhere.

Think: Recognize when Core Values are being compromised. Speak up if someone makes inappropriate or wrong comments, for instance. The more you live by the Core Values, the more people will notice it. These values, lived, will give you credibility and influence with others. Both you and those you work with will be more effective.

Act: Do the right thing. Apply the Core Values in your dealings with peers and leaders. Report illegal activities if necessary.

Reevaluate: Think about how well your life matches up with the Core Values. Are you falling short? If so, how can you improve?

When You Get Into a Gray Area

Like a ship that's not securely anchored, you may sometimes find yourself drifting into a moral or ethical gray area. The Core Values can help you navigate around these. Have the courage to examine whether your behavior is honorable. If not, commit to changing your behavior. If your fellow cadets act in a questionable way, have the courage to tell them. This will make it easier to avoid further confrontation.

"When I Think of Commitment . . . ."

Adm James Stockdale
Courtesy of the Associated Press

ARE YOU COMMITTED to making your piece of the world a better place? Are you committed to your family, your classmates, your church, your country? . . . You must be committed to doing the right thing, no matter what the consequence. . . . .

When I think of commitment . . . I think of Adm Arleigh Burke, one of the great Naval heroes in World War II and our longest-serving CNO. One of the most remarkable men of this century. Admiral Burke and his dear wife were committed to each other for 72 years, and they were committed to the Navy for 72 years. When President Eisenhower asked Admiral Burke to serve an unprecedented third term as CNO, he said, "It is your duty." And Admiral Burke rogered the call and stood for another term as the CNO. That's commitment.

When I think about commitment, I think, too, about Senator John McCain, a 1958 graduate of this great institution (the United States Naval Academy). I think about the years he spent as a prisoner of war in North Vietnam, never losing faith in his country, never losing faith in himself. His commitment to his country was unwavering and continues to this day in everything he does, particularly on the floor of the Senate. That is commitment. . . .

If you want to learn about a sense of commitment to God, country, and family that is a model for all of us young and old, you need to read *In Love and War* by Admiral and Mrs. James Stockdale. Admiral Stockdale spent seven years as a prisoner in North Vietnam. His inspiring leadership and indomitable spirit resulted in him receiving the Congressional Medal of Honor.

Commitment is the active ingredient in the word *shipmate*. It's the driving force behind acts of great physical and moral courage. If you are committed to doing right, to honoring your country, your family, and yourself, then you cannot go wrong, and you will make a difference. Commitment—it's something to think about. It's something to put into your own personal kit, and it's very important as you go forward in the Navy.

> —Admiral Jay L. Johnson, Chief of Naval Operations
> Remarks at the US Naval Academy, 31 July 1997

Table 1.1	THE NAVAL SCIENCE CURRICULUM	
Year One	Cadet Field Manual	• Military Drill • Uniforms • Military Customs and Courtesies
	Introduction to the NJROTC Course	• History of JROTC • Citizenship • Laws–Authority–Responsibility
Year Two	Maritime History	• War at Sea • US Navy • Strategy and Tactics
	Nautical Sciences	• Maritime Geography • Oceanography–Meteorology–Astronomy
	Introduction to Leadership	
Year Three	Naval Knowledge	• Sea Power • National Security • Laws of the Sea
	Naval Skills	• Shipboard Life • Rules of the Road • Navigation
Year Four	Leadership Theory	• Ethics and Morals • Case Studies
	Leadership Laboratory	• Positions of Authority • Responsibility for Others

The Naval Science Curriculum

In addition to your studies into the Navy's Core Values, your studies in Naval Science will cover eight other major areas over the next four years.

This curriculum emphasizes two different areas each year and is customized by your school to meet your needs and the needs of your classmates. In general, the program is meant to provide a balance of classroom studies, military activities, physical fitness, and orientation trips.

Team Activities

Most NJROTC units have teams that compete against other units in military drill, marksmanship, color guard performance, and academics.

The *Cadet Field Manual* is your guide to success as an NJROTC cadet. It will show you how to wear and care for a uniform and will explain uniform rates, ranks, and ribbons. The manual also explains military standards of personal appearance. The manual will tell you what you need to know about military customs and courtesies. This includes saluting and proper behavior while in uniform.

Key Term

curriculum—
a course of study

When you master these standards, you will be able not only to take part in unit activities with pride and confidence but also to assist your fellow cadets in their own mastery and understanding of these important codes of conduct.

Introduction to the NJROTC Program

This course will explain the background, purpose, goals, and objectives of the program. It will also help you build important study and time-management skills. These skills will help you in all aspects of your school and professional life, not just in your NJROTC studies. Furthermore, these traits will provide you with the tools required to succeed as a member of your community and as a citizen of the United States.

Part of learning how to be a cadet in the NJROTC program is learning how to act as a responsible citizen. You'll learn how other forms of government around the world over the past century compare with our own. You'll study the Declaration of Independence and the US Constitution, the founding documents of our republic, and explore how these documents affect your life, the lives of your classmates, and people across the planet.

Your instructors will explain the role of the armed forces in a democracy, tell you about how these forces are organized, and describe the role of the Defense Department.

You'll receive an introduction to the Navy's ships, aircraft, and weapon systems. You'll also learn something of the basic principles and theories of leadership and followership. This learning will help you prepare for more responsibility in your unit.

Maritime History

Navies have been an important part of life for thousands of years as seafaring peoples have sought to trade with or even conquer their neighbors and to explore more of the world. Your instructors will introduce you to maritime history—the history of ships and navies—with emphasis on the role of the US Navy.

A FIELD MANUAL
FOR THE
NAVAL JUNIOR RESERVE
OFFICERS TRAINING CORPS
(NJROTC)

CADET FIELD MANUAL
(6th Edition)
NAVEDTRA 37116-F

AUGUST 2005
0509-LP-103-1173

The Cadet Field Manual

Key Term

maritime—
relating to the sea

In NJROTC, you'll learn about maritime history and famous battles like the fight between the USS Monitor *and the Confederate ship* CSS Virginia *(the* Merrimack*).*
Courtesy of Bettmann/Corbis

Nautical Sciences

Part of understanding the Navy is learning the sciences that go into the operation of ships and aircraft, including sciences that apply to navigation, keeping the ships afloat, and keeping the planes and helicopters in the sky. Several different fields of study make up the nautical sciences.

Maritime geography includes the study of the world's oceans and seas. These waters cover three-fourths of the Earth's surface and have long been important for transportation, commerce, and trade.

Oceanography is the study of what happens in, on, and under the world's oceans. This is especially important to the United States, which has 10,000 miles of coastline. Oceanography also includes the study of natural resources such as the oceans' food and minerals.

Meteorology, the science of weather, is part of the nautical sciences, too. Any boat or ship set to launch needs reliable weather information to stay out of danger. In naval warfare, weather has often helped decide key battles.

Astronomy, the study of the sun, moon, planets, and stars, is also important to seafarers.

Finally, the nautical sciences include the study of *physics*—the physics of flight, the basics of electricity, the principles of buoyancy, and an introduction to electro-magnetic waves. All these principles come into play during the daily operation of a Navy ship or aircraft.

Naval Knowledge

You will learn about the concept of *sea power* as presented by Alfred Thayer Mahan (1840–1914), an influential naval historian who believed that sea power was the key to success in international politics.

In his view, the ability of a coastal nation, like the United States, to use the oceans for trade, commerce, science, industry, and national defense would largely determine that nation's role in the world.

Your studies in Naval Knowledge will consider the history of United States strategy from our country's beginnings to the modern era and how the three classic schools of strategy—sea power, air power, and land power—affect a modern-day engagement.

Your instructors will explain the national security planning process. You'll learn about how our government looks at current threats to national security and takes steps to counter them with some of the most advanced surveillance methods on the planet.

Coupled with the national security unit, you'll learn more about the responsibilities of the Merchant Marine and the Coast Guard in the maritime defense of the United States. Your instructors will explain the role of naval operations, communications, intelligence, logistics, and research and development.

To wrap up your unit on Naval Knowledge, your instructors will explain the differences between military and civilian law and how the Uniform Code of Military Justice, or UCMJ, is rooted in the Constitution. From this you'll be better able to learn about the sources and principles of international law, and why international law is important to those who go to sea.

Key Term

buoyancy—
a tendency or ability to stay afloat in water

Alfred Thayer Mahan, a naval historian, believed that sea power was the key to success in international politics.

Courtesy of the Library of Congress

Aviation Boatswain's Mate 2nd Class Joseph Dollison, left, demonstrates to NJROTC cadets from Everett (Washington) High School how to properly handle a fire hose.
Courtesy of the US Navy/Photographer's Mate 2nd Class Casey R. Jones

Naval Skills

This is where you will learn about the ins and outs of life aboard ship. You'll study shipboard organization and the roles of the commanding officer, the executive officer, and other members of the command structure. You'll also learn about standing watch and such basics of shipboard life as meals and sleeping quarters.

Naval skills include a wide variety of skill sets unique to the naval environment that fall under the definition of seamanship. This term covers handling lines, preparing to get a ship underway, preparing to anchor, handling small boats, and many other skills specialized to life on a ship. Ship driving, for instance, involves knowing the sea "rules of the road," which act in much the same way as traffic laws on a highway and are required knowledge for anyone in command of a ship. Your Naval Skills classes will provide you with both International and Island rules, which cover proper signaling (with lights and other means) as well as guidelines for avoiding other vessels.

Understanding the 24-hour clock used by all the armed forces is covered by Naval Skills, as is learning about Greenwich Mean Time (GMT). All the Navy's schedules, operational plans, and navigational aids run on GMT. This means you'll be better able to relate navigation and time, and have the opportunity to get practical experience in navigation and maneuvering.

Your classes in Naval Skills will also introduce shipbuilding. This will answer such questions as: What factors does the Navy think about when building a ship? What propulsion systems have been used and are used today? What sort of weapons systems does a Navy warship carry? This discussion will include all the various guns, missiles, bombs, rockets, and aircraft currently in use by the US Navy.

Key Term

seamanship—
skill in sailing, navigating, or managing a boat or ship

Leadership Theory

In this course instructors will present basic principles of leadership, stressing the importance of leading by example and the role of ethics and morals in leadership. Classes will draw heavily on case studies of actual situations to help students understand the role of the leader in making decisions.

Leadership Laboratory

This is where senior cadets have the opportunity to serve in positions of authority. They are expected to plan, influence, and direct unit members' efforts in accomplishing a mission. Many cadets consider these experiences the most exciting part of their NJROTC careers. They will allow you to evaluate and practice the leadership skills developed in class.

NJROTC Unit Activities

During the school year, your NJROTC unit will sponsor a number of activities to reinforce your new skills and knowledge. You'll have opportunities to practice what you've learned, sometimes in competition with other JROTC units.

Team Activities

Along with your fellow cadets, you'll learn the basics of military drill, from simple in-place movements to the manual of arms (drill with a rifle). Most units also offer students the opportunity to participate in after-school drill activities like drill team and color guard. These teams will help develop your skills in military drill as well as provide a chance to join some of your fellow cadets in testing your skills against those of other JROTC units in drill competitions

Teams are formed for competitions involving drill with or without arms, and in basic or exhibition drill. Exhibition drill is a more rigorous form of military drill whereby members perform complex maneuvers such as drill without verbal commands or the spinning and throwing of rifles. Team members can participate in individual drill competitions as well as color guard competitions. The role of a color guard team is more ceremonial than that of a drill team. The members represent the national colors and their services at events like football games or patriotic events by carrying our nation's flag. Together drill teams and color guards represent their units both in competition and in the community, participating in school and community events as examples of our nation's youth.

In addition to drill, many units offer voluntary classes in range safety and marksmanship training, using precision air rifles. Cadets who excel in marksmanship often form teams to compete with nearby units, sometimes combining drill and marksmanship competitions into a single event.

Unlike drill teams, marksmanship teams sometimes compete remotely. Such a competition is called a *postal match*. Each school team shoots, or completes its course of fire, at its own range and sends the targets to the competition sponsors for scoring. This makes it possible to hold national rifle competitions without spending time and money to travel to a central competition site.

In addition to these competitions, the Secretary of the Navy sponsors an annual national rifle competition for all NJROTC units.

Along with your fellow cadets, you'll learn the basics of military drill.

The Naval Service Training Command sponsors another kind of annual national contest as well an *academic team competition*. Each unit taking part fields a team composed of one to five cadets, all of whom take the same test locally on the same day. The NSTC then scores the results and declares the winners. These competitions can be combined with drill and rifle team meets to form a single grand event.

Another team opportunity provided to cadets is *orienteering*, which challenges cadets to use their land-navigation skills to go on a kind of large-scale treasure hunt. Those taking part must navigate cross-country over unfamiliar territory with a map and compass to locate control markers within a set amount of time. These competitions require speed, accuracy, good decision-making, and teamwork. The objective is to find as many markers as possible in the shortest time.

Orienteering events can be held by individual units, by groups of neighboring units, or on a regional or national basis.

Physical Fitness

NJROTC encourages students to be physically fit. All students take the NJROTC physical fitness exam. Those who pass are awarded the NJROTC physical fitness ribbon. Some receive a special ribbon in recognition of exceptional performance.

Throughout the year NJROTC units compete against one another in physical contests. These include individual activities—running, jumping, climbing, and running obstacle courses—as well as team games such as volleyball, basketball, softball, and tug of war.

Social Activities

Most NJROTC units have parties, picnics, and other social gatherings where cadets can hang up the garrison cap and enjoy the company of their fellow cadets. Some events are more formal than others, but no less enjoyable. Units may sponsor dining-ins, dining-outs, military balls, or honors and award ceremonies. The difference between the two kinds of dinner parties is that dining-ins are for unit members only, and a dining-out may include parents, friends, and other non-NJROTC participants.

Dining-outs may be combined with award ceremonies where unit members receive ribbons, medals, and other awards at military formations in recognition of their contributions to their units and their communities.

A military ball is a formal dinner dance sometimes shared by multiple JROTC programs. Certain rules, procedures, and protocols govern an event such as a ball; for instance, the senior officer can set a dress code.

The *receiving line* is part of a formal event during which a line of people forms to greet arriving guests individually, as at a formal gathering. Each cadet introduces his or her date to each person in the line. Members of the receiving line are usually instructors, the units' senior officers, and the official guest of honor.

For honors and award ceremonies, the entire unit assembles in formation, and individual members receive ribbons, promotions, and advancements. At some ceremonies, community organizations may present awards to cadets in honor of their contributions to that specific organization or to the community at large.

Community Activities

NJROTC cadets can take part in a wide variety of community service work as part of their citizenship training. These events often provide the community with a much-needed service as well as an extremely rewarding experience for the cadets.

Key Term

protocol—
a special form of ceremony and etiquette

NJROTC cadets engage in community service activities, such as these cadets helping clean up a beach.
Courtesy of Jeff Greenberg/ PhotoEdit

Orientation Trips

Orientation trips are one of the most important types of unit activities. Many units offer one or more of these, either during the school year or during school vacations. These trips, to military bases, ships, or air stations, bring to life the material cadets have been studying.

Each unit chooses who gets to go on orientation trips. Not all members will take part in each one.

These trips can be unforgettable experiences. Often cadets take part in Navy training programs such as damage-control exercises, dry net climbing, rappelling, obstacle courses, water survival, and flight simulations. Some orientation trips include time training and living aboard a Navy ship. Such events let cadets experience firsthand what a Navy career really offers. Other orientation trips include an experience of basic military training such as Marine Corps boot camp or Navy recruit training. All these activities provide yet another opportunity for students to build and practice leadership skills as well as to meet members our Navy's fighting force.

Leadership Experience

No other school activity offers as many practical leadership opportunities as the NJROTC program. From the first time you serve as a squad leader in your unit until your senior experience as a unit officer, you'll be challenged to lead and direct the efforts of others and to learn to accept responsibility for their successes and failures.

Leadership Academy

Some cadets get the opportunity for advanced training at NJROTC leadership academies. These academies are intended to help prepare these cadets for unit leadership roles.

Leadership Academy has four objectives:

1. To promote habits of orderliness and precision and to develop respect for constituted authority.
2. To challenge and motivate cadets to push toward and expand their physical and intellectual limits. Cadets will continually be called upon to meet high standards standards of personal appearance, self-discipline, and meticulous attention to detail.
3. To instill a high degree of personal honor, self-reliance, and confidence in each cadet by presenting a military environment in which cadets will be forced to rely upon themselves and their shipmates to study, work, and learn.
4. To enhance the basic attitude, knowledge, and skills required to practice the art of leadership.

Successful completion of Leadership Academy includes passing a physical fitness test and a series of practical leadership activities. These usually include:

> **Key Term**
>
> **meticulous—**
> *extremely careful and precise, especially with regard to detail*

- Leadership Characteristics for the Cadet Officer
- Physical Fitness and the Leader
- Field Leadership (Orienteering)
- Obstacle Course
- Commanding Troops
- Inspecting Troops
- Manual of the Sword
- Social Etiquette and Manners
- Sail Training.

Leadership Academy offers cadets the opportunity to improve their leadership skills and interact with other promising cadet leaders from units across the nation.

The NJROTC Program's Benefits

"What's in it for me? Why should I stay enrolled in NJROTC?" These are questions high school counselors hear all the time.

You may be used to thinking of your high school courses mainly as preparation for more high school courses. Algebra I prepares you for Algebra II, for instance. But much of the NJROTC course work will prepare you for life after high school—whether you go on to higher education or directly into the workforce. Your classes will help you develop the maturity and responsibility required for success and will be invaluable to you, regardless of the career path you take.

Discipline

Many people misunderstand the word *discipline*, associating it with harshness, unfairness, or undue severity.

The NJROTC program has another view of discipline. This view agrees with Webster's New Collegiate Dictionary, which defines discipline as "instruction, an orderly or prescribed conduct or pattern of behavior, self-control." The goal of NJROTC training is to develop self-discipline.

The essay on the following page was written by Kim Robertson, a 1998 graduate of the Shawnee Mission (Kansas) West High School NJROTC program.

Kim Robertson is not alone in her experience. The NJROTC program gives cadets a chance to learn how to do the right thing, accomplish goals, and guide others to do the same. No other high school activity matches the leadership opportunity of NJROTC. Wherever a cadet heads after graduation—college, the workforce, or military service—NJROTC training will provide self-confidence, self-discipline, and self-motivation.

Leadership

There's that word again—*leadership*. It keeps coming up. Experience shows that the opportunity to develop leadership skills is what those who have completed the NJROTC program value most.

The NJROTC program is a leadership lab—fostering skills that will matter in school, in your community, your house of worship, or any other organization. A leader directs others toward a common goal. Leadership is a set of skills that can be taught—if you're willing to learn them.

What's in It for Me?

ON THE FIRST DAY OF HIGH SCHOOL, an average freshman walked into the school's NJROTC classroom. She was a little reticent, a little shy, a little intimidated. As she looked around the room seeing posters of Marines jogging and huge Navy ships glistening in the sun, she wondered what had possessed her to join. She thought to herself, "I can't do this! I don't have the discipline to run five miles or make a ship that clean! I don't even have the self-discipline!"

The girl soon relaxed and got to know the other cadets in the program with her—her fellow freshmen, the older cadets, and the instructors. For the most part, everyone seemed like they were trying to help her learn what she was supposed to do. She even joined the unit's drill team, which required a lot of dedication. She found herself having to budget her time so that she could get her homework and other responsibilities done and still have time to have fun.

As her sophomore year began, she was promoted to a squad leader. This gave her new responsibilities. Her superiors expected her to get everything done, without having to worry that she might not do it correctly, or even do it at all. Also, she now had a few squad members who looked to her for help and guidance. Their belief that she could help them gave her self-confidence. She felt she must set the example for them, as her instructors had told her many times a leader must do to be successful. Since she wanted her cadets to be the best that they could be, she made herself look as sharp as possible. This required a lot of self-discipline because she hated shining her shoes. She learned in the process that she could make herself do anything, even the stuff (such as shining her shoes) that she didn't want to do, if she quit procrastinating and complaining about it and just did it. She accomplished a lot by taking this attitude.

Her sophomore and junior years passed by quickly with all of her fun times and friends and homework and responsibilities. In NJROTC, she was promoted every semester: at every promotion, she gained a higher leadership position and more responsibilities. As she went higher and higher up the chain-of-command, her self-confidence grew. She accomplished more and more due to her increasing self-discipline. These accomplishments increased her self-motivation; because she wanted to push herself to be the very best she could, both in NJROTC and outside of it.

Then it was her senior year. The timid freshman seaman apprentice had now become a confident senior officer. She now knew how to give orders and how to take them, how to handle responsibility as well as delegate it to others, how to motivate herself and others to accomplish the goals of the unit. By teaching her what to do and then trusting her to do her job well, her instructors and peers had given her a chance to develop her self-confidence, self-discipline, and self-motivation. Her leadership had helped her to become a better person. At graduation, she silently thanked everyone that had helped her along the way.

The US Naval Academy in Annapolis, Maryland
Courtesy of Lowell Georgia/Corbis

Military Career Assistance

If you're considering a military career, your NJROTC experience will be all the more valuable. You'll get to meet real Navy people and watch them at work. You can talk with them about military career opportunities and get their real-life perspectives on military life.

If you go into military service directly from high school, the NJROTC program provides advanced pay-grade enlistment. In other words, it gives you a head start up the pay scale. Currently, if you have three years of NJROTC training and the recommendation of your instructor, you can enlist at pay grade E-3. Without this experience, you would enlist at grade E-1 and serve for 18 to 24 months before promotion to E-3.

Other students considering military service can apply for the United States Naval Academy. This is a special university in Annapolis, Maryland, that educates officers for the Navy and the Marine Corps. To enter the academy, you must be nominated by one of your senators or representatives in Congress or by the vice president. Another avenue to a nomination is through your NJROTC unit via your instructors. The requirements are tough, but those who get in receive a college education at no expense to themselves or their family.

If you're interested in becoming a Navy officer, you might also want to consider the college-level Naval Reserve Officers Training Corps (NROTC). NROTC scholarships provide books, tuition, fees, and a monthly stipend at some of the finest education institutions nationwide. Prior participation in NJROTC can not only help with preparing for these programs but also increase your chances of receiving an NROTC scholarship.

The Army, Marine Corps, Air Force, Merchant Marine, and Coast Guard also have college scholarship opportunities that NJROTC graduates might want to apply for.

There are times; however, when the answer in life is "no." NJROTC experience has helped some people realize that a career in the military is *not* for them. That, too, can be a valuable lesson.

Whatever your path in life may be, NJROTC is a rewarding and worthwhile experience.

Conclusion

The Navy Junior Reserve Officers Training Corps program is a joint effort between the US Navy and local school districts across the country. NJROTC aims to instill patriotism and foster citizenship and leadership skills in America's youth. Its three- to four-year curriculum balances naval science, military activities, physical fitness, and orientation trips.

The program seeks to instill the Navy Core Values of honor, courage, and commitment and to teach young people how to learn to live those values—even those who never join the Navy. More than any other program a young person is likely to enter in high school, NJROTC provides opportunity for leadership training. Those who complete the program tend to call this its biggest benefit.

Review Questions

1 What is the mission of the NJROTC program?

2 What are the goals of the NJROTC program?

3 What are the Navy Core Values?

4 What does the acronym *LATAR* stand for?

Career Planning

What You Will Learn to Do

In this chapter you will learn how to think about your career and your life goals.

Skills and Knowledge You Will Gain Along the Way

✔ Describe selecting and charting a good career path

✔ Explain careers versus jobs

✔ Describe career direction—getting to know yourself

✔ Explain career choices

✔ Explain the US Navy as a career option

✔ Explain how to develop good study habits

Selecting and Charting a Good Career Path

You want a career that is fulfilling, rewarding, and enjoyable, too. Everybody does. After all, people spend too much of their lives on the job to want to put up with work they don't like!

Still, finding the right career is not an easy task. The world is getting more competitive and technical every day. That means new opportunities, sometimes in fields that didn't even exist when your parents were growing up. That's a good thing. But these new jobs require skills, especially in math and science. That's the challenge. And that's why you should take as many courses in these fields as you can.

You need to think about grades, too. Good grades will open the door for you to many opportunities. Poor grades will close doors. If you want to be a doctor, for instance, you have to go to college and then medical school after that. You need good grades in high school to get into a good college, and then you need good grades in college to get into medical school.

All this sounds like something way off in the future. But the future will be here before you know it, and it's never too early to start thinking about where you want to go in life.

Fortunately, you can change your mind and keep trying out new ideas throughout your school career and beyond. Still, the decisions you make now are important. If you have an idea now where you want your career to go, this will help you focus, and focus will help you succeed in school and in life.

Key Term

career—
the general course or progression of one's working life

Careers Versus Jobs

People often use the words career and job as if they meant the same thing. But they don't. A job is what someone does to make a living—just to earn money to pay the bills and cover basic needs.

There's nothing necessarily wrong with doing work just for money. Some people take jobs to help meet a special need at home, or to pay for schooling. Others take jobs to finance careers that they care about but that don't pay well. That's why some actors wait tables, and some writers drive taxis.

But you may have noticed that some people have a string of jobs that don't "go anywhere." They do the same work for pretty much the same money for a long time. They're not learning or growing, and their heart isn't in their work. "It's OK; it's just a job" can become a catch phrase in these instances.

A career, on the other hand, is much more than "just a job." A career defines your working life. It includes learning, advancement, and developing talents. You might think of a career as a kind of story—each phase leads logically, or maybe surprisingly, to the next, and goes forward to a happy ending.

Profession and occupation are two other words with much the same meaning as career. Some professions, such as medicine, require specific courses of study. Other fields are less structured, with less formal education required, or maybe more than one standard way to prepare. Some careers don't even require a college degree.

Key Terms

job—
the work someone does to make a living

advancement—
promotion, as in rank

profession—
an occupation or career, especially one such as the law, medicine, or engineering, that requires considerable training and specialized study

occupation—
an activiy that serves as one's regular source of livelihood

Regardless of what it is, any work that you would describe as a career typically involves a path for advancement. This may mean working extra hours or taking on difficult assignments. Sometimes this means going back to college for another degree. You may know of a teacher in your school, for instance, who has taken time away from teaching to earn an advanced degree. Sometimes career advancement may mean moving around within a single company to learn all aspects of its operations.

Careers generally involve moving up a ladder of responsibility over a period of years. There's more work, and harder work, but also more authority and more money on those upper rungs. Sometimes people move up within a single company; more often they move from company to company, or maybe even from industry to industry. Technological change has completely transformed some industries, and brought others into being. Your career may someday lead you into a field that doesn't even exist today!

In your work life, what counts is not where you start but where you finish. You may take a job bussing tables in a restaurant, for instance. This may be just an opportunity to make some spending money before you go off to college to study engineering. Along the way, you may work up the ladder—serving as a server, a short-order cook, assistant chef, and so on. Eventually, you discover that you have a real interest in food. You decide to train as a chef or you find that the business side of the restaurant industry interests you.

It's also possible that you may not get very high up in an organization, but still gain valuable experience in such things as self-discipline, pacing yourself at work, and treating others well. And you may find that having a boss willing to give you a good reference for being punctual, reliable, and good with customers is not a bad thing at all—even if you go off to college to study engineering.

Career Direction—Getting to Know Yourself

Know yourself. This is the key to finding a satisfying career path. The answers to two simple questions will be a big help here:

- What do I want to do?
- What am I suited to do?

Choosing a career involves your feelings, your personal needs, and your insights into yourself. You must be aware of your aptitudes and abilities, interests, values, attitude, and physical abilities.

Aptitudes and Abilities

Aptitudes are talents or skills that you have or can develop with practice or training. What do you like to do in your spare time? What subjects do you like most at school? The answers to these questions are clues as to your aptitudes. Your physical abilities—strength, stamina, good eyesight, good hand-eye coordination, for instance—are important here, too.

Do you like to take things apart and put them back together? That is a sign of mechanical ability. You might find your niche as an auto mechanic or an engineer. If you enjoy solving puzzles, you might make a good program analyst or accountant. Do you like to write? That's a talent much needed in the business world.

Key Term

insight—
the ability to grasp a hidden or inward truth

Key Terms

aptitude—
an inherent ability or talent

ability—
the mental or physical power to do certain things

Your experience in part-time jobs could provide clues as to where you'd be happiest later on in your work life. Work gives you experiences that are different from school. Do you like dealing with the public as a salesclerk in a retail store, or are you more interested in the products you were selling—electronics, clothing, books, or do you enjoy both?

Interests

Your likes, dislikes, hopes, and wishes are part of your interests. Special tests of interests (called inventories) can tell you how your interests match those of people in the field you are considering. If you think you'd like a career in sales, for instance, do you know for sure how your interests line up with those of people who have been successful in that field?

This can be useful to find out, but remember, too, that you need not just interest but aptitudes to make a go of a career. If you want to be a graphic artist, for instance, you not only have to like to draw, you have to be good at it.

Values

Values give your life meaning—they help you be the person you want to be. Many people express their values in terms of their moral, religious, or political beliefs. If service to others is a value, you might find a satisfying career in health care or teaching.

Attitudes

Some jobs and careers require certain kinds of temperaments. Unflappable calm is a good attitude for a police officer. Air traffic controllers need to be able to deal with stress. Traveling sales reps need to be able to create their own energy. They must keep their spirits up when they're alone on the road, facing clients who can all too easily say no. Firefighters need immense physical courage and energy. They need to be able to rush to where the fire is.

On the other hand, there are some people who play against type. They overcome personality limitations and find success in a field they care deeply about. A naturally shy person may be able to win election to public office. Someone else may work hard to develop courage needed for a career in public safety.

If you think you need help getting a reading on your own temperament, you can ask a guidance counselor at your school to give you something called an "attitude inventory." This may well give you some interesting insights into yourself, but it will be only a snapshot of you at a moment in time, not a life sentence. Still, an attitude inventory may identify qualities to develop or overcome. In other words, it can help you to know yourself.

Career Choices

You have several possible careers paths in front of you. Different paths will require different levels of education and different kinds of experience. You will want to think about what kind of employer you want. Do you want to work in the private sector— for a small business, maybe even a family business whose owners you know? Or would you prefer to work for a big company that's known around the country or maybe even around the world? Or do you want to go into business for yourself?

Key Term

interest—
a subject or an activity that captures a person's attention, curiosity, or concern

Key Term

values—
principles, standards, or qualities considered worthwhile or desirable

Key Terms

temperament—
a person's typical way of thinking, behaving, or reacting

attitude—
a person's feelings or state of mind

Then there's what's known as the public sector—government employees. These include people who work for the federal, state, or local government. Even school-teachers are government employees, although you may not think of them that way. They typically work for a local school district, or a city's education department.

There are other ways careers differ. Do you like to work indoors or outdoors? With a large group of people, or a small team, or on your own? Different careers have different rhythms and paces, too. Sales work, for instance, has its ups and downs. So does construction. Retailing has its end-of-the-year crunch. Schoolteachers have summers off—but very demanding workdays during the school year. Public safety workers have irregular schedules.

How do you feel about money? Do you want job security and the promise of steady income—or are you willing to accept more risk for the opportunity to receive higher earnings?

What kind of family life do you want? Will the career that appeals to you allow you to support the family you'd like to have someday?

Think about the career paths in front of you—each requires different levels of education and different kinds of experience (clockwise from top left: computer animator, doctor, builder, office worker).

Courtesy of (clockwise from top left): Kim Kulish/Corbis; Reza Estakhrian/Getty Images; ColorBlind Images/Getty Images; Digital Vision/Getty Images

The US Navy as a Career Option

Going into the Navy right after high school graduation offers opportunities found in no other career. Sailors meet people from all over the country and have endless opportunities for training. The Navy offers enlisted people more than 65 different technical skills (called ratings) from which to choose. Each rating offers formal training as well as extensive on-the-job experience.

Those who complete college before starting their Navy career can choose to become commissioned officers. Officers in the Navy receive their commissions from the President of the United States.

Two programs that interest many JROTC students who want to go to college are the US Naval Academy and the Navy Reserve Officers Training Corps (NROTC) college scholarship program, where NJROTC students have an edge.

The US Naval Academy

Your naval science instructor can make up to three nominations to the Naval Academy each year. The nominees then compete for appointment to the academy by members of Congress, the president, the vice president, and the secretary of the Navy. Your instructor can help you apply for a nomination.

The Naval Academy is located on the Severn River in Annapolis, Maryland. The academy's purpose is to prepare young men and women morally, mentally, and physically to serve as officers of the US Navy and Marine Corps.

You must meet some tough academic standards to be admitted to the Naval Academy. In addition, you must be between the ages of 17 and 23, unmarried, not pregnant, and having no legal obligation to support a child. You must also be a United States citizen, be in good physical condition, and be of good moral character.

The Naval Academy, like other colleges and universities, chooses students in large part on the basis of their scores on the SAT or ACT tests.

You should begin taking the tests by the end of your junior year of high school. Low scores can eliminate a candidate from further consideration, so taking these tests more than once to get the highest possible score is a very good idea.

Over 75 percent of the candidates for admission to the Naval Academy rank in the top fifth of their high school class. The subjects they have taken in high school usually looks like this:

- Mathematics (four years), including algebra, geometry, and trigonometry
- Science, including physics and chemistry
- English (four years)
- History
- Government
- Computer science (all Naval Academy cadets use personal computers in most courses).

Key Terms

nomination—
the naming, or submission of the name, of someone for an appointment; to the Naval Academy, for instance

appointment—
the designation of someone to an honor or a position, such as a place at the Naval Academy

US Naval Academy Midshipmen celebrate their last day at the academy before graduation.

Courtesy of US Navy/Mass Communication Specialist Seaman Matthew A. Ebarb

To enter the Academy, you will also need to pass a medical exam as well as a physical-fitness test. Every midshipman is required to participate in physical exercise every day.

The academic program at the Naval Academy includes a core curriculum as well as a choice of 18 subject areas to major in. Eight of them are in engineering; six are in science, mathematics, and computer science; and four are in humanities and social science.

All midshipmen receive professional training in naval knowledge, skills, and leadership. Midshipmen train at naval bases, take part in Marine Corps activities, and spend time on Navy ships and aircraft each summer.

The academy offers a full program of varsity athletics and intramural sports. All midshipmen must take part in one or the other.

Graduates of the academy earn a bachelor of science degree and a commission in the US Navy or Marine Corps. They are then required to serve five years on active duty in the Navy or Marine Corps.

The Naval Academy offers a fully subsidized college education—schooling at no cost to the student and his or her family—and pays a monthly salary as well.

NROTC College Scholarships

The NROTC college program offers four-year scholarships at dozens of institutions. The scholarships go to outstanding high school graduates with top grades, high class ranking, and a recommendation from an interview board of officers. The scholarship recipients take part in the NROTC program on their campus and work toward a degree in a field of study that the Navy deems valuable.

In addition to the four-year scholarships, the Navy also offers two- and three-year programs for students who are already in college and completing their sophomore or freshman years.

NROTC scholarship students receive full tuition, their laboratory and administrative fees are covered, and they get a cash allowance as well. Upon graduation and commissioning in either the US Naval Reserve or Marine Corps Reserve, they must serve on active duty for at least four years.

Naval Academy Prep School

Promising and highly motivated applicants for Annapolis can be selected for a 10-month college preparatory course at the Naval Academy Preparatory School (NAPS) at Newport, Rhode Island. The school's mission is to prepare candidates who are judged in need of additional academic preparation for admission to the Naval or Coast Guard academies. The ten-month course of instruction at NAPS, lasting from August through May, emphasizes preparation in English Composition, Mathematics, Chemistry, and Physics. Placement depends on demonstrated ability, previous education, and additional needs for success at the respective academies. If you're selected for NAPS, you join the Naval or Coast Guard Reserve before reporting to NAPS in August.

Enlisted Careers

If you want to join the Navy, stay in school. A high school diploma is required for enlistment. If you enlist, your years in NJROTC will give you a leg up toward advancement. Two years of NJROTC will let you enlist at pay grade E-2, instead of the E-1 grade, where most enlistees start out. Three years of NJROTC will let you enter the Navy at pay grade E-3. With three years of NJROTC and a letter from your Senior Naval Science Instructor confirming your time in the program, you can enter the Army or the Air Force, too, at pay grade E-3. (The Marines, by the way, do not allow three-year cadets to enter the Corps as E-3s.)

Students who haven't yet finished high school, or who have, but want to better prepare for Navy life, can take advantage of the Navy's Delayed Entry Program. It allows enlistees to report for duty up to a year after signing up.

If you choose this option, during that period you can:

- Attend meetings and classes set up by your recruiter
- Start getting in shape for Primary Training and learning basics such as Navy policies, terminology, and rank structure
- Work with your recruiter to set goals for your Navy career
- Refer friends and classmates to your recruiter. Each of your referrals who enlists gets you credits toward advancement in rate (up to E-3), which equals higher pay.

Advanced Programs

Along with regular enlistment, the Navy has three particularly demanding Advanced Programs: the Nuclear Power Program, the Advanced Electronics Program, and the Advanced Technical Program. To qualify for any of these, you must be a US citizen with a high school diploma or college degree and a good academic record. Qualifying scores on the Armed Services Vocational Aptitude Battery (ASVAB) and sometimes an advanced placement test are also required.

Men and women accepted into these programs enter the service at pay grade E-3 and enlist for six years instead of the usual four.

Men and women with Navy Advanced Program training are in great demand in the civilian world and can expect to find much opportunity open to them. If these sound interesting to you, they are three more reasons to take all the advanced math and science classes you can in high school.

Aviation Electronics Technician 3rd Class Owen Snell rebuilds an advanced targeting forward looking infrared pod (AT FLIR), in the Advanced Intermediate Maintenance Division's Shop 4 aboard the nuclear-powered aircraft carrier USS Enterprise *(CVN 65).*

Courtesy of US Navy/Mass Communication Specialist Seaman Brandon Morris

Those accepted into the Nuclear Power Program have their recruit training at Navy Station Great Lakes, Illinois. They then attend the Nuclear Field (NF) "A" school at Charleston, South Carolina. On completion of the "A" school they are advanced to the E-4 pay grade. Then comes Nuclear Power School, also in Charleston. Men and women who complete this training may be assigned to nuclear aircraft carriers. (Only men are assigned to nuclear submarines.)

The Navy Advanced Electronics Program provides training in the most sophisticated technology. After their initial electronics training, which usually takes 22 to 36 weeks, participants are promoted to E-4. They may then get further training, or may be given assignment in data systems, electronics, electronic warfare, cryptological maintenance, missile and sonar operation, or fire control.

The men and women in the Advanced Technical Program are assigned to work on small ship engines or gas turbine systems, or in damage control, interior communications electronics, or cryptology.

More Careers in the Navy

You may be surprised at the wide range of career fields in which the Navy offers training. Here is a list of some of them.

- Arts and photography
- Aviation
- Business management
- Computers
- Construction and building
- Education
- Emergency, fire, and rescue
- Energy and power
- Engineering
- Finance and accounting
- Food, restaurants, and lodging
- Human resources
- Information technology
- Intelligence and communications
- Law enforcement and security
- Legal support services
- Mechanical and industrial repair and technology
- Medical and dental support services
- Music
- News and media
- Office and administrative support
- Purchasing and supply
- Religion
- Science
- Special-operations warfare
- Telecommunications
- Transportation and logistics
- World languages

For further information on Navy enlisted careers, go to **www.navy.com/enlisted**

Developing Good Study Habits

By now the message should be clear: Finishing high school is essential to getting a good job and enjoying a successful career. Four things will help you succeed in high school:

1. Good study habits
2. Good time management
3. Good test-taking skills
4. Good skills in listening and note taking.

Studying is the way you reinforce the material presented in your classes. You review the chapter of the textbook or your class notes, or maybe work on some exercises or solve some problems. This helps you make the material your own. It's the best way to get better grades.

Studying doesn't have to be boring or hard. If you do it right, studying can be interesting and even fun. The important thing is to start studying at the very beginning of the course. Many of your classes in school will start off with the easy stuff and get harder from there. If you don't understand or don't really master the first lessons, you'll soon be completely lost. It's like coming in late to a movie. If you don't follow the opening sequences, you won't be able to get the rest of the story and that can make your job nearly impossible.

Where to Study

You may like to study at school, at a library, at home, or at a friend's house. You may have one place you go to just to study—a quiet place in your school library, for instance. This can help get you in the right frame of mind to study, because you will associate that place only with your schoolwork. You won't think of it as a place to watch videos or hang with your friends.

Any good place to study should have good light, good seating, and writing space. You should be sure to have all the necessary materials at hand—books, notebooks, lab manuals, other papers, highlighters. This is especially important if you're going to pack up your things to go study at a friend's house. You don't want to get there and realize you've left some important papers at home.

Study in a place where you know you'll be free of interruptions. And don't listen to music while you study. While this may relax you and make you feel more at ease with your studies, music can be a distraction and can keep the material from sticking.

Studying with a friend can be a real help, especially if you're working on the same assignment together. You can answer each other's questions about the material and explain the concepts to each other in your own words. This will help you fix the material firmly in your mind. This is especially valuable if you learn better by listening than by reading.

Finishing high school is essential to getting a good job—
and good study habits are essential to finishing high school.

Even if you and your friend are not working on the same material, studying together can help you keep each other on track. You have to be honest with yourself, though, about whether you're really studying together, or just wasting time interrupting each other with chit-chat. Try experimenting with "study buddies" to find out whom you work with best and how both of you can get the most out of the experience

When to Study

Set regular times to study. Here again, it pays to experiment and see what works for you. Does going over material right after class, or as soon as you get home from school, help you get a grip on it, or do you find it helps to have a break in the afternoon? Maybe you work best getting back to the books after you've had a little recreation, dinner, and a chance to check in with family and friends.

Pay special attention to big assignments, such as term papers and other projects that will take weeks or even months to complete. These can be so scary that you're tempted to put off even thinking about them. Then suddenly the deadline is just a week off and you go into a panic. Remember that even the scariest assignment can be "tamed" with a little planning. Break the work down into steps—choosing the subject of a paper, for instance, then finding the sources, gathering the data, and so on. Then plot the steps on your calendar. If you master this technique, you'll not only enjoy greater success in high school, but you'll have developed a skill that will help you the rest of your life.

Here are some other guidelines for good study habits:

1. Take regular, five-minute breaks during long study sessions. But don't forget to go back to work!
2. Don't spend all your time on one subject.
3. Start with the hardest material and work toward the easier stuff from there.
4. Make a schedule for a week and follow it. Be sure to include time for recreation, sleep, exercise, food, and friends. At the end of the week, see how well it worked. Change the parts that didn't work. Maybe you didn't allow yourself enough time to sleep, for instance, or weren't realistic about how much time your homework takes. A good weekly schedule that becomes second nature to you will be useful to you throughout your life.

Study Methods

Experts have come up with a number of methods to study that will help you read and really "get" the material in a chapter of your history book, for instance. Here are a couple of these. They go by the initials *OK4R* and *PQRST*.

OK4R

O. *Overview.* Read the title, introduction, summarizing paragraphs (often at the beginning or end of a chapter, often in bold type), and the headings. ("Study Methods" is the heading for this section of this chapter.)

K. *Key ideas.* Skim the text for the key ideas. Note italics or bold type. Look carefully at pictures, graphs, and tables.

R1. *Read.* Read the entire assignment.

R2. *Recall.* Close the book and think through, or write out, the main points. (This is where a study buddy can help.)

R3. *Reflect.* Think about the material. How does this fit in with other things you know about the subject? How does this chapter in the history book relate to the chapter you studied last week, for instance?

R4. *Review.* This step comes before your next test or quiz on the material.

PQRST

P. *Preview.* Glance through the material looking for topic sentences (statements of main points), pictures, graphs, tables, and summaries. Get the main points; don't worry about details at this point.

Q. *Question.* What questions form in your mind as you do this review? Hint: The review questions at the end of a chapter, as in this book, are good clues as to the main points of the material.

R. *Read.* Read the material. Pay attention to it all, but concentrate your thoughts.

S. *State.* Say aloud what you have read. Put into your own words the facts, thoughts, and ideas in the material. You may want to write these out, especially if you're studying in a library or other place where speaking aloud would make you feel self-conscious. But again, pay attention to what works for you. If you learn best by listening, the say-aloud step may be worth trying, even if you occasionally have to find another place to study.

T. *Test.* Sometime after your first reading and stating, test how much you remember of the material. Go back to any written notes you've made.

Tests and Exams

You should care about doing well on a test but not be so worried that you get "test anxiety." That can be disastrous. The best way to handle stress is with good preparation—and the best preparation for tests is the kind of good study behavior described above. Keep up as you go along, and you won't have to cram right before a test.

You will want to review, though, and as you review, think what questions the teacher might ask. Check the points the teacher emphasized in class. Review each section of the material and try to figure out which questions your teacher could ask you about it.

Ideas for Test Taking

Understand how the new material relates to what you already know. If you're faced with an objective test (short answers), pay attention to details. If you're taking an essay exam, you're likely to be asked to discuss (to write about) the big ideas of the material and the relationships among them.

Cramming, or trying to learn it all the night before a test, is the worst way to study. Losing sleep and disturbing your daily rhythm will work against good learning. And you're less likely to remember what you've learned in haste.

When you're actually in the classroom to take the test, read the directions carefully. Don't be afraid to ask the teacher to explain anything you don't understand.

For a better grade on a short-answer test, look the test over for 30 seconds to see how many questions there are and how much each counts. If you're graded by how many right answers you get, guess at answers you don't know. If wrong answers are subtracted from right answers, though, don't guess. Move along at a steady pace—skip hard questions and go back to them later. Don't leave blanks. An answer you're not sure of is better than none at all.

Key Term

cramming—
preparing for an exam at the last minute

When you're taking a test, read the directions carefully, and don't be afraid to ask the teacher to explain anything you don't understand.

Essay Tests

Essay tests are those requiring long written answers, often to complex questions. Unlike matching, true-false, and other short-answer tests, essay tests let you show not only mastery of the material but your writing and organizational skills, too.

With an essay test, remember to read the questions carefully first before you plunge in. In the margins of your test paper, jot key words and phrases that come to you; they will help you start writing.

Organize your answers. You may well want to use the outline structure you have learned for your term papers (I, II, III; A, B, C, and so on) on your essay tests as well. This can help reveal weaknesses in your thinking about a question. If you've been asked to provide three reasons for something, and your outline shows that most of your ideas really have to do with only one reason, you know you've got more thinking to do.

Write legibly, and review your answers before turning your paper in. Make sure you have actually answered the questions asked. With an essay test, you face a lot of blank space on the page. Sometimes in the rush to fill that space, you may write things that are interesting and true, but not an answer to the question.

The questions on essay tests are often not really questions, but commands: "Explain the causes of the American Revolution." These commands are often given in language you don't use every day: *Analyze, compare, contrast, define, elaborate, evaluate, illustrate*. Look these words up in your dictionary, and review them as you prepare for an essay test. This will prevent any unpleasant surprises on test day.

Listening and Note-Taking Skills

Good listening skills are important to success in school. *Listening* is a lot more than just *hearing*. Hearing is continuous, unfocused, and unconscious. Listening is a focused, conscious activity.

Listening is the neglected communication skill. Most people have had instruction in reading, writing, and speaking, but few have had any formal instruction in listening. You can become a better listener by understanding the four types of listening:

- passive listening
- competitive listening
- active listening
- reflective listening.

Passive listening is one-way communication. You may or may not understand what you've heard. Listening to the TV, your MP3 player, or a teacher who doesn't take questions is passive listening.

Competitive listening takes place when you are not listening closely. You listen only long enough to get the necessary information. You're already thinking about how you're going to reply. Competitive listening occurs when people "talk past" each other in an argument.

Active listening is two-way communication. You pay full attention and think about the information. You ask questions if you don't understand the speaker.

Reflective listening involves not only actively listening to the speaker, but also interpreting the speaker's feelings. It involves the sense of sight as well as of hearing, because speakers often express feelings through gestures and body language. Good friends often engage in reflective listening.

Effective Listening Techniques

To be a good active listener, you need to focus on what the speaker is saying. The following techniques can help you do this.

- *Clarify.* Ask specific questions to ensure you've understood the speaker.

  Example: *"When you say the research paper is due on the 15th, do you mean in class, or by the end of the day?"*

- *Restate.* Use the speaker's words as your own and repeat what you think the speaker has said.

  Example: *"Did I understand you correctly? Did you say that classes will be canceled if the temperature falls below zero degrees Fahrenheit?"*

- *Acknowledge.* Let the speaker know you have understood the message and that you appreciate the speaker's point of view.

  Example: *"I appreciate the fact that you can't attend every meeting. I realize that you live much farther from school than most students do."*

- *Summarize.* Touch on the main ideas or conclusions, not each individual point. You restate the main ideas and set the tone for the next subject or conversation. This can be useful when you are discussing several issues.

  Example: *"OK. We've agree that I'll work your shift on Thursday evening and you'll work mine on Friday morning, right?"*

- *Frame.* You present information in a neutral way. You can then find areas of agreement on which to focus. This helps shape the conversation.

  Example: *"I can see your point that we need new team equipment, but we won't get it soon. Do you think we can make better use of what we have?"*

Note Taking

Nobody can remember everything a teacher or speaker says. One solution is to take notes.

In note taking, don't try to write down every word a speaker says. If you take too many notes, you can't listen. Just jot down words, phrases, diagrams, or the occasional sentence that will remind you of the speaker's main points. Draw arrows and use bullet points. If a teacher says, "Some differences between the Greeks and the Romans were that the Greeks were a philosophic and poetic culture, whereas the Romans were a practical and engineering culture," you could write down "Gs—philosophic, poetic. Rs—practical, engineering." You can use your notes to help you apply the listening techniques above. Read over your notes soon after you take them, while the speaker's ideas are still fresh in your mind.

Traits of Successful Students

Successful students, wherever they are in school, follow these principles:

- They set goals, so they have a clear idea why they are in school. They know where their current studies fit into the big picture of their lives.
- They practice good study habits.
- They manage their time. Things don't just happen randomly in their lives.
- They develop good skills for taking tests and exams.

Conclusion

It's never too early to start thinking about your goals in life, especially your career goals. Whether you go to college or not, you'll want a satisfying career, not just a string of jobs. You don't have to make final decisions now, but if you begin to think about goals, you'll have a focus that will help you throughout your school career.

As you consider options, you should know that your participation in NJROTC can be a big help to you in your further schooling and career—whether you enlist in the Navy directly after high school graduation, or seek appointment to the Naval Academy.

Review Questions

1 Why is it important to think about a career path now?

2 What is the difference between a job and a career?

3 How can your time in NJROTC help you if you seek a Navy career?

4 What are some traits of successful students?

Leadership Skills

Followership

Key Terms

- followership
- readiness
- ability
- willingness
- confidence
- proactive

What You Will Learn to Do

This chapter will help you become a better leader by learning how to be a good follower.

Skills and Knowledge You Will Gain Along the Way

✔ Explain the importance of good followership
✔ Describe the readiness factors of followers
✔ Explain how to build productive relationships with leaders
✔ Describe how to be an effective follower

The Importance of Good Followership

You may have heard this before: "Before you can lead, you have to learn to follow." Good leaders emerge from the ranks of able followers. As a member of various teams and groups throughout your life, you'll have many chances to practice good followership.

Key Term

followership—
displaying the attitudes, behaviors, and actions that help a leader succeed at leading

UNIT II

But why do you need a lesson about following? To be a follower, you simply do what you're told, right? Well, the role of a good follower is more than that. Followership is often taken for granted in studies of leadership. Yet an active follower who shares the leader's goals and values is an invaluable team member. Followers—the "worker bees" or whatever you call them—are the heart and soul of an effective team.

The Follower Relationship

Throughout your life and career you will be a follower in one role or another. On a sports team, you follow the lead of your captain or coach. On a school project, you help the team leader. In your cadet unit, you follow higher-ranking cadets and your instructor. As a Navy captain, you would follow admirals. And even if you became a Navy admiral yourself, you would still have to follow the directions of our country's civilian leaders.

The relationship between follower and leader sometimes gets blurry. During a single day, a team member's role might flip back and forth from leader to follower many times. For example, suppose that your school principal asks the Adopt-a-Road team that you lead to clean up the school parking lot. Wearing your follower hat, you say, "No problem, ma'am. Our team can handle it!" Then later, wearing your "leader hat," you would assign certain parts of the job to various members of your team to complete the job.

When successful business leaders are asked to list traits they look for in effective leaders and good followers, the traits they choose in both cases are similar. The most commonly named traits are:

Leader: honest, competent, forward-looking, inspiring

Follower: honest, competent, dependable, cooperative.

Why are the two lists so similar? It's because the roles of leader and follower are closely related. In fact, followership and leadership are sometimes so closely connected that you may not even realize when you are switching roles.

Types of Followers

In your unit, you will find a number of types of followers. Some followers are *independent*. One kind of independent follower plays an active role in the unit by seeking out responsibility, carrying out assigned tasks in a responsible manner, and respectfully offering appropriate suggestions for improvement. Such cadets support the unit's goals and objectives. These cadets are known as *effective followers*.

Another kind of independent follower will take a negative approach to his or her job as a follower. Such cadets always complain, criticizing every idea or questioning every unit policy. They are known as *alienated followers*.

The opposite of independent followers are *dependent* followers. They simply go along with anything you ask them do without thought. They are the "yes" people, or the sheep. They wait for you to tell them what to do, then do it.

Between the independent followers and the dependent followers are the *survivors*. These followers are almost invisible: They stay in the background as much as possible, never volunteer, and contribute only to keep out of trouble.

Which kind of team member are you? As a leader, which type of follower would you want serving in your unit?

Qualities of a Good Follower

Good followers usually demonstrate the same qualities as effective leaders. As a good follower, you are *loyal* to the organization and its goals. You believe in your leaders and respect their decisions. You assume that your leaders have the unit's best interests in mind.

A second important quality of an effective follower is to be *smart*. You know your job in the unit and strive to know your superior's job as well. You are prepared to accept greater responsibility when needed to fill a new role in the unit.

Initiative and *common sense* are two more traits that go hand in hand in a good follower. No one has to tell you to carry out your job. As a good follower, you know what has to be done and do it.

Good followers usually demonstrate the same qualities as effective leaders.

Followers Have Power

Individual followers can play different, yet crucial roles in helping their team achieve its goals or mission. As a member of a group or team, you probably possess certain skills or knowledge that no one else does. To the degree that the team needs your knowledge and skills, you as a follower can affect team performance and exert considerable power. Your skill may even be the power of your personality. A popular follower, as an individual, can change the behavior of a group. It's up to the team leader to decide how to use each follower's individual strengths for the team's overall good.

The Readiness Factors of Followers

In Act 5, Scene 2, of Shakespeare's "Hamlet," the prince remarks, "the readiness is all." Hamlet was right. Understanding the readiness of followers is a key element of leadership.

Team members are naturally at different levels of readiness as they face each task or mission. The effective leader's job is to help followers or team members gain the knowledge and skills they need to perform at the highest level they can.

Three factors determine readiness: *ability*, *willingness*, and *confidence*.

Key Term

readiness—
how prepared a team member is to carry out a particular task or tasks

Readiness Levels

Readiness levels are the combinations of ability and willingness that a person brings to team tasks. Follower readiness breaks down into four levels. Each level represents a different combination of follower ability and willingness, and confidence.

Low Readiness

Readiness Level 1: Unable and unwilling—The team member lacks ability, commitment, and motivation. This level may also apply to a team member who is both unable and insecure, lacking the confidence to perform a task to standard.

Moderate Readiness

Readiness Level 2: Unable but willing—The team member lacks ability, but is motivated and makes an effort to complete the task. The person may also be unable but confident, as long as you are there to provide guidance.

Readiness Level 3: Able but unwilling—The team member is able to perform the task, but is unwilling to use that ability. Or the team member is able but insecure—showing ability but acting insecure about doing the job.

High Readiness

Readiness Level 4: Able and willing—The team member has the ability and commitment to perform the job. The team member is confident about completing the task.

Ability, willingness, and confidence chart the course to your readiness as a follower.

Ability of Followers

Ability is partly based on the experience a team member has gained from doing previous tasks. If you are a team leader and need to assess the ability levels of your followers or team members, first consider the task you will be assigning and its desired outcome. Then decide which followers are best suited to handle that task by their knowledge, skill, and experience.

Willingness of Followers

Willingness consists of the ability to do the work, a sense of duty in doing it, and a desire to do it. A team member who isn't comfortable with a task and isn't confident that his or her performance will meet the standard might show unwillingness.

Ability and willingness affect each other. A change in either factor will affect the way the two factors operate together.

Confidence of Followers

As team members' competence and abilities change, so will their attitudes, levels of enthusiasm, and commitment. As they learn more and become more competent, their confidence level will increase.

Confidence levels can shift and change. As a leader, you must be aware of your followers' changing levels of confidence and competence. Followers usually become increasingly confident as work proceeds, but this isn't always true. Sometimes repeated false starts or failures shake an individual's, or a team's, confidence. In any case, never label a team member. Be aware of your team members' confidence levels and intervene if they start to slip.

Building Effective Relationships With Leaders

People often think that a good leader-follower relationship is a matter of luck. Many followers say they have a "good" leader or a "bad" leader, and assume they can't do anything to change the situation. This is a mistake. The leader alone does not determine the quality of the relationship between leader and follower.

Effective followers know how to strengthen their relationship with their leaders. They also know how to enhance the support they provide to their leaders and to the team.

As a follower, how can you strengthen the leader-follower relationship? Here are some suggestions.

Always Help the Leader Succeed

Part of the leader's job is to help his or her followers succeed. But it works both ways: Followers also need to help their leaders succeed. That doesn't mean you should be an "apple polisher" or play politics. You just need to remember that you and your leader are part of the same team with the same goals. If the team succeeds, everyone benefits. If the team fails, the blame should fall on the followers as well as the leader.

Understand the Leader's World

Effective team members must know the leader's and the organization's objectives so they can share that vision. Loyalty and support are a two-way street. Just as a leader can help followers attain their personal goals, a follower can help a leader achieve the team's goals. Knowing his or her leaders' values, preferences, and personality can help a follower understand the leader's actions and decisions. Such understanding gives followers insight into how to strengthen relationships with their leaders.

The leader's job is to help his or her followers succeed. The followers' job is to help their leader succeed.

Educate Your Leader

Remember that leaders don't always have all the answers. Followers can make a great contribution to a team's success by recognizing—and trying to help overcome—a leader's human shortcomings.

A new leader, in particular, almost always needs team members' help. Such a leader may have a great deal of knowledge and experience, but may not be familiar with the operations or needs of the team to which he or she has been assigned. It's up to followers to orient and educate a new leader about team members' expertise and experience. This process is especially important if the leader comes from a different field or area of specialty.

Keep Your Leader Informed

Nobody likes unpleasant surprises. As a follower, never put your leader in the embarrassing situation of having someone else know more about the team's business than he or she does. Brief your leader often on all business related to the team's goals and mission.

Adapt to Your Leader's Style

It's the follower's responsibility to adapt to the leader's style, not vice versa. Followers need to be flexible. They need to adapt to the leader's decision-making style, problem-solving strategies, methods of communication, and styles of interaction. If your leader does not set clear expectations, ask for clarification. If you are the leader, clarify your expectations about followers' roles and responsibilities.

Be an Effective Follower

Besides working to build a supportive relationship with your leader, you can take these additional actions to be an effective follower:

Be honest. Followers need to be honest and dependable. If a follower does not have integrity, it doesn't matter how many other great qualities or talents he or she might have. No one wants to work with someone who isn't trustworthy. After integrity, leaders value dependability. They value team members who have reliable work habits, accomplish assigned tasks at the right time in the right order, and do what they promise.

Don't gripe. Part of a follower's job is to make the team work well. Ideally, the leader helps a team work well, but sometimes the team must perform despite its leader. Poor leadership is an enormous burden. But complaining about policies and poor leadership is never productive. A follower who gripes only further undermines the leader's authority and the team's ability to function.

Be proactive. Being proactive includes building a good relationship with your leader. A proactive follower considers policies and suggests to the leader ways to improve team success. A follower must buy into the task of making the team better.

Make sound decisions. Once you have taken a proactive approach to followership and are confident in your role, you will need to make sound decisions. Your decisions will affect those around you. Sound decisions will improve your leader's confidence in you. Step up and use your expertise.

Be enthusiastic. Enthusiasm is contagious energy. An enthusiastic follower can have a great influence over the team, its leader, and its overall performance.

Suppose your leader gives you a task. You may like the task or you may think it's boring or even useless. As far as the team's welfare goes, that's not important. No matter how you feel about a task, approach it with a positive attitude. Your enthusiasm will have a ripple effect on the group's or the leader's feelings concerning the task. Be upbeat and energetic when performing tasks. Success rests with the followers' enthusiasm as well as the leader's.

Be versatile and flexible. Hitting your head repeatedly against a brick wall isn't the most efficient way to get to the other side. When a problem comes up, take a few minutes to assess the issue and to reevaluate your approach. Use your brain rather than your skull. A second look will almost always reveal a better way around the wall.

Key Term

proactive—
taking the initiative and assuming part of the responsibility to make things happen

UNIT II

An enthusiastic follower helps the team and the leader.
Courtesy of Mike Brinson/ Getty Images

Conclusion

Whenever you're in the role of a follower, learn as much as you can about effective leadership by watching good leaders in action. Use your experience and success as a follower to help you become an effective leader. Remember that the differences between a good leader and a good follower are quite small. This is because good leaders and good followers share a goal—to be part of an excellent team.

Review Questions

1 What is followership?

2 What is the importance of follower readiness?

3 How can you assess follower ability?

4 Why do followers need to be willing?

5 What happens to follower confidence over time?

Chapter 2

Leadership

What You Will Learn to Do

Understand the principles of leadership and how you can become a successful leader

Skills and Knowledge You Will Gain Along the Way

✔ Discuss the two orientations to leadership behavior

✔ Define the four leadership styles

✔ Identify the primary factors of the leadership situation

✔ List the six traits of an effective leader

✔ Describe the personal qualities of an effective leader

✔ Explain the leadership opportunities in NJROTC

Key Terms

- **situational leadership**
- **relationship behavior**
- **empathetic**
- **task behavior**

The Two Orientations to Leadership Behavior

Becoming a successful leader requires training and practice, but you can begin to acquire and practice leadership skills right now—at school and in your community. Suppose, for example, a volunteer team forms at your school to help rebuild houses devastated by tornadoes. The group elects you as its leader. Now what? You need to think about the tasks ahead and the people who have volunteered to do them. It's not an easy job, but it's one you can do if you understand how leaders do their jobs effectively.

This lesson provides some advice that will help. The guidelines are based on years of research about leadership. Leaders in business, in the armed forces, and in virtually every other walk of life use them successfully.

An important concept to understand is the difference between *leadership* and *management*. Leadership is the art of influencing and directing people to accomplish the mission. Management is supervising the use of resources to achieve team objectives. In essence, you lead *people*, and you manage *things*. While both skills are important, this lesson will concentrate on leadership.

How does a leader get people to come together to accomplish a mission? You'll find no single answer to this question. A leader must tailor his or her approach to the task and the people available to do it. The leader must base the approach on the environment and on the readiness of the team and its individual members. *Readiness* is the degree to which a follower demonstrates the ability and willingness to accomplish a task. In other words, the leader must base his or her approach on the situation in which the leader and team find themselves. This is called situational leadership.

Situational leadership is flexible. It is based on the abilities, knowledge, skills, and motivational level of the team or group the leader is influencing. To be effective, a leader using this leadership style must know his or her people and how they respond to working in groups.

Another part of understanding situational leadership is knowing your orientation: Are you oriented toward *people* or oriented toward a *task*? This is important because the two orientations are connected. A leader who is people oriented focuses on interaction with his or her people. A leader oriented toward task focuses on the job to be done.

Orientation Toward People

Another name for orientation toward people is relationship behavior. Relationship behavior includes, for example, listening, praising, collaborating, and counseling. A leader who practices such behaviors can greatly improve followers' performance. If you reach a barrier in the way of team progress, relationship behaviors can help overcome the obstacle.

And that makes sense, doesn't it? People respond better if they feel their leader is supportive and empathetic. A leader who simply issues orders and then criticizes team members' performance will have a hard time gaining their cooperation. Leaders should bear in mind the old expression, "You catch more flies with honey than you do with vinegar."

Key Term

situational leadership—
a leadership model based on the concept that there is no single best way to influence and lead people

Key Terms

relationship behavior—
a leader's engagement in supportive, two-way communication with his or her team members

empathetic—
having the ability to understand; being aware of, and sensitive to, the feelngs, thoughts, and experiences of others

Orientation Toward Task

Task behavior focuses on the practical aspects of the team's job or mission. Task behaviors include directing team members on what to do, how to do it, and when to do it.

In his book *Leadership in Organizations*, Gary Yukl suggests that task behavior has limitations when used alone, because its effects on team-member satisfaction and productivity are difficult to predict. That's why, as noted above, task behavior and relationship behavior must go hand in hand.

When it comes to task behavior, a leader should survey the needs and abilities of his or her followers and then choose a leadership style accordingly. If as leader of the tornado-relief volunteers, you knew that Maria was a self-starter and needed little motivation, you could probably just make sure she understood her task and then get out of her way. You'd allow her to work independently. On the other hand, if you knew that Randy, another team member, seemed uncertain about how to accomplish his task, you would step in and use task behavior to give Randy instructions, training, and guidance.

Key Term

task behavior— *the leader's involvement in defining the duties and responsibilities of an individual or a group*

UNIT II

Four Leadership Styles

Task behavior and relationship behavior are distinct, but complementary, leadership behaviors. Considered together, they help define four main leadership styles. These four styles make up what's known as the *leadership grid*.

Table 2.1	THE LEADERSHIP GRID
Participating	**Selling**
Style 3	**Style 2**
High Relationship Orientation	High Task Orientation
Low Task Orientation	High Relationship Orientation
Delegating	**Telling**
Style 4	**Style 1**
Low Relationship Orientation	High Task Orientation
Low Task Orientation	Low Relationship Orientation

Telling (Style 1)

In the telling leadership style, the leader provides specific instructions and closely supervises team members as they perform their tasks. The telling leader has a high task orientation and a low relationship orientation.

Typical telling behaviors include:

- directing others what to do
- supervising them closely
- following up to ensure they complete their tasks.

Selling (Style 2)

Leading by selling means the leader closely supervises task completion and following up, while also providing explanations and opportunities for clarification from team members. The selling leader has a high task orientation and a high relationship orientation.

Typical selling behaviors include:

- supervising closely
- following up
- explaining relationships between tasks and team goals
- encouraging questions
- supporting progress.

Participating (Style 3)

In the participating style, the leader helps and supports team members' efforts toward completing the task by sharing ideas and responsibility for decision making with his or her team members. Participating leaders have a high relationship orientation but a low task orientation.

Participating behaviors include:

- asking team members for ideas
- listening
- encouraging others to try out their ideas
- allowing others to structure their tasks
- sharing control and accountability.

Delegating (Style 4)

In the delegating style, the leader turns over to team members responsibility for decision-making, problem solving, and implementation. Delegating leaders have both a low relationship orientation and a low task orientation.

Delegating behaviors include:

- setting task boundaries
- letting others make their own decisions
- allowing members to chart their own courses of action
- giving group members the freedom they need to do the job well
- providing help when asked
- monitoring progress.

A leader should survey the needs and abilities of his or her followers and then choose a leadership style accordingly.

Leadership Etiquette

Successful leaders:

- Make decisions that will enhance the entire organization rather than just themselves.

- Realize that they also have superiors—everyone, even a person of the highest rank, is accountable to someone.

- Serve as examples of fair play, integrity, and dependability.

- Listen to the needs, feedback, and suggestions of all organization members, not just a select few.

- Understand that leadership is not a position of glory and popularity, but of responsibility.

- Roll up their sleeves and help other members of the organization when the going gets tough.

- Know that they cannot succeed without the work, support, and dedication of all members of the organization.

- Do not seek personal recognition but rather share it equally with their followers or team members.

- Work for the success of the organization, not for individual gain.

- Know that the members of the organization gave them whatever power the leaders may possess—if the leader uses this power improperly, it can be taken away and given to someone else.

Primary Factors of the Leadership Situation

You lead people and you manage things. But how do you know how much time to spend on each? According to situational leadership theory, the situation the team finds itself in will dictate how much time the leader must devote to each activity.

Leaders should approach each leadership situation by considering four factors: *the mission, the people, the leadership style,* and *the environment.*

The Mission

Most missions involve many tasks. The team must complete each to fulfill its responsibilities. The leader must define the mission and set goals for completing the different parts of the team's tasks.

In many instances, someone outside the team, such as a teacher, coach, supervisor, or unit leader, provides the mission. The leader's job is to translate this mission into goals that the team members will accept and understand. The team members must be able to relate to these goals and adopt them as their own.

When possible, involve team members in setting these goals. This will ensure their support. A team cannot succeed without the dedicated effort of each member. The goals the leader and team set must be challenging but attainable. Unrealistic goals frustrate even the most dedicated people, while frivolous goals reduce belief in the mission's worth.

Another part of the leader's role is to set standards of job performance and to communicate them to the team. These standards must be reasonable, consistent with the mission, and clearly defined for every individual. As the work proceeds, the leader should then recognize those who meet or exceed standards. He or she must also provide training for those who fall beneath standards and take corrective action for those who ignore standards. This last step is almost never easy because the problem is often rooted in the member's attitude. If a team member ignores the standards, the leader must determine the reason and move quickly to correct the situation through training or, if needed, administrative or disciplinary action. If one person ignores standards and appears to get away with it, other members will be tempted to do the same.

Like an athletic coach, a leader assigns team members their tasks or positions based on their strengths and weaknesses.
Courtesy of Tom Carter/PhotoEdit

The People

As a leader, you must be sensitive to people—after all, people perform the mission. Understanding people helps determine the leadership action to take in a given situation by determining your followers' readiness. You cannot get the most out of people on your team unless you first know their abilities.

Ability has two main elements: *training* and *experience*.

Training

You should assess each team member's level of training. If your people don't have adequate training, you must make sure they get it. No matter how committed followers are to the mission, they cannot contribute to it if they lack proper training.

Experience

As a leader, you should also be aware of the background, experience, and ability of each of your team members regarding every task you assign them. Don't base such an assessment solely on an individual's seniority or rank. While seniority or rank may be good overall indicators, the person may have never done a certain job or been in a particular environment before. Moreover, some people learn faster than others do.

The Leadership Style

Successful leaders adapt their leadership style to meet the mission demands and to reflect the abilities and experience of their people. But in choosing a leadership style, good leaders also take into account their own individual strengths and weaknesses. For example, if you can communicate well with people on an individual basis but are uncomfortable speaking to large groups, use personal conferences as much as possible. If you write well, take advantage of this skill by writing letters of appreciation or using other forms of correspondence. If you're adept at leading discussions, bring your people together and let them solve problems.

In addition to playing to your strengths and avoiding your weakness, your leadership style must correspond to your team members' knowledge, abilities, and skills.

- When one or more of your team members doesn't know how to do the job, you must spend much time giving that member guidance and support.

- If your team members are able but lack motivation, let them participate in planning the task. Motivate them by maintaining a professional working relationship. With this encouragement from you, they'll soon show greater motivation.

- If your team members have extensive experience and are enthusiastic about the task, provide them greater freedom. If they are on the track toward meeting your goals and objectives, let them complete their task in the way they choose. As the leader, you are still responsible for the mission, so be sure to monitor the group's progress.

The Environment

There's no way to plan for every possible outcome. You'll always have surprises, and some of them won't be pleasant. One way to prepare for the unexpected is to begin by carefully considering the environment. Good leaders do this constantly. They know the leadership methods that worked in one situation with one group may not work with the same group in a different environment.

Think again about the volunteer team formed at your school to help the tornado victims. Even if the team had a great leader, super team members, and a commendable mission, it might still encounter problems. Housing or food-service difficulties, equipment or parts shortages, bad weather, and many other problems might arise. Any of these problems would create a new and unpredictable environment that the group's leader would have to deal with.

As a leader, you must alter your leadership behavior as necessary to accommodate changes in the mission's environment. Be sensitive to your surroundings. The key is to stay flexible and adapt to the situation you face.

Six Traits of an Effective Leader

Effective leaders have certain distinguishing characteristics, or traits, that make up the foundation of their approach to their work. These traits form their character, which defines them as leaders. Your character is the basis for the decisions you make and the way you treat others.

Character is not something you put on in the morning and take off at night. It is who you are 24 hours a day, seven days a week, regardless of where you are, whom you are with, or who might be watching.

Many traits go into building a strong character. For you, as a future leader, six traits are essential. They are *integrity, loyalty, commitment, energy, decisiveness,* and *selflessness.*

Integrity

Having integrity means establishing a set of values and adhering to them. Integrity means being a whole person—in mind, body, and spirit. Integrity is a total commitment to the highest personal and professional standards. A person or leader with integrity is honest and fair.

How can you spot integrity? An example of integrity in action might be the leader who has an opportunity to pass off an unpleasant task to an uncooperative team member. Instead of penalizing the team member, the leader follows the schedule and fairly assigns the task to the next person on the list. The leader decides to counsel, rather than punish, the rowdy team member. A leader with integrity treats all team members fairly, putting aside personal feelings.

Loyalty

Loyalty is faithfulness or allegiance—to superiors, peers, and subordinates. Leaders must display unquestionable loyalty to their team members before they can expect members of their team to be loyal to them. When a leader is loyal to his or her team members, they will respond in kind. Team members' behaviors reflect the actions and attitudes of their leaders.

Commitment

Dedicated service is the hallmark of the leader. A leader must demonstrate total dedication to the United States, the Navy, and the team. This commitment sets an example for team members. Commitment, a Navy Core Value, is contagious.

An example of commitment is the leader who calls on the team to rally around a team member who's having personal problems. The leader encourages other members to support their comrade. Under their leader's guidance, team members stand united to act if a fellow team member asks for help.

No team member takes on this role of support alone. The leader asks team members to express their own commitment, not only to the team member in trouble, but to the team as a unit. This level of commitment leads to increased team unity and greater loyalty among members.

Energy

Energy is an enthusiasm and drive to take the initiative. Throughout history, successful leaders have demonstrated the importance of mental and physical energy. They approached assigned tasks aggressively. Their preparation included the physical and mental conditioning that enabled them to look and act like leaders. They had the perseverance and stamina to stay the course. They got the job done.

You can fail, despite your talents, if you don't use all your energy to finish the job. That's what a well-known maker of running shoes means in an ad that urges people to "Just do it." Applying your energy to the team and its mission is the key to success.

An example of energy is the team leader who urges members to hold a scheduled outdoor training session, even during an unexpected snowstorm. The leader reminds them that the training is essential to prepare the team for its mission. Members won't be adequately prepared if they take a day off. Rather than cancel the training, the leader encourages team members to relish the opportunity to come together in adversity to perform. This kind of high-energy leadership builds respect of the team and the mission. It is the energy that eventually leads to victory.

A leader must have the self-confidence to make timely decisions and then effectively communicate those decisions to the team.

Decisiveness

Decisiveness is a willingness to act. A leader must have the self-confidence to make timely decisions and then effectively communicate those decisions to the team.

Decisiveness includes the willingness to accept responsibility for the outcome of one's acts. Leaders are always accountable—when things go wrong as well as when they go right.

Suppose, for example, that a team leader has five team members but only three slots in a training program. The leader assesses the team members individually and decides which three will benefit most from the training. In private, the leader tells each member of the decision and gives reasons for it. Because this leader has made the decision fairly, the two team members not selected should respect the decision just as much as the members who are chosen do. All members know that the leader made the decision based on careful thought, not on personal preference.

Selflessness

Selflessness is the ability to sacrifice personal needs and wants for a greater cause. Leaders put accomplishing their mission and caring for their people before their own welfare or desires. Willingness to sacrifice is essential to military service.

Selflessness includes the courage to face and overcome difficulties and physical dangers. This includes the need to make difficult decisions.

Personal Qualities of an Effective Leader

An effective leader also expresses specific personal qualities: *courage, responsibility, the ability to set an example, self-discipline, confidence, a sense of humor, tact,* and *common sense.*

Courage

While most people think of courage in terms of willingness to face physical danger, the more common form is *moral* courage to make difficult decisions. It requires courage and strength of character to confront a tough situation head-on rather than avoiding it by passing the buck to someone else and refusing to decide. These qualities are essential to effective leadership. That's one reason courage is a Navy Core Value.

Responsibility

Taking responsibility and a willingness to be accountable for your actions is one of the main requirements for a successful leader. You must be willing to answer to your superiors as well as to your followers.

The Ability to Set an Example

You will set the standard of performance, conduct, and appearance for your unit by personal example. The people you lead will imitate your standards of personal conduct and appearance. If your behavior shows that you cannot control yourself, people will ask how you can control others. Lack of self-control in a leader destroys a unit's cohesion and impairs its ability to perform.

Self-Discipline

Self-discipline is an important quality for young people to develop as early as possible. There will always be rules, regulations, and standards to be met in your home, school, community, and your unit. You will be expected to be disciplined enough to follow these rules. If you do not provide your own discipline (self-discipline), someone else will usually have to provide it for you. The self-disciplined person will always be dependable and will fulfill responsibilities without the need of direct supervision.

Self-Confidence

Much like discipline, self-confidence is a quality needed by leaders. Know yourself, know your abilities, and be decisive. Confidence comes with experience. You must practice your leadership skills to develop them. The NJROTC program offers you numerous opportunities to practice leadership skills and develop self-confidence.

A Sense of Humor

Every leader needs the ability to see the humor in a situation. A humorous remark at the right time or in the right situation can ease tension and restore a group's morale. Sometimes, as the old saying goes, laughter *is* the best medicine.

Tact

Tact is the ability to deal with others in a respectful manner. The leader who displays tact in dealing with others encourages courteous treatment in return. The use of tact is very important in times of stress, such as when you are criticizing a subordinate. Usually a calm, courteous, and firm approach will bring a cooperative response without creating ill feelings. The sarcastic or "smart aleck" approach usually does not create a positive response to directions or orders.

Common Sense

A leader can be responsible, self-disciplined, and self-confident, have a sense of humor, be tactful, and still lack common sense. Just remember to treat others the way you would like to be treated. Try to make the right choices, asking yourself the following questions.

When Making Choices, Ask Yourself:

1. If I do what I'm thinking of doing, would I be willing to have my action enacted into law and required of everyone?

2. If I were considering using someone else for my own personal gain, would I allow someone to use me in that way?

3. Would I be willing to explain to a jury why I chose this action?

4. Would I do this if I knew it would be on tonight's television news?

5. What would I think of this action if it my worst enemy did it?

6. If my reason for acting this way is that everyone else does it, would I do it if no one else did it?

7. Would I do this if I knew I would have to explain my reasons to my family?

8. Would I be content with this action if my boss or a member of my family did the same thing?

9. Would I be content to have each of my followers behave exactly as I intend to in this situation?

10. My team could win the game by violating a rule. Before I call this play, would I be upset if the losing team took the same action?

11. If what I do hurts no one very much, would I be willing to let everyone do the same thing?

12. If there is very little harm in what I want to do, what kind of person will I become if it gets to be a habit?

Qualifications for Leadership

Former Chief of Naval Operations Adm George Anderson lists these qualifications in judging officers' abilities as leaders:

Achievements—They produce results; many are industrious. The effectiveness of the work serves as a measure of their achievements.

Ability to make decisions—They evaluate information, analyze the problem, and then integrate the two into a sound and incisive decision. (This is closely allied to achievement.)

Personal appearance—They take pride in every detail of their personal appearance.

Military bearing—They conduct themselves in a professional military manner 24 hours a day, every day.

Mental alertness—They give continual attention to detail coupled with an awareness of the big picture.

Ability to express self—They express themselves clearly, both orally and in writing, to communicate their ideas and decisions.

Being a good shipmate—They do not lose sight of their relationships with others in the Navy. They realize they cannot function alone and can be effective only through others.

Imagination—They use their imagination and initiative to improve the task performance of their entire unit as well as their own performance.

Knowledge of the job—They have a complete mastery of their job plus a detailed knowledge of all its responsibilities, including those of subordinates.

Manner of performance—They know themselves, the job, the enlisted personnel, and the immediate situation. They use four approaches to get this done: 1) personally do it, 2) drive others to do it, 3) inspire others to do it, or 4) combine the three in the best manner.

Social grace—They know the rules of social etiquette, such as which fork to use; but more importantly, they know how to show a sincere interest in the people they meet.

Sense of humor—They keep everything in the proper perspective; they distinguish between the important and the trivial.

Personal behavior—They reflect integrity and honor in every facet of their behavior.

Leadership Opportunities in NJROTC

One of the many benefits of participating in NJROTC is the many opportunities you have to develop and practice your leadership skills. This section lists many of those opportunities.

NJROTC Unit Organization

An NJROTC unit with 100–150 members is organized into one company with one or more platoons. Each platoon has one or more squads. The number and title of staff officers vary for each unit and depend on the local circumstances and the decision of the naval science instructor.

Units with more than 150 cadets are organized into a battalion that has two or more companies. A unit with more than 300 cadets is organized into a regiment that includes two or more battalions. The number of team commanders varies by unit. Most units have three or more teams, including a color guard team, a drill team, and a rifle team.

Other units also have an academic team, pistol team, orienteering team, drum and bugle corps, or athletic team. Each team normally has a cadet as team captain or commander.

You will find a listing of sample job descriptions for each position in Table 2.2. The job descriptions vary with each unit. Some positions have more duties and other positions have fewer. Each unit normally provides job descriptions for each position in the unit.

Table 2.2	SAMPLE LEADERSHIP POSITION DESCRIPTIONS
POSITION	**RESPONSIBILITY**
Company Comander	• Is accountable for appearance, discipline, efficiency, training, performance, and conduct of the unit. • Ensures that all cadets receive opportunities for leadership in accordance with their experience and ability. • Carries out the orders of the naval science instructor.
Executive Officer	• Is prepared to act in place of the Company Commander if required. • Supervises the unit staff. • Carries out all tasks assigned by the Company Commander.
Operations Officer	• Schedules and coordinates all activities of the unit. • Prepares a unit annual, monthly, and weekly calendar of activities.
Administrative Officer	• Keeps unit administrative files and records. • Ensures that all unit reports are prepared and submitted as required. • Prepares all unit correspondence.
Supply Officer	• Inventories, orders, and issues all unit supplies and equipment. • Orders, stores, inventories, and accounts for all uniform items. • Maintains appearance, security, and control of unit storeroom.
Platoon Commander	• Is accountable for appearance, discipline, training, performance, and conduct of platoon members. • Ensures that all members of the platoon receive opportunities for leadership in accordance with their experience and ability. • Carries out the orders of the Company Commander.
Team Captains	• Accounts for the selection, training, motivation, and performance of the assigned team members. • Coordinates all team activities with the Operations Officer • Carries out orders and duties as assigned by the Company Commander.
	Source: Lavin, *Intro to NJROTC*, pp. 2–14

Conclusion

Every spring at the Naval Academy in Annapolis, plebes (first-year midshipmen) assemble to scale a tall gray obelisk called the Herndon monument to try to replace a plebe's "Dixie cup" hat sitting at the top with a midshipman's cap. The job is dirty, tiring, and strenuous. No one midshipman ever reaches the top by him or herself. This ritual is a symbol—not of how one person can scramble to the top solo— but of how Navy teamwork and successful leadership get things done.

Working to nurture the qualities of successful leadership in your own character is essential to becoming an effective leader. This process takes work, but the effort will be well worth it. Developing these characteristics will improve your ability to build unity, loyalty, trust, and commitment among your team members. They will imitate your example, and you will stand out because of their success.

Working to nurture the qualities of successful leadership in your own character is essential to becoming an effective leader.
Courtesy of US Navy/Photographer's Mate 2nd Class Damon J. Moritz

Review Questions

1 What are the two primary orientations to leadership behavior?

2 What are the four styles of leadership?

3 What are the primary factors of the leadership situation?

4 What are the six leadership traits?

5 Which of CNO Anderson's leader qualifications best describes you?

Motivation

- **motivation**
- **hierarchy**
- **self-actualization**
- **goal**
- **incentive**
- **mentor**
- **protégé**

What You Will Learn to Do

Understand what motivates people and how you can use that understanding to lead them effectively

Skills and Knowledge You Will Gain Along the Way

- ✔ Explain the hierarchy of human needs
- ✔ Describe goals and motivation
- ✔ Discuss the key elements of coaching and mentoring
- ✔ Explain how to practice leadership

The Hierarchy of Human Needs

To be an effective leader you need a basic understanding of human behavior. Why do people do the things they do? What motivates people to act or to do anything? A simple answer is that human behaviors result from people trying to satisfy their needs.

Experts in persuasion tell us that almost everyone ponders—even subconsciously—the question "What's in it for me?" as they go about their daily business. If you can answer that question for them, you have an important key to influencing and leading others.

The very basic needs of people are food, water, and safety. More-complex needs, such as a need for respect and acceptance, are sometimes much more difficult to satisfy.

Psychologists have long been interested in the ways personality, attitudes, and behaviors affect each other. Researchers who study human behavior have developed a number of theories to explain why people behave the way they do. These theories have two things in common. First, they all deal with both the inside and the outside of the person. Second, they all describe a series of steps, or levels, of human motivation.

At this point in your life, the desire to get good grades and to have fun with friends may be two strong sources of motivation for you. These two factors can drive you to work hard and study for tests or to organize special events like trips to the movies and trying out for sports. Both are very powerful and engaging.

To be an effective leader, you need to understand why people do the things they do.

But some motivations are more basic or more physical than others. Consider that urgent craving you get after school, compelling you to move straight toward the refrigerator or kitchen cupboard. So strong and definite are urges such as this that some psychologists say it's possible to study, describe, and rank the factors that motivate people.

Key Term

motivation— *the inner force that drives people to act*

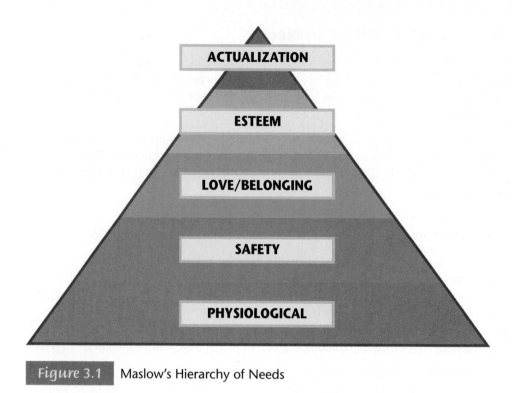

Figure 3.1 Maslow's Hierarchy of Needs

Key Term

hierarchy—
*a ranking or series
of steps that follows
a specific order;
for example, largest
to smallest, oldest to
newest, most important
to least important*

In the 1950s, psychologist Abraham Maslow proposed a "hierarchy of human needs" to describe people's motivations. Maslow's hierarchy of human needs includes the following levels:

- *physical needs*—food, water, shelter
- *safety and security needs*—personal and community security
- *belonging needs*—family, community, group acceptance
- *esteem needs*—friendship and love
- *self-actualization needs*—attainment of potential.

This hierarchy moves from the most basic needs, such as food and water, to more-complex needs. Physical needs come first; emotional and psychological needs, such as the need for love, come later. Maslow believed that people must satisfy their needs at each succeeding level before they can move on to the next.

Survival needs are the most basic of all human needs. They include those things that sustain life, such as food, water, sleep, air, and relief from pain. When these needs are met, a person will then turn to security needs.

Security needs include protection from threats, violence, disease, or poverty.

Belonging needs are the need to be liked and accepted by your family, friends, and the members of your community. People need to feel a part of some group or organization.

Esteem needs are those needs that relate to a person's desire to feel important. There are two types of esteem needs. One is self-esteem, the feeling within you that you are important; the other is the feeling that other people think you are important.

Group activities and service projects can help meet people's need to feel they belong and improve their self-esteem.
Courtesy of Yellow Dog Productions/The Image Bank/Getty Images

Self-actualization, or personal fulfillment, is the highest need on Maslow's hierarchy. Self-actualization is the need to feel that you have reached your full potential in life. Maslow believed that few people reach the point where the need for accomplishment truly becomes their primary motivation. This is because most people spend a majority of their time attempting to satisfy their lower-level needs. For instance, to become a major league baseball pitcher, you first need to have a place to live and regular meals. You must also belong to a team. As difficult as self-actualization may be to achieve, Maslow still believed that the drive to achieve one's potential was inherent in every human being.

As a person meets the needs at each level, he or she becomes more flexible and has more options. For example, you only care about higher-level needs such as esteem and belonging if you have something to eat. And if your family is in financial difficulty or you have personal problems, you may not be able to focus on getting good grades.

Goals and Motivation

Since people are so different, it's not surprising that different things often drive them. These things are their *purposes*—or goals.

The Cycle of Goal-Directed Activity

How do your goals relate to your motivation and behavior? Your motive helps you form a goal. You then choose a behavior that is directed toward that goal. If it all works, you meet your goal.

Key Term

self-actualization—
the process of becoming what you are capable of becoming

Key Term

goal—
an external aim, or end, to which one directs one's efforts

Intrinsic Motivation

Common intrinsic motivations include:

- **affiliation**—wanting to belong to a group or to have friends
- **achievement**—wanting to succeed; good grades, for example
- **power**—desiring to have control of your time, other people, situations, or things
- **wisdom**—desiring to understand
- **security**—wanting to be safe.

Extrinsic Motivation

Common extrinsic motivations include:

- **money**
- **food**
- **threats or fears**
- **status or promotion**
- **awards and recognition.**

Key Term

incentive—
something that incites or has a tendency to incite to determination or action

This process works for both tangible and intangible goals, helping you fulfill every goal you set. Suppose you're hungry—that's your motive. Your goal is to satisfy your appetite—in other words, to eat. So you adjust your behavior to one that will eventually lead to accomplishing your goal—for example, you head for the kitchen. Then, in three goal-directed activities, you put two pieces of bread in the toaster, wait until the toast pops up, and butter it. Finally, you satisfy your need and accomplish your goal: You eat the toast.

Goal-directed activities and goals form a cycle—the experience of the first cycle feeding into and contributing to the second. In the case just described, previous experience with the toaster has taught you how to get better at fixing toast, made you aware of how long the toasting process takes, and helped you learn to satisfy your hunger whenever it hits you.

Several factors may affect the progression of this cycle. One such factor is competence. For example, if you never burn the toast, other family members may start asking you to make toast for them. On the other hand, if you start getting sloppy—leaving butter all over the counter—your family members might ask you to stop.

Two Types of Motivation

Researchers divide motivation into two main types: *internal* (*intrinsic*) and *external* (*extrinsic*).

The desire to get good grades is an example of intrinsic motivation. Intrinsic motivation is a drive people feel that is based on internal factors such as the need for friendship, affiliation, achievement, power, wisdom, and security. Intrinsic motivation originates from within. The things that motivate you from within are your goals, needs, desires, beliefs, and attitudes—in other words, your personality.

Your teacher's offer of an extra-credit project might be an example of an extrinsic motivation. Extrinsic motivation is a force that drives people to act that is based on factors outside the individual. Extrinsic motivations are beyond your control, but they still have an influence on you. In other words, it's the teacher's choice to suggest an extra credit project, but it's up to you to decide whether to do it or not.

The difference between these types of motivation can get fuzzy. In fact, one motivation theory proposes that *all* motivation is intrinsic. Other theories hold that you can use external factors, or incentives, to motivate by linking them to people's intrinsic motivations.

For example, suppose that you really want a 10-speed bike. After some thought, you decide to get a job to earn money to buy one. Your intrinsic motivation to get a job is a desire for the independence and mobility that a new bike will provide. Your boss offers you an extrinsic motivation—pay—to keep you showing up for work. Together, the two motivating factors shape your perspective—or work ethic: "Working is good because it will help me earn the money I need to buy a bike, which will help me get around faster."

Positive and Negative Approaches

As you can see, many factors can motivate an individual to perform better on the job. These same factors can motivate people to act as their leader wishes them to act. The job of every leader is to motivate people to accomplish their tasks—jobs, details, projects, missions. Just remember that not everyone is motivated by the same thing. Good pay may be important to some people, while others may place higher priority on doing work that is important or interesting. Still others find self-improvement to be their motivating factor. The idea is that people are most often motivated individually rather than as a group. If someone is not performing well, the effective leader will try to determine which of the person's needs is not satisfied and then determine what will motivate that person to do a better job. This is the *positive* approach to good leadership.

A *negative* approach to motivation is punishment or disciplinary action. Military discipline is neither personal nor vindictive; it is not revenge for misconduct. The value of disciplinary action is that it teaches the offender—and others— that the behavior in question is unacceptable. This is often called the *deterrent theory* of discipline. The response must be consistent, just, and recognized as such by all parties. Most important, everyone must understand that disciplinary action is the result of the offender's behavior and is the responsibility of the offender— not of the leader who must take the appropriate action.

The NJROTC Rewards System

Another approach to motivation is a consistent, fair system of rewards for actions or desirable behaviors. Your own NJROTC unit has a well-designed system of rewards, such as ribbons and medals for individual or group achievement. Each unit establishes criteria for these awards, in addition to the criteria prescribed by the NJROTC field manual.

Another reward system is promotion. Cadets who demonstrate outstanding aptitude and leadership ability and who express a desire for increased responsibility are promoted to higher rank and assigned more-responsible positions in the unit. Some units give special awards for achievement, such as Cadet of the Month, special privileges for service to the unit, attendance awards, or honors for academic achievement. All of these are designed to motivate you and your NJROTC peers to achieve.

Key Elements of Coaching and Mentoring

Key Terms

mentor—
an individual with advanced experience and knowledge who is committed to giving support and career advice to a less experienced person

protégé—
a less experienced person who benefits from a mentor's guidance and advice

At some point in NJROTC or later in life, you may find yourself serving as a coach or mentor—helping others develop their individual talents and skills. A coach helps people grow and improve their competence by providing suggestions and encouragement. A mentor focuses on external and internal factors that will help people develop into healthy, caring, and responsible leaders.

Both mentors and coaches often lead by example. They help build a person's self-esteem and self-confidence.

A primary role of a mentor is to be a listening ear, a trusted confidant, and an adviser. A person who's lucky enough to have a mentor is called a protégé. Mentors realize that it takes time to build trust with their protégés, so they take great care to be patient. They take a gradual approach to developing the relationship.

Understanding the Mentor's Role

As a mentor, you try to put yourself in your protégé's shoes—to understand the world from his or her perspective. That requires putting aside preconceived ideas and being nonjudgmental. A mentor does not impose his or her own values on a protégé, but rather encourages the protégé to discover his or her own values.

For example, mentors might give general information about grants, scholarships, contests, competitions, and special programs that might help a protégé further his or her education and career, but they don't tell the protégé which to choose.

The Role of a Mentor

A mentor should act as a:
- trusted adviser
- clearinghouse for questions, problems, and leadership-related issues
- sounding board for decision making and problem solving
- leadership role model
- resource provider
- patient, caring, listening guide.

A mentor should *not*:
- "police" the protégé's day
- criticize or lecture the protégé
- make decisions for the protégé
- try to transform the protégé
- be judgmental
- try to "fix" the protégé, the protégé's problems, and the protégé's environment.

Coaches and mentors lead by example and help build people's self-esteem and self-confidence.
Courtesy of Yellow Dog Productions/The Image Bank/ Getty Images

Mentors must be objective. They do not recommend a specific course of action, but encourage the protégé to explore options. They avoid taking sides when a protégé has a conflict with his or her family, teachers, or friends. Mentors advise their protégés on conflict resolution, but don't try to replace a school counselor, spiritual leader, social worker, or team leader. If a protégé is having a family conflict, for example, the mentor will not advise him or her directly. Instead, the mentor will suggest that the protégé consult a guidance counselor, leader, or another trustworthy and experienced adult.

A mentor will always try to keep a positive, upbeat, and professional tone in the relationship. The mentor will also keep the relationship confidential. This means the mentor will not share any personal information about the protégé, including address, phone number, e-mail address, photos, or files unless the safety and well-being of the protégé or others is at risk.

Mentors and coaches donate their time and energy. They typically don't give or accept money or gifts. Their protégés' heartfelt thanks—and successful careers as students and leaders—are their reward.

Barriers to Mentor–Protégé Relationships

Good mentors remain aware of the purpose of the mentor–protégé relationship. They know that their role is to advise, rather than to change or reform, the protégé. They know the potential, as well as the limits, of their role.

In some cases, a well-meaning mentor may push too hard and too quickly on a protégé's problems and issues. That makes the protégé feel ill at ease. The protégé should feel totally comfortable with the mentor. A good mentor will not press the protégé to talk about issues before he or she is ready.

Some mentors fail because they focus on their own agendas and not on the protégé's needs. As a good mentor, you set the agenda for the relationship *with* the protégé, not *for* the protégé.

A mentor builds trust through active listening.

What Makes a Mentor–Protégé Relationship Successful?

The key to an effective mentor–protégé relationship is creating trust between the two people. People volunteer to be mentors because they want to help their protégés develop their leadership skills. Without mutual trust, a mentor can never truly help a protégé. Building trust requires time and is not always easy. It requires ongoing and open communication.

An important way for the mentor to build trust is through *active listening*. Active listening is two-way communication. You pay full attention and think about what people say, asking questions if you don't understand. Active listening actually requires active seeing, too. That's because sometimes people talk even when they're not saying anything. You must be patient and "read" people—their motions, their faces, their eyes, and their body language.

Active listening skills include avoiding distraction, making good eye contact, and letting the other person speak. Active listeners listen for both fact and feelings. They interpret body language effectively and acknowledge what's said. They ask good questions and smile appropriately.

How to Practice Leadership

You can practice leadership every day and in many situations, whether you are the commanding officer, a platoon commander, or a cadet in ranks. You can volunteer to serve on a committee at school, in your place of worship, or in a civic organization. You can find ways to help school officials, teachers, coaches, and fellow students. Besides those found in NJROTC, leadership opportunities abound in school clubs, Boy Scout and Girl Scout troops, Boys and Girls Clubs—and even at home, where you can take the lead in helping with household chores and responsibilities.

The following are some ways you can lead in any circumstance:

Lead by Example

The best way to lead is to set a good example for others. Live the Navy Core Values. Practice the leadership traits and characteristics you have learned. Be a good follower, and support the people who are leading you. Be faithful to your religious values or philosophy of life. Always do what is right.

The more you lead, the better leader you will become. If you continually seek out and take on opportunities to lead, your confidence in yourself and your abilities will grow. Moreover, other people—teachers, supervisors, and other adults, as well as your followers—will gain confidence in you.

This effect will snowball. People will regard you as a leader and will seek your advice.

Lead by Imitation

As an NJROTC leader in training, you wear two hats. In some situations, you can serve as an example for others. But you can also continue to imitate leadership behaviors you admire in others. Watch and study other leaders carefully. Then copy their successful actions and behaviors. Put into practice what you learn.

Try to be like successful leaders and to lead as they do, but don't forget your own leadership style. Don't try to copy something that doesn't feel comfortable to you. Although all successful leaders share certain traits, each leader expresses them in his or her own way.

Lead by Consensus

As you gain experience in leadership, you'll become more comfortable in leading by consensus. You'll relax and be willing to let your followers help you lead. Your followers will be flattered that you've asked for their input, and their productivity and interest will increase.

The best leaders don't work too hard at trying to keep control. They establish their authority, define the mission, and then let their followers do their assigned jobs. They intervene only when asked or if they see the project or mission going off course.

Leading by consensus means sharing the leadership load. It gets team members to cooperate and pull their weight. The entire team benefits—including the leader.

Evaluate Your Leadership Behavior

How do you know if you're an effective leader? You have to evaluate your leadership skills. These techniques can help evaluate whether you are leading effectively or not.

First, seek input and feedback from your own leader, other leaders, or the adults around you. Ask your parents or guardian, teachers, coaches, boss, counselor, unit leader, and other adults how you can improve your approach to leadership.

Second, talk with your team members and ask them for feedback, too. Try to get honest and critical information on how you can improve your style to better fit the needs of the group.

Continue to learn from your efforts. Use your successes as a basis for refining your leadership techniques. Use your mistakes and failures as a means for addressing larger areas for improvement.

Finally, have a conversation with yourself. Think about your leadership experiences—what seems to work and what doesn't. Evaluate your leadership in light of your team's goals: How far along is the team to achieving its goals? What obstacles stand in the way? What can you do to help the team overcome these obstacles? Is your leadership style one of the obstacles?

Seek opportunities wherever and whenever you can to practice leadership. Also look for opportunities to measure yourself—against Navy standards, against other leaders, and against yourself. You will not always succeed, but you can learn to become a better leader by evaluating your failures as well as your successes.

Conclusion

You can motivate individuals to act according to your insights, plans, and objectives if you are aware of your followers' needs. Knowledge of motivational techniques is a key for the successful leader. Good leadership does not rely on a simple system of rewards and punishment—it takes into careful account how your team members are performing, how their needs are being met, and how you can motivate them to do even better.

Review Questions

1 What are some examples of Maslow's five levels of human needs?

2 How do Maslow's needs motivate your own behavior?

3 How do your goals influence your actions?

4 How does trust develop in a mentor–protégé relationship?

5 How do you become an active listener?

6 What are some ways to assess your leadership style and effectiveness?

Chapter 3 Review

Chapter 4

Relationships

What You Will Learn to Do

Understand the workings of relationships with others in order to influence and lead them more effectively

Skills and Knowledge You Will Gain Along the Way

✔ Describe how to build on respect
✔ Discuss the values of tolerance and understanding
✔ Identify techniques for improving group effectiveness
✔ Explain conflict in groups

Key Terms

• **respect**
• **personal dignity**
• **tolerance**
• **prejudice**
• **discrimination**
• **stereotype**
• **diversity**
• **religious respect**
• **gender stereotyping**
• **justice**
• **rationalization**
• **projection**

Building on Respect

Respect for others is the foundation of our civilized culture. If you own a dog, you keep it off your neighbors' lawn out of respect for their privacy and property. If you are in a library, you don't talk loudly out of respect for others' right to work quietly.

Respect means accepting differences—tolerating and valuing other people and their customs, culture, attitudes, and beliefs.

Establishing and Demonstrating Mutual Respect

You may have heard some people say that "respect is earned." This is true in many ways. You *do* earn other people's respect on the basis of your words and deeds. To be effective, a leader must earn respect from the members of his or her group.

On the other hand, Americans believe that every human being has basic, inherent value and rights. The Founding Fathers stated this concept in the Declaration of Independence when they wrote, "We hold these truths to be self-evident, that all Men are created equal, that they are endowed by their Creator with certain unalienable Rights, that among these are Life, Liberty, and the Pursuit of Happiness. . . ." This means that people don't need to "earn" these things. They are born with them and cannot justly be deprived of them. As a citizen, you must respect the rights of others and acknowledge their value as human beings and as citizens. They must do likewise for you.

In other words, respect must be *returned*; it must be mutual. Mutual respect is the two-way relationship that develops between people or members of groups after the lines of communication are open and trust develops.

Mutual respect is what makes all relationships run smoothly—between friends, student and teacher, parent and child, husband and wife, employee and supervisor, or police officer and citizen.

People develop respect for others when they feel that others respect their personal dignity.

Key Term

personal dignity—
the internal strength that helps people feel connected, worthwhile, and valued

Personal dignity is closely linked to a person's self-worth. A lack of respect breaks down personal dignity. Such a breakdown can lead to a number of negative social behaviors, including crime, substance abuse, child neglect, family disruption, political discontent—even suicide.

So you can see that respect is a powerful force. A society cannot function if its members do not establish and practice mutual respect. Can you think of any examples of societies or groups in which a lack of mutual respect led to upheaval or disaster?

Ways of Showing Respect

Showing respect is universal: it is something you can do on both a personal and professional level. On the personal level, one of the easiest ways to show respect is simply to be courteous. In other words, use your manners. Say:

- "Please" when you ask for something
- "Thank you" when you receive something
- "Excuse me" if you accidentally bump into someone
- "Yes (or no) sir" or "Yes (or no) ma'am" to adults
- "Good morning" or "Good afternoon," especially to people older than you are.

Other examples of personal respect include:

- Holding the door for an elderly person or a child
- Standing when an older person enters the room
- Not interrupting people
- Not using a cell phone while you're conversing with someone face-to-face
- Not chewing gum or eating loudly while conversing with someone
- Taking off your hat or cap when you're indoors
- Taking off a glove before you shake someone's hand
- Removing your sunglasses before speaking to someone.

You show respect on a professional as well as personal basis by:

- Dealing with people in a cooperative way
- Communicating clearly
- Listening actively
- Giving constructive feedback
- Being flexible
- Creating opportunities to teach and learn
- Sharing behaviors and feelings
- Viewing situations as win-win scenarios
- Using inclusive language (for example, saying "we" instead of "you" or "they").

Mutual respect is what makes all relationships run smoothly.

The Values of Tolerance and Understanding

Tolerance means understanding and standing up for people's differences and helping ensure that everyone receives equal treatment.

You might say tolerance and mutual respect are like a two-way street. The traffic moves both ways: You show tolerance for others and they show tolerance for you.

But you might encounter barriers on this street, just like you come up against barriers when you're driving somewhere to meet a friend. Among these barriers are prejudice, discrimination, and a failure to value diversity.

Prejudice

The word prejudice literally means "judging ahead of time." Prejudice shuts down critical thinking. It causes you to assume you have a person or a situation figured out in advance—before you even talk to the person or see the situation for yourself. Prejudice is an irrational way of thinking—it doesn't permit reflection. It's usually based on limited experience, hunches, or heresay, rather than on facts.

Prejudices are so common that we sometimes take them for granted. That can be not only hurtful; it can be downright dangerous.

Prejudices can lead you to make blanket assumptions about an entire group of people rather than looking at them as individuals. For example, suppose someone said to you, "Athletes are stupid." How would you respond? You could roll your eyes and nod, as if in agreement. But if overcoming prejudice were your goal, you'd respond very differently. You'd have to think logically. You'd have to ask yourself a series of questions such as these:

- Who made the statement? Is it someone who plays sports or not? Does the person know any athletes?

- On what grounds did the person make the claim about athletes' intelligence? Does he or she have access to all athletes' school transcripts?

- Do you know of evidence to disprove the claim? Do you know any smart athletes? Or have you read about any great athletes were were also top scholars? If you don't personally know any athletes, is it a good idea to automatically accept another person's opinion as fact?

Reasons for Prejudice

People aren't born with prejudice any more than they are born with the ability to read. Prejudice is *learned*. You pick it up from the people around you and from the messages society sends.

People develop prejudices for several reasons. One is *fear*. People may fear people, ideas, and cultures different from their own. Another reason for prejudice is a group's feelings of superiority toward members of other groups—whether the feelings are racial, ethnic, or religious. Sometimes it's a question of men versus women.

Misunderstanding is another source of prejudice. When people of different cultures and languages come together, all kinds of misunderstandings can erupt. An innocent gesture or word in one culture can be an insult in another. For example, in America, putting your feet up on a desk can show that you are feeling relaxed and friendly, whereas in the Middle East, showing someone the bottoms of your shoes is an insult.

Still another reason is perceptions of history. Perhaps you had a bad experience with a member of another group. You then proceed to blame all members of that group for what one person did in the past. At a broader level, many ethnic and religious groups around the world have a long history of disagreements with each other over land, resources, and political power. They've sometimes fought bitter wars with atrocities on both sides. People and groups often remember the wrongs done to them far better than they remember the wrongs they've done to others.

Discrimination

One danger of prejudice is that it leads to discrimination. Discrimination is prejudice in action.

Discrimination is often based on perceived traits such as skin color, gender, or age. But the possibilities are endless. Some overweight people, for example, claim to be victims of discrimation. Left-handed people say they experience discrimination in a right-handed world. What counts are the feelings of the person being discriminated against—and your efforts to treat that individual no differently than you treat anyone else.

If someone compliments you on your new winter coat and says you have "discriminating taste," that's a good thing. It means that you tend to seek out the quality things in life. But if someone says you're "discriminatory" in your attitudes, watch out. You may be picking your friends on the basis of something other than their character, actions, or personalities. You might be judging people on the basis of stereotypes.

A stereotype can be negative or positive. It's a picture you carry around in your head about a thing or person, without ever questioning its validity.

For instance, if you hear that a friend just bought a pit bull, you might immediately assume that it's a vicious dog. If another friend bought a kitten, you might assume it was a cuddly little creature. Both assumptions are based on stereotypes. Are all pit bulls vicious? Are all kittens cuddly? Or are those labels that some people place on these animals on the basis of limited experience or stories in the media? How true are the stereotypes?

Diversity

When someone says that American society values diversity, that means Americans encourage variety and live in a society that respects differences among people.

Since the movement to give women the vote in the early 20th century and the civil rights movement of the 1950s and 1960s, America has made progress in granting equal rights to all its citizens. This social and legal progress has allowed Americans today to better exercise their right to vote and to have equal acess to education and jobs, among other things. They practice this freedom regardless of their gender, age, race, ethnicity, national origin, religion, family status, sexual preference, or physical ability.

Key Terms

discrimination—
unfair treatment based on prejudice against a certain group

stereotype—
an idea or a concept that is based on oversimplified assumptions or opinions, rather than on facts

Key Term

diversity—
variation or difference

Americans encourage variety and live in a society that respects differences among people.

The struggle for mutual respect, however, is not a battle that has been won. The United States, like all modern countries, is still working to become a more tolerant and open society.

Religious Respect

Religious intolerance has ignited conflict throughout human history, from the persecution of Jewish slaves in Egypt to the Crusader wars between Christian and Islamic soldiers during the Middle Ages to the 20th-century conflicts between Protestants and Catholics in Northern Ireland. Religious respect is essential to US society. Overcoming intolerance requires making a conscious effort to respect the beliefs—or nonbeliefs—of others. It's not condoning or condemning, but just respecting others' rights. Self-discipline and self-control will allow people to avoid religious intolerance.

Gender Stereotypes

Have you ever heard someone say that boys aren't supposed to cry? Or that girls are no good in science? If you're a boy, do people assume you love sports? If you're a girl, does everyone assume you like to cook? If so, you're experiencing gender stereotyping.

Gender stereotypes cover more than just the observable physical differences between males and females. They include cultural, social, psychological, and behavorial traits.

Gender equality is a complex issue that's still evolving. The nation's highest courts are still hearing cases involving gender rights, and state legislatures are also debating the issue. As these cases and discussions continue, the United States is working at how to be a just society—a society that practices justice. As a free people, Americans seek "justice for all."

Gender stereotypes have at least two big problems. The first one is that, like prejudices, gender stereotypes halt the thinking process. They're a trap. If you fall victim to gender stereotypes, you build your ways of dealing with people on the basis of false assumptions or misleading mental images.

The second problem is that gender stereotypes make clear communication difficult, if not impossible. Without communication, there's no understanding. With no understanding, there's no respect.

How can you avoid stereotyping people by their gender?

- Be sensitive to language that might contain gender stereotypes ("you guys," "you gals," etc.)
- Don't go with your gut reaction—it's likely to be based on preconceptions
- Take time to think
- Avoid using hurtful words or expressions
- Don't fall victim to peer pressure
- View everyone as an equal.

Just because you avoid stereotypes does not mean that you cannot have your own opinions about gender issues. But in the spirit of mutual respect, you need to be open-minded. Your ideas will naturally develop as you mature. Respect the ideas of adults in your life as well as those of your friends, but don't feel that you have to go along with everyone on everything 100 percent. Think for yourself.

Demonstrating Tolerance

Overcoming prejudice and discrimination begins with each individual. The goal is to see each person not as part of a group or a stereotype, but as an individual. How do you know if you are showing tolerance and understanding towards other people? It's really very simple. Ask yourself: Am I treating them the way I would want them to treat me?

How would you feel if others made fun of your skin color, ethnic background, hair color, religion, or the region of the United States you are from? How would you feel if you were denied a place on the team, an education, a job, an opportunity, simply because someone decided you belonged to the "wrong" group? How would you feel if others refused to be friends with you, to eat in the school cafeteria with you, or to live in the same neighborhood with you because of their prejudice?

If you wouldn't like other people doing that to you, don't do it to them. That's the foundation of tolerance and mutual respect.

Improving Group Effectiveness

Establishing mutual respect, being tolerant, and valuing diversity are important for each person on the individual level. But they're equally important at the group or organizational level.

Working Toward Common Goals

Did you ever push two bar magnets around on a tabletop? What happened as you brought them closer together? Either the magnets flipped away from each other the closer you placed them, or they snapped together, forming a bond.

All magnets are polarized—they have a south pole and a north pole. One pole is positive, and the other is negative. If you bring two positive or two negative poles together, the magnets repel each other. If you put a negative and a positive pole close to each other, the magnets attract each other.

You can compare members of a team or group with magnets. If group members can't communicate clearly and see a common goal, they tend to lack trust and respect for each other. Nothing productive will happen. They don't come together and bond. But when group or team members have a clearly defined, common goal and are able to communicate about their plan of action to achieve that goal, they come together. They bond. They're ready to produce results.

Benefits of Accepting Differences

As hard as they try, people often find it difficult to accept other people's differences. Whether they fail to understand the tenets of a religion, the political view of a certain party, or the issues that are relevant to a certain ethnicity or gender, some lack of perspective or other intangible factor seems to put people at odds with each other.

If a group or team is to function effectively, its members must work consciously to accept each other's differences. It may take a concerted effort, but the benefits of accepting other people's differences outweigh the drag that prejudicial thinking puts on team performance.

The best team is a unified whole. No team can be whole while any of its members holds wrong assumptions, false impressions, and stereotypes about fellow team members.

Communication is key to breaking down the barriers and accepting others' differences. Tapping the talents, ideas, experiences, and ingenuity of a diverse group of people is very productive. A diverse group of people can usually come up with much better solutions than can a group of people who all think the same—but to come up with the best solutions, members must trust and listen to each other. They must not only accept but also value their differences. They must see diversity as a strength.

Remembering the Titans

T. C. WILLIAMS HIGH SCHOOL

in Alexandria, Virginia, has one of the most diverse student bodies in the nation. Students from more than 80 countries, speaking dozens of languages, fill its classrooms. They pour into its football stadium every fall to cheer on their school team, the Titans.

Perhaps you don't find diversity all that unusual. Most public schools today have students from many races and ethnic backgrounds.

Scene from the 2000 movie, Remember the Titans
Courtesy of Tracy Bennett/Walt Disney/Bruckheimer Films/
The Kobal Collection

But this hasn't always been the case.
In fact, it's happened only in the past half-century. Beginning in 1954, the US Supreme Court issued a series of rulings designed to end racial segregation in public schools across the country. In a 1971 decision, the court ruled that school districts could bus students from one neighborhood school to another to achieve racial balance in the classroom.

To comply with this ruling, the City of Alexandria restructured its public school system that year. As a result, two of the city's high schools would have only freshman and sophomore students. All juniors and seniors would attend a third, T. C. Williams. The school, formerly all white, now had a mix of black and white students.

Strong rivalries had developed among the three high schools, and nowhere were these rivalries greater than in football. Football, the ultimate team sport, would be the first big test of success or failure for Alexandria's new, desegregated school system. But when the Titans came together for their first practice in 1971, little did they know that they would set the tone for the entire community in a time of racial tension.

Under the leadership of a dynamic black coach, the Titans developed a strong bond as a team. Their commitment to victory quickly overcame any prejudices based on race, economic status, or cultural beliefs. The team became a winner.

The Titans' success on the field began to extend to the rest of the school and the community. The team went on to win the division and state championships.

The Titans proved that mutual respect can be the fuel that drives not only successful teams but also strong communities. The team became the unifying symbol for the community as team members—along with adults in the community—learned to respect each other and to take pride in a joint achievement.

In 2000, the team's 1971 season was the basis of a major motion picture, *Remember the Titans*, starring Denzel Washington.

When group or team members have a clearly defined, common goal and are able to communicate about their plan of action to achieve that goal, they come together.
Courtesy of Cindy Charles/PhotoEdit

For Greater Group Effectiveness:

- **Forgive mistakes quickly**—People often learn more from failure than from success

- **Hold members accountable**—Every team member should have a role and should be responsible for carrying it out

- **Foster trust and commitment**—Both are essential to teamwork

- **Don't make excuses**—Whining and placing blame are counterprodcutive

- **Make the hard decisions**—Winning doesn't come easy

- **Seek concrete answers and solutions**—You can use them to measure effectiveness

- **Respect differences**—See them as a source of strength

- **Constantly strive toward mutual respect**—Respect is the glue that holds the group or team together.

Evaluating and Measuring Group Effectiveness

How do you tell if your group or team is working effectively? The first step is to establish clear goals. The second is to decide whether the group is meeting those goals. Are team members devoting their efforts to the team's task, or wasting them arguing among themselves over issues that have little or nothing to do with it? Figuring this out can be difficult, especially when the team's task isn't completed yet. Nevertheless, constantly seeking a measure of results—or movement toward results—is a necessary part of team-building.

Remember that along the way, the leader must measure, evaluate, and adjust as needed. Hitting the bull's-eye might take three, six, or even 10 shots, but you will finally make a direct hit. Your team will succeed.

Conflict in Groups

Although groups can have any number of conflicts, they all boil down to three basic types: conflicts in *perspective*; conflicts in *purpose*; and conflicts in *practice*.

Conflicts in Perspective

Conflicts in perspective involve what people do and why they do it. They have to do with team members' differing beliefs and values. The student who wants the highest-possible grade point average (GPA) believes that it will help him or her get into a good college. Such a student believes that a college degree is critical for success. A student who wants only a high school diploma, on the other hand, doesn't think college is important. These two students' values are different, and those values will determine how they act and react in a group.

If people try to solve perspective-level conflicts by ignoring or working around them, the conflicts will continue. That's because the participants have not addressed the underlying issues. Nonetheless, such conflicts are difficult, and sometimes impossible, to resolve. At times, people must agree to disagree and work out the best compromise possible.

Conflicts in Purpose

Conflicts in purpose involve what people want to achieve. These conflicts arise when members can't accept the team's goals and objectives.

For example, one team member might say, "I don't care what grade we receive on this assignment. I just want to get it done." Another member might say, "I want us to put together an A+ presentation so that I will keep the highest GPA possible."

Goals are easier to establish and change than team perspective. For this reason, purpose conflicts are usually easier to solve than perspective conflicts are. To deal with conflicts of purpose, the leader should set clear goals before the project begins—with input from team members.

Conflicts in Practice

Conflicts in practice have to do with the team's processes and procedures. If members can't agree on when the team will meet, where it will meet, or who will lead the meetings, they have conflicts at the practice level.

A leader's best bet in dealing with conflicts of practice is to set up operating procedures before the team begins its work. At the least, the leader can insist that practices and procedures should support the team's objectives.

Methods of Handling Conflict

People react to conflict in a group or team setting in one of two ways: *fight* or *flight*.

Some people *fight* when they perceive a conflict. They become aggressive. At their worst, they lash out, explode, argue, and become competitive. At their best, they express their own perspectives, yet continue to work with team members to arrive at a solution.

When faced with conflict, other people will resort to *flight*. These people are passive. At their worst, they pout, withdraw, passively resist, and avoid working through conflicts at all costs. At their best, they thoughtfully reflect on the issues at hand and offer their ideas to try to resolve them.

Most people have developed strategies for handling everyday conflicts. They may retreat. They may detour around the problem—a method that works sometimes, but may become habit-forming. Other situations are more difficult to deal with, however. You can't retreat. You can't pretend that the problem doesn't exist. You can't get around it. You must adjust.

What is adjustment? Does it mean giving in to avoid trouble or making a scene? Does it mean forcing others to give in to your wishes, never compromising, and relying on the other person to adjust?

Experts have identified four main ways people handle conflict—*retreating, standing still, detouring,* and *encountering.*

Retreating

Retreating is blocking or moving away from a problem or conflict. People who retreat don't want to confront conflict head on. Some people who retreat simply refuse to defend their point of view. They may give up without even trying. They may try to place the blame on others. In some cases, they may even withdraw from society to try to escape reality.

Sometimes retreat is understandable. Loss of a loved one, for example, might cause someone to retreat in fear of future loss, rejection, or loneliness.

Standing Still

Standing still is avoiding a problem or conflict by using defense mechanisms. Some people prefer to stay in one place rather than to risk defeat or rejection. They include, for example, the student with great potential who takes the easiest course, so that he or she doesn't have to work very hard. The adult who prefers to stand still says, "It was good enough for my parents, and it's good enough for me. Why change now?"

Other forms of standing still include such defense mechanisms as rationalization and projection or just daydreaming, forgetting, and regression.

Detouring

Detouring is moving around, or avoiding, a problem or conflict. People who constantly avoid important issues may think they've dealt with a problem, but the solution is temporary. The problem is bound to arise again. If your friend Mark says, "Suzanne gets good grades because she's the teacher's pet," he's detouring, rather than facing the fact that he doesn't study enough.

Compensation is one way of detouring. It involves substituting traits or attributes that give you a more pleasant picture of yourself than your undesirable traits do. A rejected or insecure person may compensate by showing off, being sarcastic, or misbehaving—just to get attention.

In some cases, compensation has favorable results. For example, a guy who doesn't make the varsity basketball team could compensate by becoming a whiz in computer science.

Encountering

Encountering is the best way to handle problems. Encountering is facing a conflict head-on and reaching a solution. The person who faces problems stands a much better chance of solving them than the person who avoids or ignores them does. You probably find it easy to advise others about how to face their problems, but when it's your own problem, it's a different story.

Key Terms

rationalization—
concealing the true motivation for one's thoughts, actions, or feelings by offering reassuring, but incorrect, explanations

projection—
the act of falsely attributing to others one's own unacceptable feelings, impulses, or thoughts

Like everyone else, you face problems and conflicts every day. You interact with others every day. You must compromise—adjust to those around you. To function in society, you must learn to meet, encounter, and resolve those problems and conflicts.

Remember that in any conflict only three outcomes are possible:

1. Win–lose—one side will win and one will lose

2. Lose–lose—both sides lose

3. Win–win—through communication, compromise, and common sense, most conflicts can be resolved with both sides winning.

Conclusion

Building positive relationships with others is one of a leader's most challenging tasks. Understanding yourself in terms of your emotions, attitudes, and prejudices is the first step. Good leaders set goals and measure their team's progress in meeting them. They understand the types of conflicts in groups and the ways people handle or avoid those conflicts.

Review Questions

1   What are three ways ways to show personal respect?

2   What are three causes of prejudice?

3   What is diversity?

4   How can you tell if your team is working effectively?

5   What are the four main ways people handle conflict? Which is the best way to handle problems?

A positive attitude can make it easier to handle life's troubles and work with others.
Courtesy of Getty Images

How many of these defense mechanisms do you recognize? Have you ever used any of them yourself? Because defense mechanisms can be used unconsciously, people sometimes use them without even knowing it. Before things can get better for Jack and Christine, Jack must realize that his attitude needs to improve.

Mature people don't fall back on defense mechanisms—mainly because they don't need them. They confront their problems directly and try to solve them. That doesn't mean they're always successful. Many times, you simply have to "grin and bear it." But growing up and developing a positive, productive attitude requires a willingness to keep working to solve an issue rather than dodge it.

Nobody comes into this world with a guaranteed perfect life. But the attitude you develop once you get here is under your control. A positive attitude can make it easier to handle life's troubles. As Norman Vincent Peale, who wrote several books about positive thinking, once wrote: "How you think about a problem is more important than the problem itself—so always think positively."

People with positive attitudes usually have other personality traits that help them meet life's challenges, frustrations, and disappointments. These people can call these traits into action to solve problems and to succeed. Some of the most important of these traits are integrity, credibility, humility, patience, respect, appreciation, and focus on task completion and on people.

Strategies for Expressing Emotions

Another factor that plays a strong role in the way people behave is their emotions. You can think of emotions as spontaneous feelings that you experience.

You may experience specific feelings such as love, joy, grief, fear, anger, or disgust. People refer to a more general kind of feeling as a "mood". We all experience people who are in a good "mood" or bad "mood." Moods are a temporary state of mind or a general feeling of some emotion.

Infants come into the world with the two most basic emotions, delight, and distress. At first they express their emotions by crying. Later they begin to include the ability to smile, gurgle, and make "baby sounds" when they are delighted.

As people grow older, they learn how to express their emotions in different ways. Children learn what type of behavior will get certain results. For example, some children try the temper tantrum to get their way. They will probably continue this technique until it no longer achieves results. Learning how to express your emotions is an ongoing part of growing up. Learning to control your emotions is a challenge for everyone in a leadership position.

The expression of emotion is very important, especially very strong emotions. Sometimes, however, circumstances require that you not express these emotions directly. You may feel like "telling off" someone or even physically striking the person, but your social conditioning tells you that this is not acceptable behavior. That is why it is essential that you learn constructive methods of expressing strong emotions. The following strategies can help you deal with your emotions in a constructive way.

Physical Activity

Emotions are a very real part of you. All of us have experienced the feeling of an intense emotional buildup. Sometimes the best way to work out such feelings is through physical activity. Some people find sports activities good emotional outlets, whereas others release their built-up emotions on creative projects. Still others find that they best release their emotional energy through some other activity, such as cleaning the house or washing the car. This way, you can work out your frustrations and have the "bonus" of a neat closet, clean house, mowed lawn, or a washed car because of your constructive release of tensions through physical activity. Hobbies such as hunting, fishing, painting, woodworking, music, and sewing are also good constructive releases.

Talking It Out

Sometimes the best therapy for releasing emotional tension is talking things out with a trusted friend, teacher, parent, or counselor. The experience of getting an issue off your chest rids you of some of the pressure. Often the other person can help you see alternatives you weren't aware of and can assist you in learning to understand your feelings more clearly.

Sense of Humor

Keeping your sense of humor is a big asset in constructively expressing emotions. Being able to laugh at yourself and to laugh *with* others is a rare combination. What some people try to pass off as humor is sometimes really just a way of poking fun at others. The jokester tries to build up his or her self-image in an attempt to feel superior at someone else's expense. The constructive sense of humor shows an appreciation for self and others and is never cutting, sarcastic, or hostile.

Positive Thoughts and Actions

Constructive emotional expression also emphasizes the positive. You read earlier about the difference between talking the talk and walking the walk. This is no different. You can resolve to "think positively," but if you have not established a healthy personal attitude as a foundation, "positive thinking" becomes an empty phrase. Improving positive attitudes begins with a healthy self-image, acknowledging rather than denying problems, and with a conscious effort to build habits for positive personal growth.

Conclusion

Your success as a leader often depends on attitudes—and you can control your attitude. Will your attitude be positive or negative? The choice is yours. A positive attitude will make you a happier and more successful family member, student, employee, and citizen. People are attracted to and will follow positive thinkers—thinkers who can solve problems for themselves and others. A positive attitude can be the leader's key to success.

Review Questions

1 How does your perspective affect your life experiences?

2 What shapes a person's perspective?

3 How do a person's perspective and affiliation need interact?

4 How do a person's goals influence his or her actions?

5 What are five common defense mechanisms?

Citizenship and American Government

Chapter 1

Citizenship and Responsibility

Above: courtesy of US Navy/Photographer's Mate 3rd Class Juan E. Diaz;
previous page: courtesy of US Navy/Mass Communication Specialist 1st Class Michael W. Pendergrass

Key Terms

- citizen
- citizenship
- law
- constituted authority
- spirit of association
- providence
- classical republicanism
- civic virtue
- established religion
- Judeo-Christian
- private morality
- separation of powers

What You Will Learn to Do

Understand what it means to be a citizen of the United States, a representative democracy

Skills and Knowledge You Will Gain Along the Way

✔ Explain authority and laws
✔ Define your role as a citizen—your rights and responsibilities
✔ Discuss the role of government

Authority and Laws

One of the purposes of the NJROTC program is to develop informed, responsible citizens. A citizen has, by birth or choice, an allegiance—a tie of loyalty—to a particular country. But citizenship is a two-way street. The citizen owes loyalty to his or her country. In turn, the country owes protection to its citizens.

Sometimes people speak of "only an average citizen" or "just a private citizen"—meaning someone with no special power or official role. But throughout American history, individual citizens have played important roles. Later in this chapter, for instance, you will read how, on 11 September 2001, individual citizens who were passengers on United Airlines Flight 93 sacrificed themselves to keep terrorists from using their plane to attack the nation's capital. Their action cost them their lives, but saved the lives of countless others.

Authority is the answer to the question, "Who says so?" In some primitive societies, tribal chieftains are in authority. They have the power to make and enforce laws and other important decisions. In other countries, a monarchy is the governing authority: A king or queen makes laws for the entire society; sometimes with the help or consent of a parliament. Some societies are under the rule of a dictatorship. In such countries, one person makes decisions for everyone. In modern representative democracies like the United States, however, the power of the government is derived not from one person but from the people, who elect legislators to create and uphold the laws of the land on the people's behalf.

In simplest terms, laws are the agreements by which people live. A single person living alone—a castaway on a desert island, for instance—would have no need of laws and could do whatever he or she wanted to do. The need for laws emerges when a group of people of almost any size decides to live together. Within your family, you might have rules about things like your evening curfew or cleaning up after dinner. In the larger world, laws regulate all kinds of behavior. For instance, there are building codes, motor vehicle standards, and restrictions on drug use, which are meant to create a standard of safety and a quality of life for all members of society. In addition, there are laws forbidding major crimes that pose an obvious threat to the safety and stability of any society, such as theft and murder.

As you might imagine, governments and those who live under them have progressed greatly over the millennia with the appearance of new religions, technologies, and philosophies. These have made the societies themselves more complex and diverse. This is why societies like the United States need laws and regulations of all kinds. In the US federal system, Congress makes the laws that apply to the whole nation while state legislatures and other local government bodies make laws that apply within their boundaries, allowing local governments to adjust to the diversity and differences of their respective jurisdictions.

To ensure that the people are always represented in the legislative process, all major members of both local and national government are elected by citizens. Ordinary citizens vote for members of the US Congress, the state legislature, the county commission, the city council, and many other positions in government. As a result, the laws these bodies pass have the force and consent of the people behind them, even though individual citizens may not know the details of most laws.

Congress is an example of what is called a constituted authority. *Constituted* means "appointed to an office or lawfully elected." Accepting the authority of the nation's constituted authoritative body is not just your role as a US citizen but also your *responsibility*. As a citizen of the United States, you have a say in how this authoritative body is structured. You exercise this input by voting for those whom you want to represent you.

Coupled with your responsibilities as a citizen are *rights*. These are assurances the authoritative body makes to those it governs. In the US system, this gives the government the consent of the people so it can continue governing. Civil rights protect people in their private lives from the arbitrary and unfair actions of the government; political rights allow people to participate in their own governance.

The Citizen's Role—Rights and Responsibilities

There are three ways to become an American citizen: by birth, by naturalization, or by act of Congress. Anyone born on US soil is automatically an American citizen. The legal term for this is *jus soli*, the law of the soil. Anyone born in a foreign country to US citizens is also a US citizen. This is known legally as *jus sanguinis*, or law of the blood.

Legal residents of the United States who are not citizens by birth can become citizens by a process known as *naturalization*. This consists of waiting a period of time, taking citizenship classes, passing a citizenship test, and then appearing before a judge and swearing an oath of allegiance to the United States.

Sometimes Congress passes a law declaring all people in a certain territory to be United States citizens. That happened most recently when Alaska and Hawaii became the 49th and 50th states of the Union. Congress granted citizenship to all people born there when they were territories of the United States.

Whether native-born or naturalized, all citizens have the same basic responsibilities. They need to respect and obey the laws of the United States. While laws sometimes need to be changed, citizens must obey them until they are changed. This duty to respect the laws of the land is not just a matter of responsibility but of loyalty to the country itself. This doesn't mean you have to approve of all actions government officials take; in fact, our own Founding Fathers greatly disapproved of the actions of their government. But they still showed loyalty to the British Empire until the number of injustices weighed against the colonies were so great that the people could no longer tolerate them. When the time came to separate from the British Empire, the leaders of the colonies did not simply fight the British and leave it at that. They still showed a measure of loyalty to the British Empire by drafting a lengthy document, the Declaration of Independence, that explained both to the colonists and to the British why they were leaving.

Characteristics of a Good Citizen

COUNTRIES EXPECT CERTAIN THINGS from their citizens besides mere allegiance. Here are some of the things good American citizens do:

- They value, respect, and defend the rights and privileges guaranteed by the US Constitution.
- They accept the basic idea of majority rule under the Constitution.
- They believe in equal opportunity for everyone.
- They respect and uphold the law and its agencies.
- They vote.
- They accept taxes as the price of necessary public services and pay them promptly.
- They accept civic responsibilities, such as jury duty, and carry them out to the best of their abilities.
- They support efforts to prevent war but stand ready to defend the country if necessary.
- They know how to work with others on social action—to win support for desirable legislation, for instance.
- They know that a democracy needs citizens who are well informed, so they pay attention to the news, especially by reading newspapers in print or online.
- They understand that democracy requires citizens to be educated.
- They respect property rights and regulations and meet their obligations under contracts.
- They support fair business practices and fair relations between employers and employees.
- They take responsibility for making our free-market economy work, with government help and regulation when necessary.
- They have some understanding of other economic systems, including their political and social aspects.
- They accept family responsibilities and uphold standards in their neighborhood and larger community.
- They understand other cultures and ways of life.
- They put the general welfare above their own when they must choose.
- They understand how people depend on one another around the world to work together to make a good life.
- They understand that in the long run, people will govern themselves better than any other group or individual would.
- They take responsibility for the wise use of natural resources.
- They rely on democratic principles as guides in evaluating their own and other people's behavior.
- They feel they have inherited an unfinished experiment in self-government, which is their duty and privilege to carry on.
- They cultivate qualities of personal character such as courage, wisdom, and generosity toward others.

THIS STATEMENT OF RESPONSIBILITIES of citizenship was developed by the Freedoms Foundation, a citizenship education organization at Valley Forge, Pa. (http://www.ffvf.org/). How do you think it compares with the Characteristics of a Good Citizen you read on an earlier page?

Preamble

Freedom and responsibility are mutual and inseparable; we can ensure enjoyment of the one only by exercising the other. Freedom for all of us depends on responsibility by each of us.

To secure and expand our liberties, therefore, we accept these responsibilities as individual members of a free society:

1. To be fully responsible for our own actions and for the consequences of those actions. Freedom to choose carries with it the responsibility for our choices.

2. To respect the rights and beliefs of others. In a free society, diversity flourishes. Courtesy and consideration toward others are measures of a civilized society.

3. To give sympathy, understanding, and help to others. As we hope others will help us when we are in need, we should help others when they are in need.

4. To do our best to meet our own and our families' needs. There is no personal freedom without economic freedom. By helping ourselves and those closest to us to become productive members of society, we contribute to the strength of the nation.

5. To respect and obey the laws. Laws are mutually accepted rules by which, together, we maintain a free society. Liberty itself is built on a foundation of law. That foundation provides an orderly process for changing laws. It also depends on our obeying laws once they have been freely adopted.

6. To respect the property of others, both private and public. No one has a right to what is not his or hers. The right to enjoy what is ours depends on our respecting the right of others to enjoy what is theirs.

7. To share with others our appreciation of the benefits and obligations of freedom. Freedom shared is freedom strengthened.

8. To participate constructively in the nation's political life. Democracy depends on an active citizenry. It depends equally on an informed citizenry.

9. To help freedom survive by assuming personal responsibility for its defense. Our nation cannot survive unless we defend it. Its security rests on the individual determination of each of us to help preserve it.

10. To respect the rights and to meet the responsibilities on which our liberty rests and our democracy depends. This is the essence of freedom. Maintaining it requires our common effort, all together and each individually.

Another responsibility, and perhaps the greatest privilege of any citizen, is the right to vote. Your 18th birthday may seem far off today, but it, and the right to vote, will be here before you know it. You may be eligible to vote with your parents and other adults in federal and state elections before you have graduated from high school. But even if not, you will probably have other opportunities to vote—in student government elections at your school and in other organizations you belong to. Exercising this right regularly is your chance to make a real difference in your society. Even if your measure or your candidate doesn't "win," you are getting into the habit of thinking through issues carefully and learning to evaluate candidates for office, something that many people around the world don't have the privilege to do.

Another important responsibility of a US citizen is to defend the country against foreign aggression. Even during wartime, of course, not all citizens need to serve in the armed forces, but all citizens do need to support the armed forces in their efforts to defend our country.

This is a tradition that goes back to the signers of the Declaration of Independence. Many of them were past military age themselves, but when they signed the Declaration, they wrote their names below the words, " . . . we mutually pledge to each other our lives, our fortunes, and our sacred honor." They were willing to sacrifice everything to establish the nation, and many of them paid a heavy price.

One of the best-known foreign observers of the United States in its early days was Alexis de Tocqueville. As a citizen of France, a society that valued liberty highly, he was impressed by the equality of opportunity he found in America. But he wondered how a society so devoted to materialism and self-interest could produce the civic spirit needed for self-government.

De Tocqueville believed the answer lay in the traditions of local self-government and the habits of free association. His emphasis on the spirit of association is one of the best-known themes in his writings about America.

The "American experiment" drew on many different ideas about the best organization of government, as well as on the thinking of many different philosophers. You'll read about some of them later in this chapter.

The Role of Government

The Founders of our republic knew history, especially the history of ancient Greece and Rome. They understood how the Greeks had described three kinds of governments:

* *monarchy*, or rule by one
* *aristocracy*, rule by a few, and
* *democracy*, rule by many.

The Founders were also familiar with the ideas of the political thinkers and philosophers of their own day in Britain, France, and Germany. In the second half of the 18th century, Europe was going through a period known as the Age of Enlightenment, which celebrated reason and science.

The Judeo-Christian religious tradition was also a powerful influence on the Founders. They represented many different strands of religious thought. But they generally took the teachings of the Bible seriously and frequently spoke of providence—by which they meant God's care for His children. The constitutional system they devised ultimately reflected all of these influences.

Perhaps the greatest right of any citizen is the right to vote.
Courtesy of Digital Vision/ Getty Images

Key Term

spirit of association— *the fondness American citizens have for banding together in organizations to address problems of common interest*

Key Term

providence— *the care, guardianship, and control exercised by a deity*

The Founders used the Roman Republic, which lasted almost 500 years, as one of their models for the new American government. This photo shows the Roman Coliseum.

Courtesy of Wilfried Krecichwost/ Getty Images

Key Terms

classical republicanism—
a theory that holds that the best kind of government is one that promotes the common welfare instead of the interests of one class of citizens

civic virtue—
the dedication of citizens to the common good, even at the cost of their individual interests

Classical Republicanism

One of the models the Founders turned to when they were setting up the American government was the Roman Republic. This republic lasted almost 500 years, from 509 BC to 27 BC, and set the model for classical republicanism. In a classical republic, citizens and their government are supposed to work together to achieve the common good rather than further their own personal or selfish interests.

One of the ideals of classical republicanism was civic virtue—or public-spiritedness, as people might call it today. This meant a willingness to put public service ahead of making money or even tending to one's family.

Cincinnatus embodied this ideal. He was a prosperous farmer called to serve as a consul, or chief magistrate, in the first century of the Roman Republic. He accepted the call, and when his service was over, he returned to his farm. One of the reasons George Washington was so admired was that people saw him as an American Cincinnatus. He was a prosperous landowner who could have made much more money had he stayed home, but he put his country first. And like Cincinnatus, he eventually retired to his farm when his country no longer needed him.

Americans saw civic virtue as one of three elements essential to making classical republicanism work. The other two were moral education and small, uniform communities.

The ancients believed that children had to be taught civic virtue: qualities such as courage, fairness, generosity, and self-control. Nowadays you might hear, "It takes a village to raise a child." The ancient Romans believed something very similar. The whole community took part in bringing up the next generation of Roman citizens. In the Roman Republic, children were also taught to practice civic religion. This meant the ritual worship of gods and goddesses, involving special ceremonies and other acts of devotion. The Romans believed that these deities kept watch over them.

Classical republicanism also favored small, uniform communities—cities or city-states where everyone knew everyone else, where no one was very much richer or poorer than anyone else, and where everyone shared a common religion.

You are probably already beginning to see some of the limits of this model. For one thing, Americans didn't worship ancient Roman gods and goddesses and they didn't like the idea of state religion, or established religion. In some places, the ruler decides the religion for the whole population. In other places, the government doesn't care what people believe but expects everyone to pay taxes to support the official religion. But many people had come to the American colonies expressly for the freedom to worship God—or not—as they saw fit. The Founders wanted no part of a state religion, writing in the first Amendment of the US Constitution, "Congress shall make no law respecting an establishment of religion, or prohibiting the free exercise thereof . . . ."

Even in its early days, the United States was a diverse country. Early Americans didn't want to be too alike. They sought economic opportunity—they wanted to make money and prosper. They also knew they lived in a vast country. The first towns and cities were very small, and it would be some time before North America would be fully explored, but the Founders needed a system of government that could expand with the new country.

The Judeo-Christian Heritage

Religion was another tradition that greatly influenced the Founders—broadly speaking, the Judeo-Christian heritage. Many of the Founders were skeptical of religious orthodoxy—strict adherence to codified beliefs. Nevertheless, many of them also believed that organized religion could help make people better citizens. They thought it could be a channel for communicating virtue, as the ancient Romans believed.

The Judeo-Christian heritage, however, emphasized private morality—the teachings of the Ten Commandments and the Sermon on the Mount—over the public virtue of the ancient Greeks and Romans. It emphasized love and benevolence, and considered each individual to have a soul, with dignity, worth, and rights of his or her own.

Contemporary Influences

John Locke, a British philosopher and hero of Thomas Jefferson, was another major influence on the Founders. Locke proposed what he called the philosophy of "natural rights." He believed that the state—what we often call "the government"—existed for the benefit of the individual. Society and government were there at the consent of the individual to protect the individual's rights.

John Locke
Courtesy of Bettmann/Corbis

Key Term

established religion— *a religion supported by the state through tax money*

Key Terms

Judeo-Christian— *relating to beliefs and practices that have their historical roots in Judaism and Christianity*

private morality— *the principles of virtue as expressed in Judeo-Christian teachings*

Baron de Montesquieu
Courtesy of Archivo
Iconografico, SA/Corbis

Another important thinker was a French nobleman, the Baron de Montesquieu. He admired the British system because it provided what he called "mixed government." While the Empire was a monarchy, to be sure—and the Americans fought a war to be free of kings—Montesquieu pointed out that the British system was relatively balanced. Unlike other monarchies, the government wasn't run by a king and a few nobles. The professional and middle classes had a say, too—even though it would not be until the 20th century that all adults would have the vote.

James Madison and Constitutional Republicanism

James Madison, the fourth US president, is known as the "Father of the Constitution." His great achievement was to draw from all these influences and create a new system of government. He came up with a new concept that included aspects of two important ancient concepts—a democracy and a republic.

In a democracy, as Madison saw it, the people administer the government themselves. This meant that *direct democracy* worked only in places like the city-states of ancient Greece. In a republic, the people's representatives administer the government. This allows it to extend over a much broader area than a direct democracy.

By combining the two, he proposed the idea of a federal constitutional republic, a government that derives its power from the people by giving them the right to elect public officials to make laws for the whole as part of a strong federal government while at the same time protecting the rights of the people by establishing written restrictions on the power of government.

Americans of the founding era seemed more representative of human nature as described by the natural-rights philosophers than the ideal expected by the civic virtue of the classical republicanism. They and their ancestors had come to the new land to take advantage of the spiritual and economic opportunities the New World had to offer. Such restless and ambitious people were ill-suited for classical republicanism's ideals of self-sacrifice and conformity.

However much they admired George Washington, the Founders also realized how exceptional he was. They built a system that took human nature and enlightened self-interest into account, and it's a good thing they did. As James Madison once said, "If all people were angels, there would be no need for government."

During the Constitutional Convention of 1787, Madison argued for a government that would encourage people to act as good republican citizens possessing the quality of civic virtue. At the same time it would safeguard their freedoms with a system of checks and balances and of separation of powers. Such a system would help ensure that no one part of the government could completely negate the others.

The result of these various influences and schools of thought was the United States Constitution and the system of government Americans enjoy today. You, as an heir of this system, enjoy the rights guaranteed to you by the Constitution. In return, you have a responsibility to protect and defend those rights both for yourself and others. The next chapter will explain more about how the Constitution came to be and what it means.

THE ARMED SERVICES have special responsibility for defending the United States from aggression. But they don't have sole responsibility. Sometimes "ordinary" citizens step up to extraordinary challenges to protect the country.

So it was with the heroic passengers of United Flight 93 on 11 September 2001. They didn't say "not my job" when the danger became apparent. They didn't wait for anyone to tell them what to do. And they made the ultimate sacrifice, giving their lives.

On that day terrorists hijacked four aircraft at almost the same time. They planned to turn the planes into guided missiles.

The terrorists used two jetliners to bring down the twin towers of the World Trade Center in New York. They slammed a third plane into the Pentagon, outside Washington, DC Nearly 3,000 people died in these attacks.

No one knows for sure what the hijackers intended to do with the fourth plane. That plane, United Flight 93, was en route from Newark, New Jersey, to San Francisco. It had 37 passengers aboard, including four hijackers.

The hijackers took over the plane at 9:28 a.m. At 9:32 a.m. one of the hijackers announced there was a bomb on the plane. This was a lie. The terrorists made the announcement to explain why the aircraft had changed its course abruptly in the air over northeastern Ohio.

Passengers and crew made phone calls from the plane. They learned about the attacks on the World Trade Center. They decided to rush the terrorists and try to retake the plane.

At 9:57 a.m., 29 minutes after the hijackers took over, the passengers made their move. As they tried to break through to the cockpit, the hijacker pilot rolled the plane from side to side. He pushed its nose up and down, trying to throw the counterattacking passengers and crew off balance.

The passengers continued their brave effort. They were seconds away from breaking through when the pilot pushed the nose of the plane earthward.

At 10:03 a.m., United 93 plowed into a field in Shanksville, Pennsylvania.

It was all over in less than seven minutes.

The hijacker pilot's objective "was to crash his airliner into symbols of the American Republic," the 9/11 Commission report stated. "He was defeated by the unarmed, alerted passengers of United 93."

"We are sure that the nation owes a debt to the passengers of United 93," the report also said. "Their actions saved the lives of countless others, and may have saved either the US Capitol or the White House from destruction."

Conclusion

Citizenship is membership in a political community. A citizen has rights and responsibilities, including voting, paying taxes, obeying laws, and supporting the national defense. In a democracy, laws have the force of the public behind them, because they are made by legislators whom the people have elected.

The American system of government is known as a federal constitutional republic. James Madison is known as "the father of the United States Constitution." He developed the concept of a federal constitutional republic by drawing on ideas from the ancient Greeks and Romans, from the important thinkers of his own day, and from the ideals of the Judeo-Christian tradition.

The system Madison developed was intended to encourage people to act as civic-minded good citizens. But this system, with its checks and balances and its separation of powers, would guard against the consequences if they did not.

Review Questions

1 What are the three ways to become a citizen of the United States?

2 What did Alexis de Tocqueville see as the source of American civic spirit?

3 How did John Locke influence the Founders?

4 What was James Madison's great achievement?

Chapter 2

Foundations of US Government

What You Will Learn to Do

Understand the Declaration of Independence and the Constitution, with the Bill of Rights and the other amendments

Skills and Knowledge You Will Gain Along the Way

✔ Discuss the Declaration of Independence
✔ Explain the United States Constitution
✔ Describe the Bill of Rights
✔ Review the other constitutional amendments

The Jefferson Memorial, Washington, DC
Courtesy of US Navy/Photographer's Mate 2nd Class Daniel J. McLain

Key Terms

- **preamble**
- **divine right**
- **unalienable**
- **constitutional convention**
- **levy**
- **veto**
- **posterity**
- **autonomy**
- **ratify**
- **amendment**
- **quartering**
- **indictment**
- **enumerate**

The Declaration of Independence

Every year Americans celebrate the Fourth of July with fireworks and parades. The Fourth is Independence Day in the United States—the "birthday" of our country.

It was on that day, 4 July 1776, that the Second Continental Congress signed the Declaration of Independence and proclaimed America's independence from the British Empire.

The Declaration of Independence and the United States Constitution are two of history's most remarkable philosophical and political documents. The Declaration's ideas and the Constitution's carefully balanced system of government have inspired people worldwide. You can find the complete text of both documents in the appendices of this book.

The Declaration of Independence cut the 13 American colonies' political ties to Britain and launched them forth on a brave new experiment in self-government. The United States wasn't much of a country when the Declaration was signed. It would take a bloody war and a failed first attempt at self-government before the original 13 colonies would become a single smoothly functioning country. Despite all of this, the Declaration gave rise to a powerful new way of thinking and started what has become known as the American experiment.

The Parts of the Declaration of Independence

Drafted by Thomas Jefferson, the Declaration of Independence has five parts. Some of them are better known than others, but this document contains words and phrases you'll hear for the rest of your life as an American citizen. They are an essential part of America's story and national identity.

The Declaration opens with the preamble, or introduction. By announcing their independence from the king of England, the colonists knew they were taking a big step—as well as an enormous risk: if the revolution failed, each of them would be tried for treason and executed. The preamble is their promise to explain themselves to the world. Even if they should fail, the world would still see why they were compelled to act: "[A] decent respect to the opinions of mankind requires that they [the American people] should declare the causes which impel them to the separation."

Next comes the really big idea—the challenge to the notion of the divine right of kings. God did not set a few men over others as kings, the patriots insisted. "All men are created equal," the Declaration thundered, "and are endowed by their Creator with certain unalienable rights." Such rights are not given: They are a basic part of human existence, and no one can take them away. Among these inalienable rights, the Declaration went on, are "life, liberty, and the pursuit of happiness."

From this notion of divine right, the Founders went on to conclude that all governments derive their "just powers" from the "consent of the governed," not the right of the governors. In other words, governments exist for people, rather than the other way around.

Key Terms

preamble—
an introduction to a document such as a constitution, explaining its purpose

divine right—
a right or responsibiliity given by a divine being or deity that is therefore beyond question by humanity

unalienable—
incapable of being taken away or transferred to another

At the heart of all these ideas was a singular concept that the first democracies in ancient Greece never truly recognized, namely, "We hold these truths to be self-evident, that all Men are created equal . . . ." It would take some time before "all men" in America received the protection of their freedoms the Declaration promised. It would take even longer before people realized that the American idea had to include "all women" as well. Nevertheless, those ideas were there at the beginning, just as the blossom is in the bud before it blooms.

The Declaration's third part is a list of grievances, or complaints, against King George III, the ruler of the British Empire at the time of the Revolutionary War. Many of these grievances seem unimportant today, but to Thomas Jefferson and his colleagues in Philadelphia during the summer of 1776, they were important enough to spur them to challenge one of the most powerful monarchies on earth. If you look carefully, you can find in the Constitution and Bill of Rights provisions to keep abuses such as those of George III from happening again. (Read the Third Amendment, for instance.)

The fourth part of the Declaration outlines steps the colonies took to resolve their differences with England. Like the list of grievances, this section may seem less important today, but the Founders wanted everyone to understand that the colonists weren't just rebels. They thought of themselves as law-abiding British subjects. They saw themselves as part of a legal tradition going back centuries. They tried to make the existing system work before they decided to create a new one.

In the fifth part, the States actually declare their independence. They declare "that these united colonies are, and of right ought to be free and independent states; that they are absolved from all allegiance to the British crown."

The signers of the Declaration of Independence had no guarantees for the future. No one could assure them it would all turn out well. The leaders of the revolutionary movement knew they would all be hanged if their bold experiment failed. Even so, they were willing to put everything they had on the line—"our lives, our fortunes, and our sacred honor."

The United States Constitution

The constitution that governs the United States today was not our country's first attempt at self-government. During the Revolutionary War through 1787, the country was governed by the Articles of Confederation.

The new country did manage some important things under this first system. It won the war for independence, for one thing. Moreover, other counties now *recognized*, or acknowledged, the United States as a real country, standing on its own. Perhaps the most lasting achievement under the Articles is plain to see on any map of the United States: the organization of the Northwest Territories, which eventually became the states of Ohio, Michigan, Indiana, Illinois, and Wisconsin. These were carved out of the territory north of the Ohio River and east of the Mississippi.

Shays' Rebellion and the Need for a Stronger Government

After Shays' Rebellion George Washington felt the United States needed a stronger government.

Courtesy of Francis G. Mayer/ Corbis

IN 1786 DANIEL SHAYS was the leader of a group of hundreds of Massachusetts farmers facing hard times. They were heavily in debt. Those who couldn't pay their debts lost their homes and their farms. Many of the farmers went to prison. It was a very unhappy situation. No one liked to see the farmers in such a tough spot. Mobs intervened to keep the farmers' property from being sold at auction.

In search of weapons to arm themselves, Shays and his men launched an attack on the federal arsenal at Springfield, Massachusetts. Shays' Rebellion failed, but the episode was a warning to the Massachusetts authorities and those who feared that others might try the same thing elsewhere. Faced with a rebellion that almost seized federal property, Congress did not have the authority to intervene in what was considered a state matter.

George Washington was one of a number of important people who felt the time had come for a stronger national government. He wrote to James Madison saying, "We are either a united people or we are not. If the former, let us act as a nation. If we are not, let us no longer act a farce by pretending to it."

The Articles of Confederation

The Articles of Confederation were the kind of arrangement you might expect from a group of colonies who had cut loose from one powerful government and didn't want to end up under the thumb of another. The Articles were also a system that appealed to a diverse group of colonies that really were separate little countries. Different people founded these colonies for very different reasons. The colonies varied widely in size, geography, and population. Some, as in New England, were seafaring communities that looked out across the Atlantic. Others were farming communities that looked westward to the American heartland. The western borders of some of the smaller colonies were already defined. Other colonies, such as New York and Virginia, claimed vast tracts of land stretching farther inland. No one knew where their western borders would be drawn.

The Articles gave the former colonies independence from one another as well as from the national government. But after Daniel Shays led a group of rebellious farmers in a 1786 attack on a federal arsenal in Massachusetts, many of the Founders began to think the national government was too weak. The possibility

James Madison—the Youthful "Father of the Constitution"

James Madison: a man with a plan
Courtesy of Geoffrey Clements/ Corbis

JAMES MADISON was one of the youngest of the Founding Fathers. But by 1787, when he was only 36 years old, his talents had been long recognized and admired. He was probably the most influential of the Framers at the Constitutional Convention in Philadelphia. This is in part because he arrived early and brought along a detailed plan. (This is a lesson that applies elsewhere in life, too.)

It also didn't hurt that he kept the most detailed notes of the proceedings. They were meant to be secret, to let the delegates debate freely, and try out ideas they would later reject. But delegates were free to take as many notes as they wished. Madison attended nearly every session and kept careful notes. Much of what we know today about what happened in the convention comes from his records.

of more armed uprisings wasn't the only thing that concerned them. The early leaders of the country had begun to notice what was missing in their weak national government. They had set it up with:

- no real taxing authority
- no executive or judicial branch
- no power to regulate trade
- no power to regulate relations between the states, or between a state and a foreign country.

There was a Congress, but it took a two-thirds majority vote to pass a law. In those early days, the states couldn't even agree on a national currency.

That is why in the late spring of 1787, a convention, or meeting, was called to amend the Articles of Confederation. Almost at once, the delegates decided to draw up a new constitution. The meeting has since been known as the Constitutional Convention. The delegates considered two possible approaches: James Madison's Virginia Plan and the New Jersey Plan.

Key Term

constitutional convention— *a special meeting held to draw up a new constitution*

The Virginia Plan proposed a strong central government with the three branches the US has today: legislative, executive, and judicial. It called for empowering the legislature of the national government to:

- pass laws that individual states could not pass, such as laws governing trade between states
- strike down state laws in conflict with national laws
- call forth the national armed forces if necessary to enforce laws passed by Congress.

Some weeks into the convention, William Paterson offered the New Jersey Plan, named for his home state. This plan called mainly for tinkering with the Articles of Confederation.

Under the New Jersey Plan, the national government would get some taxing authority and could levy import duties and a stamp tax to raise money for its operations. The national government would have the power to collect money from the states if they refused to pay as well as to regulate trade between states and between states and foreign countries. What's more, the laws passed by Congress would be the supreme law of the land. No more would federal laws face challenges from state law. The New Jersey Plan also included some form of an executive branch and a judicial branch.

As talks progressed, the delegates focused increasingly on the Virginia Plan. The New Jersey Plan, many argued, just wasn't different enough from the Articles of Confederation. Major questions remained, though. The two biggest were:

- How much power should the national government have?
- How would states' representation be determined? Should each state's representation depend on population or geographical size?

Equal representation for all states in the Congress was the rule under the Articles of Confederation. Not surprisingly, the less-populated states liked that arrangement while the more-populated states thought it was unfair. The debates were so intense that at times they threatened to derail the convention.

The Great Compromise

Major progress finally came when Roger Sherman of Connecticut dusted off a proposal someone had made earlier. This proposal called for treating all states equally in the upper house but apportioning, or assigning, the number of seats in the lower house of the legislature by population.

The convention accepted the idea in what became known as the Great Compromise (or sometimes the Connecticut Compromise). It still holds today. The 435 seats in the House of Representatives are divided among the states by population. The least-populous states have only a single House member, while the most-populous have dozens of members. In the Senate, however, sparsely populated Alaska, Vermont, and Wyoming are each entitled to two members, as are populous California, New York, and Texas.

Roger Sherman of Connecticut suggested a way to balance large and small states in the Congress.
Courtesy of Hulton Archive/Getty Images

Other Constitutional Balancing Acts

The Great Compromise was one of the more important compromises to be struck at the Constitutional Convention, but it was by no means the only one. Decisions made at the Constitutional Convention also:

- Balanced power between the state and federal governments by giving specific powers to the federal government ("the enumerated powers") and leaving the rest in the hands of the states.
- Balanced legislative powers between chambers, or houses, of Congress. All tax laws had to start in the House of Representatives. The Senate, on the other hand, won authority to approve presidential appointees, such as Cabinet secretaries and Supreme Court justices.
- Checked the president's power to conduct foreign policy by giving the Senate the right to ratify all treaties.

Each branch of government has a specific role. As you learned in the last chapter, this arrangement is called the *separation of powers*. Under it:

- The legislative branch makes the laws and levies taxes.
- The executive branch enforces the laws.
- The judicial branch interprets the laws and assures individuals' rights.

Finally, in an arrangement not unlike the rock-paper-scissors game you may have sometimes played, the branches all have ways to check one another. Congress passes laws, but the president may veto them. Congress may override the president's veto with a two-thirds majority vote. The Supreme Court may rule a law unconstitutional. The Supreme Court has also checked the powers of the executive branch at times by ruling its actions illegal, but the president appoints the Supreme Court justices, and the Senate confirms them. This system of checks and balances was created to prevent any one person or branch from gaining complete control over the government and thereby risking the same tyranny the Founders had faced before the revolution.

Finally, the states preserve a say in the union by their collective power to approve or reject proposed constitutional amendments.

Key Term

veto—
the right (of a president) to reject a piece of legislation

An Overview of the United States Constitution

The Constitution consists of a preamble that makes clear that this is the founding document of the United States. It states the intentions for which the republic has been formed, with the consent of the people through their elected officials: "We the people of the United States, in order to form a more perfect Union, establish justice, insure domestic Tranquility, provide for the common defense, promote the general Welfare and secure the Blessings of Liberty to ourselves and our posterity, do ordain and establish this Constitution for the United States of America."

Article I details the duties of the Congress and sets forth the requirements to become a senator or representative. It explains how these officials are elected and establishes the powers that each house of Congress possesses. Section 8 gives Congress the power to declare war, raise and support armies, provide and maintain a navy, and make rules for the land and naval forces.

Key Term

posterity—
future generations

The Constitutional Convention, chaired by George Washington, adopted the Virginia Plan for a stronger federal government.

Courtesy of The Granger Collection

Article II describes the president's powers and explains the requirements to become president. It also sets forth a process for electing the president and describes the president's responsibilities to the people. For example, Section 2 declares the president the commander in chief of all the armed forces.

Article III covers the judicial branch. It sets up the federal courts and their duties as well as establishes the Supreme Court as the final interpreter of the Constitution. This means that any law or action taken by the Congress or the president can be brought before the Supreme Court, and the court may deem it unconstitutional and therefore in violation of the principles on which the country is built.

Article IV describes the relationship between the individual states and between the states and the federal government, ensuring both their autonomy and their adherence to federal law.

Article V provides for changing the Constitution by amendment with the support of a two-thirds majority from both chambers of Congress and the consent of three-fourths of the states.

Article VI provides for the adoption of all previous federal government debts and proclaims the Constitution to be the supreme law of the land.

Article VII tells how the Constitution is to be ratified. By July 1788 the majority of the states had ratified the Constitution, and the United States Constitution officially became the law of the United States.

Key Terms

autonomy—
the quality or state of being self-governing

ratify—
to formally confirm or approve, as of a treaty or a constitutional amendment

The Bill of Rights

The lack of a bill of rights in the original draft of the Constitution alarmed many people and stirred up opposition to the document. Some states refused to ratify the Constitution without a bill of rights. So the Framers, seeing the support for the new Constitution falling into jeopardy, promised to draft a bill of rights as soon as the Constitution was ratified.

Thus in 1791, the Framers created the first 10 amendments of the Constitution. These amendments would become known as the Bill of Rights. They drafted these amendments not only to more clearly define the rights of US citizens, but also to limit both the states and the new federal government. The Framers wanted a government strong enough not only to resist pressure from foreign enemies and the divided interests of the several states, but also to protect the individual rights for which they had battled the British.

Key Term

amendment—
*a formal alteration
to a document such as
a constitution or a law*

As you read above, much of the Constitution is about large institutional matters—the setting up of federal courts, for instance. The Bill of Rights daily touches on ordinary individual lives. You might call it a statement of street-level liberty. Every time you attend—or choose not to attend—religious services, you are operating within the freedom of religion guaranteed by the First Amendment. Every time you gather with friends or neighbors in a public place to protest or support some cause, you use your freedom of assembly. Every time you decide for yourself what you will read, rather than letting a government censor decide, you benefit from freedom of the press.

Anyone who has spent any time in a court of law knows the importance of the provisions of the Bill of Rights. The judges, the prosecution and defense lawyers, and all the officers of the court know in detail those amendments governing search and seizure, self-incrimination, or right to counsel.

Here is an overview of these all-important first 10 amendments:

The First Amendment: Religious and Political Freedom

> *Congress shall make no law respecting an establishment of religion,
> or prohibiting the free exercise thereof; or abridging the freedom of speech,
> or of the press; or the right of the people peaceably to assemble, and
> to petition the Government for a redress of grievances.*

This amendment means there is no state religion ("establishment of religion"). Nor is there any preference for one faith over another. This also means the state may not pass laws to keep people from practicing their religion, even if a majority of people don't believe in its practice.

The First Amendment also protects a citizen's right to say what he or she feels in public, even if it's critical of elected officials or other powerful people. Freedom of the press allows newspapers, radio and TV stations, and other media to have their say, too, within some constraints: If you publish false or untruthful material with spiteful intent, that may be deemed libelous and subject to prosecution.

The Framers created the Bill of Rights with the idea that the people would practice the classical republican model of civic virtue. This means that while the First Amendment guarantees freedom of religion, speech, and the press, these freedoms come at a cost to those choosing to exercise them. Supreme Court Judge Oliver Wendell Holmes defined this cost in 1917, when he stated that if a person's words "present a clear and present danger that they will create substantive evils Congress has a right to prevent" the speech could be prohibited. In other words, if you yell "Fire!" in a crowded movie theater, your words are not protected by the Constitution because they present a clear and present danger to the public at large. This has become the paramount limitation on our rights as citizens of the United States. It underscores that each citizen must exercise his or her freedoms responsibly.

The Second Amendment: the Right to Bear Arms

A well regulated Militia, being necessary to the security of a free State, the right of the people to keep and bear Arms, shall not be infringed.

This amendment prevents the government from forbidding citizens to own weapons.

The Third Amendment: Quartering of Soldiers

No soldier shall, in time of peace, be quartered in any house without the consent of the owner, nor in time of war, but in a manner to be prescribed by law.

Before the Revolution, the British Army required people to give its soldiers a place to live in their own houses. They did this not only to save money on housing but also as another means of coercing the population into obedience. Naturally, the colonists were sensitive about the way British soldiers quite literally made themselves at home. That is why this practice, called quartering, was banned during peacetime. During wartime, service members may be lodged in private homes, but only if Congress passes the appropriate law.

The Fourth Amendment: Search and Seizure

The right of the people to be secure in their persons, houses, papers, and effects, against unreasonable searches and seizures, shall not be violated, and no Warrants shall issue, but upon probable cause, supported by Oath or affirmation, and particularly describing the place to be searched, and the persons or things to be seized.

This amendment keeps police and other government officials from searching private homes or workplaces whenever they feel like it. This freedom is fundamental to what are known as *civil liberties*—the freedom to live one's life untroubled by government and police interference.

Police may search homes, offices, and other such places only if they obtain a warrant. To do this, they must tell a judge what they are looking for and why they expect to find it in the place they want to search. The Fourth Amendment is a part of every workday for police agencies, courts, and lawyers.

The Fifth Amendment: Criminal Proceedings and Due Process

No person shall be held to answer for a capital, or otherwise infamous crime, unless on a presentment or indictment of a Grand Jury, except in cases arising in the land or naval forces, or in the Militia, when in actual service in time of War or public danger; nor shall any person be subject for the same offence to be twice put in jeopardy of life or limb; nor shall be compelled in any criminal case to be a witness against himself, nor be deprived of life, liberty, or property, without due process of law; nor shall private property be taken for public use, without just compensation.

Key Term

indictment—
a written statement charging someone with a crime or other offense, drawn up by a prosecuting attorney, and presented by a grand jury

You may not think much about the Fifth Amendment unless you get into a scrape with the law. However, it is part of the bedrock of your civil liberties. The Fifth Amendment calls for those accused of a serious ("infamous") crime to be indicted before they are tried. That ensures that there is real evidence against the defendants and discourages the police from fabricating charges.

The Fifth Amendment prevents someone from being tried again for a crime if he or she has been found not guilty (that would be "double jeopardy"). It also prevents people from being forced to testify against themselves. You may have seen movies where people have said "I'll plead the Fifth," meaning that they refuse to testify against themselves in a court case. The prosecutor in such a situation is forced to find other witnesses and evidence to win a conviction.

The final part of this amendment ensures that private property is not taken away from someone except with fair payment. If your town needs part of your backyard for a new school, for instance, the town must pay you what the land is worth, however badly it needs the school.

The Sixth Amendment: the Right to a Jury Trial

In all criminal prosecutions, the accused shall enjoy the right to a speedy and public trial, by an impartial jury of the State and district wherein the crime shall have been committed, which district shall have been previously ascertained by law, and to be informed of the nature and cause of the accusation; to be confronted with the witnesses against him; to have compulsory process for obtaining witnesses in his favor, and to have the assistance of counsel for his defense.

Like the other amendments touching on matters of criminal justice, this is one with which most citizens have little direct experience. But by offering protections to all—even those who appear to have broken the law—the Sixth Amendment protects everyone. It guarantees criminal defendants a "speedy" public trial by a fair-minded jury. The Sixth also guarantees the accused a defense lawyer. It sets standards for witnesses' presentation of evidence and ensures the accused know the accusations against them so that they might better defend themselves.

The Seventh Amendment: the Right to a Civil Trial

In suits at common law, where the value in controversy shall exceed twenty dollars, the right of trial by jury shall be preserved, and no fact tried by a jury, shall be otherwise re-examined in any Court of the United States, than according to the rules of the common law.

Most of the courtroom dramas you see on television or at the movies depict criminal cases, but civil lawsuits—disputes between citizens or companies over money—are an important part of the justice system, too. This amendment promises jury trials in the case of civil as well as criminal cases.

The Eighth Amendment: Punishment for Crimes

Excessive bail shall not be required, nor excessive fines imposed, nor cruel and unusual punishments inflicted.

Bail is the money or property given to a court to guarantee that a criminal defendant will show up for trial. This lets the accused—who is presumed innocent until proven guilty, after all—go free until the trial. This amendment says that bail shall not be "excessive." It also forbids "cruel and unusual punishments." If you have followed Supreme Court cases involving the death penalty, you know that the concept of "cruel and unusual punishment" changes over time.

The Ninth Amendment: Unenumerated Rights

The enumeration in the Constitution, of certain rights, shall not be construed to deny or disparage others retained by the people.

In other words, just because the Constitution doesn't say anything about a particular right doesn't mean that that right doesn't belong to the citizens. Every right does not need to be enumerated. Under some systems, citizens have only the rights their governments expressly give them. The Framers wanted to make certain that the United States was not one of those systems.

The Tenth Amendment: Powers Reserved to the States

The powers not delegated to the United States by the Constitution, nor prohibited by it to the States, are reserved to the States respectively, or to the people.

This amendment makes clear that any power not clearly assigned to the federal government or forbidden to the states, belongs to the states or the people. Once again, freedom, not restriction, is the starting point of the US system of government.

Key Term

enumerate—
to list, or to specify individually

Other Constitutional Amendments

Once the Bill of Rights had been ratified, additional amendments to the Constitution came slowly. There have been only 17 amendments since the Bill of Rights; the most recent was ratified in 1992. Six of the amendments define what a person is and who has the right to vote. Even after more than 200 years, the United States is still growing and changing, expanding its definition of freedom so that all might receive the freedoms defined in the Declaration of Independence and the Constitution.

Amendment XI: *Passed by Congress March 4, 1794; ratified February 7, 1795.*

This amendment clarifies judicial power over foreign nationals, and limits the ability of citizens to sue states.

Amendment XII: *Passed by Congress December 9, 1803; ratified June 15, 1804.*

This amendment changes the procedures for electing a vice president. At first, the vice president was the runner-up in the presidential race. Under the new system, voters chose a president and a vice president separately.

Amendment XIII: *Passed by Congress January 31, 1865; ratified December 6, 1865.*

This landmark amendment ended slavery throughout the United States.

Amendment XIV: *Passed by Congress June 13, 1866; ratified July 9, 1868.*

This amendment, known for its phrase "equal protection of the laws," declared the newly freed African-American slaves to be US citizens.

Amendment XV: *Passed by Congress February 26, 1869; ratified February 3, 1870.*

This amendment outlawed racial tests for voting. It also made it illegal to keep people from voting just because they had once been enslaved.

Amendment XVI: *Passed by Congress July 2, 1909; ratified February 3, 1913.*

This amendment allowed the federal government to introduce a personal income tax.

Amendment XVII: *Passed by Congress May 13, 1912; ratified April 8, 1913.*

This amendment provided for the popular (direct) election of senators. Up till this point, House members were elected by the people, but state legislatures elected senators.

Amendment XVIII: *Passed by Congress December 18, 1917; ratified January 16, 1919; repealed by Amendment XXI.*

This amendment banned alcoholic beverages in the United States ("Prohibition").

Amendment XIX: *Passed by Congress June 4, 1919; ratified August 18, 1920.*

This amendment gave women the right to vote.

Amendment XX: *Passed by Congress March 2, 1932; ratified January 23, 1933.*

This amendment pushed the inauguration of a new president ahead from March to January 20. It also moved the day a new Congress convenes from December to January 3. It clarified procedures for Congress to follow in filling either presidential or vice-presidential vacancies.

Amendment XXI: *Passed by Congress February 20, 1933; ratified December 5, 1933.*

This amendment repealed Amendment XVIII and ended Prohibition.

Amendment XXII: *Passed by Congress March 21, 1947; ratified February 27, 1951.*

This amendment put into law a practice that was followed from George Washington until Franklin Roosevelt: a limit of two terms for any president. (Franklin Roosevelt was elected four times.)

Amendment XXIII: *Passed by Congress June 16, 1960; ratified March 29, 1961.*

This amendment gives residents of the District of Columbia the right to vote in presidential elections.

Amendment XXIV: *Passed by Congress August 27, 1962; ratified January 23, 1964.*

A century after the Civil War, this amendment was enacted to defend the voting rights of African-Americans: It forbade states to require taxes (head taxes) as a condition of voting. Some Southern states had used such requirements to keep African-Americans from casting ballots.

Amendment XXV: *Passed by Congress July 6, 1965; ratified February 10, 1967.*

This amendment, passed after the assassination of President John F. Kennedy in 1963, clarified the presidential succession. It also provided for the appointment of a new vice president to succeed one who had become president. In addition, this amendment provided for temporary transfers of presidential power to the vice president (as when the president is in the hospital) and for situations in which the president cannot speak for himself to declare himself unable to serve.

Amendment XXVI: *Passed by Congress March 23, 1971; ratified July 1, 1971.*

This amendment gave 18-year-olds the vote in federal elections. Before that, states set varying age requirements for voting, but most required voters to be 21.

Amendment XXVII: *Originally proposed September 25, 1789; ratified May 7, 1992.*

This amendment makes it harder for Congress to vote itself a pay raise. If it does vote one, the extra money doesn't start until after the next election.

Conclusion

The Declaration of Independence is the document that launched the United States. It set forth a radical new vision of individual liberty and a government deriving its "just powers from the consent of the governed."

During its first years, including those of the Revolutionary War, the country was governed by the Articles of Confederation. The Articles provided a loose connection among the states and only a weak central government.

After a few years it became clear that a stronger national government was needed. A convention was called in the spring of 1787 to revise the Articles—but almost immediately the delegates decided to draw up a new constitution. The new constitution provided for a stronger federal government with executive, legislative, and judicial branches. By July 1788, a majority of states had ratified it and it took effect. Congress and the states modified it almost immediately by adding the Bill of Rights. Over the following two centuries, they added 17 amendments.

Review Questions

1 What are the five parts of the Declaration of Independence?

2 What was the significance of Shays' Rebellion?

3 What are the three branches of the United States Government?

4 What are some examples of checks and balances in the Constitution?

5 Why is the Bill of Rights important to individuals?

Chapter 3

National Defense

Key Terms

- **appropriate**
- **chain of command**
- **National Security Council**
- **operating forces**
- **shore establishment**
- **Joint Chiefs of Staff**
- **port security**
- **navigational aid**
- **interdiction**
- **exploit**

What You Will Learn to Do

Understand how the US armed forces are organized under the control of elected and appointed civilian leaders

Skills and Knowledge You Will Gain Along the Way

✔ Explain the defense structure of the United States
✔ Describe the organization of the US Navy
✔ Discuss the roles of the US Army and Air Force

Courtesy of US Navy/Mass Communication Specialist 2nd Class Todd Frantom

The Defense Structure of the United States

Both Congress and the president have important roles to play in the defense of the United States. Article I of the Constitution gives Congress the power to declare war, raise and support armies, and provide and maintain a navy, and Article II names the president as commander in chief of the US armed forces.

Because the military falls under the authority of two elected branches of government, the official actions of the military have the weight of the Constitution and the American people behind them. That is why whenever military officers are commissioned into service, they do not swear an oath to serve and defend the president or the Congress, but the Constitution. In that way, no single person or body can outweigh the military's obligation to the country and its people.

Congress makes the rules for the military and decides how much money to provide for national defense. The Congress appropriates funds, declares wars, and confirms promotions of military officers that fall beneath its authority. The president has a drastically different role. As commander in chief, the president sits at the top of the chain of command and directs the actions of the military in peace or war.

The Secretary of Defense

A president has many responsibilities and can't personally handle all of the matters presented to the White House. For that reason, the president appoints a group of top officials to handle certain aspects of the administration's policies. These men and women are known as the president's Cabinet. The Cabinet member responsible for military matters is the known as the Secretary of Defense. The secretary runs the Department of Defense (DoD). The DoD is the ultimate authority beneath the president for national defense and managing military resources. As with all members of the Cabinet, the president appoints and the Senate confirms the Secretary of Defense

The National Security Council

The Secretary of Defense serves not only in the Cabinet but also on the National Security Council (NSC). This group consists of the president, the vice president, the Secretary of State, the Secretary of the Treasury, and the Secretary of Defense. The NSC discusses national security and foreign policy questions and advises the president on such matters. An official called the national security adviser coordinates the NSC's work and reports directly to the president. The president may appoint other members to the NSC and may invite other Cabinet members to sit in on discussions of subjects that touch on their departments' respective responsibilities.

Key Terms

appropriate—
to decide to spend money for a specific use

chain of command—
the system by which authority passes down through the military ranks, with each level accountable to a superior

National Security Council—
the president's committee for considering national security and foreign policy matters with advisers and cabinet officials; the president, vice president, Secretary of State, Secretary of the Treasury, and Secretary of Defense are members

UNIT III

The Pentagon, one of the wold's largest office buildings, houses the Department of Defense.
Courtesy of Bettmann/Corbis

The Department of Defense

The Secretary of Defense has undersecretaries, assistant secretaries, and agencies that report to him or her. In addition, the secretary oversees three military departments: the Department of the Navy, the Department of the Army, and the Department of the Air Force. The person in charge of each of these is a civilian whose title is also "secretary"—Secretary of the Navy, for instance. The president appoints these individuals and the Senate confirms the appointments

The Secretary of the Navy heads the Department of the Navy and is responsible for outfitting, equipping, recruiting, and training the United States Navy and the United States Marine Corps.

The Chief of Naval Operations

Under the Secretary of the Navy is the Navy's top military officer, the Chief of Naval Operations, or CNO. The CNO is responsible for the two main parts of the Navy—the operating forces and the naval shore establishment. The CNO also serves as principal naval adviser to the president and the Secretary of the Navy on the conduct of war.

The Joint Chiefs of Staff

The CNO has counterparts in other service branches—the Army Chief of Staff, the Air Force Chief of Staff, and the Commandant of the Marine Corps. These four top military officials, plus a chairman and vice chairman, form what is called the Joint Chiefs of Staff. The chairman is the senior military adviser to the president, the National Security Council, and the Secretary of Defense.

Flag of the Joint Chiefs of Staff Chairman
Courtesy of TME Co., Inc.

The chairman does not exercise command over the Joint Chiefs or senior commanders in the field, however. Those commanders report directly through the Secretary of Defense to the president.

The US Navy

The mission of the Navy is to maintain, train, and equip combat-ready naval forces capable of winning wars, deterring aggression, and maintaining freedom of the seas.

Each of the two main divisions of the Navy is responsible for one part of its mission. The *operating forces* are supposed to win wars, deter aggression, and maintain freedom of the seas. The *shore establishment* maintains, trains, and equips the operating forces for combat.

Seal of the US Navy
Courtesy of Tim Brakemeier/dpa/Corbis

Key Terms

operating forces— *those forces whose primary mission involves combat, plus their integral supporting elements*

shore establishment— *the land-based facilities that support the fleet*

Joint Chiefs of Staff— *a committee made up of the senior officer from each branch of the armed services; it gives the president and the National Security Council professional military advice*

The aircraft carrier USS John C. Stennis *passes the* USS Arizona *Memorial while entering Pearl Harbor, Hawaii.*
Courtesy of the US Navy

The operating forces include several fleets, known by their numbers. The 6th Fleet, in the Mediterranean Sea, is the primary operating force of US Naval Forces Europe, headquartered in London, England.

The 5th Fleet operates in the Arabian Gulf, the Red Sea, the Gulf of Oman, and in parts of the Indian Ocean. Half the world's oil supply travels through these waters. The United States and its allies want to keep these sea lanes open. The US Naval Forces Central Command is in charge of this area.

The Atlantic Fleet Command is based in Norfolk, Virginia. The 2nd Fleet is the major force responsible for US security in this area and for the freedom of the naval shipping lanes there.

The Pacific Fleet Command is responsible for the entire Pacific Ocean. It maintains multiple fleets to ensure the security of this large area. The 3rd Fleet, with its base in San Diego, California, operates in the Eastern Pacific, and the 7th Fleet, based in Yokosuka, Japan, operates in the Western Pacific.

(You'll notice that some fleet numbers are missing. That's a result of some renumbering, especially after World War II, when the Navy decided not to reassign fleet numbers.)

In addition to these commands, the Navy has what are known as "type commands." That is, ships are grouped by type—surface ships under the Surface Force Command and submarines under the Submarine Command. Aircraft carriers, naval aircraft squadrons, and naval air stations are under the administrative control of the appropriate naval air force commander. Normally, a type command controls a ship when it is training. When it goes on missions, the ship comes under the operational control of a fleet commander.

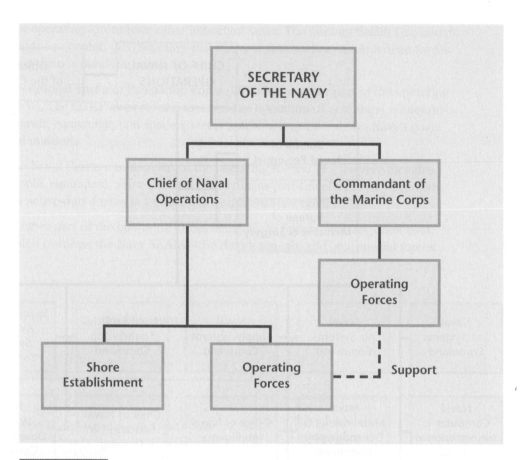

Figure 3.3 The Operating Forces of the Navy and the Marine Corps Support Each Other.

Seal of the US Marine Corps
Courtesy of Tim
Brakemeier/dpa/Corbis

Relationship With the Marine Corps

Unlike the other two military department secretaries, the Secretary of the Navy has not one but two service chiefs reporting to him: the Chief of Naval Operations and the Commandant of the Marine Corps.

The Commandant of the Marine Corps is the top Marine. He directs the three combat divisions of the Corps, with their air wings and support units. The operating forces of the Marines are divided into two commands, the Fleet Marine Force Pacific and the Fleet Marine Force Atlantic. All Marine air and ground tactical units report to one of these two commands.

As Figure 3.3 shows, the operating forces of the two branches, Navy and Marines, support each other.

The United States Coast Guard and Merchant Marine

During peacetime, the United States Coast Guard is part of the Department of Homeland Security. In time of war, the Coast Guard becomes part of the Navy. Although it is the smallest of the US armed forces, the Coast Guard has quite a list of responsibilities:

1. Law enforcement in US territorial waters
2. Port security
3. Safety and maintenance of navigational aids
4. Search and rescue for those lost at sea
5. Interdiction of illegal drug trafficking at sea
6. Pollution control in the event of a major ecological contamination like an oil spill
7. Immigration control.

Finally, the federal government has one more presence on the seas: the United States Merchant Marine. The Merchant Marine functions under the Department of Transportation's Maritime Administration. It regulates the rates and practices of shipping lines and acts as a secondary resupply service to the Navy and Coast Guard. The Merchant Marine is not part of the Navy, but in time of war it becomes a primary carrier of supplies and personnel for the armed services.

The US Army and Air Force

The **US Army** celebrates 14 June 1775 as its "birthday." On that date, the Continental Congress adopted the existing Continental Army. It appointed a committee to "draft the rules and regulations for the government of the Army."

The Army is the oldest branch of the US armed services. The Constitution calls for Congress to "raise and support armies" to provide for "the common defense." After ratification of the Constitution, Congress and President George Washington established the Department of War as part of the president's Cabinet. This arrangement continued until the National Security Act of 1947 created the Department of Defense.

The Army's mission is to provide forces able to conduct prompt, sustained combat on land as well as stability and reconstruction operations, as needed. This means that the Army must be ready to defend areas vital to US national interests at home and overseas. This is similar to the mission of the US Air Force, though the methods the two groups use to fulfill their mission vary greatly.

Seal of the US Coast Guard
Courtesy of Richard Cummins/ Corbis

Seal of the US Merchant Marine
Courtesy of TME Co., Inc.

Seal of the US Army
Courtesy of Tim Brakemeier/dpa/Corbis

Key Terms

port security—
measures taken to protect a harbor or other marine facility against crime, espionage, or sabotage

navigational aid—
a general term for lighthouses, buoys, beacons, lanterns, and radio signals; the Coast Guard maintains these to help mariners of all kinds find their way on the water

interdiction—
the blocking, intercepting, or preventing the passage of something

UNIT III

The **US Air Force** organizes, trains, and equips forces for offensive, defensive, and reconnaissance operations that are conducted either in the skies or in space. The Air Force began in the early 20th century as a branch of the Army called the Army Air Corps. After passage of the National Security Act of 1947, the Air Force became an independent department and began to receive separate funding. Its mission was broadened. This mission is to defend the United States by controlling and exploiting the air and space over hostile nations and maintaining the security of areas vital to US national interests. This involves intercepting possibly hostile aircraft, operating US military satellites, and supporting US ground forces through bombing and air-defense missions.

Seal of the US Air Force
Courtesy of Tim Brakemeier/ dpa/Corbis

Courtesy of (from left):
Ed Kashi/Corbis; Steve Kaufman/ Corbis; Adrin Snyder/Associated Press/The Daily Press

Table 3.1	US MILITARY FORCES, JUNE 2006
Air Force	352,620 Airmen
Army	496,362 Soldiers
Marine Corps	178,923 Marines
Navy	353,496 Sailors
TOTAL	1,381,401
	Source: *Information Please Almanac,* http://www.info-please.com/ips/A0004598.html

Conclusion

The United States armed forces answer to the will of the people through their democratically elected civilian leaders. The Constitution gives Congress the authority to "raise and support" the Army and to "provide and maintain" the Navy. Congress enacts the rules for the armed forces and decides how much to appropriate to them. It also has power to declare war. The president, meanwhile, leads the armed forces as the commander in chief.

The head of each military branch—the Chief of Naval Operations, the Commandant of the Marine Corps, the Army Chief of Staff, and the Air Force Chief of Staff—answers to a civilian secretary within the Department of Defense. These three secretaries—of the Navy, of the Army, and of the Air Force—report to the Secretary of Defense, who reports in turn to the president. The four top officers, together with a chairman and vice chairman, function together as the Joint Chiefs of Staff. They provide the president, National Security Council, and Secretary of Defense with professional military advice.

The mission of the Navy is to maintain, train, and equip combat-ready naval forces capable of winning wars, deterring aggression, and maintain freedom of the seas.

The operating forces are supposed to win wars, deter aggression, and maintain freedom of the seas. The shore establishment maintains, trains, and equips forces for combat. The Secretary of the Navy has two service chiefs reporting to him: the Chief of Naval Operations and the Commandant of the Marine Corps.

While their missions differ, the Navy, Marine Corps, Coast Guard, Merchant Marine, Army, and Air Force all work to defend the liberties of every American.

Review Questions

1 To whom do the United States armed forces answer? Through whom?

2 Who are the Joint Chiefs of Staff?

3 What is the mission of the US Navy?

4 Explain the difference between operating forces and the shore establishment.

5 Which two service chiefs report to the Secretary of the Navy?

The US Navy

Chapter 1

Navy Ships

Key Terms

- **strategy**
- **stability**
- **deterrence**
- **strategic**
- **tactical**
- **humanitarian**
- **displacement**
- **knot**

What You Will Learn to Do

Identify the ships of the Navy and understand how they fulfill the Navy mission

Skills and Knowledge You Will Gain Along the Way

✔ Explain the mission of Navy ships

✔ Explain ship terminology

✔ List types of Navy ships

✔ Describe shipboard customs and courtesies

Above: courtesy of US Navy/Mass Communication Specialist 2nd Class Shannon E. Renfroe; *previous page*: courtesy of US Navy/Mass Communication Specialist 3rd Class Douglas G. Morrison

The Mission of Navy Ships

The purpose of Navy ships is to carry out the military strategy of the United States.

That strategy includes three parts:

1. Peacetime engagement
2. Deterrence and conflict prevention
3. Fight and win.

The first element means that during peacetime the US has forces around the world to promote economic and political stability. This means the United States is paying attention to what's going on in the global neighborhood. The presence of American ships encourages free trade and peaceful connections among nations by ensuring the security of the seas.

Deterrence, the second element of the Navy's strategy, is derived from the adage, "If you seek peace, prepare for war." In other words, if a country places combat power where it cannot be ignored, a potential enemy is less likely to become hostile for fear of immediate reprisal.

The third element of the strategy—fight and win—means that US forces must be ready for combat at all times.

The Navy's Mission

The Navy's mission in carrying out the national strategy is to maintain, train, and equip combat-ready naval forces capable of winning wars, deterring aggression, and maintaining freedom of the seas.

Over the years, the Navy has seen this mission as having four elements:

1. Strategic deterrence
2. Sea control
3. Projection of power ashore
4. Naval presence.

Strategic Deterrence

Strategic deterrence means convincing a potential enemy that an attack on the United States is not a good idea. The best example of this is the Navy's submarine force. These fast and maneuverable underwater ships are nuclear powered and can maintain secret operations for months. Add to this capability of the strategic missile submarine force, which can deliver nuclear weapons to targets across the globe, and strategic deterrence becomes a reality. Potential enemies who know that to attack the United States would be to risk devastation will be less inclined to attack.

Sea Control

Sea control refers to keeping the seas open to the United States, its allies, and other friendly nations. It also means being able to deny a potential enemy the use of the seas. Operation Anaconda during the Civil War was a good example of sea control: the Union fleet maintained control of the Confederate sea lanes by blockading Southern ports and preventing the Confederates from trading with Europe.

Key Terms

strategy—
a country's top-level political and military plan

stability—
steadiness or order in the international or political realm

deterrence—
prevention of war by instilling fear in potential enemies

Key Term

strategic—
referring to a country's long-range weapons or plans; the big picture

UNIT IV

Projection of Power Ashore

Projection of power ashore refers to the use of the seas to carry a fight to a potential enemy beyond US borders and into its own. The United States is largely bound by water, with nearly 13,000 miles of coastline split between the Pacific, Atlantic, and Arctic Oceans. To defend its vast shoreline, the United States must be able to strike at any enemy before it reaches the shore. Over the past two centuries, the United States has refined the ways it accomplishes this mission. It has made strides such as the advancement from smooth-bore cannon mountings to Tomahawk cruise missiles, and from rowboats to tactical aircraft that allow troops to quickly land on enemy soil. Because of these and other advancements, a foreign enemy military force has landed on American soil only three times in more than 200 years.

Naval Presence

Naval presence is the ability to show the flag around the world—to be visible on the open seas anywhere on the globe. This presence can be a silent threat but it can also be quite visible—as when the Navy provides humanitarian assistance. Still, with a strong naval presence and the implied threat of action, the United States Navy helps keep the seas free and open to all and ensures compliance with the international law of the sea.

Ship Terminology

The Navy has a lot of specialized lingo. Some of these terms have to do with being a military organization while others have to do with being a nautical organization. In this section you will learn some of the basic terms.

In the Navy, a majority of a Sailor's time is spent on a ship, and several terms have been adapted to fit a Sailor's environment. Instead of saying, "upstairs," Sailors say *topside*, and they say *below* to mean "downstairs." Given the construction of the ship, terms like "floor" and "ceiling" are called *deck* and *overhead*, respectively, while walls have been labeled as *bulkheads* and hallways are *passageways*. These terms and others are as much a matter of tradition in today's Navy as they are of practicality. They are part of what distinguishes the Navy.

Directions

Navy language labels lengthwise direction on a ship as *fore* (toward the front) or *aft* (toward the rear). Crosswise is *athwartships*. The front of the ship is the *bow*. The rear is the *stern*. If you move toward the bow, you're *going forward*, in Navy talk. To *go aft* is to head toward the stern. An object closer to the bow than is another object is *forward* of that other object. If something is closer to the stern than is another object, Navy talk says it's *abaft* of the other object.

A ship's *centerline* divides it in half lengthwise. When you face forward along the centerline, everything on your right is to *starboard*, and everything to your left is to *port*. Fixtures and equipment are described in terms of the side of the ship they are on—such as the *port anchor* or the *starboard gangway*.

Key Terms

tactical—
referring to short-range weapons, or to assets used in support of ground forces

humanitarian—
referring to help given to individuals in need, such as assistance to disaster victims, without regard to military or political concerns

The exterior parts of a ship
Courtesy of Dorling Kindersley

Moving toward the centerline is going *inboard*. Moving away is going *outboard*. The section around the midpoint is called *amidships*. The widest part of the ship, usually in the midship area, is its *beam*.

Human beings live *in* a ship or *on board* a ship. Inanimate objects, stores, and equipment are *aboard* a ship. You *board* a ship or go *on board*. Supplies, on the other hand, are *taken aboard* and *struck below*. If you climb the mast, the rigging, or any other area above the highest solid structure, you go *aloft*.

An object hanging against the side, bow, or stern is *over* the side, bow, or stern. An object in the water but not touching the ship is *outboard* of or *off* the ship (off the starboard side, off the port bow, and so on).

An object in front of a ship is *ahead* of it. An object to the rear is *astern*. Cooking is done in the *galley*, not in the kitchen.

Structural Terms

The *keel* is the backbone of the ship. Most steel ships have a keel that does not extend below the ship's bottom; such keels are known as *flat keels*.

The *hull* is the supporting body of a ship. It's like an envelope. Inside it are supports that prevent it from collapsing from the pressure of the water. Vertical walls called *bulkheads* divide the interior of a ship's hull into *compartments* for machinery, berthing, mess or dining, and other purposes.

The interior and exterior parts of an aircraft carrier
Courtesy of Dorling Kindersley

Bulkheads run both transversely and longitudinally—across the beam or along the length of the ship. Some bulkheads are just partitions, like room dividers in a house. Others form watertight compartments that are essential to the ship's structure.

Large ships have a series of longitudinal side bulkheads and tanks that provide protection against torpedoes. The outer tanks are usually filled with oil or water. The inner tanks, called *voids*, are empty. The innermost bulkhead is called the holding bulkhead. If a torpedo hit the ship, the outer tanks, even though ruptured, would absorb enough of the explosion that the holding bulkhead would stay intact. Vital spaces on the ship would stay dry.

A ship's *waterline* is the water level along the hull of a ship afloat. The vertical distance from the bottom of the keel to the waterline is the ship's *draft*. *Freeboard* is the distance from the waterline to the main deck.

Decks

The decks provide additional hull strength and protection for internal space. A ship does have some rooms that are actually called rooms—the wardroom, stateroom, and engine room, for example, but most "rooms" are called something else aboard a ship. The place where you sleep is called a *berthing*, and you eat on the *mess deck*.

A deck exposed to the weather is called a *weather deck*. A deck that extends from side to side and from bow to stern is a *complete deck*. On an aircraft carrier, the uppermost complete deck is called the *flight deck*. It's where the planes land and take off.

On every other kind of ship except an aircraft carrier, the uppermost complete deck is the *main deck*. On an aircraft carrier, however, the main deck is the *hangar deck*. This is where the aircraft are stowed and serviced when they're not on the flight deck.

Ladders go from one deck level to another. They may or may not be covered by hatches. The *forecastle* (pronounced fohk-s'l), on most ships, is the forward portion of the weather deck. The *poop deck* is a partial deck above the main deck located all the way aft.

The *quarterdeck* is not an actual deck, but an area designated by the commanding officer for official functions. When the ship is in port, it's where the *officer of the deck* (officer in charge of the deck) has his or her station. Its location depends on how the ship is moored or which side is tied to the pier.

Doors and Hatches

Doors give access through bulkheads. *Hatches* give access through decks. *Watertight doors* form a watertight seal when properly closed. All doors leading to weather decks are watertight. The doors are held closed by fittings called *dogs*.

Ship Size

The size of a ship is given in terms of displacement in tons. The Navy uses full-load displacement, which describes the condition of the ship complete and ready to deploy.

Ship Identification

Each Navy ship is identified by name and designation. In the case of *USS Nimitz* (CVN 68), for instance, USS means *United States ship*. CVN is the designation for a nuclear-powered aircraft carrier. The ship's hull number (68) is a general indication of the number of ships of the same type that have been built. (Some gaps occur because of the cancellation of shipbuilding orders.) A ship's hull number never changes unless its designation also changes.

Armaments and Armor

Armament refers to a ship's offensive weapons—guns, rockets, and even aircraft. A ship's *armor* is the protective layers of steel lining the ship's hull for defense against attacks.

Ship Speed

The speeds of ships are given in knots. When a ship goes 20 nautical miles an hour, its speed is said to be 20 knots. Don't ever say 20 knots per hour!

Key Term

displacement—
the weight of the volume of water that a ship displaces when afloat; in other words, the weight of a ship by itself

Key Term

knot—
one nautical mile per hour, or about 1.15 statute (land) miles per hour

UNIT IV

Types of Navy Ships

All Navy ships are either *combatant* ships or *auxiliary* ships. Combatant ships, in turn, fall into one of two categories: warships or other combatants.

Types of Warships

Aircraft Carriers

Aircraft carriers include multipurpose carriers (CVs) and multipurpose carriers with nuclear propulsion (CVNs). Both are intended to carry, launch, retrieve, and handle combat aircraft quickly and effectively. A carrier can approach the enemy at high speed, launch planes for an attack, recover them, and retire before the enemy can even spot it. The aircraft carrier is a formidable long-range offensive weapon. It is at the center of the modern carrier battle group.

The CIWS is a self-guiding 20mm rotary barrel machine gun used as a last line of defense against incoming aircraft, missiles, or small attack ships. It fires a series of high-density rounds at a rate of more than 3,000 rounds per second.
Courtesy of the US Navy

The *Nimitz*-class CVNs displace about 97,000 tons when heading into combat. Such a ship carries about 6,000 men and women, including the carrier air group. A carrier can operate between 85 to 90 aircraft on a deck about 1,090 feet long and 25 feet wide, maintaining flight operations for a near indefinite amount of time if need be. The *Nimitz*-class CVNs carry various defensive systems in addition to aircraft such as the 20-mm Phalanx Close-In Weapon System or CIWS.

Carriers have angled flight decks designed to launch and recover planes simultaneously. They have a special hangar deck that can be used to stow planes as well as hydraulic elevators that bring planes from the hangar to the flight deck. As a self-sustaining defense and attack platform, a carrier is also equipped with a large series of repair shops, parts and munitions compartments, and fast-fueling equipment. The power plant and engines of the modern carrier are able to propel these 97,000-ton behemoths, which can move at speeds in excess of 30 knots. Combine this with a carrier's sea-keeping ability and you have a platform that can rapidly move into an enemy position and carry out sustained flight operations despite storms and other environmental factors.

USS Nimitz
Courtesy of JP Laffont/Sygma/Corbis

In times of crisis, the question is always, "Where are the carriers?" The aircraft carrier is the centerpiece of naval operating forces. Carriers support and operate aircraft that can carry out attacks on air and surface targets, as well as targets ashore. Carriers can also engage in sustained operations in support of other forces, such as search-and-rescue operations or maintenance of air cover for amphibious assaults and troops already ashore.

Aircraft carriers are deployed worldwide. They can provide anything from peacetime presence to full-scale war. They have become the symbol of United States Naval supremacy around the world.

USS Gettysburg *(CG 64) is a* Ticonderoga-*class cruiser based at Mayport, Fla.*
Courtesy of the US Navy

Cruisers

These ships, designated CGs, are the modern Navy's primary surface warfare platform. They can carry out missions either within a carrier battle group or independently. Cruising at more than 30 knots, the guided-missile cruiser acts as both an escort for surface forces and as a fire-support platform for amphibious and land operations.

As the name implies, guided-missile cruisers are designed to carry the Tomahawk cruise missile in addition to the two five-inch gun mountings and dual-CIWS emplacements to provide a heavy and sustained course of fire in the event of attack. Cruisers displace about 10,000 tons and are about 567 feet long with a beam of 55 feet, making them the largest surface warfare ships in the fleet. The *Ticonderoga*-class cruisers can employ vertical launch missile tubes that, when coordinated with the shipboard anti-air warfare combat weapons system or Aegis, can deliver a payload to a surface location from more than 200 miles away.

Today's guided-missile cruisers perform mainly in a battle-force role and can undertake a multitude of missions such as air warfare (AW), undersea warfare (USW) and surface warfare (SUW). In addition, they can conduct reconnaissance operations as well as act as flagships for surface-action groups.

Destroyers

Destroyers are known as "the greyhounds of the sea" for their speed. They evolved around the turn of the 20th century in response to a new threat at sea. This was the small torpedo boat that could dash in close to a larger ship, release torpedoes, and get away before an enemy's defense could adjust. The world's navies recognized the need to defend against these sorts of attacks, and so the torpedo boat destroyer—later just "destroyer"—came into being.

Today's destroyers (DDs) and guided-missile destroyers (DDGs) are useful in almost any kind of naval operation. They are fast and carry a variety of armaments, but relatively little or no armor, making their displacement run from about 8,300 tons to 9,000 tons. Their real advantages are speed and mobility.

Both types of destroyers operate in support of carrier battle groups, surface-action groups, amphibious-support groups, and replenishment groups. DDs perform primarily undersea-warfare duty. But they can also engage in anti-air and anti-surface warfare with their guided-missile counterparts, which can act as a cruise missile platform for precision bombing ashore. Destroyers make up the Navy's largest group of similar types of ships and are the Navy's "workhorse."

Spruance-*class destroyers*

The first *Spruance*-class destroyer was commissioned in 1975. *Spruance*-class destroyers were the first large US warships with gas-turbine propulsion. This system requires less space than others, can be replaced rapidly, and does not require a warm-up period for operation. *Spruance*-class destroyers displace more than 8,000 tons fully loaded and carry an armament of two five-inch, 54-caliber guns, eight Harpoon missiles, and a Seasparrow missile launcher, among other systems. Each ship has full helicopter facilities for two SH-60 helicopters for replenishment missions and anti-submarine warfare.

Arleigh Burke-*class destroyers*

The *Arleigh Burke*, commissioned in 1991, was the most powerful surface combatant ever put to sea. *Arleigh Burke*-class destroyers are equipped with the Aegis Combat System, which integrates the ship's sensors and weapons systems to engage missile threats against the ship and tracks the movement of aircraft from hundreds of miles away. Destroyers of this type carry 56 Tomahawk cruise missiles, among other systems for power projection ashore.

These ships displace 9,033 tons and are powered by four GE LM 2500 gas turbines, each rated at 33,600 horsepower with a power turbine speed of 3,600 revolutions per minute, driving two shafts, with controllable pitch propellers for increased maneuverability and control.

USS Spruance *(DD 963) was commissioned at Pascagoula, Mississippi, and became the first gas-turbine-powered US destroyer.*
Courtesy of the US Navy

Named for the Navy's most famous destroyer-squadron combat commander, Arleigh Burke *was the most powerful surface combatant ever put to sea.*
Courtesy of the US Navy

Frigates

Frigate is the Navy's term for ships used for open-ocean escort and patrol missions. Although similar in build to destroyers, they are slower and have only one propeller. They carry less armament, but can operate in shallower water and therefore enter ports other ship classes can't. Different classes of frigates carry different armaments depending on their mission.

The *Oliver Hazard Perry*-class of frigate carries a single CIWS in addition to a single Harpoon missile launcher, two SH-60 LAMPS helicopters, two Mk32 triple-torpedo tubes, and a pair of dual .50-caliber machine guns for close-in fire support.

Frigates are undersea warfare combatants meant to protect shipping interests for amphibious expeditionary forces, supply groups, and merchant convoys as well as to act as an anti-submarine warfare platform and coastal defense force.

USS Ford *(FFG-54) is the 48th ship of the* Oliver Hazard Perry-*class of guided-missile frigates.*
Courtesy of the US Navy

Guided-missile frigates (FFG) have an anti-air warfare capability, but with some limitations. They are meant to be money-saving surface combatant ships, but they are also known for their toughness and durability—they can take a number of hits and still survive. Given their age and the nature of their construction, however, FFGs have limited versatility. They do not have the multimission ability of other US Navy ships. For these reasons, the Navy's current five-year shipbuilding plan includes no new frigates. A plan is in place to phase out these ships with the introduction of the new DDX type destroyer.

Submarines

In the mid-1950s, nuclear-powered submarines began to replace diesel subs in the US Navy. These earlier subs, designated SS, had trouble staying at sea for very long and were prone to detection when forced to surface for oxygen and to recharge battery power. Today's submarine fleet is entirely nuclear. Its attack submarines (SSNs) and ballistic missile submarines (SSBNs) operate a nuclear reactor and air-filtration system able to sustain ship power and life support for months without surfacing. These features make them the most sustainable submarine fleet in the world.

Attack Submarines

The mission of attack subs is to locate and destroy enemy ships and submarines. They act as scouts, deliver supplies and personnel to locations in enemy territory, perform rescue and reconnaissance missions, and are the primary defense against enemy submarine attack.

Nuclear power has made the submersible surface ship a true submarine. The modern submarine no longer needs frequent refueling or resupplying. The first SSN, *Nautilus*, steamed more than 62,000 miles without refueling. The *Triton*, another early nuclear sub (commissioned in 1956), traveled around the globe underwater, remaining submerged for 83 days.

Today's submarines have special air-revitalization equipment to change the air every few minutes. Other equipment lets the submarine take oxygen from seawater to renew oxygen supplies, making the submarine truly self-sustaining.

The goal of technical superiority over numerical superiority is still the driving force in American submarine development. Many developing countries have state-of-the-art non-nuclear submarines able to slip past many surface defenses undetected. Countering their threat is the primary mission of US nuclear attack subs. While there are other methods to counter the threat of these silent predators, the saying, "The best way to find a sub is with another sub," still holds true.

In 1989 the Navy began construction of the *Seawolf*-class submarine, which was meant to be the premier anti-ballistic missile submarine defense platform. It is designed to be the fastest and quietest attack sub to date. With the fall of the Soviet Union and the end of the Cold War, the *Seawolf*-class's production level has dropped, but the mission hasn't changed. Armed with advanced sensors and an array of sound suppression and detection systems, the *Seawolf*-class is the premier attack sub to date with a capability to seek and destroy enemy submarines and surface ships and to fire cruise missiles in support of surface forces.

USS Seawolf *(SSN 21) is exceptionally quiet and fast.*
Courtesy of the US Navy

Fleet Ballistic Missile Submarines

Fleet Ballistic Missile Submarines (SSBNs) are nuclear-powered submarines armed with Trident II Ship Launched Ballistic Missiles, or SLBMs. The sole mission of the SSBN fleet, since its initial deployment in 1960, has been the strategic deterrence of any hostile nation, especially those with nuclear-launch capability. They represent the most survivable nuclear-strike platform in the US military. A single SSBN could deliver several nuclear payloads on an enemy, even if all other US airborne or land-based missiles had been destroyed.

The *Ohio*-class SSBN is roughly 560 feet in length and has a beam of 42 feet. It displaces 18,750 tons when completely submerged. Armed with four Mk-48 torpedo tubes, the *Ohio*-class can reach cruise speeds of more than 20 knots. It can carry up to 24 Trident I or Trident II SLBMs, each with multiple nuclear warheads able to independently target individual objectives on re-entry. They are the most destructive weapons platform in the US arsenal.

Guided Missile Submarines

In 1998, a contract was awarded for building the first of a new class of attack submarine called the guided-missile submarine, or SSGN. These vessels, to be referred to as *Virginia*-class, will support a new strategic concept as the first US submarine designed for dominance across a broad range of missions, including open-ocean, "blue water" missions. Built to act in the traditional role of the attack submarine, the *Virginia*-class will keep many of the *Seawolf*-class's characteristics, such as the speed and maneuverability of an attack submarine. At the same time, it will incorporate a larger variety of weapons systems, such as 12 Tomahawk cruise missile launch tubes. The *Virginia*-class attack submarine is the first to be built to engage targets ashore, on the surface, and beneath the waves.

To accompany the construction of the *Virginia*-class and further the SSGN program, some *Ohio*-class submarines will be converted to carry the same Tomahawk cruise missile platforms, making them SSGNs. This means that for the first time in naval history, a submarine force can independently destroy targets ashore, on the surface, and beneath the waves without the use of surface ships or nuclear ordinance or the need to surface.

Submarines like USS Alaska *have one mission: strategic deterrence.*
Courtesy of the US Navy

Other Combatant Ships

Mine-Warfare Ships

The Navy has two types of mine-warfare ships. These ships, the Mines Countermeasure Ships (MCM) and the Minehunter, Coastal (MHC), are designed to clear mines from vital waterways.

The MCM can find and destroy mines, whether they are moored or placed on the sea floor. Using sonar and video-imaging systems, the MCM locates the mine, cuts loose any mooring using an onboard cable cutter, and detonates the mine. In addition to these systems, the MCM carries two .50-caliber machine guns. It is 224 feet long with a beam of 39 feet and displaces 1,312 tons when fully loaded.

The MHC acts a smaller minesweeping platform designed for use in coastal waters. Limited by an underwater life span of 15 days, the MHC relies on a support ship or facilities onshore for resupply. Running 188 feet in length with a beam of 36 feet, the MHC displaces 893 tons when fully loaded. Its reinforced plastic fiberglass hull decreases displacement and allows the MHC to operate in shallower waters than the MCM can.

Amphibious Warfare

Amphibious warfare means an attack launched from the sea involving naval forces and ground combat troops, usually beginning with surface warships and airplanes bombing hostile shores. Later, amphibious ships bring in combat-ready ground forces—Marines, special operations forces, or other joint combat forces—while landing craft and helicopters move the ground troops from ship to shore. Amphibious assaults are intended to quickly capture enemy territory or to deny the enemy the use of that land.

Amphibious Command Ships

Amphibious command ships, designated LCCs, provide amphibious command and control for major amphibious operations. LCCs are more than 634 long and 108 feet in beam, displacing more than 18,500 tons. With their up-to-date command-and-control facilities, these ships have become the flagships of several Naval fleets. *USS Blue Ridge*, for example, is the command ship of the 7th Fleet in Yokosuka, Japan, while *USS Mount Whitney* is the command ship of the 6th Fleet in Gaeta, Italy.

USS Mount Whitney *is the command ship of the 6th Fleet, based in Norfolk, Va.*
Courtesy of the US Navy

Amphibious Assault Ships

A single amphibious assault ship, designated an LHA, can load up, rapidly deploy, and land a Marine battalion into enemy territory otherwise inaccessible by land, using a combination of helicopters, landing craft, and amphibious vehicles. Armed with five-inch guns and point-defense missiles, the LHA can provide limited shore bombardment and defend itself from attack during amphibious operations, but it relies mainly on escort ships for defense.

An LHA like USS Peleliu *can deploy a Marine battalion landing team using a number of different methods.*
Courtesy of the US Navy

Another kind of amphibious assault ship (LHD) is designed to land 2,000 troops and their equipment, primarily using transport helicopters. The Navy calls this technique of using helicopters instead of landing vehicles to put troops on the beach *vertical envelopment*. Because it enables placement of troops and supplies in any position accessible by air, vertical envelopment is much more effective than the older methods. You may have seen the older system in movies about the D-Day landings on the Normandy beaches during World War II. While in the landing craft, troops are vulnerable to a number of attacks, such as mortar and artillery fire or fixed gun emplacements. Helicopters allow troops to avoid such fixed defensive positions. Combined with the relatively rapid speed of deployment, vertical envelopment allows the landing troops, and not the defenders, to choose the areas of engagement, simultaneously making amphibious assault easier and coastal defense significantly more difficult.

LHDs are more than 800 feet long with a beam of more than 100 feet and a displacement of about 40,000 tons. Carrying a crew of 1,108 sailors and able to transport 1,894 Marines or other landing forces, the LHD can travel at more than 20 knots, making the determination of a potential landing zone difficult for an enemy to determine.

Although they have a long history of distinguished service, beginning in 2007 both LHAs and LHDs will be replaced under the Sea Power 21 program by updated variants.

Amphibious Transport Dock

The Amphibious Transport Dock (LPD) can carry about 700 Marines and their equipment. The LPD can launch its landing craft through an opening in the stern while the ship is underway or dead in the water. In addition, the deck over the well carrying the landing craft provides a platform for helicopters.

The LPD is 680 feet long with a beam of 105 feet and carries a crew of 400.

Dock Landing Ships

Dock landing ships, designated LSDs, were designed to transport amphibious craft and vehicles, along with crew and troops. These ships also have a helicopter platform over the well deck. They are more than 600 feet long and 84 feet in beam. Their crews total 419 officers and Sailors, and the ships can carry 504 Marines.

An amphibious transport dock like USS San Antonio *can land troops by landing craft or helicopter.*
Courtesy of the US Navy

Dock landing ships such as USS Carter Hall *carry and launch amphibious craft and vehicles as well as crew and troops.*
Courtesy of the US Navy

The Landing Craft, Air Cushioned

An air-cushioned landing craft (LCAC) travels over the water using a large pocket of air to ride over the waves while carrying troops and equipment from ship to shore and across the beach. With four gas turbine engines, it can transfer 60 to 75 tons of equipment more than 200 miles at 40 knots. It can transfer troops and equipment over 70 percent of the world's coastline.

The LCAC travels across the water on a cushion of air.
Courtesy of the US Navy

Auxiliary Ships

Auxiliary ships are the lifeline of the Navy's combatant force. The auxiliaries bring fuel, supplies, and repair parties to the combat ships, wherever they are. There are several different kinds of auxiliary ships for several different purposes. Each has a designation beginning with the letter A.

Transferring fuel, munitions, supplies, and personnel from one ship to another while ships are under way is called *replenishment at sea*. Usually the replenishment ship maintains its course and speed, and the other ship (or ships) pulls into position alongside it.

Fast combat support ships (AOEs) carry not only fuel and ammunition (the "E" in their designation stands for "explosives") but can supply dry and refrigerated stores. AOEs move fast enough to keep up with a battle group for extended periods. They are the largest and most powerful auxiliary ships in the Navy.

AOEs can carry more than 177,000 barrels of oil, 2,150 tons of ammunition, 500 tons of dry stores, and 250 tons of refrigerated stores. An AOE receives oil and other supplies from shuttle ships and then distributes these items among carrier-battle-group ships. Ships are particularly vulnerable to attack while being supplied, so the AOEs move quickly to transfer supplies and reduce that vulnerability.

Rescue and Salvage Vessels

Rescue and salvage ships have the designation ARS. Their mission is to provide fire-fighting, dewatering, battle-damage repair, and rescue towing assistance. They must often do their work in combat zones or areas of high threat. Their focus is to move damaged combat ships out of hostile areas and to tow them to repair ships or bases in safe areas.

The Navy is also responsible for salvaging ships owned by the federal government. Sometimes it salvages privately owned ships as well. This work is also part of the ARS vessels' mission.

Shipboard Customs and Courtesies

Over hundreds of years at sea, the British and American navies developed a great number of special customs and courtesies, some of which you may have already learned from your *Cadet Field Manual*. *Customs* are behaviors performed for so long that they have become common practice. *Courtesies* are expressions of consideration or respect for others. These may take the form of words or actions. In this section, you will read about customs and courtesies aboard US Navy ships.

Salutes

When aboard ship, Sailors salute the commanding officer every time they meet. That includes chance meetings as well as formal meetings. Sailors also salute any visiting officers senior to the commander on every meeting. They salute other officers only the first time they meet each day.

Side honors is a special ceremony for officials or officers boarding or leaving a ship. A group of four to eight sailors called *side boys* (whether they are men or women) line up along the gangway. Half are on one side and half on the other. The higher the officer's rank, the more side boys there are. The Boatswain's Mate of the Watch (BMOW) sounds a pipe. The side boys begin the salute at the first note of the pipe and finish together at the last note.

Another ceremony involving a salute is *passing honors*. When two naval vessels pass each other—within 600 yards for ships and 400 yards for boats—"Attention" is called. All sailors in view on the deck give a hand salute. Sailors render passing honors to US Navy vessels, US Coast Guard vessels, and those of most foreign navies.

Colors

The *colors ceremony* is the hoisting and lowering of the national flag. The national flag—the Stars and Stripes—flies on the *fantail* at the stern of a ship in port. A color detail, usually consisting of two junior personnel and a petty officer, performs the colors ceremony. The colors ceremony is performed twice a day when the ship is not underway. *Morning colors* is at 0800 hours and *evening colors* is at sunset.

Ships not underway also raise and lower a flag called the *jack* at morning and evening colors. It flies from the *jackstaff* at the ship's bow. The US jack consists of 50 white stars on a dark-blue field and resembles the upper-left corner of the Stars and Stripes.

A sailor raises the Navy Jack aboard USS Salt Lake City
in memory of the 11 September 2001 attacks on the United States.
Courtesy of US Navy

The national anthem is part of the colors ceremony whenever possible. If a band or an audiotape is available, Attention is sounded, and then "The Star-Spangled Banner" is played. At morning colors, hoisting of the ensign—the flag—starts with the music while at evening colors, the lowering of the flag starts with the music and ends at the last note. If no band or audiotape is available, a bugler plays. If no bugler is available, a whistle can signal the beginning and end of the ceremony.

When a ship is underway, it flies its ensign day and night. There is no ceremony for raising or lowering the flag.

How Cadets Render Honors During Colors

During the colors ceremony, cadets in ranks come to Attention. The person in charge of the formation salutes until "Carry on" is sounded. If not in ranks but in uniform, cadets face the colors and render a hand salute until they hear the order "Carry on." If in civilian clothes or athletic attire, they face the colors standing at Attention and put their right hand or hat in hand over their heart until they hear "Carry on." If no flag is in sight, they face the direction of the music and make the proper gesture until they hear "Carry on."

Boarding, Leaving, and Crossing Naval Vessels

There are special courtesies you must practice when boarding or leaving a Navy ship.

Boarding Your Ship

If you are in uniform, when you come to the top of the brow, come to attention, face aft to the flag (if it's flying) and salute. Then face the Officer of the Desk (OOD) and salute. While holding the salute, show your identification card and say, "I request permission to come aboard, sir/ma'am." You must salute even if the OOD is enlisted and not an officer. When the OOD returns your salute and grants permission, you may go aboard.

If you are not in uniform, the procedure is the same, but no salute is required.

When you board a ship other than your own, or when you board your own ship for the first time, you follow the same procedures as above, but also state your purpose: "Reporting as ordered," for instance.

Leaving Your Ship

This is the same as boarding, only in reverse. You step onto the quarterdeck, face the OOD, present your identification card, and salute. Say, "I request permission to go ashore, sir/ma'am." When you receive permission, step onto the brow, face aft, and salute the ensign, if it is flying. Then go ashore.

In you are in civilian dress, follow the same practice, but no salute is required.

Crossing Another Ship

Smaller ships sometimes nest beside other ships. You may have to cross one or more ships side by side to get to your ship or to get ashore. The procedure is the same as for boarding or leaving a ship except that you must ask permission to cross over.

Military Etiquette Aboard Ship

The quarterdeck is a ceremonial area. You should always treat it with respect. You should always be in the uniform of the day when you appear there, unless you are returning from leave or liberty. Never smoke, eat, or drink on the quarterdeck. Do not lounge in or around the quarterdeck. Cross it only when necessary.

When you are moving through passageways, step aside to allow those senior to you in rank to pass first. If other juniors are present, call out "Gangway" so everyone can make way for the senior person in rank.

Always call the commanding officer of a ship "Captain," regardless of rank.

Conclusion

The National Military Strategy includes three concepts—peaceful engagement, deterrence and conflict prevention, and fight and win. The Navy seeks to fulfill its mission through four areas: strategic deterrence, sea control, projection of power ashore, and naval presence.

The Navy operates a wide range of types of ships—combatants and auxiliaries—to accomplish these goals. The aircraft carrier is the center of the modern carrier battle group. In times of peace or during building tension, it projects "forward presence." In times of war, it can carry, launch, and retrieve combat aircraft quickly and efficiently, fulfilling the mission before the enemy even sees them. Under the sea, the fleet ballistic missile submarines make up the backbone of the Navy's strategic deterrence.

Review Questions

1   What are the three elements of the National Military Strategy?

2   What are the four parts of the Navy mission?

3   What weapon is at the center of the modern carrier battle group?

4   What is the sole mission of the Fleet Ballistic Missile Submarines?

5   What is the procedure for boarding your ship while in uniform? While out of uniform?

```
A — Attack
B — Bomber
C — Cargo/transport
E — Special electronic installation
F — Fighter
H — Helicopter
K — Tanker
O — Observation
R — Reconnaissance
S — Antisubmarine
T — Trainer
U — Utility
V — VTOL or STOL (vertical or short
       takeoff and landing)
X — Research
```

Figure 2.1 Aircraft Designations

Aircraft

In addition to aircraft launched from carriers, the Navy has relied on a variety of planes and helicopters to carry out fleet-support missions. In today's Navy, helicopters do many things that pontoon planes and dirigibles used to do: scouting, rescue, and patrol missions.

Modern naval aircraft fall into two categories—fixed-wing (airplanes) and rotary-wing (helicopters). Fighter and attack jet planes can strike at an enemy as well as protect the fleet from enemy aircraft and surface ships. The Navy uses patrol aircraft and long-range multi-engine aircraft in undersea-warfare missions. These aircraft also perform photographic and escort missions. Carrier-based aircraft also make reconnaissance flights. They provide the fleet with early warnings of potential trouble.

Helicopters came into their own during the Korean War. They were used in amphibious operations in support of the Marines. They also helped deliver supplies, equipment, and personnel to ships at sea. This is "vertical replenishment," as you learned in the last chapter.

A — **Attack**	G — **Permanently grounded** (for ground training)
C — **Cargo/transport**	
D — **Director** (for control of drones)	J — **Special test, temporary** (when tests are complete, the craft will get its original design back)
E — **Special electronic installation**	
H — **Search and rescue**	
K — **Tanker**	N — **Special test, permanent**
L — **Cold weather**	
M — **Missile carrier**	X — **Experimental stage of development**
Q — **Drone**	
R — **Reconnaissance**	Y — **Prototype** (for design testing)
S — **Antisubmarine**	
T — **Trainer**	Z — **Early stages of planning or development**
U — **Utility**	
V — **Staff**	
W — **Weather**	

Figure 2.2 Mission-Modification Designations

Figure 2.3 Special-Use Designations

Aircraft Model Designations

All aircraft in the US armed forces have "tri-service designations." That means a given model of plane has the same designation code, whether it's used in the Navy, the Army, or the Air Force.

Each basic designator has a letter and a number. The letter signals the basic mission of the aircraft, as shown in Figure 2.1.

The number (one, two, or three digits) shows the design number of the type of aircraft. Thus an F-14 is the 14th fighter design. If a design is modified, another letter (A, B, C, etc.) follows the design number. The B in S-3B tells us that this antisubmarine plane is a modification of the original design.

When the mission of an aircraft changes, another letter goes in front of the basic mission symbol, as shown in Figure 2.2.

Some of these mission-modification letters are, as you see, the same as the basic mission letters.

Here's how the system works: If the Navy modifies an A-6 for use as an electronic-warfare aircraft, it becomes an EA-6.

Other letters put at the very front of an aircraft's designator are called "special use" symbols. They signal that an aircraft has some special status. Six letters are currently in use this way (see Figure 2.3).

Key Terms

drone—
an unmanned aircraft or ship guided by remote control

modification—
an alteration or adjustment, as of an aircraft or other vehicle

Naval Aircraft and Missions

The Navy groups aircraft of the same type into *squadrons* for training, maintenance, and administration. Aircraft of various squadrons combine and deploy as *operational air groups* aboard ships. The battle group's mission determines the types and numbers of squadrons.

Fighter/Attack Aircraft

The single-seat F/A-18 Hornet is the nation's first carrier-launched strike-fighter. It was built with the ability to drop bombs or deny access to sea lanes. But it was also designed as a fighter plane, too—able to engage enemy pilots in the sky. The F/A-18 replaced the F-14 Tomcat, which was the Navy's primary air-to-air superiority fighter for 36 years, until 2006.

The F/A-18 Hornet proved itself during Operation Desert Storm in 1991.
Courtesy of the US Navy

The F/A-18 Hornet operates in 37 tactical squadrons from air stations worldwide, and from 10 aircraft carriers. The US Navy's Blue Angels Flight Demonstration Squadron proudly flies the Hornet in air shows across America.

The newest model, the Super Hornet, carries out an even wider variety of missions. It can act as an air-superiority fighter, fighter escort, and reconnaissance plane. It can provide close air support, air-defense suppression, and precision strikes during day or night operations. The Super Hornet has a longer range than earlier models and is even tougher than the Tomcat. It also costs 40 percent less to operate and requires 75 percent fewer hours of labor per hour of flight than the F-14.

The Hornet proved itself during Operation Desert Storm in 1991. Hornets took direct hits from surface-to-air missiles, recovered successfully, underwent rapid repairs, and resumed missions the next day.

The newest models, the E and F, rolled out at McDonnell Douglas (now part of the Boeing Company) 17 September 1995. The E is a single seat aircraft while the F is a two-seater. Both can fly almost twice the speed of sound, at altitudes up to 50,000 feet, and for ranges greater than 1,300 miles. Also being deployed is the F/A-18 G or Growler, which is meant to replace the EA-6B Prowler as the Navy's primary electronic-warfare aircraft by 2010. Carrying some of the most advanced electronic surveillance and jamming equipment in the world, this new version of the Hornet will revolutionize the battlefield. It will introduce an electronic-warfare aircraft that will outmaneuver many of the world's fighters and take the fight to enemies both on the ground and in the skies.

Electronic Warfare

The EA-6B Prowler, a twin-engine, mid-wing aircraft, is designed for carrier and advanced-base operations. The Prowler's mission is to protect strike aircraft by jamming enemy radar, electronic data links, and communications in a combat zone. The EA-6B can travel at more than 500 knots, up to a ceiling of 37,600 feet for more than 1,150 miles. Unlike most carrier-launched jet aircraft in the Navy, the EA-6B is a four-seat aircraft that carries one pilot and three electronic-warfare officers to the battlefield. Commissioned in 1977, the EA-6B is near the end of its life expectancy in the Navy; the F/A-18G will replace it by 2010.

The EA-6B Prowler
Courtesy of the US Navy

Airborne Early Warning

The E-2C Hawkeye is the Navy's all-weather, carrier-based tactical-warning and control-system aircraft. It provides airborne early warning and command-and-control function for the entire battle group. Other missions for the E-2C include surface surveillance coordination, strike-and-interceptor control, search-and-rescue guidance, and communications relay.

The Hawkeye provides its early warning by flying in front of the battle group to look for enemy surface ships and aircraft. The newest variant of this aircraft, the Hawkeye 2000, has a new mission computer, improved radar displays, and "cooperative engagement capability." This last element helps bring streams of data from several different sources to give commanders one big picture of a battle, whether at sea or on land.

The Hawkeye carries a crew of five—two pilots and three mission system operators. It can exceed 300 knots and has a range of 1,500 miles.

UNIT IV

An E-2C Hawkeye launches forth from USS Kitty Hawk *(CV 63).*
Courtesy of the US Navy

The E-6B Mercury airborne command post
Courtesy of the US Navy

The E-6B Mercury is the Navy's strategic airborne command post. It also relays communications for fleet ballistic missile submarines. It can launch land-based intercontinental ballistic missiles.

The E-6B can fly above 40,000 feet. It has a range of more than 7,500 miles and can travel at 600 miles per hour.

Undersea Warfare

The P-3C Orion is the Navy's sole land-based antisubmarine-warfare aircraft. The Navy took delivery of its first Orion in July 1962. It has gone through a designation change from P3V to P-3 and three major models: P-3A, P-3B, and P-3C. The Navy has kept repairing and refurbishing the airframes of these planes. It's upgraded the weapons, electronics, and other systems, too. The Navy is cutting back the Orion's numbers, however—down to 130 by 2010 from an original 227. Current plans call for the P-6 Multi-mission Maritime Aircraft (MMA) to start replacing the P-3 beginning in 2013.

A P-3C Orion assigned to the "Golden Eagles" of Patrol Squadron Nine (VP-9) circles Mt. Fuji in Japan.
Courtesy of the US Navy

The S-3B Viking is a twin-engine carrier-based aircraft. Its primary mission is to detect and destroy enemy submarines. It can also refuel other jets, drop mines, and conduct electronic surveillance. The Viking can fly at more than 500 miles per hour up to a ceiling of 40,000 feet. It has a range of 2,000 miles.

An S-3B Viking can fly more than 500 miles per hour.
Courtesy of the US Navy

Logistics Aircraft

The C-2A Greyhound is a twin-engine cargo-passenger aircraft. Its primary mission is carrier on-board delivery. The C-2A can deliver up to 10,000 pounds of cargo. The cabin can carry cargo or passengers or both. The Navy is overhauling this plane to extend its service life from 15,020 landings and 10,000 flight hours to 36,000 landings and 15,000 flight hours. The C-2As are getting structural enhancements, rewiring, avionics-systems improvements, and new propeller systems. Congress and the Chief of Naval Operation have required two passenger safety improvements to be part of the program, too. One is a system to avoid midair collisions; the other warns pilots when they are flying too close to the ground ("terrain").

Some other Navy logistics aircraft are:

- the C-9 Skytrain. A twin-jet version of the civilian DC-9, it provides primarily fleet logistical support

- the C-12F Huron. A twin-engine turboprop aircraft, it transports equipment and passengers between naval air stations

- the C-130 Hercules. A four-engine turboprop aircraft, it can take off from and land on short runways. It hauls cargo and people.

The primary mission of the C-2A Greyhound is carrier on-board delivery.
Courtesy of the US Navy

Key Term

logistics—
the aspect of military or naval operations that deals with the procurement, distribution, maintenance, and replacement of materiel and personnel

The C-9 Skytrain provides fleet logistical support.
Courtesy of the US Navy

Trainers

The T-34C Turbomentor is a two-seat turboprop trainer. Its mission is to provide primary flight training for Navy and Marine Corps student pilots.

The T-45A Goshawk is a two-seat jet trainer, used for intermediate and advanced pilot training. The T-6A Texan II is another single-engine turbo prop and represents the next generation of primary basic trainers.

Unmanned Aerial Vehicles (UAV)

The RQ-2A Pioneer is an unmanned aerial vehicle. It can perform a wide variety of missions: reconnaissance, surveillance, target acquisition, and battle-damage assessment. It can provide tactical commanders with real-time images of a battlefield or target.

The Navy introduced the Pioneer as a land-based system in 1986 but now uses it at sea as well. The Pioneer can travel at speeds higher than 100 miles per hour. Its ceiling is 15,000 feet and its range more than 115 miles.

The T-6A Texan II
Courtesy of the US Navy

The T-45A Goshawk
Courtesy of the US Navy

The RQ-2A Pioneer
Courtesy of the US Navy

Rotary-Wing Aircraft

The helicopter has been an important part of naval operations since World War II. Helicopters play a role in the transfer of supplies and in search-and-rescue operations, as well as undersea warfare (USW), mine warfare, and special warfare.

Undersea Warfare

The SH-60 is a twin-engine helicopter. Its primary mission is to detect and destroy enemy submarines. The Navy also uses it for search and rescue, advanced scouting, special operations, cargo lift, and intercepting drug smugglers. It can be deployed on cruisers, destroyers, and frigates as well as aircraft carriers.

Mine Warfare

The MH-53E Sea Dragon operates from carriers and other warships. Its primary mission is airborne mine countermeasures. It seeks out and destroys enemy minefields. It can also deliver troops or cargo to a ship.

The SH-60 Seahawk
Courtesy of the US Navy

The MH-53E Sea Dragon operates from carriers and other warships.
Courtesy of the US Navy

VTOL—
vertical takeoff or landing; refers to either the capability or to the aircraft that has it

rotor—
an assembly of rotating horizontal airfoils (wings), such as on a helicopter

nacelle—
a separate, streamlined enclosure on an aircraft for sheltering the crew or cargo or housing an engine

Training

The TH-57 Sea Ranger is the primary training helicopter for those preparing to become naval aviators. It can also perform some photo, chase, and utility missions.

The TH-57 Sea Ranger
Courtesy of the US Navy

VTOL

The V-22 Osprey is a helicopter that can turn into a propeller airplane once it takes off. The Osprey is a *tiltrotor* aircraft with a 38-foot rotor system and engine/transmission nacelle mounted on each wing tip. It can operate as a helicopter when taking off and landing vertically. Once airborne, the nacelles rotate forward 90 degrees for horizontal flight, converting the V-22 to a high-speed, fuel-efficient turboprop airplane. The wing rotates for compact storage aboard ship. The Osprey's ceiling is up to 25,000 feet and it can cruise at more than 272 knots.

The plane's first flight occurred in March 1989. The V-22 is the world's first production tiltrotor aircraft. Planned purchases include 360 for the Marine Corps, 48 for the Navy, and 50 for the Air Force.

The Osprey pushes the limits of VTOL (vertical takeoff or landing) technology, and as a result some people have called into question its safety record. The Marine Corps, however, is committed to it to provide its heavy lift capability for years to come.

The V-22A Osprey is a helicopter that turns into a turboprop plane.
Courtesy of the US Navy

Conclusion

Naval aviation goes back to the first years of flight. The first aircraft carriers were introduced in the 1920s. Not until World War II, though, did naval air power truly come into its own. The challenge of naval aviation is to integrate aircraft with the fleet. Today the Navy relies on a combination of jet aircraft, giant nuclear-powered aircraft carriers, helicopters, and large, long-range patrol planes.

Review Questions

1 What were two achievements of Eugene Ely?

2 What were two turning points in naval aviation during World War II?

3 What were three important developments in aircraft carriers after World War II?

4 What does the combination of letters and number in the C-12F Huron signify?

5 What is the Navy's primary fighter aircraft?

Wellness, Fitness, and First Aid

Choosing the Right Exercise Program for You

What You Will Learn to Do

Develop a personal exercise program

Skills and Knowledge You Will Gain Along the Way

✔ Classify exercises as aerobic, anaerobic, isometric, and isotonic

✔ Compare the benefits of aerobic, anaerobic, isometric, and isotonic exercise

✔ Identify the benefits of regular exercise

✔ Determine the essential components of a good exercise program

Above: courtesy of US Navy/Gary Nichols; *previous page*: courtesy of US Navy/Mass Communication Specialist 3rd Class Michael A. Lantron

Introduction

What you eat and how much you exercise can directly affect how you look and feel. When it comes to your appearance, diet and exercise help you maintain proper weight, muscle tone, and healthy hair and skin. When it comes to your health, diet and exercise can lower your risk of heart disease, high blood pressure, and other health problems, including depression. Staying healthy and looking good means following a balanced diet and exercising regularly. This chapter discusses guidelines for a healthier lifestyle that will help keep you fit and feeling great, now and throughout your life. This first chapter specifically covers exercise, including types of exercises and how to stick with an exercise program.

Some people consider exercise a chore; others think it's fun. There are even those who avoid it altogether. With the right outlook, however, everyone can find an exercise program that they enjoy. More and more people find ways to keep fit, from walking to joining fitness clubs, because they recognize the importance of exercise for physical and mental health.

Although the fitness craze has hit many older Americans, it has not yet reached most of America's youth. This is unfortunate because not only is exercise good for you, it can also be fun. You can form friendships with people you meet while exercising on the track or basketball court or at the gym or pool. You will feel better about yourself, improve your resistance to disease, and relieve stress found at school and work. Basically, being fit improves your overall health—both physically and mentally.

Do you think you are physically fit? Physical fitness is the ability of the heart, blood vessels, lungs, and muscles to work together to meet the body's needs. When you are physically fit, your body's systems work as a team allowing you to breathe easily and contract muscles in coordinated movement.

Your body is made for activity. Stimulating your muscles, bones, heart, lungs, and blood vessels with regular exercise helps you gain or maintain physical fitness. A program of vigorous exercise, however, is not the only important factor in fitness and a healthy lifestyle. Rest, sleep, and good nutrition are just as important. What muscles are required to move the furniture in the photo?

Physical fitness is necessary for performing many tasks, such as moving furniture.
Courtesy of Ken Karp

UNIT V

Components of Fitness

Each individual has his or her own potential of fitness. For example, you may not have the capability of becoming an Olympic weightlifter or a professional gymnast; yet you can reach your own personal best. Physical fitness can be broken down into four health-related areas: cardiorespiratory endurance, muscular strength and endurance, flexibility, and body composition. Each component is a necessary part of fitness.

Cardiorespiratory Endurance

The first component, cardiorespiratory endurance, is the ability of your heart, blood vessels, and lungs to distribute nutrients and oxygen and to remove wastes. When you exercise, your heart and lungs must supply more oxygen to your muscles than they need when you are resting. When you are at rest, for example, your heart pumps about 5 to 6 quarts (5.5 to 6.6 liters) of blood per minute, but it pumps about 20 to 25 quarts (22 to 27 liters) when you are exercising.

If your heart and lungs function easily during hard exercise and recover quickly afterward, you probably have good cardiorespiratory endurance. People with poor cardiorespiratory endurance might be left short of breath and have a very high heart rate after light exercise. Their lungs and heart are unable to keep up with the muscles' demand for oxygen.

Muscular Strength and Endurance

The capacity of a muscle or a group of muscles to exert or resist a force is called muscular strength. In contrast, muscular endurance is the ability of muscles to keep working for an extended time. For example, the amount of weight you can lift is one measure of your muscular strength. How long you can hold that weight—or how many times you can lift it—is a measure of your muscular endurance. You need muscular strength for all sports and most everyday activities. Acts of muscular endurance include repeated actions, such as raking leaves, shoveling snow, or doing sit-ups.

Which components of physical fitness are especially important in lifting weights?
Courtesy of David Madison

Great emphasis was placed on physical fitness in the schools of ancient Greece. Students received instruction in exercise and sports such as wrestling, running, and jumping. In fact, the word gymnasium comes from the ancient Greek word *gymnasion*, meaning "school."

Flexibility

The ability to use a muscle throughout its entire range of motion is called flexibility. This means that you can bend, stretch, and twist your joints easily. The sit-and-reach test measures the flexibility of specific groups of muscles in the back and legs, but it is also used to indicate overall flexibility. However, flexibility can vary in different joints. Some people may show poor flexibility in the sit-and-reach test, for example, yet have excellent flexibility in the shoulders and arms. Stretching exercises, if done correctly, can increase flexibility and may reduce the risk of injury during exercise.

Body Composition

The fourth component of physical fitness, body composition, is the amount of body fat compared to lean tissue, such as muscle and bone. Skinfold measurement is one method for assessing body fat. Excessive body fat has been linked with heart disease, diabetes, arthritis, cancer, and other harmful health conditions.

The Benefits of Exercise

What happens inside you when you run, swim, dance, play hockey, or enjoy some other form of exercise? As the muscles in your arms, shoulders, or legs alternately contract and relax, they use energy that comes from chemical reactions in which oxygen combines with nutrients. Because of the increased needs of your muscles, your heart beats faster, and you breathe more rapidly and deeply. The flow of blood to your heart, lungs, and skeletal muscles increases as your blood vessels dilate, or widen. Your blood pressure and body temperature rise, and you begin to sweat. How do these responses benefit your body? Refer to Figure 1.1 to help you answer this question.

UNIT V

SOME BENEFITS OF REGULAR EXERCISE

Physical Benefits

- Increases muscle strength and endurance
- Increases efficiency of heart and lungs
- Increases physical stamina
- Increases bone strength
- Increases flexibility
- Increases resistance to muscle and bone injury
- Improves posture and appearance
- Reduces blood pressure
- Reduces risk of cardiovascular disease
- Helps to reduce excess body fat
- Helps to control appetite
- Aids digestion and helps prevent constipation
- Increases resistance to disease

Psychological and Social Benefits

- Improves mental alertness
- Increases ability to concentrate
- Increases resistance to mental fatigue
- Improves self-image
- Improves self-confidence
- Helps to relieve stress and to improve relaxation
- Helps to control anxiety and depression
- Improves quality of sleep
- Increases social involvement

Figure 1.1 Regular exercise helps both physical and mental health.

Courtesy of Function thru Form

Physical Benefits

Because blood circulates more rapidly through vessels during exercise, the rate at which it brings oxygen and nutrients to, and removes wastes from, your tissues is increased. This increased circulation rate is one reason why you feel refreshed and energetic after a hard workout. In addition, over time, regular exercise may increase the number of capillaries in your body. These additional capillaries provide muscles with a greater supply of blood, not just when you are exercising but at all times.

Cardiorespiratory endurance is significantly improved by an exercise program. Your heart becomes stronger and pumps blood more efficiently. Regular exercise can also lower your blood pressure and can improve the function of your lungs. An exercise program can help prevent atherosclerosis and coronary heart disease.

As you stretch your muscles when you exercise, you can improve your flexibility by loosening stiff muscles and joints. When you run, swim, or do other endurance exercises on a regular basis, your muscles become stronger and are able to work longer. Regular exercise also strengthens your bones, making them thicker and denser. Strong bones and muscles are less likely to be injured than are weak ones. Table 1.1 shows ratings of various exercises.

Exercise can also improve or maintain body composition. A regular workout is important in keeping body fat within recommended levels. A program of regular exercise is an important factor in successful weight loss or weight maintenance.

Table 1.1	FITNESS RATINGS OF PHYSICAL ACTIVITIES			
ACTIVITY	Cardiorespiratory Endurance	Muscular Strength	Muscular Endurance	Flexibility
Aerobic dancing	3–4	2	2	3
Ballet	3	2	2	4
Baseball/Softball	1	1	1	2
Basketball	3–4	1	2	2
Bicycling (at least 10 mph)	3–4	2	3–4	1
Bowling	1	1	1	2
Calisthenics	3	3–4	3–4	3–4
Canoeing	2–3	3	3	2
Football	2–3	2	2	2
Golf	1	1	1	2
Gymnastics	1	4	3	4
Handball/Squash	3	2	3	2
Hiking (uphill)	3	1	2	2
Hockey	2–3	2	2	2
Jogging/Running (at least 6 mph)	3–4	1	3	2
Judo/Karate	1	2	1	3
Jumping Rope	3–4	1	3	2
Racquetball	3–4	1	3	2
Rowing	3–4	3	3	2
Skating (ice, roller)	2–3	1	2–3	2
Skiing (cross-country)	4	2	3–4	2
Skiing (downhill)	3	2	2–3	2
Soccer	3	2	2	2
Swimming	4	2	3	2
Tennis/Badminton (singles)	2–3	1	2–3	2
Volleyball	2	1	2	2
Walking (brisk)	3	1	3	2
Weight training	1–2	4	3	2
Wrestling	3–4	2	3	3

Rating Scale: 1 = Low, 2 = Moderate, 3 = High, 4 = Very high

Psychological Benefits

People who exercise regularly are likely to sleep better, feel more self-confident, and focus more productively on their work. Exercise may also increase creativity by releasing body chemicals that stimulate the brain's centers of creativity.

One of the most important psychological benefits of exercise is the reduction of emotional stress. Simple stretching exercises, for example, can help you relax tense muscles and allow you to sleep better. If you are feeling depressed, exercise can generally help make you feel better. In fact, many health professionals consider exercise an important part of a complete treatment for depression, whether the depression is mild or serious.

Have you ever experienced a sense of physical and emotional exhilaration after a hard workout? This feeling is at least partly the result of certain substances called endorphins. Endorphins, which are chemicals produced in your brain, help to give you a sense of satisfaction and pleasure. During vigorous exercise, cells within your brain produce greater amounts of endorphins.

Types of Exercise

No single exercise can improve or maintain all four components of physical fitness. Table 1.1 compares the fitness benefits you can receive from many activities. Notice, for example, that recreational activities such as basketball and rowing provide many health benefits. Swimming is also an excellent exercise.

Exercises can be classified into different types, depending on what their performance involves. Included among these are aerobic, anaerobic, isotonic, isometric, and isokinetic exercise.

Key Terms

aerobic—
allowing sufficient amounts of oxygen to be delivered to the muscles

anaerobic—
working in the absence of adequate amounts of oxygen being delivered to the muscles

isotonic—
exercise in which muscles contract, but very little body movement takes place

isometric—
building muscle strength using resistance without joint movement

isokinetic—
building muscle strength using resistance with joint movement

Swimming is an excellent all-round exercise that is especially good for developing cardiorespiratory and muscular endurance.
Courtesy of David Madison

Aerobic Exercise

Nonstop, repetitive, strenuous physical activity that raises the breathing and heart rates is called aerobic exercise. Aerobic exercises increase the amount of oxygen that is taken in and used by the body. Aerobic exercise works the heart, lungs, and blood vessels. As you exercise aerobically, your heart beats faster and you breathe in more air, so your blood can supply more oxygen to your hard-working muscles. This type of physical exercise improves blood and oxygen flow to vital organs, as well as lung capacity (the ability to take in and use more air). Swimming, riding a bike, running, brisk walking, and cross-country skiing are all forms of aerobic exercise. If aerobic exercises last for at least 20 minutes at a time and are done frequently, on a regular, ongoing basis, they will improve cardiovascular endurance. Aerobic exercises are therefore especially important in maintaining the health of your circulatory and respiratory systems. As the information in Table 1.1 indicates, activities that provide good aerobic exercise do not always improve muscular strength. They do, however, generally improve your muscular endurance.

Anaerobic Exercise

Anaerobic exercise, on the other hand, works the muscles intensely in fast bursts of movement and does not require as much oxygen as aerobic exercise. Instead of endurance, anaerobic exercise requires bursts of power and energy and the ability to maneuver quickly. For example, a sprinter working his or her leg muscles hard in a burst of energy to cross the finish line in a few seconds is performing an anaerobic exercise. Many sports, from tennis to football, require anaerobic work to move from one point to another as quickly as possible. Imagine that for 20 minutes you exercise like a weight lifter. Although your overall exercise time is 20 minutes, the periods of intense physical activity come only when you actually lift the weight. Anaerobic exercise is intense physical activity that lasts only from a few seconds to a few minutes, during which time muscles use up more oxygen than the blood can supply. Anaerobic exercises usually improve the flexibility, strength, and sometimes speed at which muscles work. However, it does not specifically condition the cardiovascular and respiratory systems. Most anaerobic exercises are designed to develop specific skills, agility, flexibility, or strength. Lifting weights, sprinting, push-ups, and some forms of gymnastics, for example, are usually considered anaerobic activities.

Isotonic, Isometric, and Isokinetic Exercise

Other forms of exercise concentrate specifically on firming and toning muscles and building muscle strength. Working against resistance builds muscle strength. You work against resistance when you try to open a tight lid on a jar or push a heavy piece of furniture across a room. Three types of exercise—isotonic, isometric, and isokinetic—can increase the strength and endurance of specific groups of muscles. Isometric exercise builds muscle strength by using resistance without joint movement, while isotonic exercise uses resistance with joint movement. For example, when you try to pull your locked hands apart, you perform an isometric exercise. You contract your muscles but do not move any joints. Most weight training, on the other hand, is isotonic. When you do bicep curls, you contract your muscles and bend your elbows to raise the weights to shoulder level. Isotonic exercise involves the contraction and relaxation of muscles through the full range of their motion. You can perform isotonic exercises with or without weights. Through repetition of isotonic exercises, you can develop muscle strength.

Note:

Aerobic dance programs, in which people perform a set of exercises in time to music, are offered by many community centers, YMCAs, YWCAs, and health clubs. Recreational dance can be substituted for aerobic dance as long as you dance vigorously enough to reach your target heart rate for at least 20 minutes.

UNIT V

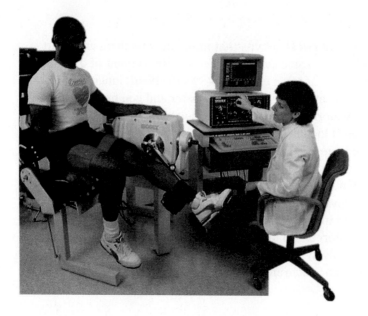

Physical therapists help people perform isokinetic exercises using special machinery to recover the use of muscles.

Courtesy of Larry Mulvehill/
The Image Works

Place your palms together and push them against each other. You are performing an isometric exercise in which muscles contract but very little body movement takes place. Pushing against a wall is another example of isometric exercise. Even though this activity involves little movement, your muscles are contracting and thus working. If you continue isometric exercises over a long period, the muscles you use will become stronger.

Perhaps you have seen an accident victim or injured athlete use a special machine in order to recover the use of specific muscle groups. They are performing isokinetic exercises. Isokinetic exercises are exercises that involve moving a muscle through a range of motion against a resistance, or weight that changes. Unlike isotonic exercises, isokinetic exercises always use special machinery to provide the resistance. Many exercise machines in gymnasiums and fitness centers provide isokinetic exercise.

Defining Your Goals

Do you want to obtain total fitness, increase your stamina, have a trimmer body, achieve better coordination, or just feel more alert? Your goals help to determine the best exercise program for you. Reexamine Table 1.1, which lists different types of exercises and their benefits. If your goal is to strengthen muscles, for example, your program might include anaerobic exercises such as lifting weights. If you want to improve your cardiorespiratory endurance, you may develop a program of aerobic exercise. Basketball, jumping rope, or brisk walking will fit into this type of program. Most likely, you have a combination of goals in mind. For example, you may want to increase both your cardiorespiratory endurance and your flexibility.

As you create your exercise program, remember that your fitness program should be fun! Choose activities or a sport that you enjoy and will look forward to. Combine exercise with social activities; for example, take a hike with a group of your friends. You can often develop an enjoyable fitness program by expanding on the activities that are already a part of your life, as shown by the weekly exercise record in Figure 1.2.

Youth Fitness Fact Sheet

- Youth fitness in the United States has not improved in the last 10 years and, in some cases, has declined.

- Approximately 50 percent of girls ages 6 to 17 and 30 percent of boys ages 6 to 12 cannot run a mile in less than 10 minutes.

- Fifty-five percent of girls ages 6 to 17 and 25 percent of boys ages 6 to 12 cannot do a pull-up.

- Boys generally perform better than girls on fitness tests, except in the area of flexibility.

- Girls' scores increase until age 14, where they plateau and then decrease (except for flexibility, which continues to improve to age 17).

- American children have become fatter since 1950 (US Public Health Service).

- Forty percent of children between the ages of 5 and 8 show at least one heart disease risk factor, e.g., obesity (overweight), elevated cholesterol, or high blood pressure.

- Only 36 percent of America's schoolchildren in grades 5 through 12 are enrolled in daily physical education, with the average number of gym classes per week in grades 5 through 12 being 3.6.

Adapted from the President's Council on Physical Fitness.

Key Term

obesity—
overweight to the point of injuring health

A WEEKLY EXERCISE PROGRAM

Sunday
- Slow 20-minute run around the pond
- Two flights of stairs taken three times

Monday
- 20-minute brisk walk to school
- Gym class at school
- 20-minute walk home

Tuesday
- Walk to school
- 30-minute swim after school
- Walk home

Wednesday
- Walk to school
- Gym class
- 40-minute basketball practice

Thursday
- 20-minute walk to school
- Basketball game

Friday
- Gym class
- 30-minute aerobics class
- 20-minute walk home

Saturday
- Leaf raking for 40 minutes
- Slow 20-minute run

Figure 1.2 What changes would you make in this weekly exercise program to suit your own needs and interest?

UNIT V

The FIT Principle

The effectiveness of your exercise depends on three factors: how often you exercise, how hard you exercise, and how long you exercise at each workout session. These ingredients make up the FIT principle, which stands for frequency, intensity, and time. To achieve fitness, you need to meet minimum standards for each FIT factor. Do you think the students playing baseketball are FIT?

Frequency of Exercise

To stay physically fit, you should exercise frequently, preferably three or more times a week. As you become more fit, some studies suggest that if the intensity of your exercise is moderate, four times a week is most effective in increasing cardiorespiratory endurance and weight loss. If you exercise vigorously, however, do not do so more than five times a week; otherwise, injuries can result.

No matter what your goal is, you should spread your exercise out over the week. Being inactive during the week does not prepare your body for an intense weekend workout. Weekend athletes are more likely to injure themselves than those who exercise regularly throughout the week.

Intensity of Exercise

If your goal is increased cardiorespiratory endurance, you must work your cardio-vascular and respiratory systems with greater-than-normal effort through aerobic exercise. The intensity of a workout is indicated by the number of times your heart beats per minute. The more intense the exercise, the faster your heart rate.

Your maximum heart rate is your heart's top speed or your heart rate when you have exercised to the point of exhaustion. For teenagers, this rate is about 200 beats per minute. You should not try to work out at your maximum heart rate, since exercise at that intensity puts a strain on your heart. Your target heart rate, which is lower than your maximum heart rate, is the approximate heart rate you need to maintain during aerobic exercise in order to benefit from the workout. Your target heart rate depends on your age, your current level of fitness, your resting heart rate, and your maximum heart rate. It is often expressed as a range, such as 145 to 170 beats per minute. Do you think that cross-country skiing is intensive exercise?

During exercise, you need to check your heart rate regularly to determine whether it is within your target heart range. To check your heart rate, you need to stop exercising briefly and count your pulse. Your heart rate slows down quickly, so take your pulse for only six seconds and multiply by ten to get an accurate count of the number of heartbeats per minute.

The "talk test" is an easy way to check your exercise intensity. If you are so out of breath while exercising that you cannot talk, your exercise level is too intense. If you can sing while you exercise, however, you probably are not working hard enough. You are working at the proper intensity if you can talk comfortably.

Cross-country skiing is good aerobic exercise.
The faster you ski, the more intense the exercise becomes.
Courtesy of David Stoecklein/The Stock Market

Exercise Time

Finally, the amount of time spent exercising affects your level of fitness. If you are just beginning an exercise program, start out with only a short period of exercise—about 10 or 15 minutes. Then increase the exercise time gradually, by no more than 10 percent a week. Increasing your exercise program needs to take place over several weeks, as illustrated in Figure 1.3. Once your workout program is well established, most research suggests that 20 to 30 minutes of vigorous exercise four times a week will lead to greater fitness. If your goal is cardiorespiratory improvement, you must exercise within your target heart range for 20 to 30 minutes each session. If your goal is to reduce body fat, your exercise period should be a minimum of 30 minutes, which is longer than the 20-minute minimum required for a cardiorespiratory workout. You should, however, exercise only at a moderate level of intensity—about 60 percent of your maximum heart rate. This is because, at a moderate level of intensity, your muscles tend to use body fat as an energy source, rather than the glucose that is used to provide energy for high-intensity exercise. In order to burn a significant amount of fat, you need to exercise for at least 30 minutes.

Phases of Exercise

A complete fitness workout should be preceded by warming up and followed by cooling down. Although skipping these preliminary and follow-up procedures does not always result in injury, the safest and most healthy exercises include these two phases.

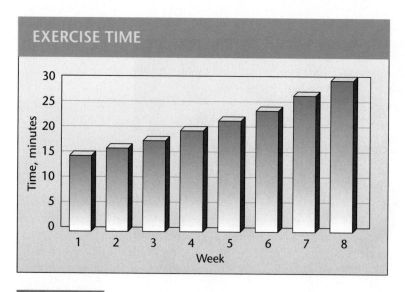

Figure 1.3 If you want to increase the time of your workout, do it gradually, at a rate of about 10 percent a week.

Reprinted from *Health Skills for Wellness*, Third Edition, by B.E. (Buzz) Pruitt, Kathy Teer Crumpler, and Deborah Prothrow-Stith, (2001), Prentice Hall, Inc.

Walking is a good way to warm up for running.
Courtesy of Ken Karp

Warming Up and Stretching

Before doing any type of exercise you must warm up. A warm-up is a 5- to 10-minute period of mild exercise that prepares your body for vigorous exercise. During a warm-up, your body temperature begins to rise, your heart rate picks up, blood flow to your muscles increases, and your muscles become more elastic and less likely to become injured.

Some people suggest that you go through the motions of your planned activity when you warm up. Rather than doing these movements at full intensity, do them at a slower pace. If you are planning to run, for example, start out by walking. Then gradually increase your speed until reaching your usual pace.

Your warm-up should include 5 to 10 minutes of stretching. As you know, stretching increases your flexibility, and proper stretching may decrease your chance of injury. However, it is very important to know your limits and stretch according to safe guidelines, such as those given in Building Health Skills in Chapter 2. Don't overstretch, as that can damage ligaments and weaken joints. Stretching should be a constant, even pull on the muscles on both sides of your body. Because muscles work in pairs, you need to stretch both muscles in a pair. As you stretch each muscle group, you should feel tension but not pain. Do not bounce when you stretch, since bouncing can tear muscle fibers.

Exercise Myths and Facts

1. **MYTH:** "No pain, no gain"; exercise to the point of feeling pain is the only way to improve your abilities.

   FACT: Pain is a danger signal, a signal that you are causing harm. Sharp or sudden pain should be a signal to stop immediately.

2. **MYTH:** Sit-ups and other abdominal exercises will decrease fat in the stomach area.

   FACT: You cannot "spot reduce" or lose fat just in one area.

3. **MYTH:** Drinking fluids before exercising can cause stomach cramps.

   FACT: Plain water will not cause cramps. Without adequate water, you can become dehydrated, which can lead to muscle cramps and other more serious problems.

4. **MYTH:** Being thin is a sign of fitness.

   FACT: Thin people who do not exercise are likely to have poor heart, lung, and muscular fitness. Cardiovascular fitness is a better indication of overall fitness than your appearance.

5. **MYTH:** If women lift weights, they will develop large muscles.

   FACT: Women actually have less muscle tissue and more fat tissue than men. They also have a balance of hormones that is different from men and that prevents the development of large muscle mass.

6. **MYTH:** Exercise is unsafe for older people.

   FACT: The health of elderly people can benefit greatly from moderate exercise.

When it is cold, your clothing should protect you from frostbite. Cover your hands and head, since you lose a lot of heat from these parts of your body. You may need a sweat suit for warmth but do not overdo it. Clothing that is too thick or heavy can inhibit the evaporation of sweat and possibly cause overheating. If you wear layers of clothing, you can regulate your temperature by taking off or adding layers as necessary.

Choosing the Right Exercise Program

Your exercise program should be based on your current fitness ratings and your own interests, needs, and abilities. Even if you think you are perfectly healthy, it makes good sense to check with a physician or other health-care professional to be sure your new activities will not put you at risk. After you have a physician-approved exercise plan, an exercise specialist, such as your physical education teacher, can help you select the best exercises. Moreover, he or she can give you specific pointers on the techniques that will make the activities safe and effective.

The type of exercise program you choose should have three parts: warm-up, conditioning, and cool-down.

The warm-up period allows for a slow increase in the heart rate and sends extra blood through muscles to warm them up. Your warm-up could include slow walking, mild stretching, or calisthenics. Remember, warm-up for five to seven minutes.

The conditioning period brings you into cardiorespiratory endurance and/or muscle strengthening activities. This is where most of your exercising occurs. These exercises should push your body to its normal limit, and when you are feeling strong, a little beyond. As exercising becomes easier, your normal limit should change. Walk or jog a little farther; do a few more sit-ups or push-ups. When weight training to gain bulk, increase to heavier weights; to build strength without bulk, keep lighter weights and increase repetitions. With muscle strengthening exercises, give your muscles a day off between workouts to rest. Or work your upper body one day and your lower body the next. The conditioning period generally lasts twenty minutes.

Figure 1.6 is a sample of a weekly physical fitness training schedule. Notice how it includes the warm-up and conditioning periods as well as a cool-down period.

The cool-down period allows your heart rate to slow down, relaxes muscles, and cools the body. Slow walking, simple calisthenics, and mild stretching are good ways to cool down. Stretching during cool-down can prevent muscle cramps and soreness. Cool-down should last four to six minutes.

Key Terms

calisthenics— *light gymnastic exercise designed to promote good health by developing strength and grace*

cardiorespiratory— *of or relating to the heart and the respiratory system*

WEEKLY PHYSICAL FITNESS TRAINING SCHEDULE

MONDAY	TUESDAY	WEDNESDAY	THURSDAY	FRIDAY
Warm-up/Stretching	Warm-up/Stretching	Warm-up/Stretching	Warm-up/Stretching	Warm-up/Stretching
Conditioning exercises, to include strength training	Aerobic conditioning activities	Conditioning exercises, to include strength training		Physical fitness assessment of goal measurement session
Running		Running	Unit fun run	
Cool-down/Stretching	Cool-down/Stretching	Cool-down/Stretching	Cool-down/Stretching	Cool-down/Stretching

Tuesdays and Thursdays are the "recovery" days. They allow the body to recover. Appropriate activities for these days include aerobic dance, kickball, volleyball, touch football, speed work, and/or fun runs.

[Sample]

Figure 1.6 What changes would you make in this weekly exercise program to suit your own needs and interests?

Sticking with an Exercise Program

Even though many people know how important exercise is to a healthy lifestyle, they have trouble sticking with an exercise program. Follow these tips and you will find it easier to keep your resolution to become or remain physically fit.

- Think of fitness as part of your daily routine, just like brushing your teeth, going to class, or eating dinner.

- Set realistic and specific goals for yourself. If you have never jogged before, do not expect to jog three miles your first time out. You may become discouraged. Plan to jog one mile and stick with it, even if you have to walk part of the way. You will find that you progress quickly, which will build your self-confidence.

- Exercise at least three times a week. If you exercise less than this, you probably will not see much progress, which will give you an easy excuse to give up.

- Keep track of your progress in a journal. It is motivating to look back at where you started and see how far you have come.

- If you are a routine person who likes for things to remain the same, keep the same exercise routine from week to week. If you get bored easily and like change, develop several exercise routines that you can alternate from week to week.

- Exercise with a friend or group. You will get support from others and feel more committed to stick with it.

- Choose a place to exercise that is convenient for you. If the place you plan to exercise is far from home or school, you may not get there as often as you should.

- Wear comfortable clothing and shoes to make your exercise experience as pleasant as possible.

- Stay positive and have fun. Remember that you are doing something good for yourself. Be serious and consistent with your exercise routine, but enjoy it as well. If you choose an exercise program that you just cannot learn to enjoy, try something else. There is an exercise program for everyone!

Caution: Before beginning any exercise or diet program, it is important that you have the approval of your physician.

Assessing Cardiovascular Fitness and Determining Target Heart Rate

When you exercise, your heart and lungs must supply your muscles with more oxygen than they need when you are resting. Your heart, for example, pumps about 5 quarts (about 5.5 liters) of blood per minute when you are at rest and 20 to 25 quarts (about 22 to 27 liters) when you are exercising vigorously. Running track is a great way to get a cardiovascular workout.

Your target heart rate is the heart rate you need to maintain during exercise in order to improve your cardiovascular fitness. The following is a simple test for assessing your cardiovascular fitness and the procedure for determining the range in which your target heart rate should fall. These are followed by some guidelines for improving cardiovascular fitness.

Test Your Cardiovascular Fitness

Before you do this test or start an exercise program, have a physical examination to make sure that you do not have any health problems that rule out vigorous exercise. The examination should include a check of your blood pressure and resting heart rate. Do not attempt this test if you are ill or if you have a history of health problems.

To test your cardiovascular fitness, you must walk and/or run one mile as fast as you can. You can alternate running with walking, but your goal is to cover one mile in as little time as possible. You will need to work with a partner. Your partner should use a watch with a second hand to measure the time, in minutes and seconds, it takes you to complete the distance of one mile.

Compare Your Results to Recommended Results

Compare your score to the scores listed in Table 1.2. To be at a good fitness level, your time should be no greater than the minimum times listed in the table.

Table 1.2	MILE WALK/RUN TIMES*	
AGE	GIRLS	BOYS
14	10:30	7:45
15–18	10:30	7:30
	*In minutes and seconds	

Note:

To prepare for the test, do the warm-up and stretching exercises described in this chapter.

UNIT V

Taking your pulse is easy and tells you your heart rate before and after exercise.

Courtesy of Boston Graphics

Take Your Resting Pulse and Determine Your Target Heart Range

To determine your resting heart rate, you will need a watch or clock with a second hand. Use your index finger or middle finger to find your pulse, either in your wrist or in your neck. Then count the number of pulse beats during one minute.

Subtract your resting heart rate from 200, which is approximately your maximum heart rate. Then multiply the resulting number first by 0.6 and then by 0.8.

Add your resting heart rate to each of the two numbers you obtained in the previous step. The two sums give you the range in which your target heart rate should be.

Choose an Appropriate Cardiovascular Exercise Program

Ask your physical education teacher to help you select appropriate activities for building cardiovascular fitness, such as those in the table. Select moderate intensity activities first; then switch to activities of higher intensity as your fitness improves.

Do these activities three to four times a week. Take your pulse rate immediately after you stop exercising to see if you are exercising in your target heart range. (Because your heart rate begins to decrease as soon as you stop exercising, count the beats in 6 seconds and multiply this number by 10 to get the total number of beats for 60 seconds.)

After you have been exercising regularly for a while, repeat the cardiovascular walk/run fitness test to monitor your progress.

Apply the Skill

1. Complete the timed one mile walk/run to determine your cardiovascular fitness level. Record your results. Be sure to do warm-up stretches before you begin.

2. Determine the range in which your target heart rate falls.

3. After a physical checkup by a qualified health-care professional, design a cardiovascular fitness program that will improve your fitness level.

Fitness Throughout Life

One of the most important and challenging things you can do for yourself is to start exercising now and continue your program for your entire life. If you begin and continue an exercise program when you are young, it will help you stay healthy and fit as you age. Some people are discouraged from achieving this goal because they think that exercise is too difficult or time-consuming. They do not realize that many activities that they already perform may actually be forms of exercise. In addition, fitness activities can actually be a lot of fun. Both aerobic dance classes and recreational dancing can help you become physically fit.

Fitness and Recreation

Do you have fun riding your bike to visit a friend? Is a brisk walk on a cool morning something that you enjoy? At school dances, do you love to jump and turn enthusiastically in time to fast music? Do you and your friends ever get together for a hike, a quick game of basketball, or a swim at a local lake or pool? If you answered yes to any of those questions, you already perform activities that contribute to your physical fitness. Recreational activities that involve exercise, such as walking, biking, dancing, and swimming, are an important part of a fitness program.

Fitness and Aging

As people age, they undergo physical changes. Their bodies become less flexible, and their bones tend to fracture more easily. Those changes do not, however, have to prevent older people from being physically fit. Studies have shown that moderate exercise can help reduce the effects of, and sometimes eliminate, many physical problems associated with old age, such as cardiovascular disease and arthritis. This is true even if exercise begins late in life.

Some older people mistakenly think that they need to avoid exercise to protect themselves from injury. In fact, bones and muscles are more likely to stay strong and function well if they are exercised regularly. Exercise can significantly reduce the risk of osteoporosis, a condition in which the bones of elderly people—particularly elderly women—become fragile. Older people who get little exercise are generally less healthy than those who remain active.

Moderation is especially important in a fitness program for older adults. Older people may not be able to exercise at as high an intensity as they once did. Older people are more likely than younger people to develop circulatory-system problems, and the target heart rate for exercise decreases as a person ages. Elderly people also need to be especially careful not to put too much stress on bones and muscles. If older people exercise carefully and moderately, however, they can continue to benefit from regular exercise.

Finding Ways to Get Fit

Do you still think you just cannot bring yourself to plan and carry out a fitness program? Then at least try to increase your daily level of activity. Make a game out of trying to add just a little more exercise each day. If you travel mostly by car or bus, bicycle or walk instead. Use stairs instead of an elevator. If you already walk quite a bit, pick up your pace or jog for a short distance. A small amount of exercise is better than none at all. People who get even a little bit of exercise have less risk of cardiovascular disease than those who are totally inactive.

Conclusion

Regular exercise is important to maintaining your health. It can make you feel and look better and help your body fight disease. Different exercise programs have different benefits, like aerobic dancing for a strong heart and weight lifting for strong muscles. No matter what exercise program you choose, remember that the most important thing is to stay active. So much in life today makes things easy for us—elevators, escalators, cars, electric appliances—that it is easy to get out of shape. In addition to an exercise program, take the stairs, walk or bike to the store, go bowling with friends instead of watching television. It can be fun, and it is all to your benefit!

In the next chapter, you will learn about the exercises designed for the NJROTC Physical Fitness Test and the Presidential Physical Fitness Award (PPFA) program.

Review Questions

1 How does aerobic exercise differ from anaerobic exercise? Give an example of each.

2 List three physical benefits of regular exercise.

3 Explain how your target heart rate affects the level of intensity of the exercise you perform to improve your cardiorespiratory endurance.

4 List two ways to reduce your risk of injury when you exercise.

Chapter 2

Evaluating Your Physical Fitness

What You Will Learn to Do

Understand the basic physical exercises paramount for success in NJROTC

Skills and Knowledge You Will Gain Along the Way

✔ Explain why stretching is important to building healthy skills

✔ Describe the proper techniques for the three basic physical fitness exercises evaluated in NJROTC

✔ Describe the Presidential Physical Fitness Award

✔ Identify the events in the Presidential Physical Fitness Award

Key Terms

- **curl-ups**
- **Presidential Physical Fitness Award (PPFA)**
- **pull-ups**
- **v-sit reach**
- **shuttle run**
- **flexed-arm hang**

Introduction

This is it! Time to put on your sneakers and start warming up for what may be the toughest part of your unit—participating in exercises designed for the Physical Fitness Test (PFT). Get ready to tackle these exercises developed to assess your physical ability: sit and reach, curl-ups, push-ups, and a run. They require endurance, speed, strength, and flexibility. What can the PFT do for you? First, it allows you to develop an understanding of and appreciation for physical fitness. Second, it shows how an exercise program can improve health and appearance, thereby improving self-confidence. Finally, there is the personal satisfaction associated with striving to achieve a goal as well as recognizing and recording your own progress.

Building Health Skills

As you go through this or any exercise program, it's important to protect your body as well as develop some health skills. These skills include knowing how to warm up, cool down, and, stretch. These activities should be viewed as essential conditioning that ensure the body can sustain periods of exercise like the PFT.

Warming Up, Cooling Down, and Stretching

Imagine that you are about to go on a five-mile bicycle ride or play your favorite sport. You know that these are strenuous activities that put stress on your bones, muscles, and tendons. How should you prepare your body for these activities? After the activity, what should you do to minimize the effects of the stress your body has just undergone?

Before a workout, use slow movements to warm up the muscles that you will use. When the muscles are warmed up, stretch them. Stretching cold muscles is not effective and can cause injury. After your workout, cool down by slowly moving the muscles you used. Then stretch these muscles as you did before the workout.

Although no single stretching routine is appropriate for every activity, the stretching exercises that follow provide a base for you to build on. It is important not to rush when you perform these movements. A pulled muscle can hold you up much longer than the few minutes of warming up/stretching and cooling down/stretching needed with each workout.

When you perform stretching exercises, do not bounce. Bouncing can tear muscle fibers, and scar tissue can form as a result.

Figure 2.1

Stretching helps to protect your muscles during exercise.

Courtesy of Susan Spellman

Figure 2.2

The hand grasp stretches your arms and shoulders.

Courtesy of Susan Spellman

Note:
To warm up for bike riding, begin by pedaling slowly and gradually increase your speed.

Warming Up/Cooling Down

Before your workout, walk, jog slowly, or do the activity that you are about to participate in at a reduced pace. This warms up your muscles, preparing them for the more intense activity of the workout itself. Similarly, right after the workout, you need to continue moving your muscles at a reduced pace for five to ten minutes, as you did in the warm-up. This cool-down period helps ease the body back to normal levels of muscular activity.

Side Stretch

Stand with feet apart, knees bent, and one hand on your hip. Extend the opposite arm overhead and stretch to the side, as shown in Figure 2.1. Hold 15 seconds. Repeat in the other direction. Do five times in each direction.

Hand Grasp

Grasp your hands behind your back and hold. Stand with your feet apart and knees slightly bent, and lean over at the waist. Pull up your arms behind you, as shown in Figure 2.2, and hold 15 seconds.

Lower Back Curl

Lie on your back with legs extended. Bring one knee up to your chest. Grasp the leg behind the knee and pull the knee closer to your chest. Next, curl your shoulders toward your knee. Figure 2.3 shows how this is done. Hold this position for 15 seconds. Switch to the opposite leg and repeat.

Calf Stretch

Stand in a stride position with your right leg forward and hands on your hips. Lean your upper body forward. Simultaneously bend your right leg and extend your left leg back in a continuous line with your upper body. Push your left heel to the ground. Figure 2.4 shows this position. Hold for 15 seconds. Repeat with the other leg. Do this five times on each side.

Hamstring Stretch

Sit on the floor and extend one leg, toes facing up. Tuck your other foot against your extended thigh. Reach forward over your extended leg and slide your hands down your leg until you feel a stretch. Hold for 15 seconds. Switch to the other leg. Repeat with each leg twice.

Take five minutes to practice these stretching exercises.

Each day for a week, do the stretching routine and record how you felt before and after the routine, including any soreness or stiffness. At the end of the week, evaluate the stretching routine and your reactions to it. What are its benefits?

Figure 2.3

Stretch the muscles in your lower back to prevent injury while working out.
Courtesy of Susan Spellman

Figure 2.4

Stretching your calves will help prevent cramping and shin splints.
Courtesy of Susan Spellman

Note:

Select a favorite sport or other physical activity and then ask your physical education teacher or coach to suggest an appropriate warm-up routine for that activity, including stretching exercises.

UNIT V

Basic Rules of Exercise

As you prepare for the PFT, remember to follow these basic rules:

* To produce positive results, exercise at least three times a week
* Begin your exercise program by warming up for 5 to 7 minutes
* Spend at least 20 minutes on conditioning then cool down for 4 to 6 minutes
* Make the sit and reach part of your warm-up or cool down.

Remember to follow an exercise program that includes aerobic exercise for the run/walk, anaerobic exercise which aids in muscle strengthening for curl-ups and push-ups, and stretching for the sit and reach. If you give it your all you and perform to the best of your abilities you will have a stronger body, feel good about yourself, and appreciate health and fitness.

Taking the Physical Fitness Test

The PFT consists of the following four events:

Sit and Reach

The sit and reach test serves as important functional measure of hip and back flexibility. After a sufficient warm-up, the sit and reach is conducted by sitting on the floor with knees fully extended, feet together, ankles at right angles, and toes pointed up. Reaching forward slowly, attempt to touch the tips of your toes with your fingertips. This position must be maintained for one second. You will have three attempts to perform the sit and reach per evaluation period.

Curl-ups

Conduct curl-ups on a flat, clean surface, preferably with a mat. Start in lying position on your back with your knees up so your feet are flat on the floor and about 10 inches from your buttocks. You should have your arms crossed so that your hands are placed on opposite shoulders with your elbows close to your chest. Have your partner hold your feet at the instep. At the command, "ready go," raise the trunk of your body, curling up to touch the elbows to the thighs; then lower your back so that your shoulder blades touch the floor/mat. This constitutes one repetition of a curl-up. You should attempt as many curl-ups as possible in the time allotted and may rest in either the UP or DOWN position. During each repletion, bouncing off the floor/mat is not allowed and the fingers much touch the shoulders at all times.

Right Angle Push-ups

Lie face down on the mat/floor with your hands under your shoulders, fingers straight, and legs parallel with your toes supporting the feet. Your feet should remain together. This is the standard starting position for push-ups. Straighten the arms to push off the ground keeping the back and knees straight. Now lower the body until there is a 90-degree angle at the elbows, with the upper arm parallel to the mat/floor.

Key Term

curl-ups—
one of the four events in the PFT consisting of a sit-up movement from a lying position up to the point where your elbows touch your thighs

A partner may hold his or her hand underneath your chest at the point of the 90-degree angle (typically one fist-length from the ground) so that you go down only until your chest touches your partner's hand, then back up. When you return to the UP position this constitutes one repetition of a push-up. At no time should your buttocks be raised. You should attempt as many push-ups as possible in the time allotted and are allowed to rest in the UP position.

Run/Walk

The run/walk is meant to measure your cardiorespiratory endurance. This event is conducted on a flat area that has a known measured distance of one mile with a designated start and finish line. Start from the standing position. At the command, "ready, go," start running the specified distance—most often a distance of 1.5 miles is used for this event. Although walking is permitted, try to cover the distance in the shortest time possible. Scores are recorded to the nearest second.

Improving Your Scores

The exercises in the PFT test your endurance and physical strength. Initially, it does not matter what you score on these events—although you should always strive for your best—except for the purpose of establishing a base score from which to build. From there, however, you should develop a routine exercise program, so that your score will improve, and along with it, your health.

More Than Healthy Rewards

The Presidential Physical Fitness Award

In 2007, President George W. Bush started the President's Challenge Program for the purpose of encouraging all Americans to make being active a part of their everyday lives. The Physical Fitness Program is not all that different from the NJROTC PFT. It includes five events that measure muscular strength/endurance, cardiorespiratory endurance, speed, agility, and flexibility. By earning a score in 85 percent or higher on all five areas of the test, you are eligible for the Presidential Physical Fitness Award (PPFA). The five events are curl-ups (or partial curl-ups), pull-ups (or right angle push-ups), v-sit reach, shuttle run, and a one mile run.

If you achieve a standard of 84 percent or below, but more than 50 percent, you qualify for the National Physical Fitness Award (NPFA). You may also use a flexed-arm hang instead of pull-ups or push-ups to receive this award. The PPFA consists of a round blue emblem embroidered with an eagle and the NPFA consists of a round red emblem embroidered with an eagle. If you are interested in participating in the President's Challenge you can find more information at www.presidentschallenge.org in *Get Fit: A Handbook for Youth,* or ask your Naval Science Instructor.

Key Terms

Presidential Physical Fitness Award (PPFA)—
an award earned by achieving a standard of 85 percent or higher on the Presidential Physical Fitness Test

pull-ups—
an exercise that consists of pulling the body up from a dead-weight hanging position on a bar to having the chin clear of the bar

v-sit reach—
one of the five events of the Presidential Physical Fitness Test that consists of stretching a number of inches past an established baseline

shuttle run—
one of the five events of the Presidential Physical Fitness Test that consists of a run back and forth between two points 30 feet apart

flexed-arm hang—
an alternative event for the pull-up in the Presidential Physical Fitness Test

UNIT V

Conclusion

The Physical Fitness Test is an introduction to a specific goal. You will see your scores improve as you continue to practice. Making healthy changes in your lifestyle and working hard to reach this goal will make you a stronger, healthier individual, both mentally and physically, and will bring you the great satisfaction of a job well done.

The following chapter introduces you to the importance of good nutrition. You will learn that "you are what you eat," and how a balanced diet is essential when planning a fitness program.

Review Questions

1 Explain the events of the PFT.

2 Describe what you can do to help your body prepare for the PFT.

3 Contrast the difference between the PPFA and the NPFA.

Chapter 3

You Are What You Eat

What You Will Learn to Do

Evaluate how diet impacts life

Skills and Knowledge You Will Gain Along the Way

✔ Explain how calories consumed versus calories used affects body weight

✔ Identify daily required food and portions

✔ Identify sources and benefits of fiber in diet

✔ Describe the importance of water

✔ Describe the possible effects of a diet high in fat and cholesterol

✔ Explain why salt, sugar, and caffeine should be used in moderation

Key Terms

- **nutrients**
- **fats**
- **deficient**
- **calories**
- **metabolism**
- **vitamins**
- **minerals**
- **carbohydrates**
- **protein**
- **osteoporosis**
- **fiber**
- **diabetes**
- **stimulant**

Introduction

A healthy lifestyle includes good nutrition as well as exercise. You need to eat well to maintain an exercise program. Just as a car will not run without fuel, your body will not work properly without the right nutrients. Eating a balanced diet also helps you maintain proper weight and lowers your risk of disease. This chapter explains the importance of a proper diet to your health.

Americans live in a fast-paced environment and frequently eat on the run. Eating on the run too often, however, may affect your nutrition and weight. You can end up consuming too many fats and too few vegetables and fruit, leaving you overweight and/or deficient in certain nutrients. Learning to eat balanced meals, even on the run, contributes to your overall well-being by helping to maintain proper weight, providing energy for physical activity, and supplying nutrients for good health.

Balancing Calories

You must eat to fuel your body. The more active you are, the more fuel your body requires. Even if you remain very still, your body uses a certain amount of energy, or calories, on basic functions that work automatically all the time to keep you alive, such as your heart beating, your lungs inhaling, and your nerves delivering information. You do not have much control over the amount of calories used for these basic functions. Some people's bodies naturally use more calories to sustain their basic functions; some people's use less. It's often said that those who use more have a high metabolism, meaning they can eat more and not gain weight.

Your body also uses calories to do everything else throughout the day, from brushing your teeth, to studying, to stretching. Unlike your basic functions, however, you can control how many calories you voluntarily use throughout the day by how active you are. For example, you will use more calories if you choose to walk for an hour instead of watching television for an hour. Also, the more effort you put into an activity, the more calories you burn. For example, walking at a brisk pace uses more calories than walking at a leisurely pace.

When your body uses the same amount of calories daily than you eat daily, your weight stays the same. If you eat more calories than your body uses, your body stores the unused calories as fat and you gain weight. If you eat fewer calories than your body needs, your body uses the stored fat for energy and you lose weight. It's a balancing act between numbers of calories eaten and calories used.

Key Terms

nutrients—
substances found in food that allow the body to function properly

fats—
nutrients made up of fatty acids that are insoluble in water and provide energy to the body

deficient—
having too little of something, such as a nutrient in the body

Key Terms

calories—
the amount of energy it takes to raise the temperature of one kilogram of water one degree Celsius; a measurement of energy

metabolism—
the chemical process by which the body produces energy and maintains vital functions

Karen and Andrea

Here's an example of making sensible choices when choosing the foods you eat.

Karen wonders why she keeps gaining weight—10 pounds over the last year. One Saturday, she and her friend, Andrea, meet at the local fast-food restaurant for lunch. While they wait in line, Andrea says she played tennis that morning. Karen admits she slept late and watched television. Andrea orders a small soda and a salad with grilled chicken and light Italian dressing; Karen orders a double hamburger with mayonnaise only, large French fries, and a large chocolate milkshake.

Andrea shakes her head and asks Karen if she ever eats fruit or vegetables. Karen shrugs and says "sometimes." Andrea explains that she eats hamburgers and French fries every once in a while; in fact, she had that for lunch a few days ago, which is why she ordered a salad today. Andrea tells Karen that eating fruit and vegetables more often than fried foods and sweets helps her maintain her desired weight, and she feels better, too. Karen thinks about this for a moment as they sit down to eat.

Perhaps if Karen had access to the following calorie counts, she would reconsider what she ordered. Keep in mind that most people need only between 2,000 and 3,000 total calories a day. Table 3.1 shows the difference between the two food orders.

Even if Karen did not want a salad, she could cut her calories considerably by ordering a single hamburger with mustard and ketchup, a small milkshake, and a regular order of fries. She could also have lettuce and tomato on the burger to eat some vegetables. Her new calorie intake would look simliar to Table 3.2.

Table 3.1		KAREN AND ANDREA'S LUNCH ORDERS	
KAREN'S ORDER	**Calories**	**ANDREA'S ORDER**	**Calories**
Plain double hamburger with bun (¼ pound beef)	540	Salad with grilled chicken	200
Mayonnaise (1 tablespoon)	100	Light Italian salad dressing (2 tablespoons)	50
French fries (large order)	360		
Chocolate milkshake (large)	540	Soda (small)	150
TOTAL	**1540**	**TOTAL**	**400**

The calories listed here are approximate; actual calories in these food items may vary at different restaurants.

UNIT V

Table 3.2 — AN ALTERNATIVE TO KAREN'S LUNCH ORDER

KAREN'S ORDER	Calories
Plain single hamburger with bun (2-ounce patty)	275
Lettuce (1/2 cup)	5
Tomato (1 slice)	5
Mustard (1 tablespoon)	8
Ketchup (1 tablespoon)	15
French fries (regular order)	220
Chocolate milkshake (small)	330
TOTAL	**858**

If Karen really wants to lose those extra 10 pounds, however, she should skip the milkshake and replace the fries with a small salad and light dressing. This would reduce her calorie intake to about 400 for lunch. She should then get some exercise like her friend Andrea. Playing tennis for an hour uses three times as many calories as watching television for an hour. If Karen sticks to eating sensibly and exercises daily, she will start using more calories than she eats, losing those extra pounds. How many calories are contained in the food you eat? Figure 3.1 gives you an idea of the calories contained in everyday foods.

THE CALORIE CONTENT OF SOME COMMON FOODS

25 — Tomato 1 medium
150 — Whole milk 1 cup
290 — Cheese pizza 1 slice
80 — Egg 1 large
80 — Apple 1 medium
20 — Green pepper 1 medium
65 — Wheat bread 1 slice
145 — Potato 1 medium
270 — Ice cream 1 cup
60 — Orange 1 medium

Figure 3.1 Of the foods shown, which two have the most calories? Which have the fewest?
Courtesy of Function thru Form

The Importance of a Proper Diet to Your Health

Just as important as eating the correct amount of calories to supply your body with energy and maintain proper weight is what you eat to get those calories. If you eat like Karen every day, you are giving your body too much fat, cholesterol, salt, and sugar, and denying your body many necessary nutrients. Many health problems are related to poor diets, and these problems can start when you are young. At your next physical examination, ask your doctor about your cholesterol, blood pressure, and blood sugar levels. You may be surprised to find you need to change your diet to improve your health.

What Should You Eat?

The United States Department of Agriculture (USDA) developed the Food Guide Pyramid to indicate how many servings of six different food groups you should eat daily to get the nutrients your body needs. If you follow these guidelines, you will get enough vitamins and minerals to keep your body's processes functioning properly, and you will have enough carbohydrates, protein, and fat to supply your body with energy. When you do not get enough of certain nutrients, you increase your risk of disease. For example, if you do not get enough calcium, a mineral found in milk products, almonds, sardines, leafy vegetables, and beans, you can develop osteoporosis.

To see the current Food Guide Pyramid, as offered by the USDA, check out http://www.nal.usda.gov/fnic/Fpyr/pyramid.html or Figure 3.2.

Figure 3.2 The Food Guide Pyramid divides foods into groups and indicates how many servings you should eat from each group every day.

Key Terms

vitamins—
nutrients that occur naturally in plant and animal tissue and are required for proper function of the body

minerals—
natural chemical elements of the earth used by the body to supply necessary nutrition

carbohydrates—
one of the various neutral organic compounds composed of carbon, hydrogen, and oxygen (including starches and sugars) produced by plants and used to provide energy necessary for growth and other functions

protein—
nutrients that are made of amino acids and that maintain body tissues and supply energy to the body

osteoporosis—
a condition characterized by a calcium deficiency in the bone mass; the body pulls calcium from the bones, causing them to lose their density and possibly leading to fractures

UNIT V

fiber—
coarse food made mostly of carbohydrates, such as bran or broccoli, that serves to stimulate and aid the movement of food through the digestive tract

diabetes—
a disease in which the body is unable to use sugars properly

Clot

Figure 3.3

Cholesterol shown in artery walls

Key Term

stimulant—
an ingredient found in beverages, food, or drugs that speeds up the activity of the mind or body; a drug that speeds up the activities of the central nervous system, the heart, and other organs; for example, caffeine in tea or chocolate

Your body also needs fiber, the only form of carbohydrate that is not an energy source. Fiber aids in digestion. It prevents cholesterol, fats, and other toxic materials from entering the bloodstream and for this reason may lessen your chances of cancer and heart disease; it also helps balance your blood sugar levels, which is important if you suffer from diabetes. To obtain fiber, eat raw or lightly cooked vegetables, fresh fruit, beans, nuts, and whole wheat or bran breads, cereals, and crackers.

One final nutrient which contains no calories is water. Water can be obtained from plain or sparkling water, fruits and vegetables and their juices, milk and yogurt, cooked cereal, rice and soups. More than 65 percent of the body is water, and, as the body loses water through normal activity and exercise, it must be replaced. Water aids in digestion, regulates temperature, carries vitamins and minerals to all parts of the body, and is important for the removal of waste products from the kidneys. Drink a minimum of five to six glasses of water a day. On the days you exercise, you may need to drink more.

Eating in Moderation

Your body needs fat for energy, but too much fat in your diet can make you gain weight and can lead to high cholesterol. Cholesterol, a type of fat, is a natural, waxy substance produced by your body and found in animal products. Your body needs some cholesterol to remain healthy, but too much is harmful. As shown in Figure 3.3, cholesterol forms plaque on artery walls, restricting the flow of blood within blood vessels. This leads to high blood pressure and an increased risk of heart disease. To lower cholesterol levels, lower your intake of fat by eating less meat, using oil-free dressings, avoiding fried foods, eating low-fat dairy products, and consuming lots of fiber.

Many foods, especially prepackaged foods and restaurant foods, already have added salt, so do not shake on more. Too much salt in your diet forces your body to retain unnecessary water and may contribute to high blood pressure.

Sugary foods like candy, soda, syrup, and table sugar supply you with calories and few (if any) nutrients. These foods contain "empty calories"; they give your body calories and nothing else. Avoid them while dieting, and do not eat them as a replacement for other foods that provide nutrition. Many fruits and vegetables naturally contain sugar, but they also provide many other important nutrients.

Limit your intake of coffee, tea, and sodas that contain caffeine, a stimulant. Although caffeine temporarily reduces drowsiness and makes you more alert, in large quantities it can upset your stomach, make you nervous and irritable, keep you awake when you want to sleep, and give you diarrhea.

Conclusion

Your body needs food for energy, just like a car needs fuel to run. How much food your body needs depends on how active you are and how many calories your body uses to keep its basic functions operating. You know you are getting the right amount of calories from food when you maintain your ideal weight. Not only does food supply you with energy, but the right foods also provide the nutrients your body needs to operate properly and lower your risk of disease. Eating a healthy, balanced diet and exercising regularly increase your chances of a long, strong, and disease-free life.

In the next chapter, you will learn more about nutrition and what it takes to properly nourish your body.

Review Questions

1   Think about what you had for breakfast.
    How could you have balanced your calories better?

2   Do you feel you have a slow or fast metabolism?
    How can you plan your meals with this in mind?

3   Looking at the food pyramid, what food group
    do you need to eat more or less of?

4   Define the term *metabolism*.

Chapter 4

Nutrition: Nourishing Your Body

Key Terms

- simple carbohydrates
- complex carbohydrates
- fat soluble vitamin
- monounsaturated fats
- polyunsaturated fats
- saturated fats
- amino acids
- water soluble vitamin
- Referenced Daily Intake (RDI)

What You Will Learn to Do

Analyze how well you meet nutrient guidelines

Skills and Knowledge You Will Gain Along the Way

- ✔ Explain the six nutrients your body requires
- ✔ Explain the difference between simple and complex carbohydrates
- ✔ Describe the role fat and cholesterol play in body functioning
- ✔ Compare saturated and unsaturated fats
- ✔ Describe ways to reduce cholesterol levels
- ✔ Compare the functions of vitamins, carbohydrates, fats, and proteins
- ✔ Identify food sources of vitamins and minerals

Introduction

Nutrition is the science of nourishing the body properly to reach the higher levels of dynamic living. This chapter introduces you to the six nutrients and shows you how to best provide them in a diet that is well rounded yet diversified. You will learn the newest methods available in how to choose your foods and how to read labels. Finally, you will better understand how to maintain a lean body, free from the damaging effects of carrying too much personal fat.

Our diets have radically changed during the past 35 years. With the advent of fast-food outlets, an increase in dual-career parents, and sky-rocketing numbers of single-parent households, most Americans now have a hurry-up lifestyle where proper eating habits take a back seat to convenience and lack of time.

Knowing that our lifestyles are busy and sometimes hurried, it is very important that young adults have at least a basic understanding of nutrients, how to obtain them, and how to control fat. This knowledge will lead to a more dynamic life and a higher quality lifestyle. The six types of nutrients are carbohydrates, fats, proteins, vitamins, minerals, and water.

We also refer to the first three nutrients, carbohydrates, fats, and proteins, as food-stuffs. They give us the energy for all of the bodily processes. When our body uses the foodstuffs, it releases energy. We measure this energy in calories.

Carbohydrates

Carbohydrates are the starches and sugars found in fruits, grains, and vegetables. They have a caloric value of four calories per gram and supply us with short- and long-term energy to accomplish everything from thinking and breathing to running a race.

The short-term carbohydrates are the sugars, or simple carbohydrates, which are quickly digested and absorbed into the blood. The most important simple sugar is glucose, or blood sugar. Before the body's cells can use other simple sugars (such as fructose, sucrose, and lactose) for energy, a change must occur converting them into glucose. Many sugary foods are sources of simple carbohydrates; however, those such as soda and candy have few other nutrients, while fruit is an excellent source of simple carbohydrates and contains many other vitamins and minerals as well.

The long-term carbohydrates are starches, or complex carbohydrates, which are made up of combinations of simple sugars. They take longer to digest because the body must break them into simple sugars (glucose) before they can enter the bloodstream. When your body has extra glucose that it does not need immediately for energy, it converts it into the complex carbohydrate glycogen and stores it in the muscles and liver to be released later when energy is needed, usually for short periods of strenuous activity. After your muscles and liver store as much glycogen as they can hold, your body changes the rest to body fat for long-term energy. Long distance runners use carbohydrate loading (eating large quantities of carbohydrates) to have the long-term energy they need to complete the race.

Key Terms

simple carbohydrates— *a sugar that is found in food and the body in its simple state, which supplies the body with short-term energy*

complex carbohydrates— *a carbohydrate that is formed by the body or by plants after the conversion of simple carbohydrates, which supplies the body with long-term energy*

UNIT V

Table 4.3	TRACE MINERALS		
MINERAL	US RDI	FUNCTIONS	SOURCES
Selenium	50–75 mcg*	Prevents breakdown of fats	Seafood, whole-grain cereals, meat, egg yolks, milk, and garlic
Manganese	5 mg*	Central nervous system; normal bone structure; reproduction	Nuts, whole grains, vegetables, fruits, tea, and cocoa powder
Fluoride	1.5–4 mg*	Tooth and bone formation	Drinking water in some places, seafood, and tea
Molybdenum	75–250 mcg*	Part of enzymes	Legumes, cereals, liver, kidneys, and dark green vegetables
Iron	18 mg	Formation of hemoglobin; part of enzymes and proteins	Liver, kidneys, meat, egg yolks, green leafy vegetables, dried druit, dried beans and peas, and whole-grain and enriched cereals
Copper	2 mg	Formation of red blood cells; part of respiratory enzymes	Oysters, nuts, cocoa powder, liver, kidneys, beans, corn oil, and margarine
Iodine	150 mcg	Functioning of the thyroid gland and production of thyroid hormones	Iodized salt and seafood
Chromium	50–200 mcg*	Helps the body use carbohydrates and fats; aids in digestion of protein	Liver, nuts, whole grains, Brewer's yeast, meat, mushrooms, potatoes, apples with skin, and oysters
Zinc	15 mg	Part of many enzymes; essential to synthesis of DNA and RNA; metabolizes carbohydrates, fats, and proteins; disposes of carbon dioxide; strengthens immune system; helps wounds heal; helps body use vitamin A	Meat, liver, eggs, poultry, and seafood

*No US RDI established. Amount is an estimated recommendation for dietary intake.

Point of Interest: Minerals

A study has found that heart-disease patients who received 150 mcg of chromium per day had a dramatic jump in the HDL cholesterol, the good stuff that helps keep arteries clear.

Water

About 60 to 70 percent of your body is water, with most of your blood, brain, and muscles being water and even 20 percent of your bones. Water carries the other nutrients, when dissolved, to all parts of the body where and when needed. It also aids in digestion, regulation of temperature, removal of wastes, joint lubrication, and biochemical processes taking place in the body all the time. Without water you would die in a few days. To maintain all the bodily functions water helps carry out, you need to consume the equivalent of six to eight glasses of water a day. If you exercise regularly, you may need as many as ten glasses, especially on the days you exercise.

Hunger and Malnutrition

As long as people can easily obtain an abundant and varied diet, it is not difficult for them to meet their nutritional needs. When such fortunate people become hungry, they can usually satisfy their need for food. However, many people in the world cannot obtain enough of the right foods, and in some cases cannot get much food at all. For them, hunger is a way of life—an ongoing, painful condition over which they have little control. Poor nutrition is a serious, worldwide problem.

Famine victims, such as this Somalian woman, search in vain to try to find food.

Courtesy of Jean-Claude Coutausse/Contact Press Images

Malnutrition

Technically, malnutrition is any condition in which a person's nutrient consumption is inadequate or unbalanced. Most cases, however, are the result of consuming too little of one or more nutrients. Malnutrition harms every system of the body and also damages emotional well-being.

When people are malnourished, they do not have the energy to perform well in school or at work. Malnourished people are also more susceptible to disease than those who eat a healthy diet. Malnourished children usually grow much more slowly than children whose diet is adequate. If malnutrition occurs during pregnancy, the baby may weigh less than normal and have serious health problems.

There are various types of malnutrition, including the vitamin and mineral deficiencies discussed earlier in this chapter. In one especially serious condition known as protein-energy malnutrition, the diet does not contain adequate protein, nor does it supply enough calories to meet the body's energy needs. The effects of this condition are especially severe on children because their bodies need protein and calories for growth. Severe cases can cause death, either directly through starvation or indirectly through the diseases to which its victims become susceptible. Protein-energy malnutrition is the most serious nutrition problem affecting people in developing countries today.

Malnutrition has various causes. In some cases, people may be undernourished because they are unaware of the foods that they need for good health. Also, diseases and other conditions may prevent the digestive system from absorbing nutrients. But, indirectly, poverty is by far the most common cause of malnutrition. Victims of severe poverty cannot afford to buy or grow the food they need.

A World Problem

Hunger and malnutrition are an especially severe problem in many of the world's poorer nations. Severe famines, for example, have devastated countries such as Somalia and Bangladesh. However, hunger is also a problem in more prosperous countries, including the United States. Although few people starve in the United States, many are not receiving adequate nutrition. Hungry people in the United States are those who have little or no income, such as homeless people, teenage runaways, families dealing with unemployment, and some elderly people.

Various programs and organizations are trying to solve the problem of malnutrition and provide food for those who need it. For example, the Food and Agriculture Organization of the United Nations combats hunger by helping people improve methods of agriculture and food distribution. The US government sponsors the Food Stamp Program that enables low-income people to purchase the food that they need. Volunteers also work hard to help those who are hungry. For example, soup kitchens, which are often staffed by volunteers, provide meals for those in need.

Conclusion

Understanding what nutrition your body needs is essential to maintaining both physical and emotional health. Without the proper balance of carbohydrates, fats, proteins, vitamins, and minerals, you open the door to all kinds of health problems—some possibly fatal. Even with a fast-paced lifestyle, it's still possible to eat correctly and give your body the fuel it needs.

Next, you will learn about dietary guidelines. You will examine the National Academy of Sciences' 2001 report on how we should eat, as well as some alternative choices that many nutritionists advocate.

Review Questions

1 How do carbohydrates help the body?

2 Compare and contrast monounsaturated fats and polyunsaturated fats.

3 What roles do proteins play in nutrition?

4 What are the effects of malnutrition?

Chapter 5

Dietary Guidelines

Key Terms

- anorexia nervosa
- bulimia
- amenorrhea
- episodic
- diuretics
- esophageal
- electrolyte

What You Will Learn to Do

Relate the National Academy of Sciences dietary guidelines to your personal diet

Skills and Knowledge You Will Gain Along the Way

✔ Identify the nine National Academy of Sciences dietary goals

✔ Identify factors that affect the nutritional requirements of individuals at various life stages

✔ Identify signs and symptoms of anorexia nervosa and bulimia

✔ Examine varying viewpoints on vitamin and mineral supplement usage

✔ Calculate your personal blueprint

Introduction

Today's hurry-up lifestyles, diverse family structures, fast-food restaurants, and personal finances have all impacted on the way we eat. Thus, by our actions, America has become a country that is overweight and suffering greatly from cardiovascular disease, cancer, diabetes, and other ailments that hinder our efforts to live a dynamic lifestyle.

This chapter explains the National Academy of Sciences' report on how we should eat, as well as some alternative choices that many nutritionists advocate.

The Lifetime Eating Plan

Nutritional needs vary at different ages. There are different needs for children (age two to adolescence), adolescents, adults, and the elderly. There are also special conditions and needs for pregnant women.

For example, the special concerns for teens are that they often have erratic eating habits, their calcium requirements are high, and after the onset of menstruation, females need more iron. General dietary recommendations are to ensure you eat sufficient calories to support your growth and activity levels with high-carbohydrate foods. Also, consume iron-rich foods and keep healthy snacks available.

Pregnant women need to increase their caloric intake and to eat adequate protein, iron, calcium, folic acid, and vitamin C. Proper nutrition is essential to avoid complications, including nausea, heartburn, constipation, and gestational diabetes. General dietary recommendations are to eat two dairy servings daily and two cups of calcium-rich vegetables; also eat green leafy vegetables, legumes, broccoli, asparagus, and whole grains. Avoid overcooking. An obstetrician may recommend supplements. Drink at least eight glasses of liquid daily. Avoid alcohol and caffeine.

The New American Diet—Step by Step

Another popular eating plan is the New American Diet. This plan yields similar dietary recommendations as those explained elsewhere in these nine guidelines. However, the basis for this plan is the development of a healthier lifestyle by following a three step approach: Phase I stresses the use of substitutions to your present diet; Phase II introduces new recipes; Phase III prescribes a new way of eating.

Eating Disorders

Eating disorders such as anorexia nervosa and bulimia are common in today's society. People with anorexia nervosa experience extreme weight loss, amenorrhea, and a variety of psychological disorders culminating in an obsessive preoccupation with the attainment of thinness. However, for 10 to 15 percent of its victims, the disease becomes episodic and relentless, resulting in death from the consequences of starvation.

Key Terms

anorexia nervosa—
an aversion to food syndrome; an eating disorder characterized by an extreme (prolonged) loss of appetite and very decreased food intake

bulimia—
a disease (or eating disorder) with symptoms of binging and purging or overeating and vomiting

amenorrhea—
an abnormal absence or suppression of the menstrual period

episodic—
occurring, appearing, or changing at irregular intervals; incidental

UNIT V

A person with anorexia nervosa normally exhibits the following characteristics:

- An unwillingness to maintain minimal normal body weight for the individual's age and height; weight loss that leads to the maintenance of a body weight 15 percent below normal; or a failure to gain the amount of weight expected during a period of growth, resulting in a body weight that is 15 percent below normal.
- An inordinate fear of gaining weight and/or becoming fat despite being significantly underweight.
- An unrealistic perception of body weight, size, or shape. The person "feels fat" or perceives that one specific part of the body is "too fat."
- An absence of at least three, otherwise normal, menstrual cycles.

On the other hand, people with bulimia experience alternate cycles of binge eating and restrictive eating. Purging usually follows binges, primarily by self-induced vomiting supplemented with the use of laxatives and diuretics. The physical and psychological results of such a struggle with bulimia include esophageal inflammation, erosion of tooth enamel caused by repeated vomiting, the possibility of electrolyte imbalances, and altered mood states, particularly anxiety and depression.

A person with bulimia normally exhibits the following characteristics:

- An episodic eating binge, characterized by rapid consumption of large amounts of food in a short time.
- At least two eating binges per week for at least three months, even possibly experiencing a loss of control over eating behavior while in the process of binges.
- Frequent purges after eating; then engages in fasting, strict dieting, or vigorous exercise.
- A constant concern over body shape, size, and weight.

If you think someone has an eating disorder,

- Express your concern about the person's health. Although the person may deny there is a problem, show that you care.
- Try to focus on feelings that the person may be experiencing, such as excessive worrying, anxiety, poor self-esteem, anger, or hurt. Encourage the person to talk about issues not related to food. Be a good listener.
- Encourage the person to talk to parents, relatives, or a health care or mental health professional.
- Talk to someone else (possibly a professional) about your concerns for that person.
- Do not label the person. That may make the person feel accused and strengthen feelings of denial.

Key Terms

diuretics—
food, medication, etc., that promotes or tends to increase the excretion of urine

esophageal—
of or relating to the esophagus (a muscular tube through which food passes from the mouth to the stomach)

electrolyte—
substance that, when dissociated into ions in solution or fused, becomes electrically conducting; obtained from minerals in the diet

Getting Help for Eating Disorders

For more information about anorexia, bulimia, and other eating disorders, contact:

National Eating Disorders Association
603 Stewart St., Suite 803
Seattle, WA 98101
(206) 382-3587
www.nationaleatingdisorders.org

The National Academy of Sciences believes there is a close association between total fat intake, saturated fat, high cholesterol, and heart disease. They developed nine guidelines for reducing the risk of chronic diseases and helping to provide protection against the possibility of early disease.

> **Note:**
>
> The American diet should consist of a total fat intake between 35 to 40 percent of the total calories consumed each day; however, the typical American diet consists of nearly 50 percent fat calories.

Guideline #1

The goals of this guideline are to reduce your total fat intake to 30 percent or less of your total calories, your estimated fatty acids (building blocks of fat) intake to less than 10 percent of your total calories, and your cholesterol intake to less than 300 milligrams. Take a look at Figure 5.1 and determine which of these foods has the lowest percent are of saturated fat.

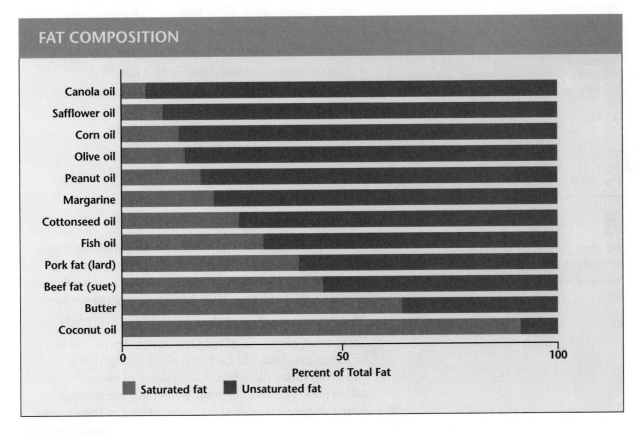

FAT COMPOSITION

Percent of Total Fat

■ Saturated fat   ■ Unsaturated fat

Figure 5.1 Which of the fat sources in the graph is lowest in saturated fat?
Courtesy of Function thru Form

Nutrition Facts
Serving Size: 1/2 cup (114 g)
Servings Per Container: 4

Amount Per Serving

Calories 260	Calories from fat 120

	% Daily Value*
Total Fat 13 g	20%
Saturated Fat 5 g	25%
Cholesterol 30 mg	10%
Sodium 660 mg	28%
Potassium 400 mg	11%
Total Carbohydrate 31 g	11%
Sugars 5 g	
Dietary Fiber 0 g	0%
Protein 5 g	10%

Vitamin A 4%   Vitamin C 2%
Iron 4%   Calcium 15%   Vitamin D 25%

* Percent (%) of a Daily Value is based on a 2000 calorie diet. Your Daily Values may vary higher or lower depending on your calorie needs:

Nutrient		2000 Calories	2500 Calories
Total Fat	Less than	65 g	80 g
Sat Fat	Less than	20 g	25 g
Cholesterol	Less than	300 mg	300 mg
Sodium	Less than	2400 mg	2400 mg
Potassium		3500 mg	3500 mg
Total Carbohydrate		300 g	375 g
Dietary Fiber		25 g	30 g
Protein		50 g	65 g

Calories per gram
Fat 9   Carbohydrate 4   Protein 4

Figure 5.2

A typical food label gives you information about the contents of the product.

*Note: Trans-fat will be added to food labels by January 2006.

Tips for achieving these goals include the following:

- Limit your egg intake. Use two or three egg whites for every yolk. Cholesterol is in the yolk, and egg white is a great source of protein.
- Use skim, nonfat, or one percent milk. Purchase low-fat or nonfat cheeses, yogurt, and other dairy products.
- Use margarine sparingly. The soft tub or liquid margarine is best.
- Read labels. Avoid foods that contain trans-fat. Trans-fat causes the same type of damage in your arteries as saturated fats and cholesterol. Trans-fat is found in foods that contain solid plant fat, such as stick margarine, cream filling in cookies, and baking shortening.
- When ordering in a restaurant, tell the waiter to ask the chef to use only half the oils or fat products he would normally use.
- Try to eat three servings of fish per week. Cold water and deep sea running fish are best because of the high omega three oils (fat that may aid in the maintenance of the heart and blood vessels).
- Eat lean meat and then sparingly.
- Bake and broil meat products, if possible.
- Use the lowest saturated fat cooking oils.
- When eating snacks, choose low-fat, low sugar content sweets.
- Learn how to read a label and calculate the fat content in food products.

Figure 5.2 shows a sample food label that might appear on a package.

Alternative Guideline #1

An alternative goal for Guideline #1 is to reduce fat intake to 20 percent or less of your total calories, saturated fat to 5 percent of your total, cholesterol intake to 100 milligrams, and use only 4 to 7 teaspoons of mono- or polyunsaturated fat a day.

Your eating habits can affect your health. Try to develop an eating plan that will keep you at your healthiest level and avoid eating disorders. A discussion of two acceptable eating plans and two common, potentially dangerous eating disorders was given at the beginning of this chapter.

Breads are excellent sources of starch.
Courtesy of Steven Mays

Guideline #2

The goal of Guideline #2 is to increase starches and other complex carbohydrates. The typical American diet consists of 22 percent complex carbohydrates and 24 percent sugar.

General dietary recommendations are to receive 60 to 65 percent of your diet from the carbohydrate group, 50 to 55 percent of that from the complex carbohydrates, and 20 percent from sugar, with most of that coming from fruits.

Note:

Almost all nutritionists agree with the National Academy's number two guideline. By choosing those percentages, you will receive more than adequate amounts of fiber.

Guideline #3

The goal of this guideline is to maintain protein intakes at moderate levels. Americans receive 68 percent of their protein from animal sources (compared to 4 to 5 percent for the Chinese). There is evidence pointing to the rise in some cancers with the increase in animal protein.

The body needs no more than 0.45 of a gram of protein per pound of lean body weight per day. Since the minimum requirement is 0.16 grams per pound, 10 to 15 percent of your food should come from proteins and the majority of that from plant sources.

Alternative Guideline #3

The American Heart Association recommends no more than two protein servings daily. However, the US Department of Agriculture recommends two to three servings of the milk, cheese, and yogurt group daily and two to three servings of the meat, poultry, fish, beans, eggs, and nuts group.

Guideline #4

The goal of this guideline is to balance food intake and physical activity to maintain appropriate body weight. Approximately one-third of the American population is overweight. Overweight teenage boys are more likely to die at a higher than usual rate by age 45. Teenage girls who are overweight are eight times more likely to have trouble in later years with daily routines such as climbing stairs, lifting, and walking.

To balance food intake and physical activity requires planning each day's food intake based upon these guidelines as well as each week's physical activities to include at least three 30-minute workouts. While in school, participating in sports programs and daily physical activities is the best way to accomplish this goal.

Alternative Guideline #4

Body weight is not the best indicator of measuring food intake versus physical activity. Measurement of body fat is a healthier indicator and a much more concise measuring tool in determining the best balance of food intake and physical activity. Also, the more fat that accumulates around the stomach represents more of a danger to the person.

Fewer than 10 percent of Americans over age 18 exercise vigorously and regularly. Exercise can decrease a person's chance of dying of heart disease, cancer, and a host of other illnesses.

Guideline #5

The main goal of Guidelines #5 is to avoid alcoholic beverages. Alcohol can produce the following problems with nutritional balance and wellness:

- Upsets metabolism
- Produces fullness, thus the person does not eat a balanced diet
- Increases nutritional needs
- Causes inadequate assimilation (digestion and absorption) of the nutrients

It is not easy to avoid the temptation of alcoholic beverages, particularly with the pressure that our peers put upon us. The best way to avoid alcoholic beverages is to make the decision not to drink an alcoholic beverage before it is offered to you.

Alternative Guideline #5

Try to avoid putting yourself into a situation that will force you to make the choice to drink or not to drink alcohol. First make the decision not to drink alcoholic beverages and let your friends know that alcohol is not for you. Whenever possible, avoid parties and other events where alcohol is served. If you have to attend these events, always plan ahead and have your decision made.

Guideline #6

The goal here is to limit the daily intake of salt to no more than 3 grams. Salt is 60 percent chloride and 40 percent sodium. Too much sodium can lead to high blood pressure in some people (those who are salt sensitive). Furthermore, salt absorbs water in the body, causing the blood pressure to increase because of the larger volume of water the heart must pass through the system. Try to avoid adding salt to your meals. It is best not to add table salt to any of your meals. All processed or manufactured food has salt added. Just read the label on any canned food and you will be surprised how much salt has already been added.

Alternative Guideline #6

There are several ways that you can cut down on your salt intake, including the following:

- The National Academy of Sciences recommends no more than 2400 milligrams ($1/2$ teaspoon; 2.4 grams) of salt a day. One teaspoon of salt is equivalent to 5 grams.
- Switch to "lite" salt, thus reducing the sodium content by one half. You can also increase potassium (too little increases blood pressure) by using "lite" salt.
- Eat less processed or manufactured food.
- Avoid snack food or use unsalted varieties.
- Limit smoked foods.
- Limit brine prepared foods such as pickles, olives, and sauerkraut.

Guideline #7

The goal for Guideline #7 is to maintain adequate calcium intake. Most Americans do not receive enough calcium from their normal diets. Ninety-nine percent of our body's calcium is present in the bones and teeth. One percent aids in the functioning of the blood, muscles, and nerves.

To meet its need for calcium, the body will pull calcium from the bones, causing them to lose their density. This condition, known as osteoporosis, can lead to hip, leg, and arm fractures. Diets that are low in calcium may also cause hypertension (high blood pressure) and some forms of cancer.

The referenced daily intake for ages 11 to 24 is 1200 milligrams a day. Adult men and women need 1000 milligrams. Pregnant and nursing women also need 1200 milligrams. To prevent osteoporosis:

- Participate in lifelong weight-bearing exercises to ensure the density of the bones
- Avoid excessive protein
- Eat a diet rich in calcium (skim milk, certain fruits, and vegetables)
- Take calcium supplements, if needed
- Avoid starvation diets
- Avoid alcohol and smoking

Alternative Guideline #7

A well-balanced diet following the Food Guide Pyramid guidelines, as shown in Figure 5.3, ensures adequate calcium intake. Make sure that there is a variety of colors on your plate each meal. For example, dark leafy green vegetables contain calcium, just as dairy products do.

Note:

For more information on the Food Guide Pyramid, see Chapter 3, "You Are What You Eat."

Figure 5.3 The Food Guide Pyramid provides guidance for a well balanced diet.

Guideline #8

The goal for Guideline #8 is to avoid taking dietary supplements in excess of the referenced daily intake in any one day.

There are two schools of thought on this guideline. One says that we can get all of our vitamins and minerals from our normal diet without supplementation. The other opinion is that by taking supplemental dosages of specific vitamins and minerals, we can protect ourselves from birth defects, cataracts, cardiovascular disease, and cancer, as well as strengthen the immune system.

Alternative Guideline #8

As an alternative to Guideline #8, you can

- Take a general vitamin/mineral supplement daily, not to exceed the RDI
- Take a calcium supplement
- Take antioxidant vitamins in supplemental form: vitamin C, vitamin E, and beta-carotene (see the following nutrition prescription for an additional alternative).

> **Note:**
>
> Always consult a healthcare professional before taking any supplements.

Your Nutrition Prescription

Vitamin and mineral supplements are indispensable anti-aging weapons, but too many people use them shotgun style—a handful of this, a bunch of that—instead of coordinating them for the most life-lengthening strategy. To ensure that you are not over- or underdoing any element, you need a prescription customized for your age, gender, health, and lifestyle. Look at the Supplement Blueprint in Table 5.1 and see how much of each supplement you take. Then answer the following six questions. For each yes answer, follow the directions for revising the Supplement Blueprint. If you end up with more than one recommendation for a particular nutrient, follow the highest single dosage.

- Are you male? Delete iron.
- Do you smoke or live/work with a smoker, or do you live in an air-polluted area? Increase C to 1000 mg, selenium to 400 mcg, beta-carotene to 25,000 IU, E to 400 IU, copper to 3 mg, and zinc to 50 mg.
- Do you exercise at least three times a week for 20 or more minutes? Increase E to 400 IU, magnesium to 400 mg, B-1 to 100 mg, and zinc to 50 mg.
- Are you on the Pill (birth-control pills)? Increase B-6 to 50 mg.
- Are you pregnant or nursing? Increase folic acid to 800 mcg, iron to 60 mg, calcium to 1300 mg, and magnesium to 400 mg. Delete A.
- Do you have high cholesterol levels and/or a family history of heart disease? Increase E to 400 IU, C to 1000 mg, beta-carotene to 25,000 IU, chromium to 200 mcg, and magnesium to 400 mg.

Table 5.1	PERSONAL SUPPLEMENT BLUEPRINT	
SUPPLEMENT	Longevity Standard	My Dose
Beta-carotene	15,000 IU	_____
Vitamin A	10,000 IU	_____
Vitamin B-1	25 mg	_____
Vitamin B-2	25 mg	_____
Niacinamide	100 mg	_____
Pantothenic acid	50 mg	_____
Vitamin B-6	25 mg	_____
Vitamin B-12	100 mcg	_____
Biotin	100 mcg	_____
Folic acid	400 mcg	_____
Vitamin C	500 mg	_____
Vitamin D	400 IU	_____
Vitamin E	200 IU	_____
Calcium	1,200 mg	_____
Chromium	100 mcg	_____
Copper	2 mg	_____
Iodine	150 mcg	_____
Iron*	18 mg	_____
Magnesium	200 mg	_____
Manganese	5 mg	_____
Molybdenum	50 mcg	_____
Selenium	200 mg	_____
Zinc	30 mg	_____

*Double-check with your doctor before adding iron to your regimen. Some people are prone to iron overload.

Courtesy of US Army JROTC

According to Ronald Hoffman, Director of the Center for Holistic Medicine in New York City, supplements are especially important for people who do not eat: 1) fresh fruits and vegetables daily; 2) dairy products more than once a week; or 3) at least two full meals a day. Some of the above recommendations are higher than the US RDI's because longevity research has leapfrogged over the old standards. However, all recommendations are well within safety guidelines. Avoid taking more than the amounts suggested; mega dosing can be dangerous. Remember, check with your doctor before starting any supplement regimen.

Guideline #9

The goal for this guideline is to maintain an optimal intake of fluoride, particularly during tooth formation, which normally continues until the beginning of the teenage years. The requirement for sufficient intake of fluoride begins during pregnancy to ensure proper tooth and bone development.

Fluoride is important to tooth and bone formation. It makes the teeth harder, and they can resist decay and breakdown. Only two-thirds of the US population receives fluoridated water. The National Research Council of the National Academy of Sciences recommends 1 milligram of fluoride for each liter of water consumed.

Alternative Guideline #9

Most cities and towns in the United States add fluoride to the communities' drinking water, which provides the fluoride needed to help fight tooth decay; however, it is also recommended that you brush your teeth with a fluoride toothpaste to ensure that you are providing adequate protection for your teeth.

Conclusion

The nine guidelines presented in this chapter are the results of one of the most comprehensive scientific analysis of potential health risks and benefits stemming from diet. Implementing these guidelines means that we will need to devote more time and attention to our daily diets and the risk factors associated with improper diets.

In the following chapter, you will learn tips and hints to help control your intake of fats in your diet. You will also learn that some fat is essential to good health.

Review Questions

1 What is the goal for total daily fat intake?

2 What are the differences between anorexia nervosa and bulimia?

3 What are the signs of anorexia nervosa and bulimia?

4 What is the general dietary recommendation for daily carbohydrate intake?

Controlling Fat

What You Will Learn to Do

Estimate your body fat content

Skills and Knowledge You Will Gain Along the Way

✔ Identify the risks of obesity

✔ Explore tendencies that encourage fat accumulation

✔ Define current and desired state for healthy lifestyle

✔ Identify steps that can lead to a lean body fat content

✔ Relate food intake and physical activity to weight control

Introduction

In today's society, obese and overweight people, young and old, seek corrective advice from all types of organizations and individuals. These "experts," for many reasons, attempt to encourage and control what we eat, how we eat, when we eat, how much of what we eat, etc.

In this chapter, you learn how it is possible, without difficulty, to carry an amount of fat that is helpful and encourages the dynamic living principle. You will see in the simplest terms a method designed to keep you healthy and promote enjoyment of living while participating in life to your fullest potential.

Fat Control

When you are obese or overweight, you increase your risk of cardiovascular disease, high blood pressure, gall bladder disease, diabetes, and certain types of cancer. Obesity also prevents you from performing actively at your highest potential and from raising your self-esteem and self-assurance.

Determining whether you are obese or overweight is not dependent on how much you weigh on a scale. All of us have our own unique and special body types, which include our inherited strengths and weaknesses and tendencies that encourage accumulation of fat in our formative years, such as the following:

- Family eating habits
- A tendency to develop more fat cells
- A large skeletal structure
- Any number of unproved theories passed down through the years.

To ensure that you follow a proper and proven method for obtaining a healthier lifestyle, we will present you with a few guidelines on learning how to control your fat intake.

The steps to controlling body fat are a combination of restricting your fat intake, getting adequate exercise, making the right food choices, and understanding how to measure your body fat and how to use that information in your overall wellness program.

Step 1: Restricting Your Fat Intake

Most of us are continually trying to lower our body fat. When you diet, the body says you need to store more fat instead of less fat. This causes, especially in females, the body to slow down, which reduces the fat burning enzymes. Therefore, with each diet you undertake, the body reduces more fat burning enzymes, making it harder for you to lose fat. But remember, fat levels that drop too low are also unhealthy and unsafe. A certain amount of essential fat is necessary to maintain the bodily functions discussed earlier.

For example, most women should not go below eight percent, as this would upset the menstrual cycle, the ability to conceive children, and eventually hormonal balance. In men, the lower limit is approximately three to four percent.

Key Term

essential fat—
fat that the body needs in certain amounts to maintain bodily functions

UNIT V

Storage fat, on the other hand, is our fat reserve that can become a problem for many of us. Women in general seem to have a greater propensity to store fat. The reason for this is probably estrogen, which increases the fat-storing capability. Evidence points to the hips, thighs, and buttocks as the body's most desirable storage areas.

The following are ratings of body fat percentages by age and gender:

Males ages 18 to 30:		**Females ages 18 to 30:**	
Athletes	6–10%	Athletes	10–15%
Good	11–14%	Good	16–19%
Acceptable	15–17%	Acceptable	20–24%
Possibly needs help	18% and over (Obese/Overweight)	Possibly needs help	25% and over (Obese/Overweight)

The average-weight adult has approximately 25 to 30 billion fat cells, whereas the average overweight adult has between 60 to 100 billion. Some overweight people can have as many as 200 billion. Many factors are responsible for the development of these fat cells. Despite all the reasons, a person's growth and/or activities may or may not use all of the foods, or calories, consumed. The body will store the non-used calories as fat. For maximum benefit, keep saturated fat to a minimum. Count your total fat intake over a seven-day period. If you foul up, just cut back the next day.

When your fat content is where you desire, the next step is to develop a lifetime guideline for healthy eating. Calculate your daily intake of carbohydrates, fats, and proteins (as you did in the Journal Exercises in the previous chapters). Then choose one of the following plans and stick to it. The two plans that best enhance the dynamic living profile are #2 and #3. Whichever plan you select will require an effort on your part to make it succeed; but it will work and you can enjoy the benefits of that change.

Plan #1 (Average American Diet)		**Plan #2 (The New American Diet)**	
Fat	37–42%	Fat	20%
Saturated Fat	12–15%	Saturated Fat	6%
Protein	10–15%	Protein	10–15%
Carbohydrates	40–45%	Carbohydrates	60–65%

Plan #3 (The Lifetime Eating Plan)		**Plan #4 (US Dietary Goals)**	
Fat	10%	Fat	30%
Saturated Fat	Low	Saturated Fat	10%
Protein	10–15%	Protein	10%
Carbohydrates	75–80%	Carbohydrates	60%

Step 2: Exercise—How the Body Burns Food (Calories/Energy)

In addition to eating a healthy diet, you must follow an exercise program to maintain a lean body fat content. Balancing how many calories you consume with how many calories your body burns daily is the key to maintaining body fat content and weight. People gain body fat when they consume more calories daily than their bodies use for energy. Keep in mind that one pound of body fat contains approximately 3,500 calories. Therefore, if a person wants to lose a pound of body fat in one week, he or she must burn 3,500 calories more than he or she consumes over the course of the week.

Your body burns calories even when it is at complete rest. Basal metabolic rate (BMR) is the number of calories burned at complete rest, and it varies based on age, health, and body size, shape, and weight. For example, after age 25, most people's BMR decreases approximately 1 percent because their requirements for energy slow down. In addition to your BMR, your body burns calories through muscle activity; and while you do not have much control over your BMR, you do have control over the amount of physical activity in which you participate. Obviously, the more active you are, the more calories you use.

Choose an exercise program that accomplishes the two goals of improving your heart and lungs, as well as working your muscles. You can increase the efficiency of the heart and respiratory system through exercises such as jogging, swimming, and biking that increase the heart rate and maintain it for a set period of time. The time will vary based on your age, abilities, and the exercise being performed.

The second goal of working your muscles includes toning your muscles and/or increasing your muscle size and improving your muscle strength. Because muscle burns more energy than fat, the more muscle tissue you have, the more calories you burn. This is also true of your BMR, meaning that even at rest, the more muscle mass you have, the more energy your body will burn. You can work your muscles through weight training and exercises such as push-ups and sit-ups.

Step 3: Food Control and Choice

People eat for many different reasons: they feel hungry, the time of day, they missed a meal, or they are following their families' eating routine. Whatever the reason to eat at any given time, it is the choice of food that will truly make the difference in whether you will develop an overweight problem or maintain the dynamic living profile.

As you learned in previous chapters, the most recent USDA-approved Food Guide Pyramid can be accessed at www.mypyramid.gov. This is an interactive website where you can enter your age, gender, and level of activity to design an eating program geared towards your body type and lifestyle. For example, if you are a 16-year-old female who gets 30 to 60 minutes of exercise per day, you should be getting 2,000 calories per day, consisting of:

- Six ounces of whole grains (breads, pastas, cereals, and so on)
- Two and a half cups of vegetables (it is recommended that you eat more dark green vegetables such as spinach and other leafy greens; orange vegetables such as sweet potatoes and squashes; dried beans and peas)
- Two cups of fruit (fresh, frozen, dried, or canned, but try to go easy on the fruit juices)
- Three cups of milk (low- or no-fat is preferable)
- Five and a half ounces of lean protein foods (broiled, grilled or baked) with a variety of chicken, fish, beans, peas, nuts, and seeds.

Key Term

basal metabolic rate (BMR)— *the number of calories burned at complete rest; measurement of it indicates an individual's general metabolism or state of health*

UNIT V

Limit your oil (butter and other fats) intake to six teaspoons per day, and try to avoid an excess of sugar. You should strive to limit your extra oils and sugars to 265 calories per day.

Step 4: Measuring Your Body Fat

This section presents two fairly accurate methods of measuring your body fat. Follow the directions and do not be discouraged. Body types differ, and you are your own special person.

Pinch an Inch Test

Remember, your body does not need large amounts of fat. When your storage, or reserve, fat begins to melt away, you can determine the right level by using the "pinch an inch" test as a simple method of measuring and maintaining your body's fat.

You can perform the "pinch an inch" test by pinching the skin fold of your triceps (women only), waist, or thighs between your fingers. If the fat is over an inch between your thumb and forefinger, you might consider continuing your fat control program.

Estimating Body Fat

Jack H. Wilmore, an exercise physiologist at the University of Texas in Austin, created the following ways to measure body fat.

Women: Measure the circumference of your hips at the widest point and plot that measurement and your height on the chart in Figure 6.1. Then, using a straight edge, draw a line connecting the two plots. Your body fat percentage is where the line crosses the percent fat column. Refer to the appropriate chart in Step 1 to see if your fat content is acceptable, good, athletic, or needs help.

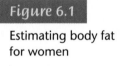

Figure 6.1

Estimating body fat for women

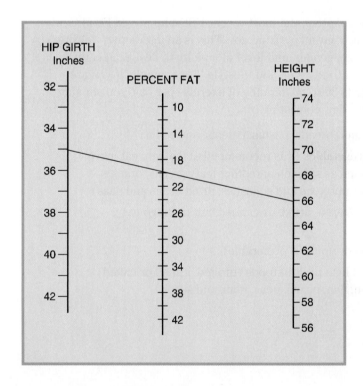

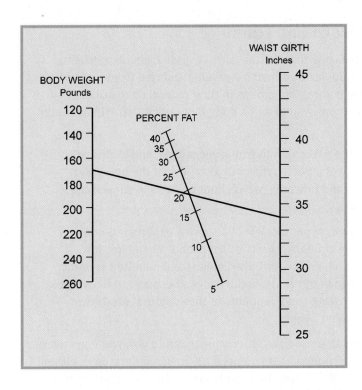

Figure 6.2

Estimating body fat for men

Men: Refer to Figure 6.2 and measure the circumference of your waist at the exact level of the belly button, making sure to keep the tape perfectly horizontal. Plot that measurement and your weight on the chart at the top of the next column. Then, using a straight edge, draw a line connecting the two plots. Your body fat percentage is where the line crosses the percent fat column. Refer to the appropriate chart on in Step 1 to see if your fat content is acceptable, good, athletic, or needs help.

The Road to Fat Control

A 1992 Consumer Reports survey with 68 nutrition experts indicated a deepening concern over America's dietary habits and implicated the leading causes of death as being associated with eating and drinking. The causes of death are coronary artery disease (heart attack), cancer, cerebral vascular disease (stroke), diabetes, liver disease, bowel disorders, and osteoporosis.

The 68 experts agreed on a reasonable diet for the American people as one that closely resembles the dietary guidelines set forth by the US RDI and the Department of Health and Human Services. Additionally, the experts were much more deliberate in defining an "ideal" diet as one that maximizes the immune system, reduces the risk of disease, and minimizes the process of aging.

By understanding the experts' opinions and responses, you can develop a formula that promotes a healthier lifestyle. If used properly, this formula can improve your immune system and lower risks of the leading causes of death; keep your body fat at a healthy level; and enhance your potential to maintain an ideal body fat content for life.

UNIT V

Carbohydrates: How to Eat Them

A definition of natural foods is one that fits the carbohydrate category perfectly. Natural foods are foods that are as unrefined as possible and free from additives and preservatives. Fruits, vegetables, and grains in their natural state are the key elements to a maximized immune system and a body fat content that will maintain itself for a lifetime.

There is growing evidence that a diet rich in fruits, vegetables, and grains will reduce the risk of certain cancers. Such a diet will also protect the heart and bones from early breakdown and infirmity, which limit millions of Americans from enjoying their potential.

Depending on your gender, body type, and level of activity, experts recommend at least three ounces of whole grains, a variety of fruits and vegetables, low- or no-fat dairy products, broiled, grilled, or baked meats, and a limited amount of fat and sugar. To be realistic in our hurry-up lifestyles, this may not be possible. However, evidence supports eating small amounts of these natural products several times a day for maximum benefit.

When you design your own eating program at www.mypyramid.gov, you can ensure you will be receiving all the carbohydrates you need (20 to 35 grams a day) without worrying about supplemental fiber. Plus, there is also room to enjoy a sweet treat. But remember, look at the label and keep the fat content at a reasonable level, and your sugar intake to nearly zero.

Protein: Don't Worry

If you are eating the recommended amounts of carbohydrates in a diversified manner, tests indicate you will receive your complete protein needs without concern. Most of your protein (about 85 to 90 percent) should come from plant sources or the complex carbohydrates. Studies indicate that populations eating a high degree of protein coming from animal products (as do Americans, with 70 to 75 percent) will have a higher incidence of problems.

Vitamins, Minerals, and Water: The Regulators

In general, the experts believe that you can receive your vitamins and minerals in sufficient amounts from a well-balanced diet. They also suggest that you drink water at a rate of six to eight glasses per day—more if you work out rigorously.

Planning a Balanced Diet

Up and down Elm Street, families begin the day with healthy breakfasts. The Gilmores eat bran muffins, orange juice, and shredded-wheat cereal with milk. Across the street, the Lins sit down to a traditional Korean breakfast of soybean soup with chunks of bean curd (tofu) and rice.

BREAKFAST MENU	Vegetable Group	Fruit Group	Dairy Group	Meat-Poultry-Fish-Dry Beans-Eggs-Nuts Group	Grain Group
Yogurt and fruit; whole-wheat toast		✔	✔		✔
Peanut butter on bread; orange juice; milk		✔	✔	✔	✔
Tortilla with beans and cheese; vegetable juice	✔		✔	✔	✔
Cream of tomato soup; crackers and cheese	✔		✔		✔

Figure 6.3 Breakfasts can be as varied as you want them to be. Which of these breakfasts would you choose?

Reprinted from *Health Skills for Wellness*, Third Edition, by B.E. (Buzz) Pruitt, Kathy Teer Crumpler, and Deborah Prothrow-Stith, (2001), Prentice Hall, Inc.

People's food choices are influenced by many factors, one of which is their culture. The term *culture* refers to the way of life of a group of people, including their customs and beliefs. Food is one important aspect of culture. As the two breakfasts demonstrate, different groups consume different foods. Look at Figure 6.3 and imagine which breakfast you would choose.

Both culture and personal preferences affect the types of food that are served in your household. Some families may dislike fish, for example, while others may choose not to eat red meat. In addition, most people respond to peer pressure when selecting food; when you eat a meal with friends, you may choose different foods than when you are by yourself or with your family. Your economic situation also plays a role in what you decide to eat. People with low incomes cannot afford to buy certain foods.

You are in control of the foods you select in the school cafeteria. Be sure to consider the nutrient value of your lunch selections.
Courtesy of Ken Karp

UNIT V

When you are making decisions about what to eat, consider the nutrition content of foods. There are many ways of meeting your nutritional needs, no matter what your preferences are. With a little imagination, you can have a variety of well-balanced meals and snacks.

Meals

What is your favorite meal of the day? Whether it is breakfast, lunch, or supper, it and your other meals should provide you with a balance of healthy nutrients.

Breakfast

Even if you are rushed in the morning, do not neglect breakfast, because many nutritionists believe that breakfast is the most important meal. After a night without food, your stomach is empty, and your body needs fuel for the day's activities. A good, balanced breakfast should provide as much as one-third of your daily food needs. If your breakfast is inadequate, you may be tempted later to eat snacks that are low in nutrient density.

Lunch

School cafeterias provide nutritionally balanced meals planned by dietitians. Some school cafeterias even offer nutritious snacks, salad bars, and special diet foods. Because lunch makes up another third of your food needs for the day, make sure that you choose nutrient-dense foods. You might, for example, eat a turkey sandwich on whole-wheat bread, a salad, a carton of milk, and an orange.

Supper

In many cultures around the world, lunch is the major meal of the day. In the United States, the biggest meal is generally the evening meal. Because you may be less physically active after this meal, supper should not account for more than the final third of your daily calorie needs. The evening meal can be an opportunity to fill in gaps in the day's Food Guide Pyramid selections. Suppose, for example, you have not eaten foods from the vegetable group at breakfast and lunch. You might volunteer to prepare a fresh green salad for dinner that includes several vegetables, such as spinach, carrots, and celery.

Snacks

Snacks can contribute significantly to your nutritional needs if you choose them wisely. However, many snack foods, such as those frequently sold in movie theaters, vending machines, and the snack-food sections of supermarkets, are high in fats and sugar and low in nutrient density. If you fill up on chips, soft drinks, and candy bars, you may have no appetite for the nutrient-dense foods that you need. Moreover, because snack foods are often high in calories, frequent snacking may result in unwanted weight gain. Finally, many snack foods, such as soft drinks and chocolate, contain caffeine, which can cause nervousness and sleeplessness.

For snacks, choose foods with a high nutrient density. Instead of an evening snack of cookies, try satisfying your craving for sweets with some fruit. Make a bagel, not a doughnut, your after-school treat. When you go to the movies, choose unbuttered popcorn instead of chips or candy.

Table 6.1	CALORIES AND FAT IN A TYPICAL FAST-FOOD MEAL		
FOOD	Total Calories	Calories from Fat	Percent Calories from Fat
Double cheeseburger	490	245	50%
French fries	330	160	49%
Chocolate shake	290	14	5%
Total for whole meal	**1,110**	**419**	**38%**

Fast Foods

Picture this: You and a friend drop by you favorite fast-food restaurant several times a week for a meal of double cheeseburgers, fries, and shakes. Table 6.1 shows a nutritional breakdown of your favorite fast-food meal.

Similar to this one, many fast-food meals are high in fat and calories. When you eat in fast-food restaurants, follow these guidelines:

- Substitute low-fat or nonfat milk or orange juice for shakes and soft drinks
- Select the salad bar in place of fries and onion rings
- Choose a grilled chicken sandwich instead of a hamburger or cheeseburger
- Sauces and dressings can add a lot of fat; use them sparingly
- Taste food before adding extra salt to it.

Improving Your Diet

The Food Guide Pyramid's recommendations can help you select specific kinds and amounts of food. In addition, nutrition experts have identified some general ways in which the American diet can be improved. Their recommendations, called the Dietary Guidelines for Americans, can help you plan a healthy diet.

- Eat a variety of foods. To obtain all the different nutrients you need, choose a wide selection of foods.
- Balance the food you eat with physical activity to maintain or improve your weight. Health problems can develop if you are too fat or too thin.
- Choose a diet with plenty of grain products, vegetables, and fruits. These foods are especially rich in starch and fiber.
- Choose a diet low in fat, saturated fat, and cholesterol. Choose lean meats, fish, poultry, and legumes instead of fatty meat. Cut away all visible fat on meats, and remove the skin from poultry. Limit fried foods, including potato chips, french fries, and doughnuts.
- Choose a diet moderate in sugars. Foods high in sugar are high in calories but often low in more useful nutrients. Limit your intake of sweet snacks and soft drinks.

- Choose a diet moderate in salt and sodium. Sodium, which is found in table salt and salty foods, has been linked to high blood pressure. Avoid eating too many salty snacks, pickled foods, luncheon meats, and canned soups. Do not add salt to foods at the table.
- Adults who use alcohol should do so in moderation. Alcoholic beverages are very low in nutrient density. In addition, as you will learn later, alcohol can damage every system in your body. Many adults choose not to drink at all, but those who do drink alcohol should strictly limit their intake.

Changing Nutritional Needs

Just as your body changes throughout life, so do your nutritional needs. During infancy, childhood, and adolescence, the body needs great amounts of all the nutrients necessary for physical growth. Teenagers need ample protein in their diets to support their physical growth. Adolescents also need significant amounts of iron; girls lose iron during menstruation, and boys need additional iron to support the development of muscle mass. The need for calcium also reaches its peak during the teenage years. Adolescent girls, in particular, are advised to eat calcium-rich foods as a means of preventing the weakening of bone that can occur later in life.

After adolescents become adults, their activity levels generally decrease, and continue to do so as they grow older. As activity decreases, so do energy needs. For this reason, adults need to watch their caloric intake carefully. Older adults, moreover, may need to increase the fiber in their diet as an aid to digestion. With proper attention to their nutritional needs, older people can live healthy and vigorous lives.

Managing Your Weight

Are you content with your weight, or would you like to change it in some way? If you are comparing yourself to athletes, film stars, and friends whose appearance you admire, you may be trying to achieve a weight that is unrealistic for you—and even unhealthy. When people have unrealistic expectations about their weight, they sometimes develop eating disorders such as anorexia nervosa and bulimia. However, some people do have good reasons for wanting to lose or gain weight. Those reasons relate to health, and not to some idealized concept of beauty or handsomeness.

Assessing Your Weight

Cassie and her best friend Thuy are the same height. Cassie weighs 10 pounds more than Thuy, but both girls have a weight that is appropriate for them. Thuy is small-boned, while Cassie has a larger bone structure. In addition, Cassie is very athletic, and some of her extra weight is in the form of muscle mass, not body fat. A person's appropriate weight depends on various factors, including body structure and level of activity. Your appropriate weight is one that you feel comfortable with, one that does not present any health risks. A physician or nutrition expert can help you determine your appropriate weight.

The amount of body fat, rather than weight, should be your concern. Various tests measure body fat. In one test, for example, an instrument called a skin-fold caliper is used to measure the fat deposits that accumulate under the skin.

Even though you do not have skin-fold calipers, you can get a rough idea of whether or not you have too much body fat. Pinch a fold of skin on your upper arm and estimate its thickness. If the fold of skin is more than one inch (2.5 centimeters) thick, you may have excess fat. However, remember that your estimate is not as accurate as a test done by a professional who is trained in evaluating weight problems.

Appetite, Hunger, and Metabolism

If an appropriate test has determined that you should change your weight, you will probably need to modify your eating habits. Once you have achieved a healthy weight, you will want to maintain it. To maintain a healthy weight, the number of calories that you eat each day should match the daily calorie needs of your body. Calories are units of energy. If you eat more calories than your body can use, it will store the excess energy as fat, causing you to gain weight. A diet that contains fewer calories than you need can make you lose weight.

Your calorie needs are partly determined by your activity level; the more active you are, the more calories you need. In addition, your basal metabolic rate—the rate at which you use energy when your body is completely at rest—affects your calorie needs. The higher your basal metabolic rate, the more calories you will burn. Various factors affect basal metabolic rate. For example, older people tend to have a lower basal metabolic rate than do younger ones. Children and pregnant women tend to have higher basal metabolic rates than the rest of the population. Regular exercise may help increase a person's basal metabolic rate.

If you are trying to change your eating habits, your task will be easier if you understand the physical and emotional factors that make you crave food. Hunger is a feeling of physical discomfort that is caused by your body's need for nutrients. Appetite, in contrast, is a desire for food that is based on emotional factors rather than nutritional need. Unlike hunger, which is an inborn response, appetite is learned. For example, suppose you smell chicken roasting. Your appetite may make you want to eat the chicken because you have learned to associate that particular aroma with a delicious taste. Your appetite may sometimes make you eat even when you are not hungry.

Appetite and hunger are not the only factors that affect people's eating behavior. Emotional stress, for example, can influence eating. Some people crave more food when they experience stress, while others lose their appetite. People may eat because they are bored or because they are with others who are eating.

Dangers of Obesity

If you frequently eat more calories than you need, you risk becoming overweight. People are overweight if they weigh more than 10 percent above their appropriate weight. The condition known as obesity (oh BEE sih tee) occurs when a person's weight is 20 percent or more above an appropriate weight. Obesity can create many serious health problems and risks, as illustrated in Figure 6.4. Obese people may suffer from high blood pressure and experience difficulty breathing. Being obese also increases a person's risk of heart attack, stroke, diabetes, arthritis, and certain forms of cancer. People who are significantly overweight should make every effort to reduce their weight to a healthier level.

Figure 6.4

Overeating can lead to obesity. People who are obese have an increased risk of developing many health problems.

Courtesy of Function thru Form

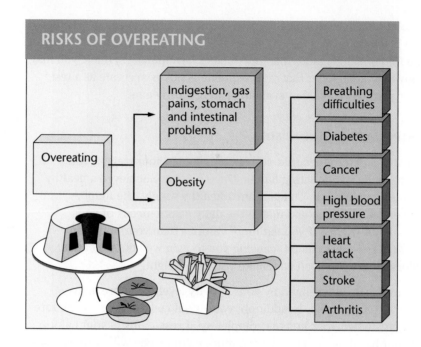

RISKS OF OVEREATING

Overeating → Indigestion, gas pains, stomach and intestinal problems

Overeating → Obesity → Breathing difficulties, Diabetes, Cancer, High blood pressure, Heart attack, Stroke, Arthritis

Reducing Weight and Fat Safely

A sensible program of weight loss involves choosing nutritionally balanced meals and snacks. Even though you want to reduce the number of calories that you consume, you still need to make sure that you are obtaining the nutrients necessary for good health. Choose low-calorie foods that are high in nutrient density.

Recognizing Eating Patterns

Before you plan your diet, keep a diary of what you presently eat. Record the foods that you consume, when you eat them, and how you feel at these times. Use calorie guides to count the approximate number of calories you consume each day.

As you review your diary, you may discover eating patterns or behaviors you were not aware of. You may even find out what triggers your overeating. Some people overeat when they are disappointed, depressed, excited, or tired.

Planning Helpful Strategies

The following are some strategies that will help you eat sensibly:

- Do not try to lose weight too fast. If you change your eating habits gradually rather than suddenly, your weight-loss program will be more successful in the long run.
- Take small portions of food and eat your food slowly so that you can enjoy its taste.
- If you tend to overeat when you are unhappy or bored, think of an enjoyable behavior that you might substitute for eating—taking a walk, for example.
- To avoid between-meal hunger, save some food from regular meals, such as bread, and later eat it as a snack.
- If you occasionally overeat, do not become upset. Just go back to your sensible eating habits.

Exercising

Your weight reduction program should involve regular exercise, such as walking, dancing, or swimming. Changing your eating habits alone is far less effective than eating changes combined with exercise. When you decrease your calorie intake but do not exercise, your basal metabolic rate goes down. Thus your body does not burn calories as rapidly as it did before you began reducing your calorie consumption, and your weight loss slows or stops.

Fad Diets, Diet Aids, and Fasting

Many people want to lose weight very quickly, so they rely on strategies such as fad diets, pills, or fasting. These approaches are unrealistic and unsafe.

Fad Diets

A fad diet is a popular diet that may help a person lose weight but without proper regard for nutrition and other matters of health. Fad diets range from high protein, low carbohydrate diets to diets with special ingredients that are supposed to help you burn fat. These diets often exclude some important nutrients.

Dieting Myths and Facts

There are many myths and facts surrounding diets and dieting.

MYTH: Eating starchy foods, such as bread and pasta, will make you gain weight.

FACT: Starchy foods, or complex-carbohydrate foods, have fewer calories per ounce than fats.

MYTH: You can lose a lot of weight just by exercising.

FACT: To lose a pound by exercising alone, you would need to run for $4\frac{1}{2}$ hours or do aerobics for more than 6 hours.

MYTH: You can lose weight if you don't eat breakfast.

FACT: Omitting any meal is likely to make you overeat at the next meal. If you skip breakfast, you will probably eat an extra-large lunch.

MYTH: You can lose weight by eating only one food, such as grapefruit, bananas, rice, or celery.

FACT: Because one-food diets are monotonous and nutritionally inadequate, dieters return to previous eating patterns and regain weight.

MYTH: Drinking caffeine always makes your appetite decrease.

FACT: Caffeine can make the level of sugar in your blood drop. This can make you hungry.

MYTH: After you lose weight, you can then resume your former eating habits.

FACT: Maintaining weight loss means changing eating and exercise patterns for the rest of your life.

The weight loss achieved with a fad diet is usually only temporary. Frequently, fad diets restrict food choices too much. People become so bored with the diet's limitations that they stop dieting and begin to overeat again.

Diet Pills

Diet aids, such as pills and candies, are supposed to suppress the appetite. However, they are usually ineffective and can be habit-forming. The major ingredient in most diet pills is caffeine, which may cause nervousness, sleeplessness, and high blood pressure. Diet aids do not provide long-term weight control. If you want to lose weight and keep it off, you need to change your eating behavior rather than rely on medication.

Fasting

When people refrain from eating all foods, they are fasting. Fasting is not a healthy way to lose weight, because muscle tissue as well as fat is lost. Long-term fasting may stunt your growth. It may also put a strain on your kidneys and cause hair loss. It has even been linked with irregular menstrual periods in girls and women.

Figure 6.5

If you are trying to gain weight, snack on nutrient-dense foods such as these.
Courtesy of Function thru Form

NUTRIENT-DENSE FOODS

Calories

135	Banana-nut bread 1 slice
280	Bean salad 3/4 cup
150	Whole milk 8 oz. (202 grams)
114	Cheddar cheese 1 oz. (28 grams)
282	Peanut butter 3 tbsp. (48 grams)
186	Brazil nuts 1 oz. (28 grams)
217	Raisins 1/2 cup
177	Sardines 3 oz. (85 grams)

Gaining Body Weight Wisely

Being too thin can be as emotionally painful as being too heavy. You are underweight if you weigh at least 10 percent less than appropriate. If you are underweight, remember that teenagers as a rule need a large number of calories for growing. Eventually, your growth rate will become slower and then stop. You may put on weight when you are in your early twenties. In addition, some people are naturally thinner than others, and thinness is not a health problem unless it is excessive. However, since underweight can be an indication of health problems, underweight people should be checked by a physician.

The goal of gaining weight can best be achieved by changing any habits that keep you too thin. Eliminate snacks right before mealtimes because they may spoil your appetite. When you do snack, choose nutrient-dense foods, as shown in Figure 6.5, that are high in calories. Never skip a meal. At mealtimes, take bigger helpings of food than usual. While you are increasing your caloric intake, do not neglect exercise. Exercising will help you gain healthy muscle tissue as well as fat.

Special Diets

People's circumstances may call for special diets. Certain physical conditions, such as diabetes and hypoglycemia, have special nutritional requirements. Lifestyle choices, such as the decision not to eat meat, may also affect how people meet their dietary requirements.

Diet and High Blood Pressure

As blood flows through your body, it exerts a force called blood pressure that pushes against the walls of your blood vessels. High blood pressure, or hypertension, is a condition in which this force becomes too strong. Sodium, found in table salt and many other foods, is thought to be a factor in high blood pressure. People with high blood pressure need to limit their sodium intake. They can do this by using herbs and spices instead of table salt to add flavor to foods. They also need to avoid salty snack foods, such as potato chips. Many processed foods, such as soup mixes and canned vegetables, contain large amounts of sodium. Therefore, people with high blood pressure need to read food labels carefully to avoid high-sodium foods.

Diets for Diabetics

Glucose is the principal carbohydrate that circulates in your blood and is used by your cells for energy. A substance called insulin enables glucose to pass from the blood into the body's cells. Diabetes mellitus is a disorder in which the body does not produce or properly use insulin, resulting in high levels of glucose in the blood. Symptoms may include sudden excessive thirst, an increase in appetite combined with a loss in weight, and frequent urination. Some people also feel fatigued, irritable, and confused. If you have a combination of any of these symptoms, you should see a physician.

Diabetes usually can be controlled. Some diabetics may need to take daily insulin injections. They also need to eat balanced meals and exercise on a regular schedule. Frequently people with diabetes carry a snack that they can eat to regulate their blood glucose levels if they are unable to eat a regular meal.

Diabetics' diets should help to control blood glucose levels by leaving out foods high in sugar and focusing on complex carbohydrates. The American Diabetes Association also emphasizes the importance of foods high in fiber and low in fat. Obesity is a factor in one type of diabetes, and those diabetics need to control their weight. For more information, go to www.ada.com (American Diabetes Association).

Diet and Hypoglycemia

If the body produces too much insulin, the level of glucose in the blood may fall dramatically. The result is a condition known as hypoglycemia, or low blood sugar. People with hypoglycemia may experience hunger, weakness, severe headaches, and shakiness as their blood glucose levels fall. Hypoglycemics need to eat several small meals per day instead of three big ones, with foods rich in complex carbohydrates and low in fat. Concentrated sweets, such as candy, should be avoided altogether.

Vegetarianism

A person who does not eat meat is called a vegetarian. Some vegetarians eat no foods that come from animal sources. Others, however, include eggs and dairy products in their diets. Complete proteins contain all the essential amino acids, but incomplete proteins do not. Vegetarians who eat no food from animal sources must make sure that their diets contain all the essential amino acids. Complete proteins can be obtained from a combination of plant foods. For example, beans and rice are a complete protein and are illustrated above.

Vegetarians are less likely than others to suffer from heart disease, a problem that can result from eating too much animal fat. In addition to protein, however, vegetarians must make sure that they are obtaining adequate supplies of the vitamins and minerals they need. Variety is therefore especially important in a vegetarian diet. Protein sources from the Meat and Beans group for vegetarians include eggs (for ovo-vegetarians), beans, nuts, nut butters, peas, and soy products (tofu, tempeh, veggie burgers). Check out http://www.mypyramid.gov/tips_resources/vegetarian_diets.html for more information on how you can eat a healthy vegetarian diet.

Nutrition and Pregnancy

A woman's diet during pregnancy must provide for her needs as well as the needs of the developing baby. When a mother's diet is inadequate, she may give birth to a premature baby or a baby who weighs less than normal. A baby with a low birth weight may be susceptible to disease and slow to develop mentally and physically.

During pregnancy, a woman needs to provide nutrients for herself and her developing baby.
Courtesy of David Dempster/Offshoot Stock

Most pregnant women should gain between 25 and 35 pounds (about 11 to 16 kilograms) during the pregnancy. To do this, they need to consume more calories than they did before pregnancy (about 300 extra calories per day). A pregnant woman also needs extra amounts of protein and the vitamin folate, since both of these nutrients are essential for the formation of the baby's cells. The minerals calcium, phosphorus, and magnesium are needed for building the baby's teeth and bones. Iron is especially important. Without it, the baby might not get enough oxygen from its mother's blood. For this reason, extra iron is often prescribed during pregnancy.

Pregnant teenagers have higher nutrient needs than any other group in the population. Since pregnant adolescents themselves are still growing, their diets need to supply both them and their babies with nutrients needed for growth. Young pregnant teenagers—those between the ages of 13 and 16—are encouraged to gain about 35 pounds (16 kilograms).

Diets for Athletes

Athletes should eat a basic well-balanced diet but with added calories to accommodate a higher level of physical activity. Most of these calories should come from an increase in complex carbohydrates. High-fat and sugar-rich foods should be avoided. During competition, athletes should drink plenty of fluids to replace water lost in perspiration.

You have probably heard of runners practicing carbohydrate loading before a long race. Carbohydrate loading consists of greatly increased carbohydrate intake, accompanied by decreased levels of exercise, in the days immediately before a competition. This practice is an attempt to make extra carbohydrates available to supply energy for the muscles. Carbohydrate loading may benefit highly conditioned athletes who participate in long-lasting sports such as marathon running. However, for most athletes, the best policy is just to eat their normal diet.

Buying Food Wisely

To choose nutrient-dense foods, you need knowledge and practice. When you buy food, do not be swayed by attractive packaging. Instead, use food labels and other information to evaluate foods.

Food Labels

The US Food and Drug Administration (FDA) requires that manufacturers of foods list certain information on a food's label. Labels must provide the name and address of the manufacturer, the weight of the food, and a list of ingredients in descending order of weight. It must also indicate the number of servings per container, based on a standard serving size for that type of food.

Nutrition Information

Food labels must also provide facts about the nutrient content of the product. The nutrition information on food labels is especially important for consumers to read and evaluate. The label indicates the following for each serving:

- The total number of calories per serving
- The number of those calories that come from fat
- The weight, in grams or milligrams, of nutrients such as saturated fat, total fat, cholesterol, sugar, dietary fiber, total carbohydrates, protein, and certain minerals
- The percentage of the Daily Values for different nutrients that are supplied by the food

Manufacturers are free to volunteer additional information. Any claims relating to nutrition or health, however, must meet FDA standards.

Food Additives

When you have read a food label, have you ever noticed a series of long chemical names in the ingredients list? These are food additives. Additives are chemicals that are added to a food to prevent spoiling, to control and improve color and texture, to replace or add nutrients, or to improve flavor. While some people may be allergic to specific additives, such as artificial colors, food additives are safe for most people.

Additives that are used to prevent spoilage or to keep foods from losing their natural color or texture are called preservatives. For example, the preservative *calcium propionate* prevents mold from growing on baked goods. Other preservatives keep peeled and cut fruits from becoming brown. Many preservatives prevent food poisoning and increase the length of time that a food is safe to eat.

When you examine a food label, you should check the fat and calorie content of the product.
Courtesy of Ken Karp/A&P Supermarket, Scarsdale, NY

During processing, nutrients are added to fortified and enriched foods such as those shown here.

Courtesy of Steven Mays

Often when a food is canned or processed in some other way, some of its vitamins and minerals may be lost. When nutrients are added to replace those that have been lost, the food has been enriched. Some breads and cereals are enriched with the vitamins *thiamin, riboflavin, niacin,* and the mineral *iron.* If vitamins, minerals, and even proteins are added to a food that does not normally contain them, the food is fortified. Milk, for example, is fortified with vitamin D. The types of foods shown above are frequently enriched or fortified.

Sometimes manufacturers use additives to improve the texture or taste of foods. A leavening agent makes baked goods rise. An *emulsifier* (ih MUHL suh fy ur) is used to keep fats from separating from the other ingredients in a food. Emulsifiers in salad dressing, for example, keep the fat from floating to the top.

Evaluating Foods

Wise shoppers check the nutrient content of foods. Price and freshness are other characteristics to consider.

Nutrients

Carefully read the label on a packaged food. Check the number of calories and whether the food contains large amounts of fat or sugar. Compare similar foods to determine which are more nutritious. If you are choosing breakfast cereals, for example, look at the amount of dietary fiber, vitamins, minerals, and protein in different products.

Reading a Food Label

Every time you go into a supermarket, you see thousands of different food products: cereals in brightly colored boxes, snack foods in shiny foil bags, and frozen dinners in packages that can be used in a microwave oven. Attractive and convenient packaging is designed to make you want to purchase the product. In addition, before you even enter a store, advertisements in magazines, in newspapers, and on television try to convince you to buy certain foods.

To judge the nutritional value of a food, do not rely on advertisements or nice looking packages. Instead, read the food label carefully. The US Food and Drug Administration (FDA) requires packaged foods to be labeled with a list of ingredients and nutrition information.

To use food labels to make healthy food choices, use the following steps:

1. Read the ingredients. Be aware of the ingredients that a food contains.
   - Become familiar with terms for different kinds of ingredients. For example, even if the word *sugar* does not appear on the label, the product may contain sugar; words ending in *-ose* are generally the names of different sugars.
   - Notice that ingredients are listed in order by weight from most to least.
   - If you have specific dietary restrictions, it is especially important to check the ingredients list first. For example, people who have an allergy for a particular food need to make sure that the product does not contain that ingredient.

2. Notice the number of servings per container. Serving sizes are standardized for over 100 different food categories, so you can compare similar food products for the number of servings they provide. For example, if you need enough lasagna to feed four people, a brand that provides four servings in one container may be a better purchase than one that provides only three servings per container.

3. Note the calories in one serving. Keep in mind that recommended daily caloric intake levels vary depending on a person's age, sex, weight, basal metabolism, and activity level. Active teenagers usually need more calories than do older people.
   - If the number of calories is high and you are trying to lose weight, you might want to choose a different food.
   - If you are trying to gain weight, a high-calorie food may be a good choice, as long as it provides useful nutrients.

4. Look at the percentages of the Daily Values. The food label indicates what percentages of the Daily Values for different nutrients are supplied by that product. For example, if the label says "Vitamin C—20%," that food supplies 20 percent of the vitamin C that the average person should obtain each day. Notice that the Daily Values are based on a diet of 2,000 calories per day.
   - Check the percentages of valuable nutrients, such as dietary fiber, iron, calcium, and vitamins. Is this food a good source of many nutrients that you need?
   - Also note the percentage of nutrients that you should limit, such as saturated fat and cholesterol. If a food is high in those nutrients, you may want to avoid it.

5. Read any health-related descriptions or claims. The FDA sets standards for the use of descriptions such as "high fiber" and "low fat." You can use those descriptions for guidance. Also notice any health claims on the package. For example, a label can indicate that high-calcium foods may help prevent osteoporosis.

Freshness

Many foods, such as meat and baked goods, have a date on their packages. This product date is an estimate of how long the product is usable. Reduced-price foods may not be a bargain if the product date has already passed.

Price

To find out which of two competing products is the better buy, compare the unit price, or cost per unit of measurement. The unit price is usually expressed in ounces or pounds. Suppose, for example, a 20-ounce loaf of bread and a 16-ounce loaf of bread both cost $1.50. The 20-ounce loaf has a unit price of about 8 cents per ounce, while the 16-ounce loaf costs about 9 cents per ounce. If both these loaves have approximately the same nutrients, which is the better buy?

Advertising and Food Choices

Advertising can have a strong influence on food choices. Often advertisers use special techniques, such as humor and lively music, to make products appealing. A television commercial for frozen waffles, for instance, may show a smiling, healthy-looking family. Yet the label on the waffles may reveal that the product is not particularly nutritious. As a smart food consumer, be aware that advertisements can mislead you.

Conclusion

The science of nourishing the body properly is a continually revolving door of facts, information, and misleading information. Much of the data is very conflicting and difficult to sort out, although there is some material that has remained consistent throughout the years. A basic understanding of this information will enable you to stay properly nourished.

To begin building a healthy diet, the Dietary Guidelines of Americans provides the following advice:

- Eat a variety of foods to obtain the energy, proteins, vitamins, minerals, and fiber you need for good health.

- Maintain a healthy weight to reduce your chances of having high blood pressure, heart disease, a stroke, certain cancers, and the most common kind of diabetes.

- Choose a diet low in total fat, saturated fat, and cholesterol. Because fat contains over twice the calories of an equal amount of carbohydrates or protein, a diet low in fat can help you to maintain a healthy weight.

- Choose a diet with plenty of vegetables, fruit, and grain products that provide the needed vitamins, minerals, fiber, and complex carbohydrates, which can also help you to lower your intake of fat.

Introduction

Exercise, rest, and good hygiene and nutrition can help you stay healthy and avoid many illnesses and infections. In other words, you can prevent disease and injury by taking good care of yourself. You learned about the importance of nutrition and exercise to your health in the previous chapter. This chapter covers the importance of good hygiene habits. In particular, it discusses hygiene and sanitation when attending JROTC summer camp or camping on your own, with friends, or family. In these cases, you may not have the modern conveniences of clean, running water or indoor plumbing, but you must still know how to take care of yourself to help prevent illness and maintain good health.

Personal Hygiene

Most likely, there are certain habits that you perform routinely at the start of each day. You are probably so accustomed to doing them that you do not give them a second thought. First, you wake up after resting your body during the night. Then you shower if you did not shower the night before, wash your face, and comb your hair. It is now time for breakfast—some toast and cereal perhaps. And, last but not least, you brush your teeth and leave for school.

Now, stop for a minute and think about the activities that we have just described. They involve rest, nutrition, and cleanliness, three elements that are important to maintaining good health and are a part of personal hygiene.

It is easy for most of us to practice personal hygiene in our homes where there are sinks, showers, toilets, and clean water, all of which help with sanitation. In some situations, however, practicing personal hygiene and maintaining sanitary conditions take more effort and require greater care. For example, if you are camping, you may have to work harder at hygiene and sanitation depending on conditions at your campsite. Also, when you are staying in close quarters with several other people, like at JROTC summer camp, hygiene and sanitation become extremely important. The poor sanitation or hygiene habits of one person can lead to a disease or illness that affects an entire group.

Personal hygiene is important to maintaining your personal health and establishing your health image to other people. A neat, clean, physically fit person illustrates a healthy image and a positive leadership posture.

Principles of Hygiene

It is not always simple to apply the basic principles of personal hygiene. It takes a conscience effort to follow these principles and to stay healthy.

Key Terms

hygiene—
practices or conditions that aid in good health; the science that deals with maintenance of good health and the prevention of infection and disease

sanitation—
the promotion of hygiene and prevention of disease by working to keep a clean and healthy environment

Key Term

personal hygiene—
an individual's practice of taking care of him- or herself in order to maintain good health

Field Sanitation

The following story illustrates the importance of maintaining all aspects of health and sanitation when out in the field.

On Togatabu Island in 1942, the 14th Artillery and the 404th Engineer Battalions were part of a task force preparing to attack Guadalcanal. Fifty-five percent of the engineers and 65 percent of the artillerymen contracted a disease called "Filariasis," transmitted by mosquitoes. Both units had to be medically evacuated without seeing any enemy action because they were not combat ready. The use of insect repellent and insecticides and the elimination of standing water would have prevented the spread of this disease.

Often in military history, the health of the troops influenced the course of battle more than strategy or tactics. "Historically, in every conflict in which the United States has been involved, only 20 percent of all hospital admissions have been from combat injuries. The other 80 percent have been from diseases and nonbattle injuries." (*Field Hygiene and Sanitation*, FM 21–10)

Hand Hygiene

Hand washing needs to be second nature. It is important to wash your hands after contact with an animal, after using the toilet, before eating, or before touching a person at risk for infection. A good routine needs to include removing any jewelry, wetting hands with warm water, using an anti-bacterial soap if available, washing hands vigorously for at least 30 seconds, rinsing hands, and drying hands on a clean towel or using a hand drying machine. Hand hygiene is also important in the field.

Oral Hygiene

After each meal or at least twice a day, you need to eliminate food particles and dental plaque from your teeth as well as clean your gums. Visiting the dentist twice a year is also recommended. Use fluoride toothpaste and brush up and down in a light circular motion, in front, behind and across the top of the teeth for at least three minutes. Avoid putting objects and fingers in your mouth as well as sugar and sweets that encourage germ proliferation.

Washing your hands is essential, particularly in the field.
Courtesy of Corbis

Personal Hygiene

A dirty body is a hotbed for developing germs. Dust, sweat and other secretions, and warmth are all factors that encourage germs to multiply. A shower with effective soap and shampoo should follow any physical activity. Showering daily is necessary to maintain good personal health. Clean clothes should be worn and underwear changed daily; the fabric in clothes is a breeding ground for many germs. Imagine how you would feel if you did not bathe for a week. Now imagine how others would feel about having to be around you during that time. Uncleanliness or disagreeable odors affect the morale of others, so the solution is for everyone to take personal responsibility for their own hygiene.

Nasal Hygiene

Nasal secretions are highly contagious. Runny noses and sneezing are sources of germ dissemination. Frequent nose blowing using a disposable paper tissue clears the nostrils and limits the spread of germs. Repeated blowing of the nose can cause irritation, so use a soft tissue and blow softly.

Food Hygiene

Food poisoning is on the rise. Some of these cases can be linked to the food processing industry and centralized distribution of food. You can reduce your risk of food poisoning by following simple yet effective hygiene practices. High-risk foods include eggs and egg products, poultry (particularly chicken), and food eaten raw. It is estimated that 50 percent of domestic food poisoning cases are due to poor hygiene in the home. Refrigeration is a means of reducing the spread of germs, but not of eliminating germs. Refrigerators need to be cleaned on a regular basis. Food that needs refrigeration needs to be kept at the recommended temperature; food that does not need to be kept refrigerated should be stored as indicated on the packaging, and the date indications on food packaging should be followed.

Cooking food is an excellent way of keeping germs from spreading. Cooking food at sufficiently high temperature will eliminate many germs. Rigorous hygiene is also required in the kitchen. Always wash hands before handling food. Wash frequently any cloths and towels used in the kitchen. Avoid using wooden chopping blocks, salad bowls and spoons because nicks or cracks can create an ideal place for germs. Kitchen utensils should not be used to prepare different dishes unless they have been cleaned in between. Tables and worktops should be cleaned with an anti-bacterial product between preparing different types of food. You should also watch for the country of origin of the food you eat; note the best before dates on food labels; and use the most effective practices in food preparation.

Pet Hygiene

Most people today spend a great deal of time with a pet or pets. Our pets carry a number of germs as well as affect allergy sufferers. However, it is easy to apply simple rules of hygiene without affecting the bond between people and pets. Animals need to be cleaned regularly. It is also essential to disinfect a pet's scratch or bite with an antiseptic. Clean everything that your pet touches on a regular basis. Floor areas used by an animal should also be cleaned, paying particular attention to allergen traps such as carpets and bedding. Hands should always be washed after touching an animal.*

*Adapted from the Institut Pasteur's website, January 4, 2005.

Stay Physically Fit

People who are physically fit are less likely to get sick or injured, so participate regularly in a fitness program. Physical fitness training will also help you become adjusted to a field environment. Remember to use caution when exercising in extremely hot or cold weather, particularly if you are going to run long distances.

Get Enough Sleep

The average person needs eight hours of sleep a night. Make sure you get enough sleep so you have the energy to effectively complete the required tasks of your day. You may have a harder time sleeping when you are away from home, bunking with others, or camping. Follow these suggestions to get as much rest as possible.

- Sleep as much as you can before going someplace where you may not be able to sleep comfortably or as much as you should
- Take catnaps whenever you can but expect to need a few minutes to wake up fully
- When in the field, follow your leader's instructions and share tasks with other cadets so everyone gets time to sleep
- After going without sleep, catch up as soon as possible
- Learn and practice techniques to relax yourself quickly.

If you have not gotten enough sleep in the field and are required to remain awake and alert, try these suggestions:

- Play mental games or talk with other cadets to stay alert during dull watches or critical jobs such as driving at night
- Take short stretch breaks or do light exercises in place
- Do not trust your memory; write things down and double check your communications and calculations
- Watch out for your mind playing tricks (like seeing things that are not there) when you are very tired; check strange observations before acting.

Learn to Reduce Stress

Stress begins in the mind but causes physical reactions in the body. Although stress can be beneficial in small doses by supplying you with bursts of energy to complete a project on time or compete in an important game, stress that continues over long periods of time can weaken your immune system and lead to exhaustion and illness. People under too much stress may not care for themselves properly or be able to complete tasks effectively.

To keep yourself healthy and efficient, you must learn to relax and reduce stress. The following hints may help:

Staying physically fit will help you succeed in the field.
Courtesy of David Madison

dysentery—
any of several intestinal disorders usually caused by infection and characterized by stomach pain and diarrhea with passage of mucous and blood

purified—
free from undesirable elements or impurities; cleaned

disinfect—
to destroy harmful germs; to purify

- Maintain a positive attitude
- Do not try to do more than is possible or take on tasks for which you are not prepared
- Talk with friends or family when you encounter difficulties
- Take time each day to do something that you enjoy, even if it is only for 15 minutes
- Do not worry about things that are out of your control but concentrate on what you *can* do
- Exercise regularly
- Recognize that stress is a normal reaction to many situations, like taking a test, giving a speech, or participating in field training
- Take a deep breath, relax, and do not let stress interfere with accomplishing the task at hand.

To help reduce stress in a group or among friends or fellow cadets, give each other moral support if things are tough at home, school, or in the unit. Welcome new replacements into your group and be active in establishing friendships. By building a feeling of esprit de corps, you can minimize stressful feelings of loneliness and isolation. When in the field, attempt to care for other cadets and work together to provide everyone food, water, sleep, shelter, protection from heat, cold, and poor sanitation.

Basic Principles of Sanitation

Poor sanitation can contribute to conditions that may result in diarrhea and dysentery. Intestinal diseases are usually spread through contact with bacteria and germs in human waste, by flies and other insects, or through improperly prepared food and water supplies.

Use Purified Water

When you are staying outdoors, in the field, or traveling in foreign countries with questionable water supplies, use only water that is purified. Fill your canteen with treated water at every chance. To treat or disinfect water, bring it to a boil for 5 to 10 minutes. When heated water is not available, disinfect water using one of the following methods:

Always use purified water in the field.
Courtesy of Burke/Triolo Productions/Botanica/Getty Images

The Preferred Method: Iodine Tablets

1. Fill a one-quart canteen with the cleanest water available.
2. Put one iodine tablet in the water; two in cold or cloudy water. Double these amounts in a two-quart canteen.
3. Place the cap on the canteen, wait 5 minutes, then shake. Loosen the cap and tip the canteen over to allow leakage around the canteen threads. Tighten the cap and wait an additional 25 minutes before drinking.

Treating with Chlorine

1. Fill a one-quart canteen with the cleanest water available.
2. Mix one ampule of chlorine with one-half canteen cup of water. Stir the mixture with a clean device until the contents dissolve. Take care not to cut your hands when breaking open the glass ampule.
3. Pour one canteen capful of the chlorine solution into your quart of water.
4. Replace the cap on your canteen and shake. Slightly loosen the cap and tip the canteen over to allow leakage around the threads. Tighten the cap and wait 30 minutes before drinking.

Another Alternative: Tincture of Iodine

1. Fill a one-quart canteen with the cleanest water available.
2. Add five drops of 2 percent Tincture of Iodine to the water. If the water is cold or cloudy, add 10 drops.
3. Mix thoroughly by shaking the canteen. Slightly loosen the cap and tip the canteen over to allow leakage around the threads. Tighten the cap and wait 30 minutes before drinking.
4. Very cloudy or cold water may require prolonged contact time. Let it stand several hours or overnight if possible.

Guard Against Food Poisoning

Wash your hands for at least 30 seconds after using the bathroom or before touching food. Inspect all cans and food packages prior to using them and throw away any cans with leaks, bulges, or holes. Do not eat foods or drink beverages that have been prepared in galvanized containers, which may result in zinc poisoning. When camping or in the field, wash your mess kit in a mess kit laundry or with treated water or disinfectant solution.

Bury Your Waste

On a march, personal disposal bags should be used if available; if not available personal cat holes can be used. Always dispose of your waste immediately to prevent flies from spreading germs from waste to your food and to keep unwanted animals out of your bivouac area. Chemical toilets should be used in bivouac area.

Key Term

iodine—
a nonmetallic element having important medical uses

Key Terms

ampule—
a small, sealed glass container that holds one dose of a solution, usually a medicine, to be administered by injection

chlorine—
a gaseous greenish-yellow element used as a bleach and disinfectant in water purification

Key Term

galvanized—
coated with zinc

Key Term

bivouac—
a temporary camp or shelter

UNIT V

Cleaning and protecting feet in the field is an important part of personal hygiene.
Courtesy of Michael DeYoung/Corbis

Keep Your Body and Uniform Clean

Bathe every day, if possible, or at least once a week. A daily bath or shower helps maintain cleanliness and prevent body odor, common skin diseases, and infection. When you are in the field, however, bathing daily may not be possible. In this case, make sure you take a full shower at least once a week (or at the earliest opportunity) and use a washcloth daily to wash

- Your face
- Your armpits
- Your genital area
- Your feet
- Other areas where you sweat or that become wet,
  such as between your thighs or, for females, under the breasts.

Powders, such as talcum powder, help to keep your skin dry when in the field. Apply it to places where you tend to sweat and to your feet and inside your socks each morning, especially if you have had prior foot infections. Change to clean clothing regularly. Protection of your feet is extremely important and requires daily attention.

Good personal hygiene practices reduce infestation of insects such as body lice and mites. Make sure the clothing you wear in the field is loose and does not restrict circulation. Avoid wearing nylon undergarments. Wear cotton, which is more absorbent and allows the skin to dry. Wash your uniform frequently or at least once a week. Use the quartermaster laundry or a stream, lake, or washbasin. Air-dry uniforms, especially underwear and socks.

Key Term

lice—
small, wingless, parasitic insects that live on warm-blooded animals, especially in hair, and suck the animal's blood

Other Instructions for the Field

There are other precautions that you can take to ensure your health and well-being while in the field and ensure the health of those around you.

Follow Medical Advice:

Take medications, such as antimalaria pills, that help prevent diseases. Use any medication that is prescribed by medical personnel.

Protect Yourself at Night:

Use your bed net when sleeping and ensure that it is in good repair. Always follow label directions and precautions when using DoD-approved insect spray.

Wash Your Mess Kit/Eating Utensils:

Protect yourself from diarrhea by washing your mess kit/eating utensils. Use a mess kit sanitation center or use treated water or disinfectant solution.

Domestic and Wild Animals or Birds:

Do not handle or approach animals in the field. Unless approved by veterinary personnel, do not collect or support with food and shelter any stray or domestic animals in the unit area.

Poisonous Plants:

Avoid contact with poisonous plants by properly wearing the uniform and avoid areas where poisonous plants grow. Only eat plants that have been approved by medical personnel.

UNIT V

Conclusion

Practicing good personal hygiene and sanitation are common sense actions that everyone should perform. They are particularly important in the field where cadets have a responsibility to both themselves and others, and leaders must plan and enforce preventative measures.

Remember, correct cleanliness habits, regular exercise, good nutrition, and adequate amounts of rest and relaxation can directly affect a person's well-being. By practicing these preventative measures, you can significantly reduce time lost due to illness and injuries.

The following chapter deals with a common problem in today's world—stress. Knowing how to control stress can help with your emotional and physical health.

Review Questions

1 How do you keep clean in the field?

2 What is the correlation between physical fitness and hygiene?

3 What are some results of poor sanitation?

4 Describe one method of disinfecting water.

Chapter 8

Understanding and Controlling Stress

What You Will Learn to Do

Assess how stress impacts your life

Skills and Knowledge You Will Gain Along the Way

✔ Differentiate between stress and anxiety in overall health

✔ Identify the physical and psychological effects of stress

✔ Practice prevention of stress overload including relaxation and anger management techniques

✔ Identify leadership strategies that promote healthy stress levels within a group

✔ Explore positive ways to deal with depression and anxiety

Key Terms

- **dilated**
- **fight-or-flight response**
- **migraine**
- **anxiety**
- **depression**
- **meditation**
- **visualization**
- **manic-depressive illness**
- **generalized**

If a stressor continues for a long time, your body enters the exhaustion state, and illness can result.

Courtesy of Brent Petersen/The Stock Market

Introduction

Stress in small doses is a normal, healthy part of life; however, stress that continues over long periods of time can lead to exhaustion and possible mental or physical illness. This chapter discusses what causes stress, how it can affect you, and ways that you can manage it. Handling stress in your life and recognizing symptoms of stress in others will make your life more enjoyable and your leadership more effective.

The media often portrays the teen years as a carefree time, with few major responsibilities and lots of new and exciting experiences. Many young people know, however, that this is only one side of the coin. You may not have the responsibilities of your parents, but your responsibilities are growing as you grow older. New challenges and experiences, while exciting, can also be a bit scary. Expectations for the future can be exhilarating, but they can also result in anxiety and pressure to succeed. As teenagers make their way to adulthood, they experience a range of emotions and changes that can make their high school years very stressful.

What Is Stress?

Stress is the way your body reacts and adjusts to the psychological and physical demands of life. It can be brought on by situations that cause feelings such as fear, irritation, endangerment, excitement, and expectation. Surprise tests can cause stress. Stress in small amounts is beneficial and needed for motivation, improvement, and growth. It can give you a burst of energy to complete a project or run a race, the control and strength to get through a difficult time, or the inspiration to write a poem or paint a picture. Stress can be an important factor in your achievement and progress.

Yet times of stress should be followed by times of relaxation to ensure recovery from stress. Experiencing constant stress without a break has a negative effect on people. Stress followed by a period of rest can actually make a person better prepared for the next stressful event. Stress followed by more stress without recovery in between can exhaust a person, making him or her less prepared to handle the next stressful event. Eventually, constant stress can affect a person psychologically and physically, disrupting normal behavior and resulting in illness.

A surprise test is just one stressor you may encounter today.

Courtesy of Ken Karp

Physical Effects of Stress

When your mind perceives a situation as stressful, it triggers a series of physical and chemical reactions in your body. These include increased blood flow to the muscles and brain; decreased blood flow to the skin and digestive organs; a shut down of the immune system; and the release of fuel, such as fat, into the bloodstream. While these internal reactions to stress will not be obvious to you, noticeable results of these reactions include increased heart and breathing rates, muscle tension, dilated pupils, cold hands, and dry mouth.

These reactions happen as part of a fight-or-flight response developed in primitive humans to deal with physical threats by either fighting or fleeing. Either way, primitive man's mind and body placed emphasis on physically responding to stressful situations by providing extra fuel and blood to the muscles while slowing or shutting down other functions.

For modern man, most stressful situations are not life threatening and do not require a physical response, yet being stuck in a traffic jam or pushing hard to finish a report still causes the same physical reactions as those needed for fight or flight. Luckily, once modern man deals with the stress, finishes the stressful activity or the source of stress goes away, the body and all of its functions return to normal.

On the other hand, if the source of stress continues, the person does not deal with the stress effectively, or the person faces stressful situation after stressful situation, his or her body will not recover its normal state. Eventually, the body's continual reaction to prolonged stress may result in the following physical problems:

- Insomnia
- Grinding or clenching of teeth, especially when sleeping
- Diarrhea
- Indigestion
- Ulcers
- Nausea
- Backaches
- Headaches
- Migraines
- Uncontrollable tics or twitches
- Stuttering
- Allergies
- Asthma
- High blood pressure
- Heart disease.

Of particular note is the connection between continual stress and heart disease. Because most of modern man's stressful situations do not require physical action, the fat pumped into the bloodstream to act as fuel for the muscles is left unused, collecting on artery walls and contributing to heart disease.

Key Terms

dilated—
having been widened; expanded

fight-or-flight response—
an involuntary reaction to an immediate danger or threat, which prepares a person physically either to respond to the danger or run away

Key Term

migraine—
a severe, recurring headache, usually affecting only one side of the head, characterized by sharp pain and often accompanied by nausea, vomiting, and visual disturbances

UNIT V

Psychological Effects of Stress

Generally, the first indications a person may have of stress overload are certain feelings, like irritability or worrying. If the person pays attention to these feelings and takes action to reduce stress, the effects of stress will not continue. If, however, the person ignores these initial warning signs and seeks no relief from stress, he or she will experience more psychological effects and probably begin to experience some of the physical effects discussed previously.

Psychologically, continual stress may cause the following:

- Irritability
- Excessive worrying
- Anxiety
- Inability to relax
- Forgetfulness
- Disorganization
- Inability to concentrate
- Inability to complete tasks
- Lack of energy
- Trouble with relationships
- Changed eating habits; over- or undereating with corresponding weight gain or loss
- Use or increased use of alcohol and other drugs
- Lowered self-esteem
- Feelings of discouragement
- Excessive feelings of guilt or self-blame
- Emotional overreaction, like exploding or crying without reason
- Waking from sleep with a sense of doom
- Disinterest in the world and life
- Dissatisfaction with things that were previously satisfying
- Tendency to avoid people and activities, even those that were previously enjoyed
- Unexplained feelings of helplessness or hopelessness
- Depression.

When stress continues to go unchecked, negative feelings, like depression and hopelessness, can intensify over time. In severe cases, people can become depressed enough to try to commit suicide. It is important, therefore, to listen to your feelings, relate them to what is happening in your life, and respond to them promptly before the effects of stress get out of hand.

Key Terms

anxiety—
eager, often agitated desire; one's anxiety to make a good impression, for example

depression—
psychiatric disorder characterized by an inability to concentrate; insomnia; loss of appetite; anhedonia; feelings of extreme sadness, guilt, helplessness, and hopelessness; and thoughts of death

Causes of Stress

Causes of stress and levels of stress experienced under certain circumstances vary from person to person depending on their personalities and tolerance for different situations and experiences. For example, an outgoing person may find public speaking easy and enjoyable, while a shy person may find it difficult and frightening. On the other hand, the shy person may be quite content to study alone, while the outgoing person may find studying alone nerve-wracking. Neither of these people is better or worse than the other; they are simply two different people reacting differently to the same situations. Do not compare yourself with others when it comes to stress. What is important is that you understand what causes you stress and learn to manage it before the stress "mismanages" you.

Read through the following items that are common causes of stress for many young people. Think about which ones are stressful for you and whether or not they are things that you can control. Recognizing what causes your stress is a step toward managing it.

Personal Habits

Personal habits can contribute to stress. Listed below are four negative personal habits. Do any apply to you?

- Poor time management
- Poor diet
- Irregular sleep habits
- Lack of exercise.

Social Activities

Social activities create situations that can be very stressful for young people. Which apply to you?

- Conflicts with family or friends
- Peer pressure to use alcohol, tobacco, or drugs
- Peer pressure to engage in a sexual relationship
- Pressure to be popular
- Lack of money.

Major Life Changes

Major life changes affect all people. Have you been effected by any of these major life changes recently?

- Death in the family
- Severe illness in the family
- Parents' divorce
- Parent remarries
- Moving
- Changing schools.

Environmental

The environment can affect you mentally as well as physically and can create stress in your life. Are you currently being exposed to any of the following items?

- Air and noise pollution
- Feeling confined
- Overcrowding
- Poor lighting
- Uncomfortable temperature
- Feeling unsafe in your neighborhood, home, or school.

Responsibilities

Personal responsibilities are placed on everyone at one time or another and can be very stressful. Are you experiencing any of the following items?

- Participating in too many activities
- Having unrealistic expectations of yourself
- Constant deadlines
- Concern about grades
- Concern about college and career decisions
- Having to work and go to school
- Having to care for younger brothers or sisters.

Stress Strategies

There is no way to completely eliminate stress from life. In fact, as previously explained, a stress-free life would not even be desirable, because stress in reasonable amounts aids performance, creativity, and problem solving. Letting stress get out of hand, however, is a common problem in today's hectic world. Fortunately, once you recognize signs of stress overload in yourself and identify its cause, you can either eliminate the source of stress or, if it is not possible to eliminate it, learn to manage the stress associated with it.

Preventing Stress Overload

The best way to ensure stress does not get the best of you is to follow lifelong habits that promote mental and physical well-being. Getting plenty of sleep, eating well-balanced meals, and exercising regularly will help you cope better with stressful situations; maintaining a positive outlook will help you face difficulties with more confidence. In addition to these common sense approaches, the following can also promote well-being and prevent stress overload.

- Manage your time with daily, weekly, and/or monthly schedules. In addition to scheduling time for school, study, extracurricular activities, and so on, make sure you allow enough time for sleep, unhurried meals, relaxation, and other things you enjoy.
- Take care of your problems as soon as possible; avoiding them will not make them go away. The longer you put off dealing with a problem, the more anxious you will feel about it, and the more stress you will create for yourself.

- Keep a journal of the situations you find stressful. For each situation, explain why you find it stressful, how you handled it, and whether or not you believe you could handle it better in the future.

- Develop a hobby and/or participate regularly in an activity you enjoy.

- Take some time every day to do something you find relaxing—whether it is sitting quietly alone and thinking, talking with a good friend on the phone, or laughing at your favorite sitcom.

- Talk over problems with people you trust and who you know are good listeners. Keeping all your thoughts and feelings to yourself can be very stressful. Although you may believe you can handle all your problems on your own, everyone needs at least one person to confide in.

- Accept that throughout life you will encounter stressful situations that you cannot or should not avoid, but recognize that you also have control over how you approach and respond to those situations. For example, while Shelley dreads going to the dentist, she realizes it is important, and instead of dwelling on how much she hates it, she focuses on the benefits of dental care to her overall health and on how good her teeth will look and feel after the dental appointment. Approaching stressful situations positively and looking to the ultimate outcome of the situation can lower the amount of stress you experience.

- When you do have a choice, do not participate in activities you find stressful and unrewarding. Often, young people will take part in activities because their friends do, they believe their parents want them to, or they just believe they must do it all. Only you know which activities are enjoyable and worthwhile to you, which bring you negative stress, and how many things you can do before getting overloaded. Be honest with yourself and with those who care about you in making decisions about participating in certain activities. If taking aerobics with your friends makes you feel more uptight than healthy and relaxed, and you would really rather get your exercise going for a walk alone, let your friends know how you feel and then do what is best for you.

- Be prepared when you know you will have to face a stressful situation. For example, if you know that you must give a class presentation, plan for it and rehearse it until you feel comfortable with it. By preparing for it, you will be calmer during the time leading up to the presentation and will feel more confident when giving it.

- Do not use tobacco, alcohol, or other drugs. Using drugs does not solve any problems and, more often than not, causes new ones.

- Do not be overly self-critical; remember that making mistakes is part of the growing process and that learning from them will make you more successful in the future.

- If you can, limit the number of changes you make in your life at any one time. For example, if in the same week that you start a new job after school, you also start getting up earlier each morning to jog before school, you are probably putting too much pressure on yourself. To limit your stress level, get used to the new routine of having an after-school job before you add anything else to your schedule.

- Learn a relaxation technique like meditation, visualization, or deep breathing.

Key Terms

meditation—
a contemplative discourse, usually on a religious or philosophical subject

visualization—
to make visible

UNIT V

Relaxation Techniques

Try using these relaxation techniques when you notice the warning signs of stress.

Deep Breathing

To relax through deep breathing, follow these steps:

1. While closing your eyes, take a deep breath in through your nose so that your abdomen expands.
2. Slowly exhale through your mouth, letting all the air out of your lungs and allowing your stomach to contract.
3. Repeat for 5 to 10 minutes.

The Worry Box

Relaxing through "the worry box" can be done by following these steps:

1. Start deep breathing.
2. Visualize a box that has a lock and key.
3. Imagine yourself putting all your worries and fears in the box, then closing the lid, and locking it with the key.
4. Imagine yourself putting the key somewhere out of sight—like under a mattress or on the top shelf of a closet—and, therefore, out of mind.

Meditation

Meditation can help you clear your mind and relax. To do so, follow these steps:

1. Find a quiet place where you can be alone for at least 10 minutes.
2. Sit on the floor with your legs crossed. Some people put one or both of their feet up onto their inner thighs when meditating. Keep your back and neck straight. Relax your arms with your hands in your lap or on your knees—palms up or down, whichever feels most comfortable to you.
3. Close your eyes and try to empty your mind. Many people do this by concentrating on their breathing or on a single word, image, or sound.

Quick Calming Response

To calm and center yourself quickly, follow these steps:

1. Turn inward and listen to a sound or word that you find relaxing and choose to use when stress overload hits.
2. As you repeat the sound or word inside yourself, slowly take deep breaths in and out, visualizing the release of the "tense air" from your body with each exhaled breath.

Progressive Relaxation

To try progressive relaxation, do the following:

1. Sit or lie down in a comfortable position and begin deep breathing.
2. As you inhale, tighten the muscles in your head and neck area.
3. Relax the tensed muscles as you slowly exhale.
4. Continue with all parts of your body, working your way from head to foot.

Being physically active when under stress helps to release the built-up tension in your muscles.
Courtesy of (*left*) Ray Morsch/The Stock Market; (*right*) Larry Lawfer

Letting Off Steam

Sometimes, stressful situations can make you feel frustrated and angry.
To keep the stress from getting the better of you and possibly "losing your cool,"
try the following:

- Take several deep breaths, releasing tension with each exhale

- Close your eyes and visualize yourself in a calming situation or place

- Take a break; if possible, remove yourself from the problem or situation
  until you feel more relaxed and under control

- Analyze the importance of the situation. Does it really matter if someone
  cuts you off in traffic or bumps into you and does not excuse him or herself?
  Is it worth feeling angry about or wasting your time and energy on?
  Is it better just to forget it and move on?

- If something is important to you and you can take action, confront the person
  or situation calmly. If it is not possible to confront the person or problem directly,
  let off steam, depending upon the situation, by either talking to someone you trust
  or writing an angry letter, then throwing it away.

- Work off tension with a physical activity, like screaming into a pillow,
  taking a walk, or lifting weights.

Stress and Leadership

As a leader, learn to manage your own stress effectively, so that you do not create a negative environment for your followers. Recognize that your behavior can directly affect the stress level of your group of cadets. Stress in groups can be increased to counterproductive and unhealthy levels when leaders

- Act unpredictably
- Constantly find fault with their followers, which eats away at their followers' self-esteem and results in increased anxiety
- Set up win-lose situations in which either they are right and their followers are wrong or vice versa
- Demand too much or too little of their followers.

Leaders can keep a group's stress to healthy levels by

- Allowing some participation in the decision-making process, which creates a feeling of trust and usefulness in followers, and promotes team spirit and cooperation within the group
- Giving credit where it is due and praise when warranted
- Offering constructive criticism when necessary
- Having a good working knowledge of the tasks the group needs to perform
- Monitoring and tracking tasks as they are performed and offering guidance when necessary.

As a leader, you must also be aware of any indications that cadets are feeling or acting "stressed out." If you realize someone is showing signs of stress, let them know that you have noticed they have not been themselves lately, or ask if everything is okay with them. Your concern will probably encourage them to talk to you about how they are feeling, and just the fact that they are talking about it and you are listening can help to relieve their stress.

Depression

People often say, "Oh, I'm so depressed," when they are having a bad day or because some unhappy event has recently occurred. Sadness and grief are normal reactions to certain events in life. A person who is having a passing blue mood is not truly depressed. For minor low moods, stimulating or enjoyable activities, like running or reading a good book, are often all that is needed to raise a person's spirits.

Feeling sad is a normal response to a disappointing event in your life.
Courtesy of James Whitmer

Major depression, on the other hand, is a serious illness that requires treatment. It affects the whole body and involves thoughts, feelings, bodily functions, and behaviors. Most people usually recover from bad events in life after a reasonable amount of time; depressed people do not. And while some cases of depression can be traced to a specific stressful experience, other cases of depression seem to have no apparent reason for occurring.

An episode of depression can occur once in a person's life or many times. A depressed person's symptoms may last for months, years, or a lifetime. Depression can be so severe that the person cannot function at all. Some people who are chronically depressed are able to function but never feel really well, content, or happy. They may be unaware that they are even depressed because they are so used to feeling that way.

Depending on the individual and the severity of the illness, a depressed person will experience a variety of these symptoms to different degrees. Note that many of these symptoms are similar to symptoms of stress.

- Constantly feeling sad or "empty"
- Feeling hopeless, worthless, and helpless
- Unable to make decisions, remember things, or concentrate
- Loss of interest in normally pleasurable activities
- Irritability
- Disinterest in school, at home, and in other activities
- Not caring about appearance
- Avoiding people; staying alone most of the time
- Problems falling asleep and then problems getting up
- Loss of appetite
- Feeling tired and "slowed down" all the time
- Chronic aches and pains and digestive problems
- Frequent thoughts of death and/or suicide
- Suicide attempts.

It is important to remember that depression is a real illness and not caused by personal weakness. Potential for developing some kinds of depression may be inherited, and therefore, biologically related. For instance, manic-depressive illness seems to occur in people whose genetic makeup is different than those who do not become ill; however, not everyone who has the genetic makeup for the illness gets it. This suggests that other factors, such as stress, also play a role in the development of the disease.

As with stress, physically active people who eat well and get plenty of sleep tend to feel less depressed than people with less healthy lifestyles. Therefore, if you are feeling mildly depressed, take a look at your current eating, sleeping, and exercise habits and try to make some changes there. In addition, do things you enjoy, try something different that you have always wanted to do, talk to friends, spend time outside because the color green and the sun are known to boost spirits, and try not to pressure or push yourself for awhile.

Key Term

manic-depressive illness—
bipolar disorder

UNIT V

Likewise, if you know someone who is exhibiting signs of depression, take the time to listen to how they are feeling and offer them your support. Give them the suggestions listed above for lifting their spirits and breaking out of negative habits. Be patient. Often, depressed people are not fun to be around and may even try to push you away, but they really need a friend to understand and encourage them to try to make some changes.

If after giving these suggestions a try, you think his or her depression is worsening or becoming long-term, encourage your friend to seek help. Likewise, if you yourself are depressed and believe it is worsening and continuing, seek help. Doctors, psychologists, counselors, mental health clinics, hospitals, family services, social agencies, and private clinics are among the many people and places that offer help for all types of emotional disorders, including depression.

Anxiety

Anxiety is a feeling that everyone experiences occasionally when dealing with things they fear or worry about. Unlike depression, which makes people feel tired and unenergetic, anxiety makes people feel nervous and energetic, almost as if they cannot sit still. Like stress, anxiety in small amounts and for short durations can be beneficial. It can give you a spurt of energy and sharpen your mind. Too much anxiety, however, can be harmful and lessen your ability to perform. For example, while a little anxiety before giving a speech can heighten your powers of recall, projection, and expression, too much anxiety can make you freeze, forgetting information and stammering through the presentation.

To keep anxiety from getting the best of you, admit to yourself those things you fear and/or worry about. Then, when you know you will have to deal with one of them, make sure you are thoroughly prepared for it: practice for the speech, study for the test, rehearse the dance routine, work out faithfully before the big meet, and so forth. Being unprepared will only fuel your anxiety. When you start to worry or feel afraid, remind yourself that it is a waste of your energy, then visualize yourself doing well instead. Prior to the event or situation, focus on its positive outcomes, use the relaxation techniques discussed previously, and avoid caffeine, which only increases anxiety.

Key Term

generalized—
generally prevalent

Although it is normal to be mildly anxious about something that frightens or worries us, feeling anxious without a specific reason can indicate an anxiety disorder. When a person experiences anxiety over a long period of time that is related to so many worries and fears that the anxiety has become generalized, the person is suffering from free-floating anxiety. Often, the effects of free-floating anxiety are the same as stress overload.

When a person experiences anxiety attacks, which are strong, sudden attacks of anxiety for no apparent reason that last only a few minutes, he or she feels panic and extreme stress accompanied by dizziness, faintness, rapid heartbeat, excessive perspiration, and nausea. A person having an anxiety attack is not able to function until the attack passes. Some people have severe anxiety attacks so frequently that they are constantly fearful and unable to cope with many things in life. People suffering from excessive anxiety, whether free floating or anxiety attacks, should seek help from a counselor who can help them reduce or learn to deal with their anxiety.

Conclusion

Humans experience a wide range of emotions and not all of them are pleasant. Yet, even certain uncomfortable emotions such as stress and anxiety are beneficial in small doses. Sometimes, though, because of hectic, hurried schedules and pressures to do too many things or things we do not necessarily enjoy, stress can get out of hand. When you start feeling and showing warning signs of stress overload, step back and take a look at what is going on in your life. Ask yourself what is causing your symptoms of stress, then take care of it or reduce the stress you associate with it.

Meanwhile, to be prepared for the stressful events that will surely pop up throughout your life, maintain a healthy lifestyle so that you are better able to handle whatever life throws your way. Keep negative stress and anxiety at bay by doing things you enjoy, learning ways to relax, and thinking positively.

Remember, if these uncomfortable emotions ever become extreme, your mental and physical well-being may be threatened. They can even become initial indications of mental illness and physical disease.

Review Questions

1   Differentiate between stress and anxiety.

2   What are the physical and psychological effects of stress?

3   List positive ways to deal with depression and anxiety.

4   Define the term *depression*.

Drug Awareness

Key Terms

- drugs
- misuse
- abuse
- substance
- controlled substance
- addiction
- ferment
- distilled
- gateway
- intoxicated
- dependency
- stimulants
- narcotic
- hallucinogen
- inhalants
- nicotine

What You Will Learn to Do

Assess the effects of drug and substance abuse on life today

Skills and Knowledge You Will Gain Along the Way

✔ Identify commonly abused substances
✔ Recognize the differences among drug use, misuse, and abuse
✔ Explain reasons why people might use, misuse, or abuse alcohol or drugs
✔ Identify the risks associated with alcohol and various drugs
✔ Explain the effects of alcohol and drug use, misuse, and abuse on daily life

Introduction

Data presented by the *TeenGetGoing* website (www.teengetgoing.com) advocated by the JROTC program notes that teen alcohol and drug trends suggest that 90 percent of teens will "use" alcohol and/or other drugs during adolescence. Fifty percent of teens will abuse alcohol and/or drugs, and 15 percent will become addicted while still in adolescence. Look around your classroom. What kind of numbers does this represent? This chapter presents the latest information about alcohol and drugs, defines drugs, and explains the difference between drug use, drug misuse, and drug abuse. You will learn several types of drugs that people abuse, their side effects, and indications of overdose which will allow you to process this information in a way that is meaningful both to you and your community.

Drug Use, Misuse, and Abuse

Used under proper conditions, drugs can relieve pain, cure illness, and save lives. When abused, however, drugs can ruin lives and even cause death.

Think about the word *drug* for a moment. It can bring many images to mind, such as over-the-counter aspirin to stop a headache, a news report about someone who was arrested for cocaine possession, a prescription for antibiotics from your doctor, a drug-related death covered on the front page of the paper, medical research to develop drugs to cure illnesses, the war on drugs, and so on. So exactly what is a drug?

Broadly defined, a drug is any substance taken into the body that changes how the body functions, whether mentally or physically. This includes medications used for the prevention and treatment of disease, as well as any controlled substance to which a person can become addicted. Whether or not a drug is legal or illegal is no indication of whether or not it is addictive. For example, nicotine, which is found in tobacco products, and alcohol are addictive drugs. And just because a drug has a medical purpose does not mean it is not addictive. Many medications, when misused or abused, can cause addiction.

What Can You Do to Remain Drug-Free?

- Fill your life with activities and people you enjoy.
- Believe in yourself.
- Practice saying no before you are actually in a situation where someone offers you drugs, so you will not hesitate to say no when the time comes.
- Think through the consequences of abusing drugs. Where will drugs lead you in life? How long will your body remain healthy if you abuse drugs? How many of your plans can drugs ruin?
- Remember that drugs do not solve problems; they create them.

Key Terms

drugs—
chemicals that cause a change in a person's body or behavior

misuse—
the incorrect or improper use of a substance

abuse—
improper or excessive use or treatment

Key Terms

substance—
something, such as a drug or alcohol, deemed harmful and usually subject to legal restrictions

controlled substance—
a substance whose manufacture, possession, or sale is controlled by the law

addiction—
physical or psychological dependence on a substance, habit, or behavior that can lead to health, social, or economic problems; dependence on a drug

UNIT V

Drug use is taking a legal drug as recommended or prescribed for medical reasons. *Drug misuse* is taking a legal drug for medical reasons but not as recommended or prescribed. For example, people who double the recommended dosage of a pain reliever because they think it will make their headache go away quicker are misusing a drug. *Drug abuse* is taking a legal or illegal drug for a nonmedical reason in a way that can injure your health or ability to function.

Why Do People Abuse Drugs?

Some people try drugs out of curiosity or as an act of rebellion. Others cannot resist the peer pressure to try drugs. After people have tried a drug, whether or not they continue to abuse it depends on their individual personalities and situations and on the kind of drug abused.

Most drugs that people abuse produce feelings of pleasure and well-being. When people are unhappy, lonely, stressed, or are missing something in their lives such as friends, love, or satisfying work, they may abuse drugs to avoid their problems or fill a void. But when the effects of the drug wear off, they realize the problems and the voids are still there. So they turn to the drug again.

This cycle is what leads to addiction, a trap that can ruin a person emotionally, socially, economically, legally, and physically. Some drugs are far more addictive than others. For example, a first-time user of crack cocaine has a 1 in 3 chance of becoming an addict. This is why it is important to stop before you ever start taking drugs.

Many people take drugs without knowing what effect they have on the mind and body. Knowing ahead of time what a drug can do is often enough to convince a person not to try it, especially if one of the potential dangers of abusing a drug is death.

Alcohol

Alcohol, which is legal for those 21 years of age and older, is the most widely consumed and abused drug in the United States. It is socially acceptable in our society for adults to drink in moderation. In excess, however, alcohol is a dangerous drug. Drinking and driving remains the number one cause of death among high school students. Heavy alcohol use kills about 50 high school and college students each year because of alcohol poisoning.

The number one cause of death among high school students is drinking and driving.
Courtesy of George DiSario/The Stock Market

Alcohol Statistics

- Ninety percent of teenage automobile accidents involve alcohol
- Drinking and driving accidents are the leading cause of death among 15- to 24-year-olds
- Seventy percent of teenage suicide attempts involve alcohol

Alcohol is a natural substance formed when sugar and yeast react and ferment. Some alcohols are distilled; other are simply fermented. Alcohol is a drug; it is a *depressant* that is absorbed into the bloodstream and transmitted to virtually all parts of the body. Many people don't realize that alcohol is a drug. Some hold the view that experimentation with or use of alcohol is normal or acceptable behavior. However, the use of alcohol can cause alcohol addiction and often progresses to further drug abuses. Accordingly, some experts attach the term gateway to this substance. The use of drugs such as cocaine and heroin is unusual in those who have not previously used alcohol.

Alcohol abuse can cause serious chemical dependencies, harmful physical and psychological effects, and much suffering by family and friends. As awareness of these ill effects reaches new heights, more and more Americans are joining forces to fight alcohol abuse every day.

When a person drinks alcohol, it follows the same pathway as food through the digestive system. Unlike food, however, alcohol does not have to be digested by the stomach to be absorbed into the blood. After alcohol reaches the blood, it is circulated throughout the body and affects every part, including the brain and the rest of the nervous system.

Alcohol's Effects on the Body

The effects of ethyl alcohol (ethanol) on the human body can range greatly depending on the:

- Size of the individual
- How empty the stomach is at the time of alcohol consumption
- State of health and fatigue
- Mental attitude
- Speed and amount of consumption.

These different quantities of beer, liquor, and wine contain equal amounts of ethanol.
Courtesy of Ted Cordingley

It is also important to note that the three most common types of alcoholic drinks—beer, liquor, and wine—contain the same amount of alcohol. Although alcohol may make a person feel "high," alcohol is actually considered a "downer" drug. It slows down or depresses the central nervous system, causing slowed reactions, slurred speech, impaired coordination and judgment, and sometimes unconsciousness. Because alcohol affects reaction time, coordination, and judgment, people under its influence are more accident prone and less likely to make wise decisions. For these reasons, drinking and driving are a very dangerous and illegal combination.

Long-Term Effects

The long-term effects of alcohol abuse include alcoholism; cancers of the liver, stomach, colon, larynx, esophagus, and breast; high blood pressure; heart attacks; strokes; stomach ulcers; birth defects; premature aging; and a diminished immunity to disease due to nonfunction of infection-fighting cells. In men, hormone levels change, causing lower sex drives and enlarged breasts; women's menstrual cycles become irregular, possibly resulting in infertility.

The list of effects goes on to include shrinking of the muscles, including the heart; kidney, bladder, and pancreas damage; brain damage affecting vision and memory; depression; and mental illness. Obviously, long-term damage from alcohol abuse can be irreversible and result in death.

Tolerance

When the body becomes accustomed to or builds up a resistance to a drug, the body has developed tolerance to the drug. Tolerance causes a drinker's body to need increasingly larger amounts of alcohol to achieve the effect that was originally produced.

Dependence

When the body develops a resistance to a drug and requires the drug to function normally, dependence occurs. The drinker's body develops a chemical need for alcohol. Dependence occurs as tolerance builds. Dependence is also called addiction.

A dependent person who stops taking a drug will suffer from withdrawal. The signs of alcohol withdrawal include shakiness, sleep problems, irritability, rapid heartbeat, and sweating. The drinker also may see, smell, or feel imaginary objects.

The major psychological symptom of dependence is a strong desire or emotional need to continue using a drug. This need is often associated with specific routines and events. For example, some people drink whenever they face a difficult task or when they feel angry about something.

Brain Damage

Long-term alcohol abuse destroys nerve cells in the brain. Destroyed nerve cells usually cannot grow again. The loss of many nerve cells causes forgetfulness, an inability to concentrate, and poor judgment. These losses interfere with normal everyday functions.

Digestive Problems

Ongoing drinking irritates the tissues lining the mouth, throat, esophagus, and stomach. The irritation can cause the tissues to swell and become inflamed. Repeated irritation increases the risk of cancers of the mouth, tongue, esophagus, and stomach. Alcohol also affects the intestines and can cause recurring diarrhea. Large amounts of alcohol cause the stomach to produce too much stomach acid. The overproduction of acid may lead to indigestion, heartburn, or ulcers.

Liver Damage

Alcohol interferes with the liver's ability to break down fats. As a result of heavy drinking, the liver begins to fill with fat. The excess fat blocks the flow of blood in the liver, and the fat-filled liver cells die. Cirrhosis of the liver is a disease in which useless scar tissue replaces normal liver tissue. Because there is no blood flow in the scarred area, the liver begins to fail. Heavy drinkers suffering from cirrhosis may have high blood pressure, get infections easily, have swelling of the abdomen, and show a yellowing of the skin and eyes. Cirrhosis is the last stage of liver disease and can result in death.

Heavy drinkers often develop alcoholic hepatitis, or inflammation of the liver, caused by the toxic effects of alcohol. Hepatitis causes weakness, fever, yellowing of the skin, and enlargement of the liver. Recovery may take weeks. Sometimes hepatitis can lead to liver failure and even death.

Heart Disease

Excessive drinking contributes to increased blood pressure and heart rate, and irregular heartbeat. These problems can cause disruption in blood flow and possible heart damage. Also, alcohol causes fat to be deposited in heart muscle. Fatty heart muscle, in turn, causes the heart to pump blood through the body less efficiently. Alcohol abuse leads to heart disease, the leading cause of death in the United States.

Fetal Alcohol Syndrome

Pregnant women who drink put the health of their child at risk. A disorder called fetal alcohol syndrome (FAS) refers to the group of birth defects caused by the effects of alcohol on the unborn child. FAS occurs when alcohol in the mother's blood passes into the fetal, or unborn baby's, blood. Babies born with FAS often suffer from heart defects, malformed faces, delayed growth, and poor motor development. Alcohol prevents FAS babies from ever developing the reasoning abilities of healthy babies. Tragically, it is the leading preventable cause of mental retardation in America.

If a woman who is pregnant does not drink, her baby will not be born with FAS. Any woman who is pregnant or planning to become pregnant should not drink alcohol at all.

UNIT V

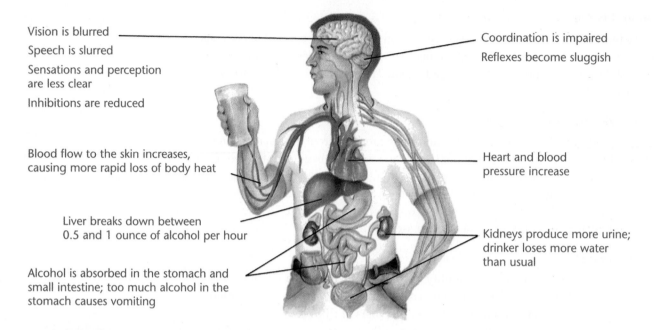

Vision is blurred

Speech is slurred

Sensations and perception are less clear

Inhibitions are reduced

Blood flow to the skin increases, causing more rapid loss of body heat

Liver breaks down between 0.5 and 1 ounce of alcohol per hour

Alcohol is absorbed in the stomach and small intestine; too much alcohol in the stomach causes vomiting

Coordination is impaired

Reflexes become sluggish

Heart and blood pressure increase

Kidneys produce more urine; drinker loses more water than usual

Figure 9.1 How the body reacts to the toxic effects of too much alcohol in the stomach
Courtesy of Fran Milner

Short-Term Effects

The short-term effects of alcohol include those that happen within minutes, and sometimes within days, of drinking alcohol. Figure 9.1 identifies the short-term effects of alcohol on the body.

Bloodstream

When alcohol enters the blood, it causes the blood vessels to widen. More blood flows to the skin's surface. The drinker feels warm for a short time as the skin flushes; however, the drinker's body temperature drops as the increased blood flow to the surface allows body heat to escape. People who drink alcohol in cold weather to get warm actually accomplish the opposite.

Brain

After reaching the brain, alcohol immediately has a depressant effect and slows the speed of some brain activities. People who drink alcohol may describe the change as relaxing. What they actually experience are physical changes such as a loss of sensation and a decrease in sharpness of vision, hearing, and other senses. Alcohol also affects the parts of the brain that control muscle coordination, which is why drinkers may lose their balance or stumble.

If drinking continues, alcohol depresses the part of the brain that controls breathing and heartbeat. Breathing rates, pulse rates, and blood pressure, which initially increased, now decrease. A drinker may lose consciousness, slip into a coma, or die from alcohol poisoning.

Heavy drinkers and many first-time drinkers may suffer blackouts. Blackouts are periods of time that the drinker cannot recall. Other people recall seeing the drinker talking, walking, and in control. The following day, however, the drinker has no memory of some events from the day before.

Liver

In the bloodstream, alcohol is carried to the liver. The liver chemically breaks down alcohol into energy and the waste produces carbon dioxide and water. The carbon dioxide is released from the body in the lungs. The water passes out of the body as breath vapor, perspiration, or urine. When people drink alcohol faster than the liver can break it down, they become intoxicated.

Kidneys

Alcohol prevents the release of body chemicals that regulate how much urine the kidneys make. The kidneys produce more urine than usual, and the drinker loses more water than usual. The drinker becomes very thirsty. In extreme cases, a drinker may lose water needed for the body to function properly.

Motor-Vehicle Crashes

Almost half of the fatal crashes and about two-thirds of all crashes involving personal injury in the United States are related to alcohol use. In addition, more than one-third of accidents involving pedestrians who are struck and killed by motor vehicles are caused by drunk drivers.

Driving while intoxicated is illegal in all of the 50 states. Driving while intoxicated means a driver exceeds the level of blood alcohol concentration allowed by law in a state. Drivers who cause motor-vehicle crashes usually undergo blood, urine, breath, or saliva tests to determine their blood alcohol concentration (BAC, discussed on the next page). If their BAC is above the legal limit, drunk drivers can have their driver's license taken away and can be prosecuted.

Synergism

Some drugs can interact to produce effects that are many times greater than the individual drugs would produce. When drugs increase each other's effects when taken together, the interaction is called synergism.

As previously stated, alcohol is generally a depressant drug. When a person drinks alcohol and takes another depressant, such as sleeping pills, the combination can cause drastic changes in the body. Together the depressants' effects are more than doubled and can cause a dangerous slowing of breathing and heart rates. In extreme cases, synergism of alcohol and other depressants can lead to coma or death.

Overdose

Taking an excessive amount of a drug that leads to coma or death is called an overdose. Severe intoxication causes the heart and breathing to stop, resulting in death from alcohol overdose. Many drinkers assume that they will pass out before drinking a fatal amount. This is not necessarily true. Alcohol continues to be absorbed into the blood for 30 to 90 minutes after the last drink. The drinker's BAC can increase even if the drinker becomes unconscious. First-time drinkers who participate in a drinking contest may die from alcohol poisoning.

Blood Alcohol Concentration

The amount of ethanol in a person's blood is expressed by a percentage called the blood alcohol concentration (BAC). BAC measures the number of milligrams of ethanol per 100 milliliters of blood. A BAC of 0.1 percent means that one-tenth of 1 percent of the fluid in the blood is ethanol. A BAC of 0.1 percent reduces a person's muscle coordination, perception, and judgment.

A variety of factors can affect a person's BAC, including the following:

- Gender
- Age, weight, and height
- Amount of food in the stomach
- Concentration of alcohol in beverages consumed
- Volume of alcohol consumed
- Rate of consumption and absorption.

The rate at which a person's liver can break down alcohol is fairly constant. In one hour, the liver can break down the amount of ethanol in a can of beer, a shot of liquor, or a glass of wine. Thus, someone who has three cans of beer in the last 45 minutes of a 3-hour party will become more intoxicated than someone who drinks those three cans of beer over the three-hour period. The effects of BAC on the body are shown in Figure 9.2.

BLOOD ALCOHOL CONCENTRATION: EFFECTS ON THE BODY

NUMBER OF DRINKS	EFFECTS	BAC RANGE*	APPROXIMATE TIME TO ELIMINATE ALCOHOL
(1 drink)	Inhibitions, reflexes, and alertness diminished. Judgment and reasoning affected.	.02–.03%	1 1/2 hours
(2 drinks)	Drinker gets the mistaken idea that his or her skills and abilities have improved. Self-control declines.	.04–.06%	3 hours
(3 drinks)	Unable to think clearly. Judgment, reasoning, and muscular coordination are impaired.	.06–.09%	4 to 5 hours
(4 drinks)	Most behaviors, including hearing, speech, vision, and balance, are affected.	.08–.12%	5 to 7 hours

*The BAC will vary depending on the alcohol content of the drinks and rate of consumption.

Figure 9.2 In some states, a person with a BAC of 0.1 percent is legally drunk. Other states have lowered the legal BAC to 0.08 percent.

Reprinted from *Health Skills for Wellness*, Third Edition, by B.E. (Buzz) Pruitt, Kathy Teer Crumpler, and Deborah Prothrow-Stith, (2001), Prentice Hall, Inc.

Drinking and Driving?

D	DEFINE the problem
E	EXPLORE alternatives
C	CONSIDER consequences
I	IDENTIFY values
D	DECIDE and act
E	EVALUATE results

JANELLE ATTENDED A PARTY with some of her friends. She planned to get a ride home with Dave, but she had seen him drink four beers since he arrived. Dave was showing some signs of intoxication, and Janelle was not sure if he should drive. Unfortunately, she did not know anyone else at the party who could give her a ride, and Janelle knew that her parents had gone out with friends for the evening. Besides, three of her friends were getting a ride from Dave. "I'm probably getting worried for nothing," thought Janelle. "What could happen in the few miles to my house?"

1. Use the DECIDE process to decide what you would do if you were in Janelle's position. Explain your decision.

2. What role might peer pressure play in influencing Janelle's decision?

3. Suggest a realistic plan that you and your friends could use to avoid situations like the one described above.

Courtesy of Ken Karp

Reprinted from *Health Skills for Wellness*, Third Edition, by B. E. (Buzz) Pruitt, Kathy Teer Crumpler, and Deborah Prothrow-Stith, (2001), Prentice Hall, Inc.

Provided the person does not continue to drink, the BAC decreases. The intoxicating effects of alcohol slowly diminish. As reflexes and coordination return to normal, a person gradually becomes steadier. Many people refer to this process as "becoming sober" or "sobering up."

You may have heard that cold showers, exercise, fresh air, or coffee will help a person sober up more quickly. But this is not true. Nothing can speed up the liver's ability to break down alcohol. Coffee or fresh air may keep a person awake, but they do not eliminate the intoxicating effects of alcohol.

Behavioral Effects

In addition to the physical effects of alcohol, certain behavioral, or learned, effects are connected to drinking. A person's mood and reason for drinking can alter the effects of alcohol. Sometimes the person's mood and reason for drinking make the effects stronger; sometimes they make the effects weaker. The environment in which alcohol is consumed may influence its effects as well.

At a quiet family dinner, family members may consume wine with no negative effects. The calm nature of the event and the fact that both parents and children expect each other to behave politely creates an environment in which people drink responsibly.

At a party in which "getting drunk" is the main theme, alcohol consumption often leads to negative behaviors. The loss of coordination may be exaggerated for comic effect. People who have been drinking may insist that they are still perfectly able to drive. They may not want to admit that they cannot drink as much as others.

As alcohol takes effect, drinkers begin to lose judgment and self-control. At the same time, alcohol decreases drinkers' natural fears. When these two effects are combined, the person's inhibitions are reduced. Inhibitions are the controls that people put on their emotions and behavior in order to behave in socially acceptable ways.

After they lose their inhibitions, drinkers may behave in ways they normally would never consider. For example, a person under the influence of alcohol may express anger in violent or destructive ways. Shy people may behave in outgoing ways, and serious people may act foolishly.

Alcoholism

Some drinkers cannot control their drinking. Their major goal in drinking is to get drunk. People who have an addiction to alcohol suffer from the disease of alcoholism. Psychologically, alcoholics consider drinking a regular, essential part of coping with daily life. Physically, an alcoholic's body requires alcohol to function. An alcoholic's drinking patterns eventually control every aspect of his or her life.

No one is sure why some drinkers become alcoholics, but anyone who drinks even one drink is at risk of becoming an alcoholic. Because alcoholism tends to run in families, there appears to be some genetic basis for it. On the other hand, the attitudes in the home in which a person grows up may play a role in whether or not a person develops a drinking problem.

Drugs

A drug is any chemical substance that changes the function of the mind or the body. Aspirin is a drug; allergy medication is a drug; marijuana is a drug; beer is a drug; the nicotine in cigarettes is a drug. A drug is neither good nor bad; it is what a person does with a drug that makes the difference.

Use, misuse, and *abuse* are terms thrown around quite a bit when talking about drugs. Use is taking a legal drug as prescribed or recommended for medical reasons. Misuse is taking a legal drug for medical reasons but not as recommended or prescribed. Abuse is taking any drug, legal or illegal, for a nonmedical reason in a way that can injure your health or ability to function. Taking drugs is a serious matter; there is no such thing as recreational drug use. Abusing drugs is not a sport or a hobby and always involves an unnecessary risk to your health.

When people talk about drugs, you often hear that someone is a drug *addict* or that a drug can or cannot cause dependence. Addiction and *drug dependence* mean basically the same thing; however, the term *addict* tends to make people think of a desperate individual living in the back alleys of a big city. But anyone from any background in any place can be addicted or drug dependent. People who are dependent cannot refuse the drug they have been abusing.

A person has a physical dependence on a drug when, after being deprived of the drug for any length of time, he or she experiences symptoms like nausea, vomiting, anxiety, watery eyes and nose, and an overwhelming desire to use the drug. Such symptoms are typical of withdrawal sickness. Withdrawal happens because the body's chemistry has been changed, causing the user to be unable to function comfortably without the drug.

Most people who are physically dependent are also psychologically dependent. Some have psychological dependence without the physical dependence, which can be an equally strong dependence. With this type of dependence, the user feels a powerful motivation to continue abusing a drug for the temporary pleasure or relief of discomfort the drug gives. Because the mind and the body work together very closely, it is often difficult to tell the difference between physical and psychological dependence. The mental craving for a drug may be so powerful that it seems to be a physical need.

Marijuana (Pot, Grass, Weed, Dope, Reefer)

Marijuana (Acapulco Gold, Ganga, Grass, Mary Jane, Pot, Weed, Reefer, Stick, Smoke) comes from the dried flowers, leaves, and small stems of the cannabis plant. It is smoked in cigarettes, known as joints, and also in pipes. Marijuana use is illegal in the United States, but in the past it was used medicinally to reduce swelling of the eyes caused by glaucoma and to counteract the intense nausea brought on by certain cancer treatments. Its legalization, especially for these medical purposes, has been a controversial subject in this country for years.

The tetrahydrocannabinol (THC) produced by cannabis is the main psychoactive substance that produces marijuana's mind-altering effects. THC is quickly absorbed into the lungs and then travels through the blood to affect the brain. It distorts the senses, including hearing, taste, touch, and smell, alters the sense of time and place, and affects emotions. THC affects sleep patterns and remains in body fat for at least a month after only one joint has been smoked. It causes users to crave food (getting the munchies) and to enjoy eating, which is unusual for a drug. It also tends to dull sexual urges and pleasure.

Marijuana is considered a gateway drug, meaning that people who use marijuana often go on to use other drugs.
Courtesy of Schleikorn/
Custom Medical Stock Photo

There are several hundred other chemicals in marijuana that vary between different types of cannabis plants and between plants grown during different seasons. The active chemicals in marijuana affect the brain, altering hearing, taste, touch, smell, and a sense of time and space. The effects of marijuana vary from person to person depending on each person's expectations and how much they smoke and because the chemicals in different marijuana plants vary. People may experience anything from a mild euphoria to uncontrollable laughter to hallucinations. Marijuana can also contain dangerous substances such as pesticides and molds and is sometimes mixed with PCP to make the user believe it is more potent.

Because marijuana is widely abused today and has been around for thousands of years, many people believe that its use poses no harm. However, research studies prove this notion wrong. The effects of marijuana use include the following:

- Short-term memory loss and shortened attention span, both of which interfere with the ability to learn. Heavy, long-term use is often called "burn out" because the user's thinking is slow and confused.
- Increased heart rate and irregular heartbeat.
- Weakening of the immune system.
- Reduced hormone levels resulting in lower sperm counts in males and irregular menstrual cycles in females.
- Development of "amotivational syndrome," which results in apathy and loss of ambition and drive.
- Impaired judgment, unsteadiness, lack of coordination, and slowed responses, which make driving a dangerous activity.
- Lung damage and increased risk of lung cancer. This risk is higher than that of smoking tobacco cigarettes because marijuana is inhaled more deeply and then held in the lungs for a longer period of time. Joints also lack filters to cut down on harmful chemical effects.
- Possible depression and moodiness. Some users feel tired and unhappy the morning after smoking marijuana and may respond by smoking a joint to feel better. This cycle may lead to psychological dependency.
- Possible intense fear and anxiety, called a "pot panic" and even paranoia and psychosis. This may occur if the marijuana contains higher levels of THC.
- Development of a tolerance to marijuana resulting in the need for greater amounts in order to feel any effects. This may also contribute to psychological dependence.

The harmful health effects of marijuana use may include rapid and irregular heart-beat, short-term memory loss, shortened attention span, a weakened immune system, fatigue, and a higher risk of lung cancer. In extreme cases, marijuana abuse can result in paranoia and psychosis. Similar to alcohol, marijuana abuse can affect driving ability. As with any illegal drug, marijuana is not tested for safety and purity. It may contain pesticides and molds and may be mixed with other dangerous drugs.

Because of all the effects marijuana has on the mind, the body, and the ability to learn, its use may be particularly harmful to young people, since they are still maturing physically, sexually, and mentally. Marijuana's effects may prevent you from becoming a healthy, normal adult.

Key Term

dependency—
addiction to a substance

Cocaine, Crack, and Bazuco

Cocaine hydrochloride (Cocaine, Coke, Peruvian Marching Powder, C, Snow, Flake, Rock, White, Blow, Nose Candy) comes from the leaves of the coca bush and is an illegal drug that looks like white crystalline powder. It is often diluted with other ingredients and then inhaled through the nose, injected, or smoked.

Cocaine is a stimulant that affects the nervous system, providing short bursts of euphoria, a feeling of excitement, increased blood pressure and pulse rate, and alertness. People often use it to increase mental activity and to offset drowsiness, fatigue, or as an appetite suppressant; however, the intense high of cocaine is followed by an intense low. Repeated abuse of cocaine can result in a strong physical and psychological dependency. The body will ignore all other drives, including hunger, in its drive for cocaine.

Cocaine is derived from the leaves of the South American coca shrub.
Courtesy of Dr. Morley Read/
Photo Researchers

Regular use can lead to hallucinations of touch, taste, sound, or smell. Tolerance develops rapidly with repeated use. As the effects of cocaine wear off, the user feels exhausted, depressed, and sometimes paranoid, similar to the crashing of amphetamines. Cocaine is considered to be one of the most potentially addictive drugs.

Cocaine stimulates the central nervous system. Immediate effects include dilated pupils and elevated blood pressure, heart rate, respiratory rate, and body temperature. Occasional use results in a stuffy nose, while chronic use decays the mucous membranes of the nose. Injecting cocaine, or any drug, with a shared needle may spread AIDS, hepatitis, and other diseases. Cocaine produces both psychological and physical dependency.

Dealers cut cocaine with other substances, usually table sugar, mannitol, lactose, dextrose, and other drugs (PCP, lidocaine, amphetamines). Strychnine, a poison, has been found in cocaine; talc, which damages the lungs, is also often used.

Occasional use of cocaine can lead to heavy, uncontrollable use, with the dependence becoming so strong that users will not quit even when cocaine severely damages their lives. When users do quit, they may not experience strong physical withdrawal symptoms, but they become depressed and irritable, are tired but unable to sleep, and constantly crave the drug.

Crack (Crack, Freebase Rocks, Rock) looks like brown pellets or crystalline rocks that resemble lumpy soap and is often packaged in small vials. It is smoked. Bazuco is a drug similar to crack. Both of these drugs are illegal.

Crack is street cocaine commonly processed with boiling water and baking soda, which produces a very pure form of cocaine. The effects and the risk of addiction to crack are so great, however, that it is like a completely different drug. It is many, many times more dangerous than cocaine hydrochloride. Its effects are felt within 10 seconds. Cocaine in this form creates a very intense high and a fast, strong addiction. The user also experiences an incredible low after the high has worn off, often throwing him or her into a deep depression. To offset this depression, the user then smokes more crack, which starts the compulsive cycle that leads to a severe dependency. The only person who benefits from this vicious cycle is the drug dealer who now has a desperate customer in constant need of his or her product.

The physical side effects of crack include dilated pupils, increased pulse rate, elevated blood pressure, insomnia, loss of appetite, hallucinations of touch, paranoia, and seizures. A major concern with crack is that dependency is almost immediate. The first experience is often very pleasurable. Then the extreme low afterward is a strong motivator to use the drug again right away, this time to relieve bad feelings. Users of crack are addicted before they know it, turning their lives upside down.

Bazuco, another form of cocaine, is equally if not more dangerous and addictive than crack. Its use originated in Colombia and other South American countries and has now made its way to the United States. It is made from the intermediate step between the coca leaf and the cocaine hydrochloride, called cocaine sulfate. It is mixed with a number of other substances, among them marijuana, methaqualone, and acetone. Its effects are similar to those of crack, as are its dangers and its quick addiction.

The use of any type of cocaine can cause death by disrupting the brain's control of the heart and respiration.

Amphetamines and Methamphetamine (Speed)

Amphetamines (Speed, Bennies, Glass, Uppers, Ups, Black Beauties, Pep Pills, Copilots, Bumblebees, White Crosses, Benzedrine, Dexedrine, Footballs, Biphetamine) look like capsules, pills, or tablets. Methamphetamines (Crank, Crystal, Meth, Crystal Meth, Methedrine, Ice) can be in the form of a white powder, pills, or a rock that resembles blue paraffin. Forms of both drugs are used medically to treat obesity, narcolepsy, and hyperactivity in children.

Amphetamines

Similar to cocaine, amphetamines are stimulants. They stimulate the nervous system, increasing physical activity, energy, mental alertness, and self-confidence, and producing euphoria. Medically, amphetamines are used to treat obesity, narcolepsy, and hyperactivity in children. For example, the amphetamine Ritalin is used to stimulate the brain center that helps hyperactive children sit still and pay attention.

As a drug of abuse, amphetamines are often referred to as "speed." Many people abuse amphetamines to increase energy and alertness, and in some cases to combat fatigue brought on by use of alcohol, marijuana, or depressants. The body builds up tolerance to amphetamines, however, and greater and greater doses are required to achieve the same effects. Addiction may become severe.

Key Term

stimulants—
drugs, drinks, or other substances that speed up the activity of the mind or body; a drug that speeds up the activities of the central nervous system, the heart, and other organs

Medically, amphetamines are taken orally, but many abusers inject the drug directly into a vein, increasing the risk of overdose and infection. Needles shared to inject the drug can spread hepatitis and HIV. After an injection of amphetamines, the user experiences an intense, short-lived euphoria. An addict may inject the drug several times a day for several days feeling little need for food or sleep. Mental depression and overwhelming fatigue follow abuse, which may cause the abuser to turn to amphetamines again for relief.

In addition to fatigue and depression, the other side effects of amphetamine abuse include extreme anxiety, temporary mental illness, and malnutrition. High doses can cause hallucinations, increased body temperature, high blood pressure, convulsions, kidney failure, lack of oxygen, bleeding of the brain, and death. Withdrawal symptoms include irritability, depression, disorientation, long periods of sleep, and not caring about anything.

Methamphetamine

Methamphetamine is a nervous system stimulant similar to amphetamines that is used medically in much the same way as amphetamines. This drug is abused to produce heightened awareness, alertness, and self-confidence. A smokable form of methamphetamine is "ice." Like crack, it produces an intense high without the use of needles and is extremely addictive. Abuse of methamphetamine may result in bizarre behavior, sleeplessness, depression, high blood pressure, increased body temperature, convulsions, heart problems, seizures, and strokes.

Methcathinone, also called "cat" and "star," is a designer drug similar to methamphetamine that can cause paranoia, slurred speech, tremors, extreme weight loss, and sleeplessness.

Barbiturates, Methaqualones, and Tranquilizers

Barbiturates (Downers, Barbs, Blue Devils, Red Devils, Yellow Jacket, Yellows, Nembutal, Seconal, Amytal, Tuinals, Luminal, Amytal, Pentothal, Phenobarbital) look like red, yellow, blue, or red and blue capsules. Methaqualones (Ludes, Quaaludes, Quads, Sopors, Sopes, 714s) look like tablets. Tranquilizers (Valium, Librium, Equanil, Miltown, Serax, Tranxene, Thorazine) look like tablets or capsules.

Barbiturates

Barbiturates are a group of depressant drugs that include phenobarbital (goofballs), pentobarbital (yellow jackets), amobarbital (blue devils), and secobarbital (red devils). They lower body temperature and blood pressure, slow breathing and heart rate, and as such, have many medical uses. For example, doctors prescribe phenobarbital to reduce the frequency of convulsions in epileptics. Barbiturates are also used medically as an anesthetic and to treat insomnia. The effects of barbiturates vary from person to person and even change within one person from one use to the next.

When abused, the symptoms they produce are similar to those of alcohol. Small amounts can produce calmness and relaxed muscles, but larger doses cause slurred speech and staggering walk. Like alcohol, they distort perception and slow reaction time, which can cause serious accidents like car crashes. Very large doses can cause respiratory depression, coma, and death.

Signs of barbiturate abuse include fatigue, blurred vision, confused or slurred speech, lack of coordination and balance, a reduction of mental and physical activity, and decreased breathing. Abusers will often act like they are drunk, but there will be no smell of alcohol. Long-term abuse may result in double vision, depression, and forgetfulness.

Signs of an overdose of barbiturates include dilated pupils, a rapid pulse, shallow breathing, and clammy skin. An overdose can cause coma and death. Because barbiturates cause confusion and forgetfulness, accidental death occurs when a person has taken barbiturates, becomes confused, forgets, and takes more barbiturates. Accidental poisoning occurs when barbiturates are combined with alcohol. Withdrawal symptoms include anxiety, insomnia, tremors, delirium, and convulsions.

Barbiturate abusers often become extremely depressed, tired, and hopeless. They may reach for the rest of the bottle to "end it all" when in this mental state, or they may become confused, forget how many pills they have taken, and accidentally overdose. For this reason, barbiturates are one of the leading causes of drug-related deaths. The combination of barbiturates and alcohol can multiply the effects of both drugs, thereby multiplying the risks. This multiplication of the effects of two separate drugs when taken together is called the synergistic effect. It can be fatal.

Methaqualone

Methaqualone production has been banned in the United States since 1984 due to its widespread misuse and minimal medical value. Abusers take it to produce a feeling of elation; however, its side effects are headaches, nosebleeds, dizziness, loss of coordination, and leg and arm pain. Tolerance and psychological dependence can develop when used regularly. Using methaqualone with alcohol is known as "luding out" and can cause death.

Tranquilizers

Tranquilizers are used medically to treat anxiety, insomnia, and convulsions. It is very easy to become both physically and psychologically dependent on them. When mixed with alcohol, they can cause death.

Narcotics

Most narcotics are opiates, which come from the seed pods of opium poppies. Many are used medically to relieve pain and treat insomnia. Narcotics abuse initially produces a feeling of euphoria that is often followed by drowsiness, nausea, and vomiting. Users also may experience constricted pupils, watery eyes, and itching. An overdose may produce slow and shallow breathing, clammy skin, convulsions, coma, and death. Tolerance develops rapidly and dependence is likely. The use of contaminated syringes to inject certain kinds of narcotics may result in diseases such as AIDS and hepatitis. Narcotics include opium, codeine, morphine, and heroin. Other types of opiates include Percocet, Percodan, Tussionex, Fentanyl, Darvon, Talwin, and Lomotil and come as tablets, capsules, or liquids.

Opium

Opium (Paregoric, Dover's Powder, Parepectolin) can look like dark brown chunks or a powder. It comes from a specific type of poppy, generally grown in the Middle East. Opium is one of the weaker narcotics, but it has side effects that make it undesirable as a medication, including slowed heart rate, breathing, and mental abilities, and loss of appetite.

Codeine

Codeine comes in different drugs such as Empirin, Tylenol, and certain cough medicines. It is either a dark liquid varying in thickness or comes in capsules or tablets. Similar to opium, codeine is one of the weakest narcotics. Doctors prescribe it for coughs and pain relief.

Morphine

Morphine (Pectoral Syrup) is an opium derivative, and comes in the form of white crystals, hypodermic tablets, and injectable solutions. Morphine is a very strong painkiller, but because it is also very addictive, it is used in medicine only for severe cases, such as in the later stages of terminal cancer when patients are in extreme pain. Unfortunately, as a drug of abuse, morphine usually results in addiction. Withdrawal from it has painful and severe effects, and getting an addict off the drug generally requires the help of a professional.

Heroin and Methadone

Heroin (Smack, Horse, Junk, Harry, H, Brown, Black Tar, Antifreeze) looks like a white to dark brown powder or a tar-like substance. Methadone Hydrochloride (Dolophine, Methadose, Methadone) comes in the form of a solution.

Heroin is a concentrated form of morphine and is so addictive that it is illegal in the United States even for medical use. Unfortunately, it is the most abused narcotic in this country, and its use is on the rise as of the late 1990s. Users of heroin often start by sniffing or smoking the drug in powdered form. Because tolerance develops quickly, they often turn to "mainlining," the practice of injecting a heroin solution into their veins to intensify the drug's effects.

Heroin dulls the senses, easing tensions, fears, and worries. A stupor follows that lasts for several hours in which hunger and thirst are reduced. After 12 to 16 hours without heroin, the user will experience severe withdrawal symptoms, including sweating, shaking, chills, nausea, diarrhea, abdominal pain, leg cramps, and severe mental and emotional pain. To relieve these symptoms, the user must take another dose of the drug. People addicted to heroin often die young, some from overdoses caused by unreliable drugs, others because they cannot distinguish between safe and dangerous doses.

Signs of an overdose include shallow and slow breathing, clammy skin, and convulsions. An overdose can result in coma and death. When addicted, a person must have more of the drug to keep from experiencing withdrawal symptoms, which are severe and can include panic, shaking, chills, sweating, cramps, and nausea.

Hallucinogens

Hallucinogens alter the physical senses, producing visions, sounds, and smells that are not real, and distorting the concepts of time and space in the user's mind. Because these drugs confuse fact and fantasy, a user may become irrational and resort to violence or suicide to avoid an imagined situation or attacker. Hallucinogens are not physically addictive, but users often become psychologically dependent on these drugs.

Lysergic Acid Diethylamide (Acid)

Lysergic acid diethylamide (LSD, Acid, White Lightning, Blue Heaven, Sugar Cubes, Microdot, Twenty-Five, Sid, Bart Simpsons, Barrels, Tabs, Blotter, L, Liquid, Liquid A, Microdots, Mind Detergent, Orange Cubes, Hits, Paper Acid, Sugar, Sunshine, Ticket, Wedding Bells, and Windowpane) can come as brightly colored tablets, imprinted blotter paper, thin squares of gelatin, or as a clear liquid.

A "trip" from an average dose of LSD can last as long as eight to 10 hours. LSD's effects are unpredictable, tolerance to it develops quickly, and its use frequently results in psychological dependence.

LSD is a powerful hallucinogen that scrambles and confuses the senses. A tiny drop taken with sugar or food can cause a person to trip or experience false visions, smells, and sounds for hours. Sensations may be confused and feelings may change rapidly. Music may appear as colors and colors as flavors or odors. Some people say these experiences are exciting; others say they are nightmares. Those having a bad trip may take dangerous or irrational actions to escape from this imaginary situation. In addition to these affects, LSD can cause nausea, vomiting, and misinterpretations of time and distance. Some people experience flashbacks of LSD's effects days, weeks, and years after the original trip. An overdose of LSD can result in psychosis, accidental death, and suicide.

Phencyclidine Hydrochloride

Phencyclidine hydrochloride (PCP, Angel Dust, Hog, Superjoint, Busy Bee, Green Tea Leaves, DOA [dead on arrival]) can be in the form of a liquid, capsules, white crystalline powder, or pills. Of the various types of hallucinogens, only PCP has a medical use as a tranquilizer for animals.

PCP interrupts the functions of the neocortex, which is the section of the brain that controls the intellect and keeps instincts in check. The effects of PCP are unpredictable, but users frequently report a sense of distance and alienation from the world and others. Sometimes a user may feel drunk, but at other times the same dose may cause depression, paranoia, hallucinations, and suicidal thoughts. Time and movement are slowed down; muscular coordination worsens; senses are dulled; and speech is blocked and incoherent.

PCP stays in the system for a long time. Chronic users report persistent memory problems and speech difficulties as well as psychological and behavioral changes. Some of these effects may last six months to a year following prolonged daily use. Mood disorders such as depression and anxiety also occur, and users may exhibit paranoid and violent behavior. In fact, many deaths attributed to PCP do not occur from the drug itself, but from accidents, like falling from high places, drowning, or car wrecks, which are related to the behavior PCP produces. Large doses of PCP can cause convulsions and coma, heart and lung failure, or ruptured blood vessels in the brain. Treatment for an overdose is very difficult and requires hospitalization.

PCP, used as a tranquilizer for animals, can cause frightening hallucinations when used by humans. Abuse can result in seizures, coma, and death or in violent, unpredictable behavior. Some abusers have committed murder and suicide.

Psilocybin (Mushrooms, Shrooms) and Mescaline (Mesc, Buttons, Cactus)

Two other hallucinogens are psilocybin, produced from a type of mushroom, and mescaline, produced from a type of cactus. Similar to other hallucinogens, use of these drugs can cause hallucinations, perception problems, nausea, vomiting, and, in extreme cases, mental illness, suicide, or accidental death. Mescaline effects, while compared to a mild LSD trip, are often accompanied by sweating and severe abdominal cramps. Eating mushrooms poses another danger because many mushrooms look alike and some are poisonous enough to cause death.

Inhalants (Air Blast)

Inhalants are toxic chemicals like glue, freon, nail polish, spray paint, and gasoline that are huffed (sprayed into a cloth and held over the mouth and nose) or bagged (sniffed from a bag, bottle, or can) to achieve a brief, mild euphoria. All of these products contain labels warning against inhaling their fumes because of the hazards involved. Some inhalants used medically are also abused, such as amyl nitrate, which relieves heart pain, and nitrous oxide, which relieves anxiety.

> **Key Term**
>
> **inhalants—** *medications or chemicals that are inhaled*

Risks involved with inhaling these chemicals include nausea; dizziness; vomiting; headaches; unconsciousness; pneumonia; permanent brain and nerve damage; bleeding of the brain; eventual liver, brain, and kidney cancer; and death due to heart failure and suffocation. Effects of inhalants are unpredictable and depend on what chemical or chemicals are inhaled and how much. Brain damage and death may result after only one use depending on the inhalants involved.

Ecstasy (XTC, Love Drug)

Ecstasy (MBDB, MDE, MDEA, and 2CB) is a "designer drug" that closely resembles cocaine. It produces euphoria that lasts several hours, heightens pleasure, and may even produce hallucinations in high doses. Ecstasy is taken orally and may cause mood swings, overly friendly behavior, insomnia, anxiety, and nausea. In extreme cases, abuse may result in seizure and death.

Rohypnol (Roofies, Forget Pill, Date-Rape Pill)

Rohypnol (GHB; includes G, Liquid Ecstacy, Somatomax, Scoop, Georgia Home Boy, and Grievous Bodily Harm) is used legally as a medical sedative in Europe and Latin America. As a drug of abuse, it is called roofies, the forget pill, and the date-rape pill. At first, it produces an alcoholic type of high, but then heavy sedation and short-term memory loss that lasts up to eight hours. It earned its reputation as the date-rape pill by being slipped into the drinks of females, who were taken advantage of in a state of sedation brought on by the drug and then unable to remember exactly what happened to them. In addition to the drawback just discussed, dangers of abusing rohypnol include impaired motor skills and slow respiration.

Steroids

Although anabolic steroids are available only by prescription in the United States, many steroid supplements are available over the counter and are marketed under several names. Steroids and steroid supplements are often taken to increase performance in sports. Some people take them to develop muscles. Abusers of steroids take many times the recommended dosages in an effort to bulk up. Steroid abuse has been increasing in recent years, especially among middle-school students. Steroid use has been associated with chemical dependence and withdrawal syndrome. Athletes who turn to steroids risk withdrawal syndrome and permanent damage to their bodies.*

Tobacco

Many people hold the view that experimentation with or use of tobacco is normal or acceptable behavior. However, the use of tobacco often progresses to further drug abuses. Accordingly, some experts attach the term *gateway* to this substance. Use of drugs such as cocaine and heroin is unusual in those who have not previously used tobacco.

The hazards of tobacco include cancer and other diseases; it can also have ill effects on others. As awareness of these ill effects reaches new heights, more and more Americans are joining forces to fight tobacco abuse every day.

In addition to smoking cigarettes, pipes, or cigars, people who use tobacco products can also do so orally in the forms of chewing tobacco (by placing a wad between the cheek and teeth and sucking on it) and snuff (by placing a pinch between the lower lip and teeth).

*Adapted from *TeenGetGoing* website, www.teengetgoing.com/Drug/Sdrugs.asp, accessed January 5, 2005.

Three major components make up tobacco, each having their own ill effects. One such component, tar, causes a variety of cancers and contributes to emphysema and other respiratory problems. For this reason, people often choose to smoke low-tar cigarettes, but even low-tar cigarettes can be unsafe because smokers often smoke more while using these brands. Carbon monoxide, also found in tobacco, restricts the oxygen-carrying capacity of the blood, and can often cause insufficient heart operation. Nicotine, the substance in tobacco believed to cause dependency, is absorbed into the bloodstream, reaching the heart and brain within a few seconds of the onset of smoking.

Key Term

nicotine—
the drug in tobacco that may act as a stimulant and cause addiction

Note:

Nicotine in its pure state is a toxic poison and is also used in insecticides.

Some of the diseases associated with long-term tobacco smoking include chronic bronchitis, emphysema, coronary heart disease, and lung cancer. Lung cancer is the leading cause of death among women today. Cigarette smoking is a major independent risk factor for heart attacks (sometimes fatal) in both men and women. Pipe and cigar smokers are more prone to dying from cancer of the mouth and throat than nonsmokers. Smoking also reduces the effectiveness of prescription and over-the-counter medications.

Note:

Infections, especially pneumonia and acute bronchitis, are twice as common in young children whose parents smoke than in children with nonsmoking parents.

Although chewing tobacco and snuff are not smoked, they increase the risk of disease and damage to the delicate lining of the mouth and throat. As a result, individuals who use these products are more likely than nonusers to develop mouth cancer, throat cancer, and gum disease. Chewing tobacco and snuff can also contribute to heart disease and strokes. The harmful effects of one can of snuff are equal to that of about 60 cigarettes.

Despite the labels required by federal law warning individuals about the hazardous effects of using tobacco products, use continues.

Recent research has indicated that nonsmokers who breathe in second-hand smoke (smoke that escapes from the burning end of a cigarette as well as the smoke exhaled by the smoker) can have an increased risk of lung cancer, heart disease, and respiratory disorders. Inhaling second-hand smoke makes the heart beat faster, the blood pressure go up, and the level of carbon monoxide in the blood increase. Smoke from an idling cigarette contains even more tar and nicotine than an inhaled one, in addition to more cadmium, a substance which has been related to hypertension, chronic bronchitis, and emphysema.

As the public becomes more aware of the dangers of inhaling second-hand smoke, the legislation protecting the rights of nonsmokers continues to increase. Smoking is increasingly being banned in both public and private places.

The Chemicals in Tobacco Smoke

With each puff on a cigarette, cigar, or pipe, a smoker inhales over 4,000 different chemicals. Of these 4,000 chemicals, at least 1,000 are known to be dangerous. Table 9.1 lists some of the harmful chemicals found in cigarette smoke. Among all the dangerous substances, nicotine, tar, and carbon monoxide can be identified as the most deadly ones found in tobacco smoke.

Nicotine and Addiction

The drug in tobacco that may act as a stimulant and cause addiction is nicotine. A stimulant is a drug that speeds up the activities of the central nervous system, the heart, and other organs. In its pure form, nicotine is one of the strongest poisons known. Taken in large amounts, nicotine can kill people by paralyzing their breathing muscles. Smokers usually take in small amounts of nicotine. However, over several years the effects of much smaller amounts on the body are numerous and severe.

Table 9.1	HARMFUL CHEMICALS IN TOBACCO SMOKE	
acetaldehyde	butylamine	methyl alcohol
acetone	carbon monoxide	methylamine
acetonitrile	dimethylamine	methylfuran
acrolein	dimethyl-nitrosamine	methylnaphthalene
acrylonitrile	ethylamine	nicotine
ammonia	formaldehyde	nitric oxide
aniline	hydrocyanic acid	nitrogen dioxide
benzene	hydrogen cyanide	phenol
benzopyrene	hydrogen sulfide	pyridine
2,3-butadione	methacrolein	toluene

Central Nervous System

- Changes brain-wave patterns

Respiratory System

- Allows harmful gases and particles to settle in air passages
- Causes hacking cough
- Causes shortness of breath

Other Effects

- Decreases release of fluid from pancreas
- Increases levels of sugar, lactic acid, and fat-derived substances in blood

Cardiovascular System

- Increases heart rate
- Increases blood pressure
- Increases volume of blood pumped per beat
- Increases force of heart contractions
- Increases coronary blood flow
- Increases blood flow to skeletal muscles
- Narrows blood vessels in skin
- Narrows veins

Peripheral Nervous System

- Activates sympathetic nervous system
- Decreases response level of some reflexes

Endocrine System

- Stimulates release of several hormones from adrenal glands
- Decreases levels of hormone involved in preventing blood clotting

Figure 9.3   Nicotine and cigarettes affect many body systems.
Courtesy of Fran Milner

When tobacco is smoked, nicotine enters the lungs, where it is immediately absorbed into the bloodstream. Seconds later, the nicotine reaches the brain. Chemical changes begin to take place. Nicotine causes the heart to beat faster, the skin temperature to drop, and the blood pressure to rise. Nicotine constricts blood vessels, which cuts down on the blood flow to hands and feet. Beginning smokers usually feel the effects of nicotine poisoning with their first inhalation. These effects include rapid pulse, clammy skin, nausea, dizziness, and tingling in the hands and feet. Nicotine and cigarettes have many adverse effects on the body, as shown in Figure 9.3.

The degree of reaction varies from person to person, depending on the person's tolerance to nicotine. The effects of nicotine poisoning stop as soon as tolerance to nicotine develops. Tolerance can develop in new smokers after the second or third cigarette. The smoker begins to experience a "lift," a physical reaction to the chemicals in nicotine. As tolerance builds, however, the user may need more and more tobacco to produce the same feeling. The Surgeon General, the country's highest medical authority, has called nicotine an addicting drug, just like heroin and cocaine.

In a short time, tobacco users develop an addiction to nicotine. A tobacco addict who goes without tobacco for a short time may experience nicotine withdrawal. Nicotine withdrawal is a reaction to the lack of nicotine in the body, which causes symptoms such as headache, irritability, restlessness, increased coughing, nausea, vomiting, a general feeling of illness, and intense cravings for tobacco. Withdrawal effects may begin as soon as two hours after the last cigarette. Physical craving for a cigarette reaches a peak in the first 24 hours.

UNIT V

Tobacco users also suffer psychological withdrawal symptoms when they stop smoking. They feel emotionally and mentally uncomfortable without tobacco. By using tobacco at certain times—when under stress, for example—tobacco users actually condition themselves to rely on tobacco whenever a stressful situation arises. When tobacco users go without tobacco, they may feel unable to handle stress. Many tobacco users begin to depend on tobacco at particular times of the day, such as when they awaken or after they finish a meal. Others begin to depend on tobacco in social or work situations, such as parties or meetings.

Tar

The dark, sticky mixture of chemicals that is formed when tobacco burns is known as tar. Smokers can see evidence of this substance on their fingers and teeth, which turn brown when tar sticks to them. The tar also sticks to the cells of the respiratory system, where it damages the delicate cells that line the respiratory tract. The cells have tiny hair-like structures, or cilia. The cilia beat back and forth and sweep dust and other foreign particles away from the lungs. If the cilia are damaged, foreign particles can enter the lungs, leading to disease.

The tar in tobacco smoke contains hundreds of chemical carcinogens, or cancer-causing agents. Cancer of the lungs, throat, and mouth are caused by the inhalation of tar in tobacco smoke.

Carbon Monoxide

Carbon monoxide is a poisonous, colorless, odorless gas that is found in cigarette smoke. You may be familiar with the dangers of carbon monoxide. Deaths that result from leaving a car engine running in a closed area are caused by carbon monoxide poisoning.

Carbon monoxide has a greater attraction for the oxygen-carrying molecules (hemoglobin) in the red blood cells than oxygen does. When carbon monoxide is inhaled, it takes the place of, or displaces, large amounts of oxygen from hemoglobin. The more carbon monoxide present in the blood, the less oxygen in the blood. Carbon monoxide also makes it hard for the oxygen that is left in the blood to get to the muscles and organs. When a person smokes, the heart works harder but accomplishes less. Because their blood contains too little oxygen to function properly, smokers often experience shortness of breath when they are active.

Chemicals in Smokeless Tobacco

Most tobacco users smoke cigarettes, cigars, or pipes. And yet there has been an increase, especially among teenage boys, in the use of smokeless tobacco. Smokeless tobacco is tobacco that is chewed or sniffed through the nose. Some people who use smokeless tobacco think that the products are safe because no smoke is produced or inhaled. What they may not realize is that smokeless tobacco contains many of the same harmful chemicals found in tobacco smoke, including the highly addictive drug nicotine.

There are two different kinds of smokeless tobacco products. Chewing tobacco is poor-quality tobacco leaves mixed with molasses or honey and placed between the cheek and gums. Snuff is finely ground tobacco that may be held between the lower lip and teeth or sniffed through the nose. One can of snuff delivers as much nicotine as 60 cigarettes. The nicotine in chewing tobacco enters the bloodstream through the membranes of the mouth. The nicotine in snuff gets into the body through the membranes of either the mouth or the nose. After it has entered the body, nicotine from smokeless tobacco has the same effects as nicotine from cigarettes.

Conclusion

When drugs are properly used, they can cure illness and save lives. When abused, however, drugs and alcohol can destroy lives and cause death. It is important to understand that, although people often abuse drugs and alcohol to find happiness and fulfillment, these substances only create more problems and unhappiness. To keep from falling into the trap of drug and alcohol abuse, stay smart, strong, and active. Say no. Recognize the different drugs that are abused in our society and what affect they have on people's health and lives. Understand the dangers of alcohol abuse, not only to the drinker but to family and friends. You can set an example of an informed, drug-free individual.

Review Questions

1 What is the difference between drug use, misuse, and abuse?

2 List three risks associated with the use of alcohol.

3 Is there any "safe" cigarette? Why or why not?

4 Define the term *gateway*.

First Aid for Emergency and Nonemergency Situations

- first aid
- Good Samaritan Law
- evaluate
- consent
- Heimlich maneuver
- rescue breathing
- cardiopulmonary resuscitation (CPR)
- cardiac arrest
- stroke
- automated external defibrillator (AED)
- arteries
- veins
- hemorrhage
- dressing
- pressure bandage

What You Will Learn to Do

Determine first aid procedures and apply them as needed

Skills and Knowledge You Will Gain Along the Way

✔ Assess first aid situations

✔ Demonstrate life-saving skills in emergencies

✔ Determine first aid procedures for a bleeding victim

✔ Give first aid treatment for shock, fractures, strains, and sprains

✔ Give first aid treatment for burns, wounds, bruises, and poisoning

✔ Give first aid treatment for heat- and cold-related injuries

✔ Give first aid treatment for bites, stings, and poisonous hazards

Courtesy of US Navy/Mass Communication Specialist 1st Class Carmichael Yepez

Introduction

Most people encounter at least one situation requiring the use of first aid at some time in their lives. Whether a friend falls when rollerblading and breaks an arm or your younger brother cuts himself on broken glass and requires stitches, someone should administer first aid until the injured person receives proper medical attention. That someone can be you if you acquire basic first aid knowledge of what to do and what not to do in different accident situations. Remember that first aid may mean the difference between life and death, permanent and temporary disability, or long- and short-term recovery for an accident victim.

In addition to the first aid taught in this chapter, consider taking a first aid class from a qualified instructor. Many schools, hospitals, and fire departments offer first aid classes that provide demonstrations and hands-on experience with medical models of victims. Hands-on training is especially important before actually performing mouth-to-mouth resuscitation and *cardiopulmonary resuscitation* (CPR), both of which can be hazardous to a victim if performed improperly.

- pressure point
- trauma
- clammy
- closed (simple) fracture
- open (compound) fracture
- splint
- dislocation
- sprain
- ligament
- strain
- mottled
- compresses
- caustic
- acids
- bases
- alkalis
- systemic
- neutralize
- solvents
- abrasion
- incision
- laceration
- amputation
- avulsion
- dehydration
- ventilation
- heat cramps
- heat exhaustion
- heatstroke
- frostbite
- hypothermia
- superficial
- subcutaneous
- insulate
- venom
- tetanus (lockjaw)
- antivenin
- rabies
- allergic reaction

The Need for First Aid/Your Response

Definition of First Aid

First aid is the immediate care given to an injured or ill individual to keep him or her alive or stop further damage until qualified medical treatment can be administered. It is caring for people involved in accidents, catastrophes, and natural disasters such as hurricanes, tornadoes, and earthquakes. First aid includes dealing with the situation, the person, and the injury, as well as encouraging the victim and showing a willingness to help.

Good Samaritan Law

The Good Samaritan Law is designed to protect the rescuer and encourage people to assist others in distress by granting the rescuer immunity against lawsuits. This law protects people from lawsuits as long as the rescuer is acting in good faith, without compensation and administers first aid correctly and without malicious misconduct or gross negligence.

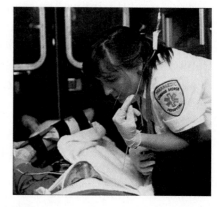

EMTs are protected from litigation under the Good Smaritan Law.
Courtesy of Dorothy Littell/Stock Boston

First Aid Kit

Administering first aid is easier with a first aid kit. It is a good idea to keep one in your house and car and take one along on camping trips and hikes. A well-stocked first aid kit contains an assortment of bandages, Band-Aids, tape, aspirin or aspirin substitutes, antiseptic cream and cleanser, safety pins, scissors, tweezers, cotton, and tissues. To protect against infectious diseases, include rubber gloves and face shields in the kit. Rubber gloves will keep you from coming into contact with blood and body fluids, and face shields will allow you to give mouth-to-mouth resuscitation and CPR without direct contact.

Evaluating the Victim

When you encounter an injured person, you must evaluate that person to determine what kind of first aid, if any, is needed. This preliminary check of the person follows a series of steps designed to pinpoint and correct the most serious health risks first and then continue with less life-threatening problems. These steps are explained in more detail later in this lesson. Basically, check for breathing and heartbeat first; severe bleeding second; signs of shock third; and finally for broken bones, burns, and head injuries. Depending on what problems your evaluation of an accident victim reveals, perform the life-saving steps in a sequence that parallels this evaluation sequence:

1. Open the airway
2. Assess breathing
3. Assess circulation
4. Assess disability.

When evaluating a conscious victim, ask the victim if you can help and get consent to provide first aid; then get as much information as possible about the situation and how the victim feels. If the victim is unconscious and others witnessed the accident, get as much information from the witnesses as possible. Check the victim for medical alert identification. Many people with heart disease, epilepsy, diabetes, and allergies to medications wear medical alert identification bracelets or necklaces that can give you a clue as to their medical condition.

Have someone at the scene dial 911 for emergency medical services (EMS). If you are alone and the victim's condition is life-threatening, give first aid first, and then call 911. When calling 911, calmly state your name and exact location, the telephone number from which you are calling, details of what has happened, and the condition of the victim or victims. A dispatcher will route your call to the appropriate service—either the EMS, police department, fire department, or a combination of these services.

Other important rules to follow at the scene of an accident include the following:

- Remain calm but act quickly. This will reassure the victim and help him or her to remain calm as well.

- Do not move an injured person. If the person has a neck or spine injury or broken bones, moving him or her could worsen the condition. Only move a victim if there is potential danger in remaining at the accident location. If you must move the victim for this reason, pull him or her in a straight line from the shoulders, keeping the head and body in line. Support the head and pull the victim as short a distance as possible.

- If there is more than one injured person at an accident scene, evaluate them quickly; then help the most seriously injured first. For example, help the person with severe bleeding before you help the person with a broken arm.

Key Term

consent—
approval for what is to be done or proposed by another

Dispatchers answer 911 calls and route them to the proper response service.
Courtesy of Frank Siteman/ Rainbow

UNIT V

The Life-Saving Steps

The following steps identify evaluation procedures and specify treatment if necessary.

1. **Check to see if the victim is conscious.**
   a. Ask in a loud but calm voice, "Are you okay?"
   b. Gently shake or tap the victim on the shoulder.
   c. Watch for response. If the victim does not respond, go to Step 2.
   d. If the victim is conscious, ask where he or she feels different than usual or where it hurts. Go to Step 3.
   e. If the victim is conscious but is choking and cannot talk, stop the evaluation and begin treatment for clearing the airway of a conscious victim.

2. **Check for breathing and heartbeat.**
   a. Look for rise and fall of the victim's chest.
   b. Listen for breathing by placing your ear about one inch from the victim's mouth and nose.
   c. Feel for breathing by placing your hand or cheek about one inch from the victim's mouth and nose.
   d. At the same time, check for a pulse in the victim's neck.
   e. If there is a pulse but no breathing, stop the evaluation and begin treatment to restore the breathing.
   f. If there is no pulse, stop the evaluation and begin CPR.

3. **Check for bleeding.**
   a. Look for spurts of blood and blood-soaked clothing.
   b. Look for entry and exit wounds.
   c. If bleeding is present, stop the evaluation and begin treatment for stopping the bleeding.

4. **Check for the following signs of shock:**
   a. Sweaty, but cool skin
   b. Paleness
   c. Restlessness or nervousness
   d. Thirst
   e. Loss of blood
   f. Confusion
   g. Faster than normal breathing rate
   h. Blotchy or bluish skin
   i. Vomiting or nausea.

If any of these signs are present, discontinue the evaluation and treat for shock.

5. **Check for fractures (broken bones).**

   a. Check for the following signs of neck or back injury:

     • Pain or tenderness of neck or back area

     • Wounds of neck or back area

     • Paralysis.

   b. Ask the victim if he or she can move.

   c. Touch the victim's arms and legs and ask whether he or she can feel it.

   d. If you suspect a neck or back injury, immobilize the victim by doing the following:

     • Tell the victim not to move.

     • If you suspect a back injury, place padding under the natural arch of the lower back.

     • If you suspect a neck injury, place padding under the victim's neck and place objects such as rocks or shoes on both sides of the head.

   e. Check the victim's arms or legs for fractures or broken bones. Signs are as follows:

     • Swelling

     • Discoloration

     • Unusual angle or position of arm or leg

     • Bones sticking through the skin.

If you suspect a fracture, stop the evaluation and begin treatment for fractures.

6. **Check for burns. If you find burns, cover them with a clean dry cloth.**

7. **Check for head injury. Some possible signs of head injury are as follows:**

   a. Pupils of eyes unequal size

   b. Fluid from ear(s), nose, or mouth, or wounds to the head or face

   c. Slurred speech

   d. Confusion

   e. Sleepiness

   f. Loss of memory or consciousness

   g. Staggering when walking

   h. Headache

   i. Dizziness

   j. Vomiting

   k. Paralysis

   l. Convulsion or twitching.

Emergency personnel are trained to help victims of all types of injuries.
Courtesy of Spencer Grant/ Photo Researchers

When first aid is administered correctly and in a timely manner, it could mean the difference between life and death for the victim. The photo on this page shows emergency medical personnel assisting with an injured person.

If a head injury is suspected, keep the person awake. Watch the victim for signs that would require restoring breathing or treating for shock.

Call the Emergency Number

Call or send someone to call for an ambulance. Calling your emergency number is often the most important thing you can do in an emergency. It is often critical to get professional medical help on the scene as soon as possible. In many communities, you can dial 911 for help in any type of emergency; otherwise, dial your local police or sheriff for medical emergencies, or dial 0, the operator, for assistance. Be prepared to follow these steps:

1. Speak slowly and clearly.

2. Identify yourself and the phone number from which you are calling.

3. Give the exact location of the accident. Give the town, street name, and number. If you are calling at night, describe the building.

4. Describe what has happened. Give essential details about the victim(s), the situation, and any treatments you have given.

5. Ask for advice. Let the person on the other end ask you questions and tell you what to do until help arrives. Take notes, if necessary.

6. Don't hang up first. The person on the other end may have more questions or advice for you. And they might want you to stay on the phone with them until help arrives. Whatever the case, let the other person hang up first.

When to Call 911 or Your Local Emergency Number

Call for an ambulance if the victim:

- Is or becomes unconscious
- Has trouble breathing
- Has persistent chest pain or pressure
- Is bleeding severely
- Has persistent pain or pressure in the abdomen
- Is vomiting
- Has seizures, slurred speech, or persistent severe headache
- Appears to have been poisoned
- Has injuries to the head, neck, or back
- Has possible broken bones.

Also call if there is:

- A fire or explosion
- A downed electrical wire
- Swiftly moving or rapidly rising water
- Poisonous gas present
- A vehicle collision.

The First Life-Saving Steps

In emergency situations, the people involved may find it difficult to remain calm and think clearly. In the midst of this confusion, one simple trick you can use to remind yourself of the first and most important problems to check for and steps to take are the letters ABC.

- **A** stands for airway. Is the victim's airway blocked? If so, clear the airway.
- **B** stands for breathing. Is the victim breathing? If not, restore breathing.
- **C** stands for circulation. Is the victim's heart beating? If not, restore the heartbeat.

Clearing the Airway of a Conscious Victim

Choking occurs when a person inhales something into the airway leading to the lungs, blocking the airway off and preventing breathing. In many choking cases, people inhale particles of food while eating. In an accident, injured people may choke on dirt, broken teeth, or dentures.

Heimlich maneuver—
an upward push to the abdomen given to clear the airway of a person with a complete airway obstruction; procedure used to expel an object lodged in the airway of a choking victim

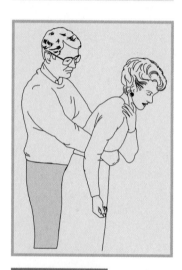

Figure 10.1

The Heimlich maneuver can save the life of a choking victim.

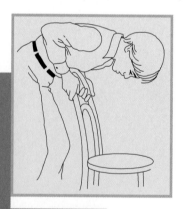

Figure 10.2

You can save your life when choking if you know how to dislodge the obstruction.

A person whose airway is completely blocked off cannot make any sound because no air is getting to the vocal cords. If a person can speak or cough, some air is getting through to the vocal cords and lungs, and you should let the person try to clear the airway on his or her own. If the person can make no sound and indicates choking by grabbing the throat, the best method to clear the person's airway is the Heimlich maneuver, shown in Figure 10.1. After performing the Heimlich maneuver, be sure the victim seeks professional medical help.

To perform the Heimlich maneuver on a choking victim, follow these steps:

1. Stand behind the victim and wrap your arms around the victim's waist.

2. Make a fist with one hand and place the thumb side of the fist against the victim's abdomen slightly above the navel and well below the breastbone. Grasp the fist with the other hand.

3. Give six to ten quick backward and upward thrusts; repeat this until the airway is clear.

For an exceptionally overweight person or pregnant woman, use the same procedure, except place the fist in the middle of the breastbone.

If you are the victim of an airway obstruction and no one is around to help, lean forward over a railing, sink, or the back of a chair, as shown in Figure 10.2, and thrust yourself down until you dislodge the obstruction.

Note:

Don't slap the victim's back. This could make matters worse. For more information about the Heimlich maneuver, check out http://www.heimlichinstitute.org/howtodo.html.

Clearing the Airway of an Unconscious Victim

If a person is unconscious and you know that individual has an obstructed airway, perform the following maneuver with the victim lying on his or her back. Figure 10.3 shows the position for this action.

1. Kneel astride the victim's thighs. Place the heel of one hand against the victim's abdomen, slightly above the navel, but well below the victim's breastbone, with your fingers pointing toward the victim's head.

2. Place your other hand on top of your first hand and press into the abdomen with a quick forward and upward thrust. Repeat this six to 10 times.

3. Open the victim's mouth and sweep out any foreign matter using a hooked finger. Be careful not to push anything down the throat.

For an obese individual or a woman in the advanced stages of pregnancy, use the following procedure:

1. Kneel to the side of the victim's body. Locate the lower edge of the victim's ribs and run the fingers up along the rib cage to the notch where the ribs meet the breastbone.

2. Place the heel of the hand two finger widths above the notch and place the other hand over the first, interlocking the fingers.

3. Position your shoulders over your hands and, with the elbows locked, press down 1 1/2 to 2 inches, 6 to 10 times.

4. Open the victim's mouth and sweep out any foreign matter using a hooked finger. Be careful not to push anything down the throat.

Restoring the Breathing

If you discover a victim who is not breathing, it is necessary to start breathing for the victim by forcing oxygen into his or her lungs as soon as possible. This process, called rescue breathing or mouth-to-mouth resuscitation, can prevent brain damage and death. Applying this first aid step will most likely start the victim breathing independently; if not, continue it until you are replaced by a qualified person or medical help arrives. When you are giving mouth-to-mouth resuscitation to a victim, you are a life-support system! Figure 10.4 shows the basic position for applying mouth-to-mouth resuscitation.

The following steps describe how to give mouth-to-mouth resuscitation to adults. Procedures that are different for infants and small children are italicized.

1. Roll the victim gently over if he or she is not already facing up. Open the mouth and check to see if it is clear. Using a hooked finger, sweep out anything you find in the mouth, being careful not to push anything down the throat.

2. Tilt the victim's head back sharply by pressing down on the forehead and lifting on the jaw. This straightens out the passageway to the victim's lungs. *For infants and small children, do not tilt the head back. Instead, place a finger under the chin and lift it slightly.*

3. Keeping the victim's head tilted sharply back, pinch the nose closed, cover the victim's mouth completely with your mouth, and give the victim two full breaths, as shown in Figure 10.5. *For infants and small children, do not pinch the nose closed. Instead, cover both the mouth and nose with your mouth and give small, slow, gentle breaths.* Each breath should last 1 to 1 1/2 seconds. Pause between breaths to let the air come out of the victim and to breathe in yourself. If the victim's chest does not rise when you breathe into his or her lungs, reposition the head slightly farther back and repeat the breaths. If the victim's chest still does not rise, perform abdominal thrusts to clear the airway as described in the previous section, "Clearing the Airway of an Unconscious Victim"; then repeat the breaths.

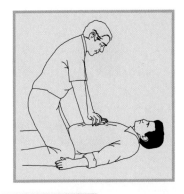

Figure 10.3

Kneel over an unconscious victim to clear the airway.

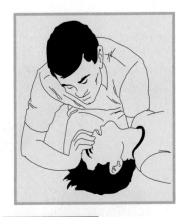

Figure 10.4

Tilt the victim's head and pinch the nose to perform rescue breathing.

Key Term

rescue breathing— *the act of forcing air into and out of the lungs of a person by another person*

UNIT V

Figure 10.5

Cover the victim's mouth completely with your mouth and give the victim two full breaths.

Figure 10.6

After two breaths, check for a pulse as you check for breath sounds.

Key Term

cardiopulmonary resuscitation (CPR)— *an emergency method to keep blood and oxygen flowing through a person whose heart and breathing have stopped*

4. After the two breaths, listen and feel for breathing by placing your cheek close to the victim's mouth. At the same time, check the victim's pulse by placing two fingers in the groove of the neck next to the Adam's apple, as shown in Figure 10.6. This is the location of the carotid artery, which normally produces a strong pulse.

5. If there is no pulse, start CPR immediately as described in the next section.

6. If there is a pulse but no breathing, continue mouth-to-mouth resuscitation at the rate of one breath every five seconds or 12 times a minute. *For infants and small children, give one slow breath every three seconds.*

7. If the victim starts to breathe, stop mouth-to-mouth resuscitation and let the victim breathe on his or her own. Check for other injuries, treat as required, and observe the victim closely until medical help arrives.

Cardiopulmonary Resuscitation (CPR)

As in mouth-to-mouth resuscitation, when you perform cardiopulmonary resuscitation (CPR), you are a life-support system for the victim. CPR is a first aid procedure performed to restore breathing and heartbeat. It is a combination of mouth-to-mouth resuscitation and a procedure known as closed chest heart massage. Mouth-to-mouth resuscitation supplies oxygen to the lungs, while the closed chest heart massage manually pumps blood through the victim's body, circulating it to the heart and brain. These actions help keep the heart and brain alive until the heartbeat is restored or medical help arrives.

CPR can be performed by a single rescuer or by more than one rescuer because CPR can be tiring and is easier if two rescuers are available. The CPR procedures discussed in this lesson are for a single rescuer. Before beginning CPR, you should turn the victim face up, clear the airway, give two full breaths as described in mouth-to-mouth resuscitation, and check for a pulse. Only proceed if there is no pulse, and therefore, no heartbeat present.

Performing CPR on an Adult

To perform CPR on an adult, follow these steps:

1. With the middle and index fingers of the hand nearest the victim's legs, locate the lower edge of the rib cage on the side of the victim's chest closest to you.

2. Slide your fingers up the edge of the rib cage to the notch at the lower end of the breastbone. Place your middle finger in the notch and the index finger next to it on the lower end of the breastbone.

3. Place the heel of the hand nearest the victim's head on the breastbone next to the index finger of the hand used to find the notch.

4. Place the heel of the hand used to find the notch directly on top of the heel of the other hand. Only let the heel of your hand touch the victim's chest; keep your fingers lifted off of the victim's chest. If you place your hands correctly, they will be positioned slightly above the lowest part of the breastbone, known as the xiphoid process. Avoid pressing on the xiphoid process because it breaks easily.

5. Position your shoulders over your hands, with elbows locked and arms straight.

6. Press down on the breastbone $1\frac{1}{2}$ to 2 inches at a very quick, continuous rate. This squeezes the victim's heart against the spine and forces blood through the body.

7. While compressing, count aloud "one and two and three and four . . ." until you get to 15. It should take you about ten seconds to do 15 compressions. Push down as you say the number and release the pressure as you say "and." Compress up and down smoothly without removing your hands from the chest.

8. After the 15th compression, give the victim two full breaths. Be sure to pinch the nose closed and tilt the victim's head back to straighten the airway. Then return to the chest compression.

9. When you complete four cycles of 15 chest compressions and two breaths, check for a pulse again. If there is no pulse, continue CPR.

Performing CPR on an Infant

Performing CPR on an infant is slightly different than performing it on an adult. Follow these steps:

1. Place your hand closest to the infant's head gently on the infant's forehead and leave it there throughout the procedure.

2. Place the middle and ring fingers of the hand nearest the infant's legs on the infant's breastbone about one finger width below the infant's nipples.

3. Give five compressions with those two fingers at a rapid pace, pushing the chest down about $\frac{1}{2}$ to 1 inch.

4. Follow the five compressions with one breath as described in the italicized text in Step 3 of mouth-to-mouth resuscitation. Rapidly repeat the five compressions and one breath 20 times a minute until breathing and heartbeat resume.

Performing CPR on a Child

To perform CPR on a child, follow these steps:

1. As with an adult, find the notched center of the child's ribcage with the hand closest to the child's legs. Measure two finger widths above the notch using the other hand, and then place the heel of the hand used to find the notch on the child's breastbone above the two fingers.

2. Place the hand that you used to measure two finger widths gently on the child's forehead and leave it there throughout the rest of the procedure.

3. Using the heel of your hand and keeping your fingers off of the child's chest, give five compressions 1 to $1\frac{1}{2}$ inches deep, followed by one breath as described in the italicized text in Step 3 of mouth-to-mouth resuscitation. Repeat this sequence 12 times a minute until breathing and heartbeat resume.

Heart Attacks

A heart attack occurs when the blood supply to part of the heart muscle is severely reduced or stopped. This happens when one of the coronary arteries (the arteries that supply blood to the heart muscle) is blocked by an obstruction or a spasm. Common signs and symptoms of a heart attack include the following:

- Uncomfortable pressure, fullness, squeezing, or pain in the center of the chest that lasts more than a few minutes or that goes away and comes back
- Pain spreading to the shoulders, neck, or arms
- Chest discomfort with lightheadedness, fainting, sweating, nausea, or shortness of breath.

When a person's heart stops beating, the victims is said to be in cardiac arrest. CPR can keep the individual alive. If a person has a heart attack, call emergency medical services (EMS). Monitor the ABCs and give CPR as necessary.

Stroke

A stroke occurs when blood vessels that deliver oxygen-rich blood to the brain rupture or when a blood clot forms and blocks the flow of blood in the brain. Common signs and symptoms of a stroke include the following:

- Paralysis on one side of the body
- Blurred or decreased vision; pupils of unequal size
- Problems speaking, slurred speech
- Difficulty breathing
- Mental confusion
- Dizziness or loss of balance
- Sudden, severe, or unexplained headache
- Loss of consciousness.

If a person has a stroke, call EMS. Lay the victim down on one side and cover with blanket. Monitor the ABCs and give CPR as necessary.

> ### Note:
>
> To learn more about strokes, check out www.strokeassociation.org to see the American Stroke Association website.

Automated External Defibrillators (AED)

Recently there has been a breakthrough in how emergency medical technicians (EMTs) treat victims of sudden cardiac arrest. The automated external defibrillator (AED) is a device that uses a computer chip to analyze the heart rhythm and determines whether a shock is needed. This device allows victims suffering a sudden cardiac arrest a greatly improved chance of survival. Because of the ease of operation, people can be trained in AED use in a few hours, and some say the techniques are easier to learn than CPR. Many AEDs offer voice prompts, which provide operators with clear and concise instructions. Most AEDs have only three buttons: On/Off, Analyze, and Shock. Many airlines have installed AEDs on all their planes, and several cities are locating them in areas where there are large concentrations of people, such as malls, arenas, and stadiums.

Controlling Bleeding

In an accident situation, you may encounter injured persons bleeding from wounds such as scrapes, cuts, or punctures as well as tears or gashes in the skin. The deeper a wound is, the more serious it becomes. Minor wounds to the outer layer of skin do not bleed heavily but still require cleaning to avoid infection. Deeper wounds in which arteries and veins are cut can be life threatening. These kinds of wounds may involve great loss of blood, and blood may often pulse or spurt out of the wound. Severe bleeding, or hemorrhage, can result in shock or death if not treated promptly. It is essential to stop the loss of blood in these cases. If a victim loses too much blood, even CPR will not keep the person alive because there will not be enough blood to deliver oxygen from the lungs to the body.

Types of Bleeding

There are three types of bleeding you may encounter in an emergency situation:

- **Arterial bleeding.** Blood loss from an artery. Characterized by bright red blood that spurts with each heartbeat, arterial blood loss is severe and hard to control. Give it first priority for treatment.
- **Venous bleeding.** Blood loss from a vein. Venous bleeding is characterized by a steady flow of dark blood.
- **Capillary bleeding.** Blood loss from the capillaries (the smallest blood vessels); usually characterized by a slow flow of blood.

First aid treatment in all of these cases includes stopping the flow of blood and preventing infection.

UNIT V

Figure 10.7

Apply direct pressure to the bandage to stop bleeding.

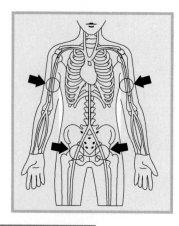

Figure 10.8

Use pressure points on the body to help slow or stop bleeding.

Key Terms

dressing—
ointment and bandages applied to a wound

pressure bandage—
a snug bandage used to control bleeding

pressure point—
a point on the body where a major artery lies near the skin surface and passes over a bone

Direct Pressure

In most cases, applying continuous, direct pressure to a wound is the best way to control bleeding. To apply direct pressure, place a dressing over the wound and apply pressure to the dressing, as shown in Figure 10.7. A dressing should be:

* As sterile as possible (If a sterile dressing is not available, use a clean cloth—a washcloth, towel, or handkerchief)
* Larger than the wound
* Thick, soft, and compressible so pressure is evenly distributed over the wound
* Lint free.

If a clean cloth or gauze is not available, use clothing, your bare hands, or your fingers—whatever is the cleanest. Continue applying pressure and the bleeding should begin to slow or stop within 30 minutes.

Stopping Infection

Even the slightest wound requires immediate cleansing. The best way to clean wounds is to wash them with soap and water. At home, use water from the faucet. On a hike, use water from a canteen or the clear running water of a stream. If available, use an antiseptic cleanser instead of soap. Wait until the skin around the wound dries and then put on a bandage. If available, apply an antiseptic cream to the wound before bandaging it.

For a minor wound, cleaning and bandaging it is probably all that is required. Deep wounds, wounds made by animal or human bites, and wounds contaminated by dirt, rust, or other items require medical treatment. Clean and bandage these wounds, and get medical assistance as soon as possible. If a wound contains glass or other objects stuck into the flesh, do not remove them unless they wash out of the wound easily.

Controlling Bleeding to Extremities

In most cases, direct pressure is the best way to stop bleeding of wounds to the extremities (arms and legs). As you apply direct pressure, keep the injured limb elevated above the heart to slow the flow of blood out of the body. After initially applying direct pressure, you may want to apply a pressure bandage by wrapping a bandage snugly around the limb, using overlapping turns with a roll of gauze. Do not tie the pressure bandage so tightly that it restricts blood flow to the lower part of the limb. If fingertips or toes appear bluish or if there is no pulse below the dressing, loosen the material used to secure the dressing immediately. After you apply a pressure bandage, only qualified medical personnel should remove it.

Pressure Points

In the case of severe bleeding that does not slow or stop using direct pressure, finger pressure may be applied to the pressure point on the injured limb between the wound and the heart. Pressure points, shown in Figure 10.8, are locations on the body where arteries are close to the surface. By applying pressure at these points, you slow or stop the flow of blood through the artery.

As with mouth-to-mouth resuscitation and CPR, it is better to have first aid training on pressure points before actually using this technique to stop bleeding. If done incorrectly, you may damage healthy tissue fed by the artery you are constricting.

Tourniquet

If heavy blood loss continues, as from amputation, it may be necessary to use a tourniquet.

Figure 10.9

Fold a cloth so it is long enough to go around the injured limb.

> **Caution:**
>
> Because a tourniquet is a constricting band that stops the flow of blood below it, it can kill the limb to which it is applied; therefore, only use a tourniquet if no other method works to stop the bleeding and you believe the injured person's life is in danger.

To apply a tourniquet, follow these steps:

1. Fold a cloth until it is approximately two inches wide and long enough to go around the injured limb (see Figure 10.9).

2. Tie the material in a loop and position it two to four inches above the wound, but not over a joint.

3. Pass a rigid object, such as a stick, under the tourniquet loop and twist it until the bleeding stops (see Figure 10.10).

4. Tie off the end of the stick with another piece of cloth or string to prevent it from unwinding (see Figure 10.11).

5. Mark the victim's forehead with a "T" to alert medical personnel that you have applied a tourniquet.

If it is necessary to cover the victim with a blanket, do not cover the tourniquet to make it easier for medical personnel to spot. After you apply a tourniquet, do not loosen or remove it. As with a pressure dressing, only qualified medical personnel should remove a tourniquet.

Figure 10.10

Use a stick or other rigid object to tie off the tourniquet.

> **Note:**
>
> Remember, use a tourniquet only as a last resort when all other attempts to stop the bleeding fail.

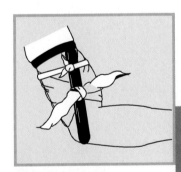

Figure 10.11

Secure the end of the stick to keep the tourniquet from unwinding.

UNIT V

Controlling Bleeding to the Head and Torso

There are different way to control head and torso bleeding. This section details how to use the methods.

Scalp Injuries

For wounds to the scalp, use a pressure dressing. If brain tissue is exposed, tie the dressing loosely over the wound. Do not press the brain tissue back into the open wound.

Facial Injuries

Control bleeding from facial wounds by using a pressure bandage. Position the victim to prevent him or her from breathing blood. Victims who have sustained a severe blow to the head should be kept under close observation as they may have brain damage and could require rescue breathing.

Chest Injuries

A chest injury may result in an open chest wound, which could lead to air leaking from a lung and the collapse of a lung. If conscious, have the victim breathe out and apply some material such as plastic wrap or foil to the wound. Bind a pressure bandage tightly to the wound to prevent leakage of air and slow down blood loss. Have the victim sit up, if possible, or lay that person on the injured side.

Abdominal Injuries

When an open abdominal wound has exposed visceral (internal) organs, cover the abdomen loosely with dressings. Do not force the organs back into the body cavity and do not give victims with abdominal wounds any food or water.

Treating for Shock and Immobilizing Fractures

Whenever you treat someone for a severe injury, you must also treat for shock–even if the injured person shows no signs of it–since shock can follow all major injuries. By treating for shock, you lessen its severity. If left untreated, shock can become life threatening. There are cases of people who died from shock even though their injuries would not have killed them; therefore, knowing how to deal with shock is a very important part of first aid.

After treating for shock, take care of broken bones or suspected broken bones. If there is a question of whether or not a bone is broken, treat it as if it were broken. Follow the first aid procedures for splinting a fracture carefully because more damage can occur if a fracture is handled improperly.

Shock

Shock from an injury is different from electric shock, although it can be brought on by electric shock, as well as blood loss, burns, psychological trauma, heart attack, and other injuries involving pain. Shock disrupts circulation. In an attempt to correct damage from an injury and to protect its blood supply, the body routes blood away from outer tissues to organs inside the body. This may keep adequate blood, and therefore oxygen, from reaching the brain. In severe cases, the injured person can lose consciousness and blood supply to vital organs like the heart, causing death.

Shock usually occurs within the first hour after a severe injury. How severe shock becomes depends upon several factors including the type of injury, how much blood is lost, and characteristics of the injured person's nervous system. Increased pain, rough handling, delayed treatment, and emotional reactions such as fear and panic can worsen shock.

Signs of Shock

When a victim is in shock, the skin is pale or bluish and cold to the touch. For a victim with dark skin, check the color of the mucous membranes on the inside of the mouth or under the eyelids, or check under the nail beds. The skin may be clammy from perspiration. Other signs that may develop in the early stages of shock include the following:

- Restlessness or nervousness
- Thirst
- Bleeding
- Confusion or loss of awareness
- Breathing rapidly
- Nausea and/or vomiting
- Blotchy or bluish skin around the mouth and lips
- Fainting.

Fainting, or blacking out, is a mild form of shock caused by a lack of blood to the brain. Fright, bad news, breathing polluted air, or standing too long can result in fainting. Before fainting occurs, a shock victim may turn pale, shake, or suddenly fall to the ground.

Treating Shock

Procedures for treating shock include improving circulation of the blood, ensuring an adequate supply of oxygen, and maintaining normal body temperature. To treat a victim for shock, follow these steps:

1. Position the victim on his or her back, unless a sitting position allows easier breathing. If the victim is vomiting, position that person on the side to let fluid drain from the mouth.

2. Elevate the victim's feet higher than the heart, unless the victim has an abdominal or chest wound or an unsplinted leg fracture.

Key Term

trauma—
a behavioral state resulting from mental or emotional stress or physical injury that has a lasting effect on the mind; a physical wound or injury

Key Term

clammy—
damp, soft, sticky, and unusually cool

UNIT V

3. Loosen clothing that may bind around the neck and waist.
4. Keep the victim from becoming cold or overheating.
5. Reassure the victim and do not give him or her any food or drink; however, if you know that help is not going to arrive for over an hour, give the victim small amounts of fluids at room temperature every 15 minutes. Add an eighth of a teaspoon of salt, if available, to each half glass of fluid. This will help the victim retain more fluids in his or her system.

Fractures

Bone fractures resulting from falls are common injuries. A closed or simple fracture is a break in the bone that does not penetrate the skin. An open or compound fracture occurs if the sharp edges of a splintered bone have cut through the skin. Both types of fractures are shown in Figure 10.12.

In the case of an open fracture, it is obvious that a bone is broken. In the case of a closed fracture, indications of a broken bone include swelling, discoloration, and unusual positioning of the limb in question.

Do's and Don'ts

When treating fractures, what you do is important, and what you don't do is equally as important.

- **Do** call for medical assistance immediately
- **Do** keep the victim from moving
- **Do** treat for shock while waiting for medical assistance
- **Don't** try to set the bone
- **Don't** put the victim in a car to rush him or her to a hospital as that is the easiest way of turning a closed fracture into an open one
- **Don't** give stimulants if there is severe bleeding.

Splints

The most important action to take when dealing with a fracture is to immobilize the injured bone to prevent further damage. The best way to immobilize bones is with a splint, shown in Figure 10.13.

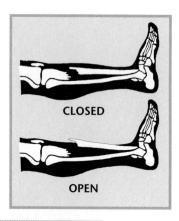

Key Terms

closed (simple) fracture—
a fracture in which the broken bone does not push through the skin's surface

open (compound) fracture—
a fracture in which the broken end of a bone pierces the skin

Figure 10.12

Closed (simple) and open (compound) fractures

Key Term

splint—
to support and immobilize a body part with a stiff material

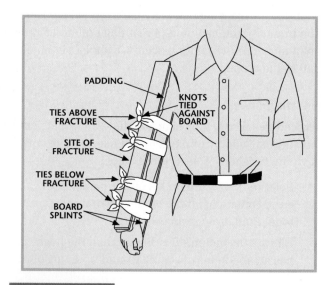

Figure 10.13

Splints help immobilize bones to prevent further injury.

For open fractures, control the bleeding before splinting. Keep the exposed bone moist by covering it with a moist, sterile dressing. The rules of splinting are as follows:

1. Pad all splinting material. Make splints from sticks, boards, cardboard, rolled newspaper, or any other unbendable material.

2. Splint the broken leg or arm in the position in which you found it. Do not try to straighten or reposition the fracture. In most cases, support an arm from above and below and a leg from the sides.

3. Use splinting material that is long enough to immobilize the joint above and below the break. For example, immobilize the ankle and the knee for a fracture in the vicinity of the calf.

4. Tie the splints above and below the suspected fracture. Make two ties above and two below the break. Never make a tie directly over the break.

5. Tie all knots on the outside of the splints.

6. Check that circulation is not restricted by splints tied too tightly.

If no splinting material is available, immobilize a leg fracture by placing padding between the injured leg and the uninjured leg and tying them together. Using the uninjured leg as the splint, draw two ties above and two below the suspected break.

Slings

For arm fractures in which the entire arm is not splinted, use a sling (see Figure 10.14) to support the weight of the arm. If necessary, pin the victim's shirttail up to serve as a field expedient sling.

Joint Injuries

Joint injuries occur when excess stress or strain is placed on the joint. This can happen during normal activities such as walking or running and is common in sports activities. Dislocations and sprains are the most common joint injuries.

Dislocations

A dislocation occurs when a joint comes apart and stays apart with the bone ends no longer in contact. The shoulders, elbows, fingers, hips, kneecaps, and ankles are the joints most frequently affected. Dislocations have signs and symptoms similar to those of a fracture: severe pain, swelling, and the inability of the victim to move the injured joint. The main sign of a dislocation is deformity; its appearance will be different from that of a comparable uninjured joint. The procedures for treating a dislocation include the following:

1. Do not try to set the joint. Immobilize and support the injured joint as if treating for a fracture.

2. Use the RICE procedures (discussed later in this lesson).

3. Seek medical attention.

Figure 10.14

Placing a sling on an injured arm can support the injury.

Key Term

dislocation—
the separation of a bone from its joint

UNIT V

Sprain

A sprain is an injury to a joint in which the ligaments and other tissues are damaged by violent stretching or twisting. Attempts to move or use the joint increase the pain. The skin about the joint may be discolored because of bleeding from torn tissues. It is often difficult to distinguish between a severe sprain and a fracture, because their signs and symptoms are similar. If you are not sure whether an injury is a sprain or a fracture, treat it like a fracture. It is better to immobilize a sprain than to take the chance of a victim sustaining further damage from an unsplinted closed fracture. Treatment for a sprain consists of **R**est, **I**ce, **C**ompression, and **E**levation (RICE). Seek medical attention.

Muscle Injuries

Muscle injuries are as common as joint injuries. These can be very painful and need treatment as soon as possible after the injury occurs. The most common muscle injury is a strain.

Strain

A muscle strain, or muscle pull, occurs when a muscle is stretched beyond its normal range of motion, resulting in the muscle tearing. Signs and symptoms include: sharp pain, extreme tenderness when the area is touched, slight swelling, and difficulty moving or using the affected part. When treating for strain use RICE.

RICE: Procedures for Bone, Joint, and Muscle Injuries

As discussed earlier in this lesson, RICE is the acronym for the first aid procedures—rest, ice, compression, and elevation—for bone, joint, and muscle injuries. What is done in the first 48–72 hours following such an injury can greatly affect the recovery.

1. **Rest.** Injuries heal faster if rested. Rest means the victim stays off the injured part.

2. **Ice.** An ice pack should be applied to the injured area for 20–30 minutes every two to three hours during the first 24–48 hours. When the skin becomes numb, remove the ice pack.

3. **Compression.** Compression of the injured area may squeeze some fluid and debris out of the injury site. Compression limits the ability of the skin and of other tissues to expand. Applying compression may be the most important step in preventing swelling. The victim should wear an elastic bandage continuously for 18–24 hours.

4. **Elevation.** Gravity has an important effect on swelling. The force of gravity pulls blood and other tissue to the lower parts of the body. After fluids get to your hands or feet, they have nowhere else to go; therefore, those parts of the body tend to swell the most. Elevating the injured areas, in combination with ice and compression, limits circulation to that area, which in turn helps limit internal bleeding and minimize swelling. Whenever possible, elevate the injured part above the level of the heart for the first 24 hours after an injury.

First Aid for Burns

Burns come from sources such as heat, electricity, and chemicals. In situations where people are injured by these sources, your first aid knowledge should include how to treat them. This lesson covers different types of burns, how to treat them, and ways to prevent them.

Burns

There are several types and degrees of burns that require different treatments. Heat, electricity, and chemicals can produce different burn injuries with their severity depending upon the burn's depth, size, and location. Burns can be painful and may result in shock and infection. They can be very serious if they are spread over a large area of the body, there are other injuries involved, or the victim is very young or very old.

Degrees of Burns

For burns caused by sources of heat, there are different categories of degrees (first, second, or third) based on the burn's depth. The deeper the burn, the more severe and the higher the degree the burn is. All electrical burns are third degree.

Characteristics of First-Degree Burns

There are several characteristics of first-degree burns.

- Least severe
- Injury to only the top layer of skin
- Reddening of the skin
- Mild swelling
- Pain due to irritated nerve endings
- Quick and complete healing if properly treated
- Caused by brief contact with hot objects, brief exposure to hot water or steam, and overexposure to sun (light sunburn) or wind.

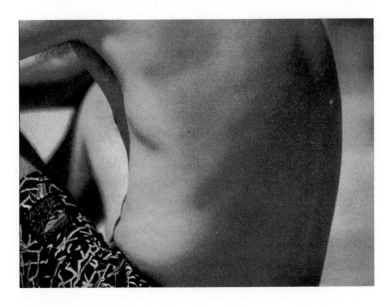

Most sunburns are first-degree burns.
Courtesy of Sinclair Stammers/
Photo Researchers

mottled—
*marked with irregular
spots or splotches
of different colors
or shades of color*

Characteristics of Second-Degree Burns

There are several characteristics of second-degree burns:

- Involve deeper layers of skin
- Cause skin to turn red and/or mottled
- Appear moist and oozing from the loss of fluid through damaged skin layers
- Produce blisters and swelling
- Is usually the most painful type of burn because nerve endings are still intact even though tissue damage is severe
- May cause shock due to extensive loss of fluid from the burned skin, especially if burns cover a large area
- Should heal within two weeks with little or no scarring if properly treated
- Caused by a deep sunburn, prolonged contact with hot objects, scalding, and flash burns from flammable liquids suddenly bursting into flame.

Characteristics of Third-Degree Burns

The specific characteristics of third-degree burns are as follows:

- Deepest and most severe type of burn
- May look white or charred (may appear to be a second-degree burn at first)
- Results in deep tissue destruction, reaching all layers of the skin and sometimes even structures below the skin
- Often cause little or no pain because nerve endings are destroyed
- Often cause shock
- Will be covered by scar tissue after healed
- Caused by immersion in extremely hot water, prolonged contact with flames, and electric shock.

Treatment of Heat Burns

Treat heat burns based on their degree; therefore, before treating a burn, determine its degree and treat accordingly. When deciding the degree of a burn, in addition to the previous descriptions, it may help to know the source of the burn and/or how hot the source was, as well as how long the victim was exposed to it. If a victim appears to have a combination of burns of different degrees, determine the degree of the most burned part—usually in the middle of the burned area—and treat for that degree. If you are not sure about the degree of a burn, treat it as a third-degree burn.

Keep in mind that the goal of burn treatment is to relieve the victim's pain, prevent him or her from going into shock, and prevent infection of the burned area.

Treating First-Degree Burns

To treat first-degree burns, follow these steps:

1. Loosen tight clothing and remove jewelry from the burned area before it swells. Have the victim put his or her jewelry in a safe place after removal.

2. Cool the burned part with water by either holding it under cold, running water, pouring cold water over it, immersing it in cold water, or applying cold wet compresses to it. Cooling the burn with water helps remove heat from the skin, relieves pain and swelling, and cleans the injury. Continue this cooling treatment for between five and 15 minutes until the pain subsides.

3. Gently pat the burned area dry with a clean cloth.

4. Cover the injury with a sterile bandage or clean cloth to keep air off of it, thereby reducing pain, and to provide protection against infection. Keep the bandage loose to keep pressure off of the injury.

5. After a first-degree burn is completely cooled, especially a sunburn, use a lotion or moisturizer to relieve pain and prevent drying of the skin.

Treating Second-Degree Burns

To treat second-degree burns, follow these steps:

1. For second-degree burns, follow steps one through four for treating first-degree burns. If you use running water to cool the injured part, ensure the water is not so forceful that blisters on the burned skin are broken.

2. Elevate the burned part.

3. Ensure the victim drinks plenty of liquids to avoid dehydration.

4. Seek medical treatment for second-degree burns to the face, hands, feet, or genitals or that are more than two to three inches in diameter.

> **Note:**
>
> For extensive second-degree burns, monitor the victim for signs of shock and treat accordingly until he or she receives medical treatment. See the previous section, "Treating for Shock and Immobilizing Fractures," for signs and treatment of shock. For second-degree burns to the face, especially if accompanied by smoke inhalation, the victim may have respiratory burns that can lead to swelling and blockage of his or her airway. Monitor the victim's breathing and treat accordingly until he or she receives medical treatment.

Key Term

compresses—
folded cloths or pads applied to press on a body part to stop bleeding or cool a burn

UNIT V

Treating Third-Degree Burns

To treat third-degree burns, follow these steps:

1. Remove the victim from the source of heat if he or she is still in contact with it. (See the following section for removing a victim from a source of electricity.)

2. Call for emergency medical services (EMS). All third-degree burns require medical treatment regardless of their size. Until the victim receives treatment, follow Steps 3 through 9.

3. Ensure that the victim is breathing. If not, begin mouth-to-mouth resuscitation.

4. Remove any clothing that is still smoldering to stop further burning. If the victim is wearing jewelry that is near or on a burned area, remove it if it comes off easily. Place the jewelry in the victim's pocket, purse, and so on, if available. If not, reassure the victim that you will give his or her jewelry to emergency medical personnel when they arrive.

5. If necessary, expose the burned area by cutting and gently lifting away any clothing. If any cloth sticks to the burn, leave it in place.

> **Note:**
>
> If you are in a chemically contaminated area, do not expose the burned area; simply apply a dressing over the victim's clothing.

6. Cover the burned area loosely with cool moist compresses, sterile bandages, or clean cloth.

> **Note:**
>
> Unlike treatment for first- and second-degree burns, do not cool a third-degree burn with water because this can increase the risk of shock.

7. Elevate the burned part.

8. Treat the victim for shock. Pay special attention to the victim's body temperature, which can change rapidly due to the skin being burned.

9. Monitor breathing of victims with burns to the face and burns resulting from fire accompanied by smoke inhalation. Treat accordingly.

Don'ts When Treating Burns

It is important to know what to do when treating burns, but it is equally as important to know what not to do. The following list details actions that should never be done when treating burns.

- Do not put butter, oil, or grease on a burn; these ointments can keep heat in the burn and cause more damage, as well as increase the chance of infection.
- Do not use cotton or cottony bandages on burns as they may stick to the injury.
- Do not put ice or ice water on a burn; this can result in frostbite and cause more damage to the skin.
- Do not break any blisters that have formed; blisters help protect against infection.
- Do not put pressure on a burn.
- Do not try to remove stuck clothing, debris, or loosened skin from a burn.
- Do not try to clean a wound with soap, alcohol, or any other antiseptic product; only water should be used and only on first- and second-degree burns.
- Do not let a victim walk on burned feet even if he or she tells you it does not hurt; third-degree burns can cause little pain because nerve endings are destroyed, but damage is severe and pressure from walking will only increase it.

Prevention of Heat Burns

There are many things you can do to prevent heat burns, including the following:

- Use caution when handling matches and starting a fire, particularly with a flammable liquid.
- If you have young brothers and sisters, store matches out of their reach.
- Use caution around hot liquids, steam, and heating and cooking equipment.
- Ensure hot tap water is not scalding before stepping into a tub or shower or putting your hands under a running faucet.
- Ensure your home has a fire extinguisher and smoke alarms.
- Never use water on an electrical fire; use a chemical fire extinguisher.
- If anyone in your household smokes, remind them not to smoke in bed.
- Keep a box of baking soda in the kitchen to smother grease fires.
- Turn pot handles on the stove so they are not sticking out where someone may bump them in passing.
- For electric cookware, do not let cords hang off the counter, where they can be caught and pull the cookware off as well.
- If a pilot light goes out on a gas appliance, make sure all burners and the stove are turned off and ventilate the area before relighting it or before using electrical switches, which make tiny sparks.
- Do not leave flammable items (such as newspapers or dishcloths) near the fireplace or on or near the stove.
- Turn off space heaters before going to sleep or leaving the house.
- Know what actions to take if a fire starts in your home and practice them with family members.

Treatment of Electrical Burns

Although an electrical shock will often produce only a minor mark on the skin, the injury can be a serious, deep-tissue burn, so treat all electrical burns as third degree. The current from an electrical shock passing through a victim's body can also result in unconsciousness and may slow or stop his or her breathing and/or heartbeat; therefore, treat electrical shock as a potentially life-threatening injury.

If you believe a person has been electrocuted, assess the situation first, *before* touching the victim. He or she may still be in contact with the electrical current, and if you touch him or her, you could become a victim of electrical shock as well. Follow these steps to avoid a double accident and provide first aid treatment:

1. If the victim is still in contact with the source of electricity, stop the current.

   Shut off the electrical current by unplugging a cord, removing a fuse from the fuse box, or turning off the circuit breaker, as appropriate. Remember that in many cases, just turning off a wall or appliance switch does not stop the electrical flow. Even though you have shut off the electrical current, to be completely safe, move the victim away from the electrical source before continuing. Proceed to step 3.

   If you cannot turn off the electricity or you are outside and the shock is due to a downed power line, either call the power company yourself if you have a phone near you, or if there are other people around, have someone else call the power company. Meanwhile, since it may take you less time to separate the victim from the current than to wait for the power to be cut off, proceed to step 2. Or, if you are alone and/or there is no phone readily available in this situation, proceed to step 2.

2. Separate the victim from the source of electrical current (see Figure 10.15).

   Push the victim off of or away from the source of electricity—or push the source of electricity off of or away from the victim—using a dry nonconducting material (wood, plastic, cardboard) like a broom, stick, or chair. If available, also stand on something dry and nonconducting, like newspaper or a rubber mat, as you disengage the victim.

   If pushing does not work, use a dry rope or dry clothing to lift or drag the victim off of or away from the source of electricity. This method works better if there are two rescuers: one to lift the victim off and the other to push the electrical source away.

Special Precaution:

If the ground is wet, do not attempt to move a victim in contact with an electrical current. Water conducts electricity, and you can be electrocuted as well. In this case, the current must be stopped before you can administer first aid.

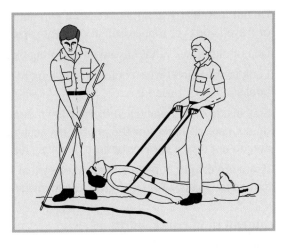

Figure 10.15

Removing a victim
from the source
of an electrical current

3. Check the victim's breathing and pulse. Be prepared to administer mouth-to-mouth resuscitation or cardiopulmonary resuscitation (CPR) if the victim's breathing is shallow or nonexistent or his or her pulse is dangerously slow or nonexistent.

4. After you are sure the victim is breathing, take the time to call EMS if you or someone else has not already done so.

5. Check the victim for two burn sites—one where the electricity entered the body and one where it exited the body. Treat the burns by following steps 4 through 9 for treating third-degree burns, including treating for shock and monitoring breathing.

Note:

About 1,000 people die each year in the United States from electrical shock.

Prevention of Electrical Burns

Electrical burns can be prevented if you know what to do. How to prevent electrical burns:

- Do not use electrical appliances in the tub, while showering, or in or near swimming pools.
- Do not use electrical equipment outdoors if it is raining or the ground is wet.
- Ensure electrical equipment you use outdoors is made for outdoor use, with three-way ground plugs and heavier wiring.
- Ensure outdoor electrical outlets have weatherproof covers.
- If you have very young brothers or sisters, ensure there are child safety plugs in all electrical outlets.
- Do not overload an outlet by plugging in several appliances in a "piggyback" fashion (see Figure 10.16).

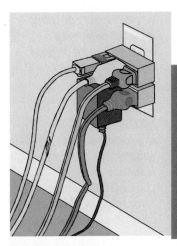

UNIT V

Figure 10.16

An unsafe electrical outlet

- Do not use electrical appliances or equipment that have exposed wiring or frayed cords or that overheat or create sparks.

- Do not climb trees that have wires running through or near them.

- Look for overhead wires before using long tools like tree trimmers, pool skimmers, or ladders.

- Stay inside during electrical storms; keep away from windows; do not use appliances or the phone, because lightning can travel through wires; and do not take a shower or bath, because lightning can also travel through pipes.

- If you are caught outside during an electrical storm, avoid trees, poles, and metal objects; find low ground and crouch down.

Treatment of Chemical Burns

Chemical burns occur when the skin or eyes come in contact with liquid or dry chemicals that are caustic or irritating. You may have products around your house, such as rust and paint removers and drain and cement cleaners, that contain acids designed to eat away certain materials and bases (also called alkalis) used to cut through grease. If used carelessly or improperly, these products may also do the same to your clothes and skin.

The seriousness of a chemical burn depends on the:

- Length of time the chemical is in contact with the skin or eyes

- Concentration of the chemical; the more concentrated, the more damaging

- Temperature of the product containing the chemical; the higher the temperature, the quicker the damage.

Treatment of chemical burns involves stopping the chemical action immediately by removing the chemical from the skin or eyes and by removing contaminated clothing that can transmit absorbed chemicals to the skin. Treatment will vary depending on the type of chemical involved, so if there are first aid instructions on the label of the chemical product causing the burn, follow those instructions. If not, use the following basic guidelines for treatment.

Treating Chemical Burns to the Skin

To treat chemical burns to the skin, follow these steps:

1. Depending on the extent of chemical coverage on the victim or in the area, consider wearing gloves and/or safety goggles, if available, to protect yourself from chemical injuries while assisting the victim.

2. Remove any contaminated jewelry or clothing from the victim, including shoes and socks where chemicals can collect.

Key Terms

caustic—
capable of destroying or eating away by chemical action; corrosive

acids—
chemical compounds with a sour taste that have a pH value of less than 7, react with metals to form hydrogen gas, and have the capability to eat away or dissolve metals and other materials

bases—
chemical compounds with a slippery or soapy feel that react with acids to form salt, have a pH value above 7, and are used as cleaning materials

alkalis—
any base, such as soda or potash, that is soluble in water, combines with fats to form soap, neutralizes acids, and forms salts with them

3. Remove the chemical from the skin.

   For liquid chemicals, flush them from the contaminated skin with large amounts of cool running water for at least 15 minutes.

   For dry chemicals, brush them off the skin using a clean, dry cloth. Take care to keep the chemicals from blowing into your eyes or the victim's eyes and avoid brushing the chemicals onto your own skin. Then, if large amounts of water are available, flush the contaminated area for at least 15 minutes. If large amounts of water are not available, do not apply any water to the contaminated area because small amounts of water can react with dry chemicals causing more burning.

Note:

If the victim says he or she feels the burning has intensified after you have finished flushing the contaminated area, flush for several more minutes, or longer, as necessary.

4. Cover the burned area loosely with dry, clean bandages or cloths.
5. Minor chemical burns generally heal without further treatment; however, call EMS for:
   - Any chemical burn to the face, hands, feet, genitals, or joints
   - Second-degree chemical burns over two to three inches in diameter
   - All third-degree chemical burns
   - If there is a systemic reaction to the chemical burn and/or chemical exposure.

Key Term

systemic—
affecting the body in general; acting throughout the body after absorption or ingestion

Note:

For extensive or severe chemical burns, monitor the victim for signs of shock and treat accordingly until he or she receives medical treatment. For a victim with chemical burns to the face or who may have inhaled chemicals, monitor his or her breathing in case of possible respiratory burns and swelling. Treat accordingly until medical help arrives.

UNIT V

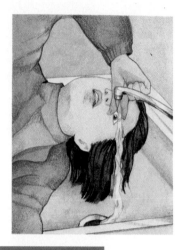

Figure 10.17

When flooding the eye, be careful the chemical does not get into the other eye.

Courtesy of Susan Spellman

Key Term

neutralize—
to counteract the activity or effect of; to make chemically neutral

Treating Chemical Burns to the Eyes

To treat chemical burns to the eyes, follow these steps:

1. Position the victim's head so that the injured eye is lower than the uninjured eye. This will prevent the chemical from getting into the uninjured eye (see Figure 10.17). If both eyes are injured, proceed to Step 2.

2. If there is only one injured eye, hold the eyelids of the injured eye open and flush with water from the inner corner of the eye (closest to the nose) to the outer corner (closest to the ear). Flush for at least 15 minutes. If both eyes are injured, flush both at the same time.

3. To keep the victim from moving his or her injured eye(s), have the victim close both eyes, then cover them with cloth pads or gauze taped loosely into place. Because eyes move together, both eyes must be closed and covered to keep the injured eye still.

4. Call EMS or transport the victim to the emergency room.

Don'ts When Treating Chemical Burns

Follow the don'ts listed earlier in this lesson in "Don'ts When Treating Burns." In addition, do not put any other chemicals on a chemical burn in an attempt to neutralize the chemical causing the burn—for example, putting an acid on an alkali and vice versa.

Prevention of Chemical Burns

Chemical burns can be prevented, if you know what to do. To help prevent chemical burns:

- Before using any chemical product, read the label—including precautions or warnings—then follow the instructions for use.

- If you have younger brothers or sisters, ensure chemical products are stored out of their reach.

- Use chemical products in a well-ventilated area.

- Do not mix different chemical products; they may react with each other, causing hazardous conditions. For example, mixing bleach and ammonia results in dangerous fumes.

- To avoid confusion and accidental misuse of chemical products, leave them in their original containers with their labels intact.

First Aid for Poisons, Wounds, and Bruises

Whenever there are small children left alone in the kitchen, accidents can happen, especially when cleaning products are left out in the open. The first part of this section introduces the treatment and prevention of injury from poisons. As an addition to your first aid abilities, the lesson ends with a discussion of different types of wounds and their treatment, as well as the treatment of bruises.

Poisons

As consumers, we buy more than a quarter of a million different household products, including materials used in and around the house for medication, cleaning, cosmetic purposes, exterminating insects, and killing weeds. These items are valuable in the house and for yard maintenance, but misuse, especially when products are used in inappropriate applications or quantities, can cause illness, injury, and even death.

Each year more than 6,000 people die and an estimated 300,000 suffer disabling illnesses as a result of unintentional poisoning by solid and liquid substances. Poisonings can happen to anyone, at any time, in any situation. Poisonings at home, however, can be prevented. Although child-resistant packaging has greatly reduced the number of fatalities among children less than five years of age, parents, grandparents, and other caregivers must still be cautious. Following label directions for all products, including medication dosages and the proper storage of potentially toxic products, are important precautions to heed.

- Poisonings from solids and liquids such as drugs, medicines, poisonous houseplants, and commonly recognized poisons caused 6,300 deaths in the home in 1998 alone.
- An additional 500 deaths in the home in 1998 were due to poisonings from gases and vapors such as carbon monoxide.
- These deaths are not all among children. Another age group at risk is adults age 25 through 44. Many adults are unintentionally poisoned when they do not follow label directions on medications or household chemicals.

Poisoning is the effect of one or more harmful substances on the body. Poisons can be inhaled or ingested. Fortunately, most poisonings happen with products of low toxicity or with amounts so small, severe poisoning rarely occurs; however, the potential for severe or fatal poisoning is always present.

Inhaled Poisons

Inhaled poisoning occurs when a person breathes a poisonous substance into his or her lungs. Inhaled poisons include the following:

- Smoke
- Gas used in outdoor cooking equipment and appliances in homes and recreational vehicles
- Hazardous fumes from household products such as paint and paint thinners, gasoline, solvents, and glues, as well as from chemicals used in industrial processes
- Carbon monoxide, which is always produced by wood, coal, and charcoal fires and by gasoline engines, can also be produced by gas, oil, and kerosene appliances such as furnaces, space heaters, water heaters, and stoves.

UNIT V

Car exhaust is a source of carbon monoxide poisoning.
Courtesy of Ted Cordingley

Carbon monoxide, in particular, is a very dangerous poisonous substance, because it is odorless, colorless, and tasteless, making it difficult to detect. When a person inhales carbon monoxide, it replaces oxygen in the blood, which results in oxygen starvation throughout the body. Exposure to low amounts of carbon monoxide can cause flulike symptoms; continued exposure can cause permanent brain, nerve, and heart damage; exposure to very high concentrations can kill a person in a few minutes.

Running a car engine in a closed garage, using a charcoal grill indoors, and burning a fire in a fireplace with a blocked chimney can all result in carbon monoxide poisoning. In addition, because carbon monoxide forms when there is a lack of oxygen resulting in incomplete fuel combustion, operating fuel-burning equipment without an adequate supply of oxygen (proper ventilation) can result in carbon monoxide poisoning. For example, hundreds of people in the United States each year suffer carbon monoxide injuries from using portable heaters, lanterns, and camping stoves inside tents, campers, and vehicles.

Symptoms of Inhaled Poisoning

Symptoms of inhaled poisoning may not show up immediately. If you suspect inhalation poisoning, keep the victim under observation. If you know the victim has inhaled a poisonous chemical, get medical help whether or not symptoms are present. Symptoms will vary depending on the type and amount of poison inhaled but can include any of the following:

- Dizziness
- Weakness
- Drowsiness
- Headache
- Mental confusion
- Breathing difficulties
- Heartbeat irregularities

- Unusual breath odor
- Discoloration of the lips and mucous membranes
- Nausea
- Vomiting
- Rashes or burns on the skin
- Unconsciousness.

Treatment for Inhaled Poisons

Before rushing in to rescue a victim in a smoke-, gas-, or fume-filled environment, quickly assess the situation so that you do not end up a victim as well. If the poisonous substance is overwhelming and the danger to you is too great, do not attempt to rescue the victim unless you have been trained for rescue in this type of situation. Immediately call EMS and stay clear of danger.

However, if after assessing the situation you believe you can safely remove the victim from the poisonous environment, do so by following these steps.

1. If you are alone, call for help first before attempting the rescue. This will notify others of the situation; a precaution that will ensure help is on its way in case you are also overcome by the poison.

2. Take several deep breaths of fresh air, then take a final deep breath and hold it as you go in. If available, a damp cloth held over your nose and mouth is a good safety precaution.

Note:

Do not use light switches, light a match, or use any other equipment or appliance that produces flames or sparks while you are in a gas- or fume-filled area.

3. If you can see fumes or smoke, keep your head out of them. For example, fumes from car exhaust are heavy and settle near the floor, so keep your head above them; but in the case of smoke, which rises, keep your head below it.

4. Move the victim out into the fresh air. If for some reason this is not possible, open doors and windows to ventilate the area, returning out into the fresh air as necessary to ensure your safety. Do not administer first aid until you and the victim are out of the hazardous environment or the area is ventilated.

Check the victim's airway, breathing, and circulation (ABCs) and perform mouth-to-mouth resuscitation and CPR as necessary. After you are sure the victim is breathing, call the EMS if you or someone else has not already done so. Even if the victim seems fine after he or she is in fresh air, call for medical help as symptoms may show up later. While you are waiting for medical help, treat the victim for any burns he or she may have suffered and monitor for shock.

Oral Poisoning

Oral poisoning occurs when a harmful substance, such as a common household cleaning product, is swallowed. First aid for oral poisoning depends on the substance swallowed.

Symptoms of Oral Poisoning

Symptoms and signs will vary depending on the type and amount of poison inhaled but can include any of the following:

- Abdominal pain and cramping
- Nausea or vomiting
- Diarrhea
- Burns, odor, and stains around and in mouth
- Drowsiness or unconsciousness
- Poison containers nearby.

Treatment for Oral Poisons

Procedures for treating oral poisoning:

1. Determine critical information:
   - Age and size of victim
   - What was swallowed
   - How much was swallowed
   - When it was swallowed.
2. If a corrosive or caustic substance was swallowed, immediately dilute it by having the victim drink at least one or two eight-ounce glasses of water or milk.
3. For a responsive victim, call a poison control center immediately. More than 70 percent of poisonings can be treated through instructions taken over the telephone from a poison control center.
4. For an unresponsive victim, or if the poison control center number is unknown, call EMS and monitor the ABCs.
5. Place the victim on his or her left side to position the end of the stomach where it enters the small intestine straight up. Gravity will delay advancement of the poison into the small intestine, where absorption into the victim's circulatory system is faster.
6. Induce vomiting only if a poison control center or physician advises it. Inducing must be done within 30 minutes of swallowing.
7. Save poison containers, plants, and so on to help medical personnel identify the poison.

Wounds

Wounds are soft tissue injuries that break the skin. Generally, they can be classified as follows:

- *Scrapes* (abrasions) are caused by sliding contact between the skin and a rough surface. They are generally shallow injuries with little bleeding.
- *Cuts* (incisions) are straight, even wounds made with sharp objects like knives or razor blades.
- *Tears* (lacerations) are caused by objects with sharp, irregular edges or by exerted force that leaves jagged, torn tissue.
- *Punctures* are caused by pointed objects such as pins and nails that make small holes in tissue, often with little bleeding.

All wounds can be minor or serious depending upon their size, depth, location, and source. Minor wounds involve only the outer skin layer. They stop bleeding in a few minutes on their own or with gentle pressure and can be treated with just first aid. Serious wounds require first aid followed by medical treatment. Consider a wound serious if the following characteristics are evident:

- The skin is cut or torn all the way through so that it gapes open
- Fat, muscle, or tendons are visible
- Bleeding is heavy and does not slow or stop after applying pressure for 15 to 20 minutes
- Soil or other debris cannot be washed from the wound
- There is loss of function such as the inability to move a cut finger
- It is on the face; even a small wound may leave a scar
- It is on the bottom of the foot
- Its source is a rusty or dirty object, or an animal or human bite.

Some extremely serious injuries that generally contain a combination of the four kinds of wounds and always require immediate medical attention are amputations, avulsions, and crushing injuries. They are generally the result of motor vehicle or industrial machinery accidents or explosions.

- An *amputation* is the complete removal of an extremity, such as a finger or leg.
- An *avulsion* is tissue torn from or pulled away from and hanging off of the body. This type of injury may also result from an animal bite.
- *Crushing injuries* occur when parts of the body are caught between heavy objects or when the body is thrown against a heavy object or vice versa. In addition to wounds, crushing injuries include bone fractures, as well as possible injuries to internal organs and internal bleeding.

Key Terms

abrasion—
a part of the skin that has been lightly torn or scraped

incision—
a wound that is made by cutting into the body

laceration—
a wound that is torn and ragged

Key Terms

amputation—
the removal of an external part of the body, most often a limb or part of it, when it has been severely crushed or following the death of the extremity due to impaired blood circulation

avulsion—
the tearing away of a body part accidentally or surgically

UNIT V

Treatment of Wounds

Clean a minor wound by flushing it with cool water and washing it with mild soap. Dry it thoroughly with a clean cloth, apply a thin layer of antibiotic ointment to keep the wound moist and protect against infection, and cover it with a bandage to keep it clean. Change the bandage whenever it gets wet or dirty, and consider leaving the bandage off at night when sleeping because exposure to air also helps the healing process. Contact a doctor if the wound does not appear to be healing after several days or shows signs of infection like redness, draining, or swelling.

For any wound caused by a rusty or dirty object or an animal bite, ask if the victim has had a tetanus shot within the past 10 years. If not, suggest that he or she get one to guard against tetanus infection.

For extremely serious injuries such as amputations, avulsions, or crushing injuries, call EMS, control the bleeding, monitor breathing, treat for shock, and provide comfort to the victim until medical help arrives. Remember that tourniquets should only be used in extreme, life-threatening situations, and pressure points should only be used if you are trained to do so.

Bruises

Bruises are injuries that discolor but do not break the skin tissue. They can be caused by a fall, a blow, or bumping into something. Though sometimes very ugly and lasting for several weeks, they are usually not very serious. Wrap ice or an ice pack in a clean towel and apply it to the bruise. To reduce swelling, elevate the bruised part for 20 to 30 minutes if the injury is mild or for a few hours if it is severe. Seek medical attention if swelling increases unusually, pain increases, the bruise site appears deformed, or there is an inability to move a body part associated with the bruise.

Heat Injuries

Participating in any vigorous outdoor exercise or activity on an extremely hot day can lead to serious injuries if you are not prepared. Knowing how to recognize the signs and symptoms of heat related injuries can help you prevent a life-threatening accident.

Causes

For your body to work properly, its temperature must be normal, which is around 98° Fahrenheit. You risk health problems, and even death, if your body gets too cold or too hot.

Heat injuries can occur when people are exposed to high temperatures and high humidity. When it is hot, your body cools itself by perspiring; sweat evaporates to carry heat away from your body. However, you risk heat injuries when you lose large amounts of water, salt, or both through perspiring and do not replace the lost fluid, which results in dehydration. You also risk injury in high humidity when sweat does not evaporate as rapidly as needed to keep the body cool, causing heat to build up. The body will then perspire even more in an attempt to cool itself, losing dangerous amounts of fluids in the process.

Figure 10.18

Heavy perspiring will occur when running or jogging on a hot day.

Key Term

dehydration—
the condition that results when fluids are lost from the body and are not replaced; symptoms can include thirst, weakness, exhaustion, and confusion, and may result in death

People who may be at risk of heat injuries include those who exercise or work outside in high temperatures and high humidity, those whose bodies do not regulate heat well, such as older people, overweight people, or babies.

Factors to Consider

When perspiring, the body can lose more than a quart of water per hour. Therefore, because the body depends on water to cool itself, you should drink plenty of water when working or playing in hot weather. Salt, which helps the body to retain water, is also lost through perspiring. In most cases, however, you do not need to consume extra salt because you obtain adequate amounts through a balanced diet. In fact, consuming salt during hot weather activities may pull water away from muscles and other tissues where it is needed and into your digestive tract.

In addition to water intake and diet, consider the type of clothing you wear in hot weather. Wear clothes that fit loosely but also protect the body from sunburn. Wear natural fabrics, like cotton, through which perspiration evaporates better. Some activities require extra clothing or equipment, such as football or hiking with full camping gear. Soldiers may have problems acclimating to hot weather because of the type and amount of clothing and equipment they must wear. In all of these cases, protective gear and equipment may reduce ventilation needed to cool the body. So, ensure clothing or uniforms fit well but are not tight, and remove extra pieces of clothing and equipment as soon as they are no longer needed.

Types of Heat Injuries

Overheating of the body progresses through stages. At first, a person may suffer heat cramps. If the person ignores the symptoms and continues exercising, working, or playing in the heat, he or she may experience heat exhaustion. If heat exhaustion is left untreated, heatstroke may follow and can be fatal.

Heat Cramps

Heat cramps are muscular pains and spasms caused by the loss of salt from the body through heavy perspiring. Other symptoms may include stomach cramps, wet skin, and extreme thirst. To treat heat cramps:

1. Move the victim to a shady area, or improvise shade.
2. Loosen the victim's clothing.
3. Slowly give the victim large amounts of cool water.
4. Monitor the victim and give more water as needed.
5. Seek medical aid if cramps continue.

Key Term

ventilation—
*circulation of air;
a system or means
of providing fresh air*

Key Terms

heat cramps—
*a condition that is
marked by the sudden
development of cramps
in the skeletal muscles
and that results
from prolonged work
in high temperatures
accompanied by profuse
perspiration with loss
of sodium chloride
from the body*

heat exhaustion—
*a condition that occurs
when a person is
exposed to excessive
heat over a period of
time, caused by the
loss of water and salt
from the body through
excessive perspiration*

heatstroke—
*a life-threatening
condition caused
by prolonged exposure
to high heat*

UNIT V

Heat Exhaustion

When people work or exercise heavily in high temperatures or in a hot, humid place, the body loses fluids through heavy sweating. Heat exhaustion occurs when fluids are not adequately replaced or when sweat does not evaporate because of high humidity or too many layers of clothing, causing the body to sweat even more. When the body loses a great amount of fluid, less blood flows to vital organs, resulting in a form of shock. The symptoms of heat exhaustion are as follows:

- Heavy sweating
- Weakness or faintness
- Dizziness or drowsiness
- Cool, pale, moist skin
- Headaches
- Loss of appetite
- Heat cramps
- Nausea with or without vomiting
- Confusion
- Chills
- Rapid breathing and pulse
- Body temperature above normal but below 102°F.

Treat heat exhaustion as follows:

1. Move the victim to a cool, shady area, or improvise shade.
2. Loosen the victim's clothing.
3. Pour water on or apply cold, wet cloth to the skin. Fan the victim if it is a hot day.
4. Have the victim slowly drink at least one quart of water.
5. Elevate the victim's legs.
6. Monitor the victim until symptoms are gone. If symptoms continue, seek medical aid.
7. If possible, keep the victim from participating in heavy activity for the rest of the day.

Heatstroke

Heatstroke, also known as sunstroke, is a medical emergency that can be fatal if not treated as soon as possible. The victim's cooling mechanism stops working when the body perspires so much that no fluids remain to produce sweat. Because the body can no longer sweat and sweating is its defense against overheating, body temperature rises and skin becomes red and flushed. If body temperature rises high enough, brain damage and death can occur; therefore, when you encounter a heatstroke victim, you must cool the victim as fast as possible.

Heat exhaustion may occur after a person participates in vigorous exercise on a hot day.

Courtesy of Bob Daemmrich/ Stock Boston

The symptoms of heatstroke are as follows:

- No sweating
- Hot, dry, red skin
- Headache, dizziness, nausea, and vomiting
- Fast, weak pulse and shallow respiration
- Seizures and mental confusion
- Unconsciousness or sudden collapse
- Very high body temperature.

Treat victims of heatstroke as follows:

1. Move the victim to a cool, shady area, or improvise shade.
2. Loosen the victim's clothing. Remove any outer garments and protective clothing.
3. Pour water on the victim or immerse in water, and fan the victim so sweat can evaporate. If you cannot immerse the victim, massage the arms and legs with cool water.
4. If the victim is conscious, have him or her slowly drink at least one quart of water.
5. Seek medical aid and transport the victim to a medical facility as soon as possible. Perform any necessary life-saving measures.

Prevention of Heat Injuries

You can prevent heat injuries by taking just a few simple precautions and exercising a little common sense. If possible, limit your exposure to high temperatures and avoid working or exercising outside in hot, humid weather. During work or training periods, or in extremely hot climates, drink at least one quart of water every hour. Also, remember to dress for the hot weather and the activity being performed.

In the military or in the field, prevention of heat injuries is both an individual and leadership responsibility. Leaders should identify people who have a high risk of injury—basic trainees, overweight individuals, and individuals who have symptoms of fatigue or a previous history of heat injury. If possible, leaders should schedule heavy or strenuous activities during cooler morning or evening hours.

Cold Weather Injuries

It is common to think that people are susceptible to cold weather injuries only in areas where snow and frost are present. If you are not prepared, prolonged exposure to low temperatures, wind or moisture—whether it be on a ski slope or in a stranded car—can result in cold-related injuries such as frostbite and hypothermia, no matter where you live.

Key Terms

frostbite—
an injury caused to body tissue by frost or extreme cold

hypothermia—
too little body heat with abnormally low internal body temperature

Factors to Consider

When thinking about cold weather injuries, there are several factors you need to consider. These factors include weather, stress, clothing, physical makeup, psychological factors, and more. This section discusses these factors.

Weather

Low temperature, high humidity, precipitation, and high wind may affect the loss of body heat. Wind chill (the temperature of both the wind speed and air temperature combined) speeds up the loss of body heat and may aggravate cold injuries. By studying the wind chill chart shown in Figure 10.19, you can determine the chilling effect that wind speed has on temperature.

Stress

When in a stressful situation, people are more likely to experience fear, fatigue, dehydration, and lack of nutrition. These factors increase the possibility of cold injury.

Clothing

When outside during cold weather, you should wear several layers of loose-fitting clothing and dress as lightly as the weather permits. This reduces the danger of excessive perspiration followed by a chill. It is better if the body is slightly cold and producing heat rather than overly warm and sweltering toward dehydration. Wet clothing adds to the possibility of cold injury.

Figure 10.19

The wind chill chart

HOW TO USE THE WIND CHILL CHART

Find the wind speed in the left-hand column, then read across to the column under the actual temperature. This number is the equivalent temperature which would be acting on any exposed skin. For example, if the wind is blowing at 20 mph and the actual temperature is 10° F, the effect on bare skin would be the same as a temperature reading of -25° F under calm conditions. Any movement has the same cooling effect as the wind. Running, skiing, or riding in an open vehicle must be considered in using the wind chill chart.

★GPO : 1983 0 - 417-503

WIND CHILL CHART FOR FAHRENHEIT TEMPERATURES

ESTIMATED WIND SPEED IN MPH	ACTUAL THERMOMETER READING (° F)											
	50	40	30	20	10	0	-10	-20	-30	-40	-50	-60
	EQUIVALENT TEMPERATURE (° F)											
CALM	50	40	30	20	10	0	-10	-20	-30	-40	-50	-60
5	48	37	27	16	6	-5	-15	-26	-36	-47	-57	-68
10	40	28	16	4	-9	-24	-33	-46	-58	-70	-83	-95
15	36	22	9	-5	-18	-32	-45	-58	-72	-85	-99	-112
20	32	18	4	-10	-25	-39	-53	-67	-82	-96	-110	-124
25	30	16	0	-15	-29	-44	-59	-74	-88	-104	-118	-133
30	28	13	-2	-18	-33	-48	-63	-79	-94	-109	-125	-140
35	27	11	-4	-21	-35	-51	-67	-82	-96	-113	-129	-145
40	26	10	-6	-24	-37	-53	-69	-85	-100	-116	-132	-148

WIND SPEEDS ABOVE 40 MPH HAVE LITTLE ADDITIONAL EFFECT.	LITTLE DANGER FOR THE PROPERLY CLOTHED PERSON; MAXIMUM DANGER OF FALSE SENSE OF SECURITY.	INCREASING DANGER OF FREEZING EXPOSED FLESH.	GREAT DANGER

TRENCH FOOT AND IMMERSION FOOT MAY OCCUR AT ANY POINT ON THIS CHART.

Physical Makeup

Physical fatigue leads to inactivity, personal neglect, carelessness, and less heat production. These, in turn, increase the risk of cold injury. Individuals who have had a cold injury before have a higher risk of being injured again.

Psychological Factors

Mental fatigue and fear lessen the body's ability to rewarm itself and thus increase the possibility of cold injury. Depressed or unresponsive individuals are also at a higher risk of cold injury because they are less active and tend to be careless about protecting themselves.

Other Factors

Individuals are also at risk of cold injury if they are

- In contact with the ground for an extended period
- Immobile for long periods of time, such as while riding in a crowded vehicle
- Standing in water
- Out in the cold for days without being warmed
- Deprived of an adequate diet and rest
- Careless about personal hygiene.

Types of Cold Injuries

People exposed to severe cold can suffer from the following conditions: frostbite, immersion foot/trench foot, hypothermia, snow blindness, and dehydration.

Frostbite

Frostbite is the most common injury resulting from exposure to the cold. Ice crystals form in body tissues exposed to temperatures below freezing. The crystals restrict blood flow to the injured parts and are like daggers that puncture cell membranes as they grow larger. Body parts most easily frostbitten are the cheeks, nose, ears, chin, forehead, wrists, hands, and feet. People suffering from frostbite may not realize it because the injured part may be numb from the cold.

There are different degrees of frostbite depending on the extent of tissue damage. A superficial cold injury can usually be characterized by numbness and tingling or "pins and needles" sensations. It involves the skin and the tissue just beneath the skin. Deep frostbite, on the other hand, involves freezing of the subcutaneous tissue and possibly even muscle and bone. With a deep cold injury, victims are often unaware of a problem until the affected part feels like a stump or block of wood. Severe frostbite may result in infection or gangrene and may require surgical removal of the injured part.

Key Terms

superficial—
not serious; on the surface; shallow

subcutaneous—
beneath the top layer of skin

UNIT V

Figure 10.20

Signs of frostbite as it appears on your feet

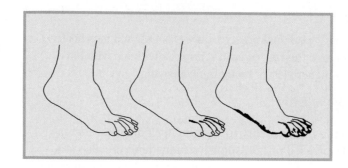

Signs of Frostbite

Signs of superficial frostbite, as shown in Figure 10.20, include the following:

- Redness of the skin on light-skinned individuals; grayish coloring of the skin on dark-skinned individuals
- Blisters appearing in 24 to 36 hours
- Sloughing of the skin.

Signs of deep frostbite include the following:

- Signs of superficial frostbite
- Painless or numb unthawed skin that is pale-yellowish and waxy looking
- Frozen, swollen tissue that is similar to wood to the touch
- Blisters in 12 to 36 hours.

Treatment of Frostbite

Treat superficial frostbite as follows:

1. Move the victim out of the cold and wind.
2. Keep the victim warm; rewarm the affected parts gently and slowly. Explain to the victim that he or she will experience pain when warmth restores feeling to the injured part.
   - Cover cheeks, ears, and nose with the victim's and/or your hands
   - Put the victim's fingertips under his or her armpits
   - Place the victim's feet under the clothing of another person next to that person's belly.
3. Insulate injured parts by covering them with a blanket or dry clothing.
4. Loosen tight clothing and remove wet clothing.
5. Encourage the victim to exercise carefully, avoiding further injury.
6. Seek medical treatment.

Deep frostbite is very serious and requires extra care to reduce or avoid losing all or parts of the fingers, toes, hands, or feet. If possible, transport the victim to a hospital or contact emergency medical services immediately; it is preferable that deep frostbite injuries be rewarmed under medical supervision. If this is not possible, rewarm the injured parts, protect them from refreezing, and seek medical help as soon as possible.

Avoid frostbite or hypothermia by dressing appropriately for outdoor activites in cold weather.
Courtesy of Paul Mozell/ Stock Boston

Key Term

insulate—
to use materials to protect or isolate from the elements of weather

The Don'ts of Treating Frostbite

Although there are many things you can do to help a frostbite victim, there are also several things you should not do.

- Do not attempt to thaw the affected part if you believe you cannot keep it warm until the victim receives medical treatment. It is extremely dangerous for an injured part to refreeze after warming. It is less dangerous to leave the part frozen than to warm it and have it refreeze.
- Avoid having the victim walk on frostbitten feet, especially if they thaw. If the victim must walk, it is less dangerous while his or her feet are frozen.
- Do not rub the injured part with snow or apply cold water packs.
- Do not warm the injured part by massage; ice crystals in the tissues will damage more cells when rubbed.
- Do not expose the injured part to open fire; the frozen part may burn because of lack of feeling.
- Do not have the victim move the injured part to increase circulation.
- Do not break any blisters.
- Do not use ointments or other medications.
- Do not let the victim use alcohol or tobacco. Alcohol reduces the body's resistance to cold, and tobacco decreases blood circulation.

Immersion Foot/Trench Foot

Immersion foot and trench foot result from long exposure of the feet to wet conditions at temperatures between approximately 32° and 50°F. Keeping your feet in damp or wet socks and shoes or tightly laced boots for long periods of time may affect circulation and contribute to injury. Inactivity also increases the risk of immersion foot/trench foot. This injury can be very serious, leading to loss of toes or parts of the feet.

Signs of Immersion Foot and Trench Foot

Symptoms of immersion foot/trench foot in the primary stage include affected parts that are cold, numb, and painless. These parts may then begin to feel hot with burning and shooting pains. In the advanced stage of immersion foot/trench foot, the pulse decreases and the skin becomes pale with a bluish cast. Redness, blistering, swelling, heat, hemorrhages, and gangrene may follow.

Treatment of Immersion Foot and Trench Foot

Treat immersion foot/trench foot as follows:

1. Gradually rewarm the affected foot by exposure to warm air. Explain to the victim that he or she may experience pain and burning when you rewarm the foot.
   - Do not massage or moisten skin
   - Do not apply ice
   - Do not expose injured parts to open fire or other sources of heat; warm the affected area by covering with loose, dry clothing or other coverings instead.

2. Protect the affected foot from trauma or infection.

3. Elevate the foot to relieve swelling.

4. Dry the foot thoroughly; avoid walking.

5. Seek medical treatment.

Hypothermia

Hypothermia is a general cooling of the body to a temperature below 95°F caused by continued exposure to low or rapidly dropping temperatures, cold moisture or wind, snow, or ice. With hypothermia, the body loses heat faster than it can produce it. Inadequate insulation, fatigue, poor physical condition, dehydration, faulty blood circulation, alcohol, trauma, and immersion in cold water can bring on this condition. People at high risk of hypothermia include infants, older people, people with limited mobility due to illness or other medical conditions, very thin people, and people with heart and lung problems.

Remember, cold weather affects the body slowly and almost without notice. Even when well protected by clothing, a person may suffer cold injuries if exposed to low temperatures for long periods of time. As the body cools, it goes through several stages of discomfort and problems.

Signs of Hypothermia

The signs of hypothermia include the following:

- Shivering or trembling, which will eventually stop as body temperature drops (indicates mild hypothermia)
- Cold skin
- Weakness
- Dizziness
- Drowsiness and mental slowness or confusion
- Uncoordinated movements and slurred speech
- Low body temperature; in severe hypothermia, 90°F or below
- Stiff or rigid muscles
- Decreasing pulse and breathing rate
- Unconsciousness
- Shock, coma, and death—all of which may result as body temperature drops and the body freezes.

Treatment of Hypothermia

Except in the most severe cases, the treatment for hypothermia is directed toward rewarming the body evenly and without delay. Treat mild hypothermia as follows:

1. Rewarm the victim slowly.
   - If possible, move the victim inside, remove any wet clothing, and cover him or her with blankets. Avoid warming the victim quickly with hot baths, electric blankets, or heat lamps.
   - If you cannot move the victim inside, remove any wet clothing and rewarm him or her beside a campfire or using the body heat from another person.

2. Keep the victim dry and protected with clothing, blankets, towels, a sleeping bag, or even newspapers.

3. Keep the victim awake.

4. Do not raise the victim's feet or legs because blood in the extremities is colder than in the rest of the body and may further chill the body's core.

5. Give the victim warm liquids gradually. Do not give the victim alcohol. Do not force liquids on an unconscious victim.

6. Be prepared to start basic life-support measures.

7. Seek medical treatment immediately.

Treating a person with severe hypothermia is extremely dangerous because of the possibility of shock and disturbances of the heartbeat while rewarming. If possible, as you begin to rewarm the victim, transport him or her to a hospital or contact EMS immediately. If this is not possible, treat the victim gently because the heart is weak when the body is cold. Stabilize the victim's body temperature by keeping him or her from losing more body heat and continue to keep the victim warm until you can get him or her medical treatment.

Snow Blindness

Snow blindness is the effect the glare from an ice field, or snowfield, has on the eyes. It is more likely to occur in hazy, cloudy weather because people tend to protect their eyes when the sun is shining and believe protection is unnecessary on cloudy days. If a person waits until he or she feels discomfort or pain to use protective eyewear, a deep burn of the eyes may have already occurred.

Signs of Snow Blindness

There are several signs of snow blindness:

- A sensation of grit in the eyes
- Pain in and over the eyes made worse with eye movement
- Watery and red eyes
- Headache
- Increased pain with exposure to light.

Treatment of Snow Blindness

Treat snow blindness as follows:

1. Cover the eyes with a dark cloth to discourage painful eye movement.

2. Try to give the eyes complete rest without exposure to light. If this is not possible, protect the eyes with dark bandages or very dark glasses.

3. Seek medical treatment. In most cases, once exposure to sunlight stops, the eyes heal in a few days without permanent damage.

Dehydration

Dehydration from cold weather occurs when the body loses too much fluid, salt, and minerals. As mentioned in the previous lesson, you can lose large amounts of fluid and salt through sweating. This loss creates an imbalance of fluids, and dehydration occurs when fluids are not replaced.

Dehydration can occur in both hot and cold climates. In cold weather, sweat evaporates quickly and heavy layers of clothing absorb it, making dehydration more difficult to detect because the signs of sweating are less noticeable; therefore, the danger of dehydration during strenuous cold weather activities can become a serious problem. The symptoms of cold weather dehydration are similar to those of heat exhaustion. Treat dehydration as follows:

1. Move the victim out of the wind and cold, and keep him or her warm.
2. Loosen the victim's clothes to promote circulation.
3. Ensure the victim receives proper fluid replacement, rest, and prompt medical treatment.

Prevention of Cold Injuries

You can prevent many cold weather injuries by taking proper care and precautions when participating in cold weather activities. Be sure to receive adequate nutrition, hot meals, and warm fluids. Get enough rest. Practice good hygiene. Wear the right clothing and protective gear. Do not forget to protect your eyes, ears, and face. Wear layers of clothing so you can remove outer layers if you begin to perspire. Avoid tight clothes that interfere with circulation. Replace or remove any clothing that gets wet as soon as possible.

You may not feel cold injuries because of cold's numbing effect, so always try to go out in cold weather with a partner. You can check each other for signs of injury. Exercise and keep active to maintain steady circulation and improve resistance to the cold. Many cold weather injuries can be avoided by planning ahead, staying alert, and using common sense.

Bites, Stings, and Poisonous Hazards

With so many outdoor activities to participate in, such as hiking, camping, bicycle riding, skate boarding, and skiing, it is common to come across emergencies involving bites, stings, and poisonous hazards. It is estimated that one of every two Americans will be bitten at some time by an animal. Dogs are responsible for about 80 percent of all animal-bite injuries. Additionally, bee, wasp, and other types of insect stings can be not only painful but also fatal if the person is allergic. Depending on where you live, the type of first aid you need to know for snakebites and plants will vary. Knowing what to do when in the outdoors can mean the difference between life and death.

Snakebites

If you spend much of your time outdoors, it may be common for you to come across snakes; however, your chances of snakebites are remote if you remain alert and careful. There are both poisonous and nonpoisonous snakes, so the severity of a snakebite depends on whether the snake is poisonous or not. Beyond that, the severity of snakebites depends on the type of snake, the location of the bite, and the amount and type of venom injected.

Courtesy of Z. Leszczynski/ Animals Animals

Courtesy of Z. Leszczynski/ Animals Animals

Courtesy of Joe McDonald/ Animals Animals

Courtesy of Z. Leszczynski/ Animals Animals

Left to right: rattlesnake, copperhead, water moccasin, and coral snake

Types of Snakes

There are approximately 130 different varieties of nonpoisonous snakes in the United States. They have oval-shaped heads and round pupils. Unlike pit vipers, nonpoisonous snakes do not have sensory pits with which to sense the body heat of their prey.

Poisonous snakes exist throughout the world, primarily in tropical to moderate climates. In the United States, there are four kinds of native poisonous snakes. Three of these four—the rattlesnake, copperhead, and cottonmouth (water moccasin)—are pit vipers.

Pit vipers in other parts of the world include the bushmaster and fer-de-lance in Central and South America, the tropical rattlesnake in Central America, and the Malayan pit viper in eastern Asia. These snakes are shown in Figure 10.21.

Figure 10.21

Common pit vipers

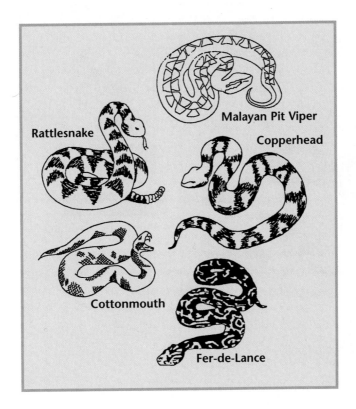

venom—
*a poison produced by
animals such as snakes
and spiders that is
transmitted by a bite
or sting*

Pit vipers have slitlike pupils; flat, triangular-shaped heads; small, deep, heat-sensing pits between their nostrils and eyes; and in most cases, hemotoxic venom. When a pit viper bites, it injects this venom from sacs through long, hollow fangs. This produces a severe burning pain, along with discoloration and swelling around the fang marks. The hemotoxin destroys blood cells, which causes the discoloration of the skin. Blisters and numbness in the affected area follow this reaction. Pit viper bites attack the circulatory system, possibly causing weakness, rapid pulse, and shortness of breath, as well as nausea, vomiting, and shock.

Corals, cobras, kraits, and mambas belong to the cobra family (see Figure 10.22). The coral snake is the only one native to the United States. Rings of red, yellow, and black color encircle its body. Although other nonpoisonous snakes have the same colors, only the coral snake has a red ring next to a yellow ring. The cobra, found in Africa and Asia, forms a hood with its neck when on the defensive. The krait, found in India and Southeast Asia, is brightly banded; the mamba in Africa is either almost black or green.

These snakes look very different, but all four inject their venom—a neurotoxin— through short, grooved fangs leaving a characteristic bite pattern, shown in Figure 10.23. There is minimal pain and swelling compared to a pit viper bite, but because their powerful venom affects the central nervous system, it can cause blurred vision, drooping eyelids, slurred speech, drowsiness, and increased salivation and sweating. Nausea, vomiting, shock, respiratory difficulty, paralysis, convulsions, and coma develop if the bite is not treated promptly.

Sea snakes are found in warm water areas of the Pacific and Indian Oceans. They have small heads, thick bodies, and tails flattened along the sides. Their fangs are only one-quarter inch long, but their venom is very poisonous.

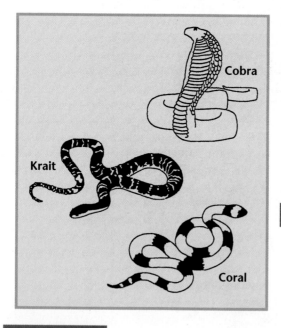

Figure 10.22

Members of the cobra family

Figure 10.23

Poisonous snakebites leave characteristic bite patterns.

Types of Venoms

Basically, venoms are categorized as neurotoxins that affect the nervous system and can cause death by paralysis, hemotoxins that digest tissue including blood cells, or cardiotoxins that affect the heart directly.

Treating Snakebites

Snakebites are rarely fatal if treated within an hour or two of injury, but they can cause pain and illness and may severely damage a bitten hand or foot. Although snakes do not always inject venom, all snakes may carry tetanus (lockjaw); therefore, anyone bitten by a snake, whether poisonous or nonpoisonous, should receive immediate medical attention.

One of the most important parts of treating snakebites is identifying the type of snake making the bite. The type of antivenin used in medical treatment of snakebites varies depending upon the type of venom injected. If you can identify the type of snake causing the injury, let EMS know when you call for help or phone the information ahead to the hospital if you plan to transport the victim yourself. If you cannot identify the snake, try to kill it without risk to yourself or delaying first aid; then show it to emergency medical personnel or take it to the hospital for identification along with the victim.

To treat snakebites, follow these steps:

1. Get the victim away from the snake.

2. Reassure and keep the victim quiet and still. This will keep circulation to a minimum and keep the venom from spreading.

3. Immobilize the affected part in a position below the level of the heart.

4. Remove rings, bracelets, watches, and other jewelry from any affected limb. In case of swelling, this will make the victim more comfortable and will keep the affected limb from losing blood flow.

5. Wash the bite thoroughly with soap and water. Do not apply any ointments.

6. Place an icepack or freeze pack, if available, over the area of the bite. Do not place ice directly on the skin or wrap the limb with ice. You are only trying to cool the bite area, not freeze it.

7. For bites to the arms, legs, hands, or feet, apply constricting bands two to four inches away from the bite (see Figure 10.24). For an arm or leg bite, place one band above and one below the bite. For a hand or foot bite, place one band above the wrist or ankle. To ensure a band is not too tight, you should be able to insert a finger between the band and the skin.

Key Terms

tetanus (lockjaw)— *an acute infectious disease caused by the poison of a certain bacterium that enters the body through a wound, resulting in muscle contractions, rigidity, and death; it is preventable by immunization*

antivenin— *an antitoxin used to counteract venom*

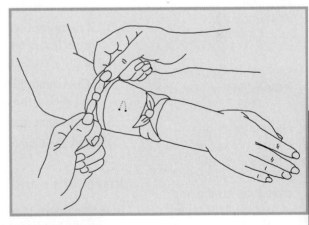

Figure 10.24

Place constricting bands on either side of the snakebite.

UNIT V

8. If swelling from the bite reaches the band, tie another band a few inches farther away from the bite and the old band; then remove the old band.

9. Do not give the victim any food, alcohol, tobacco, medication, or drinks with caffeine.

10. Seek medical aid immediately.

Prevention of Snakebites

Most snakes are shy and passive. Unless they are injured or disturbed, they tend to avoid contact with humans. You can prevent snakebites by using caution and common sense. If you are working outside clearing dense undergrowth, wear gloves, long sleeves, long pants, and boots for protection. When hiking in the wilderness, wear boots and long pants. Try to walk in open areas or stay on established paths. Look where you are stepping or placing a hand if climbing or pushing away tree limbs. Check before sitting on a rock or fallen tree. If possible, stay away from brush, rocks, and undergrowth. If you must handle a snake, even a freshly killed one, use a long tool or stick.

Human and Animal Bites

Mouths of people and animals are full of bacteria, so human and animal bites that break the skin spread germs and may result in serious infection and disease. A person bitten by a diseased animal may come down with tetanus, rabies, and various types of fevers. If you think an animal is carrying a disease, notify the proper authorities to have it captured.

To treat a victim of an animal bite, follow these steps:

1. If bleeding is severe, control it first, before continuing with other first aid. Refer to the section on Controlling Bleeding for procedures to control bleeding.

2. Cleanse the wound thoroughly with soap or a detergent solution and water. Continue to cleanse and flush the wound with water for five minutes.

3. If there is minor bleeding, cover the wound with gauze or a clean cloth, press firmly on the wound, and if possible, raise the injury above the level of the victim's heart.

4. When minor bleeding stops, cover the wound with a sterile dressing and secure the dressing in place.

5. Immobilize an injured arm or leg.

6. Seek medical assistance as soon as possible.

Insect Bites and Stings

In the outdoors, you may come in contact with various types of biting and stinging insects, including bees, mosquitoes, ticks, fleas, and spiders. Most of these insect bites and stings result in minor reactions, such as itching, redness, swelling, and irritation; however, scorpions and certain spiders can inject powerful poisons when they bite, and some people may have an allergic reaction to an insect bite or sting, particularly made by bees or wasps. In these cases, seek medical treatment immediately.

Key Term

rabies—
a viral disease affecting the central nervous system of mammals that is transmitted by a bite from an infected animal; it can result in paralysis and death if left untreated

Key Term

allergic reaction—
a physical reaction, often marked by sneezing, breathing difficulties, itching, rash, or swelling, that some people have when they come in contact with certain substances

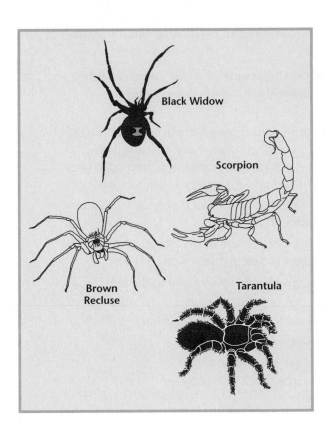

Figure 10.25

Some biting and stinging insects can cause serious health problems.

Black Widow

Scorpion

Brown Recluse

Tarantula

The black widow, brown recluse, tarantulas, and scorpions, shown in Figure 10.25, are some of the more harmful insects you may encounter. Venom from the black widow is neurotoxic and may cause stomach and muscle cramps, breathing difficulties, nausea, sweating, vomiting, and convulsions. Tarantula venom is basically neurotoxic and may produce symptoms similar to those of a black widow bite, but in some cases can affect the heart and may digest tissue, producing a severe local wound. The brown recluse spider can produce severe tissue damage around the bite, possibly leading to gangrene. Although stings from certain types of scorpions are painful but not dangerous, some can cause nausea, fever, stomach cramps, and possibly convulsions and shock.

In most cases, bee and wasp stings produce minimal swelling, pain, redness, itching, and burning at the site of the sting. Multiple stings may cause headaches, fever, muscle cramps, and drowsiness. Symptoms from an allergic reaction may include the following:

- Extreme pain at the site of the sting
- Itching and hives
- Weakness
- Anxiety
- Headache
- Breathing difficulties
- Nausea and vomiting
- Diarrhea
- Collapse, shock, and even death from a serious allergic reaction.

UNIT V

CHAPTER 10   First Aid for Emergency and Nonemergency Situations

Take the following basic first aid measures regardless of what caused the bite or sting:

1. Remove any stinger left in the skin by scraping the skin's surface with a fingernail or knife. Do not squeeze the stinger because it may inject more venom.

2. For tick bites, remove the tick with your fingers if it will come off the skin easily. Do not pull the tick off if it will not come easily; this may leave the head of the tick in the skin which can cause infection. Instead, cover the tick with Vaseline or thick oil to make it let go and then remove it.

3. Wash the area of the bite/sting with soap and water. Apply an antiseptic, if available, to minimize the chances for infection.

4. Use an icepack or cold compresses on the site of the bite/sting to help reduce swelling. Do not apply the ice directly to the skin.

5. Apply calamine lotion or a baking soda and water paste to the bite to relieve pain and itching.

6. Treat more serious allergic reactions as you would snakebites.
   - Apply constricting bands above and below the site
   - Be prepared to perform basic life-support measures
   - To positively identify the insect, attempt to capture it without putting yourself at risk
   - Seek medical aid right away.

7. If signs of infection such as pus, red streaks leading away from the bite, swollen glands, or fever occur within hours or several days after an insect bite, immediately seek medical attention.

Prevention of Insect Bites and Stings

Wear insect repellent when biting insects are present outside. Reapply repellent every few hours when participating in activities that cause heavy perspiration. Wear appropriate protective clothing when hiking or camping in the wilderness or working in a yard, garden, or other woodsy or overgrown area.

Poisonous Plants

Most plants are harmless, but a few can cause allergic reactions on contact. For example, plants of the poison ivy group, including poison oak and poison sumac, produce an oily substance that irritates the skin of many people. Reactions to this substance include a rash characterized by redness, blisters, swelling, and intense burning and itching, as well as headaches and fever. Although the rash usually begins within a few hours after contact, it may appear 24 to 48 hours later.

Courtesy of Gil Fahey/The Picture Cube

Courtesy of Spencer Grant

Courtesy of Perry D. Slocum/Earth Scenes

Poison ivy, oak, and sumac can cause severe allergic reactions in some people.

In general, treat someone who has come in contact with a poisonous plant as follows:

1. Remove contaminated clothing. Set it aside to be washed.

2. Wash all exposed areas of the skin thoroughly with soap and water, then apply rubbing alcohol.

3. Apply calamine or other soothing skin lotion to relieve itching and burning. Avoid covering the rash with a dressing.

4. Seek medical treatment if a severe rash occurs, if the rash is on the face or mouth and may interfere with breathing, or if there is a known history of allergic reactions.

Prevention of Exposure to Poisonous Plants

Become familiar with what poison ivy and other poisonous plants look like so you can recognize a poisonous plant and avoid contacting it. The following are other precautions you should take to limit your exposure to poisonous plants:

* Dress appropriately when participating in outdoor activities
* Avoid areas where you aware that poisonous plants grow
* Do not eat plants or parts of plants that you do not recognize
* Do not put grass, twigs, stems, or leaves in your mouth.

Conclusion

First aid is the help you give an injured person until qualified medical personnel arrive and can give treatment. The type of first aid an individual requires depends on his or her injuries. You determine those injuries by carefully and quickly evaluating the person. In doing so, you follow a sequence that deals with the most life-threatening problems first—breathing and heartbeat, then bleeding, then other injuries—shock, broken bones, burns, and head injuries.

Remember that while it is important to administer first aid as quickly as possible in most cases, some rescue situations require careful assessment before you jump in to save someone. You don't want to become a victim yourself. Remaining calm, thinking logically and clearly, and knowing what steps to take will help you successfully perform first aid.

Being able to adjust to new environments and protect yourself from harmful conditions is very important when you participate in outdoor activities. Extreme temperatures and humidity; animal, snake, and insect bites; and poisonous plants can harm you if you don't take precautions. Be aware of potential hazards, know how to treat nature-related injuries, and exercise common sense. If you do, you can cope successfully with the environment and enjoy your time in the great outdoors.

Review Questions

1 What is the Good Samaritan Law?

2 Why is it important to have rubber gloves and a face shield in your first aid kit?

3 What are the ABCs of lifesaving steps?

4 What are the common signs of a stroke?

5 What are the three types of bleeding?

6 What is something you should not do when treating a fracture?

7 What are the signs of shock?

8 What are the three types of burns?

9 What are common types of inhaled poisons?

10 What are the types of heat injuries?

11 How do you treat hypothermia?

12 What are the symptoms of an allergic reaction to an insect bite or sting?

Geography and Survival Skills

Geography, Map Skills, and Environmental Awareness

Key Terms

- latitude
- longitude
- degree
- meridian
- parallel
- prime meridian
- relief
- topographic map
- terrain
- marginal information
- bar scale
- legend
- orient
- orienteering
- declination
- true north
- magnetic north
- grid north

What You Will Learn to Do

Understand the principles and tools of map reading and land navigation

Skills and Knowledge You Will Gain Along the Way

✔ Identify the components of a globe

✔ Explain the characteristics of topographic maps

✔ Use the Grid Reference System to locate points anywhere in the world

✔ Use terrain features to orient a map and determine your location

✔ Measure distance using maps

✔ Calculate direction on topographic maps

✔ Use a compass and grid to locate a position on a topographical map

✔ Apply map reading and land navigation skills to determine location

✔ Relate map-reading skills to orienteering

Previous page: Courtesy of US Navy/Photographer's First Mate 1st Class Marthaellen L. Ball

Introduction

For you to be a better citizen, it is important that you know about the world around you. How often while watching a news program, have you heard the name of a country and wondered where it was? Or while enjoying a movie filmed in a beautiful location have you thought that you would like to visit there someday? An understanding of the globe can help you readily identify a location and provide you with a visual or mental picture of it.

An overview of the globe will give you a basic understanding of the world in which you live. This overview will include the seven continents, four oceans, two poles, as well as longitude and latitude lines.

The Globe: An Overview

A Globe Defined

A globe is a sphere-shaped model of the earth. It is a representation of the earth as it really is, round or like a ball. Looking at photos of the earth taken from space, you will only see half of the earth, or one hemisphere. A globe shows the whole earth. It shows the water and land formations on the earth's surface and helps you to understand natural events such as day and night and the seasons.

The Continents

Continents are the seven large landmasses on the planet. It is believed that there was only one continent over 225 million years ago. This continent slowly broke apart, shifted, and drifted over millions of years until it assumed the shapes and positions of the seven continents that exist today. The seven continents (shown in Figure 1.1) from largest to smallest are Asia, Africa, North America, South America, Antarctica, Europe, and Australia.

Asia is the largest continent in both size and population. It covers almost a third of the world's land area (16.9 million square miles) and has about three-fifths of its people (3.7 billion). It has 49 independent countries. Asia extends from Africa and Europe in the west to the Pacific Ocean in the east. The northernmost part of the continent lies within the frozen Arctic. In the south, Asia reaches into the steaming tropics near the equator.

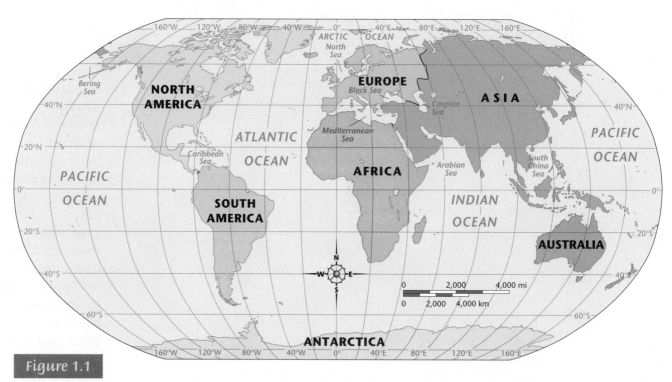

Figure 1.1

The world continents, oceans, and seas

Courtesy of MapQuest.com, Inc.

Asia has some of the world's longest rivers, largest deserts, and thickest forests and jungles. The highest and lowest places on the earth are in Asia. The photo above depicts the highest, Mount Everest, which rises 29,028 feet above sea level and is along the Nepal-Tibet border. In contrast the Dead Sea shore, located between Israel and Jordan, is the world's lowest land, lying about 1,310 feet below sea level.

Africa is the second largest continent in area and population. Africa covers about one-fifth of the world's land area (11.6 million square miles) and is home to one-eighth of its people (824 million). The continent is an immense plateau, broken by a few mountain ranges and bordered in some areas by a narrow coastal plain. It is a land of striking contrasts and great natural wonders. Tropical rain forests inhabit western and central Africa. The world's largest desert, the Sahara, stretches across northern Africa. It occupies an area almost as large as the entire United States. Africa also has the world's longest river—the Nile. It flows more than 4,000 miles through northeastern Africa. Much of the rest of the continent is grassland located in eastern and southern Africa.

The Panama Canal
Courtesy of Photo Researchers

North America is the third largest continent in area (9.3 million square miles) making up about one-sixth of the world's land area. It extends from the Arctic Ocean in the north to South America in the south. It ranks fourth among the continents in population. (Asia, Africa, and Europe are larger in population.) The continent is roughly triangular in shape with the Arctic, Atlantic, and Pacific Oceans bordering its three sides. At its northern end, North America stretches more than 5,400 miles from Alaska's Aleutian Islands to the Canadian province of Newfoundland. At the southern end of the continent, the narrowest parts of Panama are only about 30 miles wide.

South America is the fourth largest continent in area (6.8 million square miles). Only Asia, Africa, and North America are larger. It ranks fifth among the continents in population (346.9 million). Asia, Europe, Africa, and North America all have more people. South America covers about 12 percent of the world's land area and has about 6 percent of the total world population.

The Amazon River Basin
Courtesy of Photo Researchers

South America has nearly every type of landscape and climate, even though it is only 600 miles from Antarctica. The world's largest tropical rain forest grows in the Amazon River Basin (Figure 1.1.5). This basin occupies about two-fifths of the continent. By contrast, the Atacama Desert in northern Chile is one of the driest places in the world. Also to be found are snowy peaks and active volcanoes rising along the crest of the lofty Andes Mountains of western South America. Not to be forgotten are the rolling grasslands that stretch endlessly through much of Argentina and Venezuela. South America's varied landscape also includes spectacular waterfalls, huge lakes, and rocky, windswept islands.

South America is almost totally surrounded by water. The Caribbean Sea lies to the north and the Atlantic Ocean borders South America on the northeast and east. To the south, the Drake Passage separates South America from Antarctica. The Pacific Ocean is located on the west coast. South America borders land only at the Isthmus of Panama. This narrow strip of land links Central America with Colombia, in the northwestern part of South America.

Antarctica is an ice-covered continent located in the South Pole—the earth's most southerly region. Its nearly barren land forms the coldest and iciest region in the world. It is slightly colder than the region around the North Pole because the North Pole is located in the Arctic Ocean. The South Pole lies near the center of the Antarctic continent, on a high windy plateau of ice and snow. Antarctica's deepest ice is more than 10 times the height of the Sears Tower, one of the world's tallest buildings.

Antarctica covers about 5.4 million square miles, making it larger in area than either Europe or Australia. But it would be the smallest continent if it did not have its icecap. This icy layer, which averages 7,100 feet thick, increases Antarctica's surface area and also makes Antarctica the highest continent in terms of average elevation.

Stormy waters of the Atlantic, Indian, and Pacific Oceans isolate Antarctica from the other continents. The world's lowest temperatures have been recorded in Antarctica. Ice and snow cover 98 percent of the continent. Underneath the ice, Antarctica has mountains, lowlands, and valleys—much like the landforms of other countries.

The ice sheets of Antarctica
Courtesy of National Geographic Society

Monaco:
A Mediterranean location
Courtesy of National Geographic
Society

Ayers Rock
in the Australian desert
Courtesy of Comstock Stock
Photography

Europe is one of the smallest of the world's seven continents in area but one of the largest in population. It covers an area of about 4 million square miles and has a population of 707.8 million. Only Asia and Africa have more people. About one-eighth of the world's people live in Europe. Europe extends from the Arctic Ocean in the north to the Mediterranean Sea in the south and from the Atlantic Ocean in the west to the Ural Mountains in the east. Because Europe and Asia occupy the same landmass, they are sometimes collectively called Eurasia. The photo opposite shows Monaco, a popular European travel destination on the Mediterranean Sea.

Australia is the only country that is also a continent. As a country, Australia is the sixth largest in the world. As a continent, however, it ranks smallest in size. It is a stable landmass that lies between the Indian and Pacific Oceans. The northern third of Australia lies in the tropics and is warm the year round. The rest of the continent has warm summers and cool winters. About a third of the country is desert. Since it lies south of the equator, its seasons are the opposite of those in the Northern Hemisphere.

Oceans

Did you know that the ocean is one continuous body of water interrupted by landmasses? It has been assigned four different names based on where it is divided by these landmasses: Pacific Ocean, Atlantic Ocean, Indian Ocean, and Arctic Ocean.

The Pacific Ocean is the largest and deepest of the four oceans and covers a third of the globe, over 64 million square miles or 165.8 billion square kilometers. Its average depth is 12,900 feet. It is so large that all seven continents could fit in it and there would still be room for one more continent the size of Asia. It separates North and South America from Asia and Australia.

The Atlantic Ocean is the second largest body of water on the globe, covering 33 million square miles or 867.7 billion square kilometers. It is continually widening and has an average depth of 11,700 feet. The Atlantic Ocean is bordered by Europe and Africa on the east and by North America and South America on the west.

The Indian Ocean is the third largest ocean and covers an area of about 28.3 million square miles or 73.3 billion square kilometers. At 12,600 feet deep, it is deeper than the Atlantic Ocean but smaller in size. It is the only ocean that is bordered by land on the north rather than water. On the eastern border is Indonesia and Australia. Africa is to the west and Antarctica is to the south.

The Arctic Ocean is the smallest and shallowest of the four oceans. It is about 5 million square miles or 13 million square kilometers and averages about 4,000 feet deep. It is located at the top of the globe and is bordered primarily by northern Asia, Europe, and North America.

These four oceans are salt water and cover more than 70 percent of the earth's surface. They contain the highest mountain range, deepest valley, and some of the most unusual animals on earth.

Global Grid

North Pole

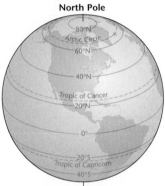

South Pole

Parallels of Latitude

North Pole

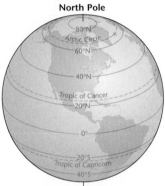

South Pole

Meridians of Longitude

North Pole

South Pole

Poles

The points on the globe representing the northernmost and southernmost points of the earth are the North Pole and South Pole. These poles are located on each end of the earth's imaginary axis. The areas around them are sometimes referred to as polar regions because they are around the North and South Poles. The North Pole is located in the Arctic and the South Pole is located in Antarctica. They are the coldest places on earth—frozen deserts covered in ice all year long. The North Pole is the farthest point north. When looking down at a globe of the earth, it is shown at the top. When you look down on a globe of the North Pole, the landmasses of North America, Europe, Asia, and even parts of Africa can be seen. The South Pole is the farthest point south. A map centered on the South Pole features the continent of Antarctica surrounded by ocean. Because it is over land instead of water, the Antarctic region is much colder than the Arctic. The closest continents visible from this vantage point are South America, Africa, and Australia.

Longitude and Latitude

Lines of latitude and longitude are imaginary lines that form a grid covering the whole globe. This grid, as shown in Figure 1.2, helps geographers find the location of places anywhere in the world. Lines of latitude run east to west around the globe. Lines of longitude run north to south, meeting at the poles. Taken together, latitude and longitude lines form a grid. Every place on earth has a unique position on this grid. Mogadishu, Somalia is located at 2°N latitude and 45°E longitude. New Orleans, Louisiana, is at 30°N and 90°W.

The concept of latitude and longitude has its origin in ancient times, nearly 2,000 years before the earth could be photographed from space. The Ancient Greeks used observation and mathematics to determine that the earth was round and not flat. They then developed a method for locating places on the earth. They came up with a system to divide the globe into 360 segments, called degrees. The imaginary vertical lines used to divide these parts are the longitude lines or meridians. They run from the North Pole to the South Pole and are equal in length. The imaginary horizontal lines on the globe are the latitude or parallel lines. These lines are parallel to each other and form complete circles around the globe. The horizontal lines of latitude and the vertical lines of longitude are further broken down into degrees, minutes, and seconds so that any point on earth can be located using the two lines that meet at that point on a globe.

In 1884, the prime meridian, or the longitude line numbered 0 degrees, was established at an international conference. It is the starting point for measuring distances east and west around the globe. The prime meridian at 0 degrees and the 180th meridian or longitude line on the opposite side bisect the globe into eastern and western halves. Longitude lines east of the prime meridian are numbered 1 degree to 180 degrees east (E). This part of the earth is the Eastern Hemisphere. Longitude lines west of the prime meridian also numbered 1 degree to 180 degrees west (W) represent the Western Hemisphere. The prime meridian passes through the Royal Naval Observatory in Greenwich, a section of London, England.

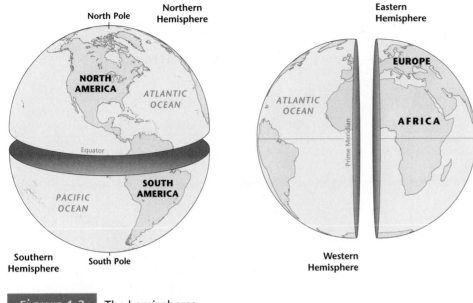

Figure 1.3   The hemispheres

Courtesy of MapQuest.com, Inc.

The equator, or 0 degrees latitude, is an imaginary line that circles the globe at its widest point halfway between the North Pole and South Pole. The equator is the longest latitude line or parallel. Latitude is measured from 0 degrees to 90 degrees from the equator to the North Pole. This part of the earth from the equator to the North Pole is known as the Northern Hemisphere (Figure 1.3). Latitude is also measured from 0 degrees to 90 degrees from the equator to the South Pole. This part of the earth from the equator to the South Pole is known as the Southern Hemisphere. When any latitude line is given, it must be stated in north or south latitude.

Introduction to Maps

Have you ever found yourself on the wrong road or in the wrong neighborhood? If you asked for directions in this situation, were you told, "Go right," or "Turn left"? After following these directions for a few blocks, the question arises, "Turn right . . . where?" These types of situations call for map reading skills.

Knowing how to read and understand maps are valuable skills that can strengthen your awareness of the world around you. Your effective use of maps requires a basic understanding of them, as well as of their scales, symbols, and colors. This section introduces you to this information and explains how to orient a map by matching man-made or natural features with map symbols.

Maps are in common use throughout the world today. For instance, when a family takes a vacation, a map is used to guide the driver from one city to another. The airline pilot and the sea captain use special charts or maps to navigate. Rarely do experienced navigators become lost because they apply their map reading abilities to read, understand, and use maps effectively.

Key Terms

latitude—
the angular distance north or south of the earth's equator, measured in degrees along a meridian, as on a map or globe

longitude—
lines that run from the North Pole to the South Pole and are equal in length on a map or globe

degree—
a unit of latitude or longitude, equal to 1/360 of the globe

meridian—
an imaginary circle on the earth's surface passing through the North and South Poles; a line or parallel of longitude

parallel—
lines that do not intersect

prime meridian—
the line of longitude that passes through Greenwich, England, designated as zero degrees longitude, and from which longitude east and west are measured

Figure 1.4

A geographic map—
Mexico's population
distribution
Courtesy of MapQuest.com, Inc.

Definition of a Map and Map Reading

A map is a line drawing of a portion of the earth's surface, drawn to scale as seen
from above. Obviously any attempt to plot each feature to its exact shape and scale
would result in a map too big to read. Therefore, maps are drawn "to scale" with
each set measurement on the scale representing a set amount of the earth's surface.

In general, maps provide information about the existence and location of man-made
and natural features; show distance, elevation, and different types of landforms;
and depict man-made and natural features by the use of symbols, lines, colors,
and forms or shapes.

There are many different types of maps. However, the most common types are:

• City or state road maps

• Geographic maps/atlases

• Topographic maps.

City or state road maps, also known as tourist maps, provide information on street
names, important buildings, route numbers, distance, and transportation centers.
In many cases, they include the location of recreational or historical areas, as well.

Geographic maps show an overall view of the mapped area in relation to climate, population, relief, vegetation, and hydrography (water features) (see Figure 1.4). An atlas is a collection of geographic maps of regions, countries, continents, or the world. These maps are generally not as accurate as city or state maps. And compared to topographic maps, their accuracy is significantly inferior; therefore, they should be used for general information only.

Topographic maps show terrain and landforms in a manner which can be measured. They also show the horizontal positions and elevations of these features. Elevation on these maps is normally indicated by vertical contour lines. Topographic maps are the ones most commonly used in the military. Beginning with the next section, you will examine topographic maps in detail and will use them throughout the remainder of this chapter so that you can begin to understand how to read and use them.

Road Maps

You can compare a map to any piece of equipment—before you use it, you must first read the instructions. Most mapmakers place the instructions on a map (known as the marginal information) around the outer edge of a map. All maps are not the same, so it is necessary to read the marginal information carefully every time you use a different map (see Figure 1.5). The following discussion describes and illustrates the most commonly used elements of marginal information that are found on road maps.

- **Sheet or Map Name.** Whenever possible, a map is named after the most prominent cultural or geographic feature in that area (for example, Orlando or the Official Transportation Map for the State of Florida). Although the most prominent feature on the map may be a state or other large geographical region (for example the Mid-Atlantic States), the map sheet normally contains numerous inserts of smaller sections in order to show them in more detail. These inserts can be found around the margin or on the reverse side of the map sheet.

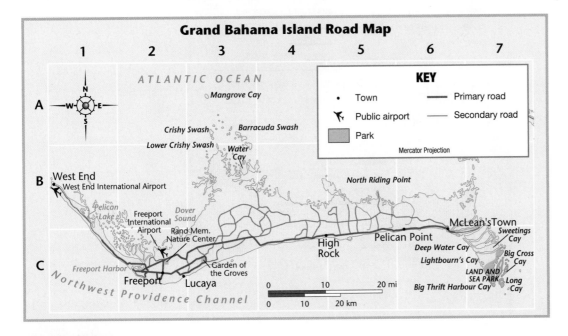

Figure 1.5 A road map
Courtesy of MapQuest.com, Inc.

Figure 1.6

An example of a bar scale

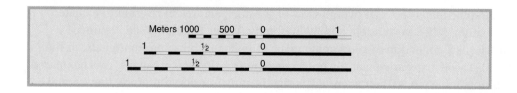

- **Bar Scales.** Bar scales are special rulers used to measure ground distance on a map. Although these scales may vary with each road map, the most common units of measurement are miles and kilometers. Figure 1.6 shows an example of a scale used on the Official Transportation Map for the State of Florida.

- **Printing Note.** This note indicates the agency responsible for printing the map. The printing date determines when the map was printed, not when the information was obtained.

- **Legend.** The legend is part of the mapmaker's dictionary. It is a shorthand method of illustrating and identifying mapped features using symbols to show some of the more prominent features on the map. These symbols are not the same on every road map.

Map Symbols

Because all features on a map cannot represent their true position and shape, mapmakers must use symbols to represent these features. These symbols are made to look as closely as possible to the actual features themselves as they are seen from above. The legend indicates the meanings of the symbols that are used on a map. A few of the commonly used symbols that you will find on road maps are identified in Figure 1.7.

Figure 1.7

Commonly used map symbols

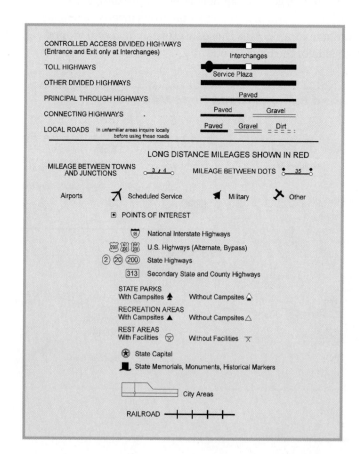

- **Roads.** Indicated by parallel or solid lines. Thickness and color of these symbols indicate the road size.
- **Interchanges.** Indicated by a heavy solid line for major access roads and parallel lines for intersecting secondary roads. Legends also illustrate full, partial, and no access at these interchanges.
- **Railroads.** Commonly shown by single or parallel lines with horizontal tick marks.
- **Buildings.** Symbols for buildings may vary from map to map according to the purpose of the map or building. Schools and churches are commonly represented by a solid square with a flag or cross affixed. Hospitals may be shown by a cross. Universities and colleges may sometimes have a special symbol as a point of interest.
- **Points of Interest.** Indicated by a special marking and its name; for example, a historical marker.
- **Airports.** Normally shown by a picture of an airplane.
- **Water Features.** Normally shown in blue and take the approximate shape of the feature.
- **Special Features.** Significant natural features (forests, recreational areas, national monuments, and so on), military reservations, or Indian reservations are normally highlighted with a specific color and do not have a standard shape. Many road maps also have a chart indicating the services that are available at the recreational areas and parks shown on the map.

You may also find the following symbols on road maps that can provide helpful information to you when using the map.

- **Route Markers.** Represented by a shield or some other shape containing the number of the road in its center. Although the map may show these route markers with white numbers and/or letters on a black shield or shape, the actual colors of the signs as seen on the highway are indicated in the previous bulleted list.
- **Interstate Highways.** There are a number of interstate highway types, and these are generally shown as:
  - **Principal Routes.** Red, white, and blue signs with one- or two-digit numbers. East-west routes have even numbers (I-4 or I-70), whereas north-south routes have odd numbers (I-5 or I-95).
  - **Loop or Belt Routes.** Red, white, and blue signs with three-digit numbers; the first number is always even (I-295). These routes circle or bypass major cities.
  - **Spur Routes.** Red, white, and blue signs with three-digit numbers; the first number is always odd (I-580). These routes lead into major cities.
  - **Business Routes.** Green signs marking routes from principal, loop, or belt highways that go to or through cities.
- **Boundary Symbols.** Shown as broken or intermittent lines that vary in pattern to denote different boundaries.

- **Mileage Markers.** Shown between towns and road junctions or between dots with the mileage indicated in red or black. State and regional maps also show long distance mileage between major cities by printing that information in red (with red directional arrows), and centering it between the two cities. An example of this long distance mileage indicator may appear as follows:

TAMPA

199 Miles

320 Kilometers

WEST PALM BEACH

- **Official Highway Mileages.** This chart shows the actual ground mileage between the major cities that are located on the map.
- **City/Street Names.** This information lists alphabetically (wherever space permits on the map—including on the reverse side of it—and printed adjacent to its corresponding feature) the names of cities on state and regional maps and the names of streets on city maps. Beside each city or street listing is a letter/number code (for example, D-9). Along the outer edge of the margin are letters ranging from "A" to "P" (or beyond) and numbers ranging from "1" to "15" (or beyond). Note that the letter "I" is usually omitted so as not to be mistaken for the number "1."

The following example shows how to locate features on a road map using this letter/number code.

> **Note:**
>
> For this example, the map sheet will have the letters along the vertical (left and right) edges of the margin and the numbers along the horizontal (top and bottom) edges.

To find the feature at D-9, use a finger on one hand to locate the letter "D"—it should be close to the top left or top right edges of the map. Next, use a finger on your other hand to locate the number "9" across the top or bottom margin. Now, move both fingers in from the margins toward the map. Where they meet is the general location of the feature. Street names may still be hard to find on a cluttered map, but you have narrowed the search to a specific area.

- **Special Traffic Regulations/Traffic Control Devices.** This section contains some of the traffic regulations and/or signs (control devices) used within the state that may be different from other states within the region.

> **Note:**
>
> It is the motorist's responsibility to know the regulations and meanings of all control devices within the region in which he or she is driving. Ignorance is not an acceptable excuse under the law.

Map Colors

Colors on a road map provide contrast to map features, making them easier to identify. Map symbols are usually printed in different colors with each color identifying a class of features. However, colors may vary from one map to another. When used differently, mapmakers indicate these colors and their uses in the marginal information.

The following describes the basic colors used on most road maps and the features they represent. Occasionally, mapmakers may use other colors to indicate special information.

- **Black.** Indicates the majority of man-made features: buildings or roads.
- **Blue.** Identifies water features: lakes, swamps, or rivers.
- **Brown.** Identifies elevation and relief features: mountain ranges.
- **Green.** Identifies vegetation: woods, grassland, brush, orchards, or vineyards.
- **Red.** Classifies man-made features: populated areas, main roads, special features, or boundaries on older maps.

Orienting a Map

Finding your way requires the ability to read and interpret a map, compare it to the features on the ground, and move to the desired location. One method of comparing your map to the ground is to orient it so that the map symbols fit the location of the features as they appear on the ground. A properly oriented map can also indicate direction; that is, after you have it correctly oriented to the ground, the top of it will usually point toward the north.

The following situation shows you how to orient a map without using a compass.

While participating in a bike rally, Barry traveled off the main road and became lost. He knew for certain he was lost when he came upon the main entrance to North Fork State Park on his right. Across from this entrance was a small bridge which crossed the North Fork River. Because Barry had a route map for this bike rally, he took the following steps to orient it.

1. Barry determined his location using at least two known points. He chose to use the man-made features of the bridge and the park entrance and the natural feature of the river.

2. Next, he located these same features on his map. With the map in a horizontal position, he rotated it until the symbol for the river was pointed in the same direction as (or aligned with) the river in front of him.

3. Barry then checked to ensure that the park entrance was correctly aligned with its actual location. From where he was located, the park entrance was on the right side of the road. He checked to see if the map symbol for the park entrance was also on the right side of the road.

With his map properly oriented, he realized what direction he had to take to rejoin the bike rally.

Key Term

orient—
to align or position oneself (or a map) in relationship to one's surroundings

In many cases, orienting a map may mean turning it upside down or holding it with one of its edges pointing toward you. Holding a map like this may make it harder for you to read street names or other symbols, but it properly aligns the features on the ground with those on the map. After you know where you are (by using the two or more known points discussed in the above story), keep the map oriented until you are at your destination or in an area familiar to you.

The next time you are on a trip to a place where you have never been before, try this method. It works! You will be able to navigate your way to your destination much more easily.

Care of Maps

Because you may have to keep a map for a long time, exercise care when using it. Three important considerations in the care of maps are:

- Properly refold it after each use
- Use a pencil if it becomes necessary to mark on it so that you can easily erase any marks
- Avoid spilling liquids on it.

Global Positioning System

The Global Positioning System (GPS) is a high-tech worldwide radio-navigation system formed from a network of 24 satellites and their ground stations. GPS provides more precise and efficient methods of surveying and mapmaking. Today, GPS makes it possible to accomplish the same work in a fraction of the time. Mapping is the science of using GPS to pinpoint locations and then create maps of any location in the world, including both natural and man-made features.

Introduction to Topographic Maps

This section presents an overview of topographic maps. It describes their characteristics and examines the marginal information, symbols, and colors used on them. The remainder of this chapter focuses on the use of topographic maps.

Compared to road maps, topographic maps show more detail of an area's natural features. Because of its detail, especially of terrain features, elevation, and relief, the military prefers this type of map.

After you have mastered the basics of map reading in this chapter, you will have the opportunity to demonstrate your knowledge of these skills during outdoor practical exercises. Whether you are practicing basic land navigation techniques, participating in orienteering, or performing land navigation at summer camp, knowing how to use topographic maps can help you in the following ways:

- Finding your way if you become separated from a group
- Successfully, and safely, navigating a group, especially during cross-country movements
- Determining distances from one location to another
- Pinpointing locations in a given area
- Determining the type of terrain in which you or your unit must operate
- Planning trips or operations.

Key Term

orienteering—
a competitive form of land navigation in which each participant uses a map and compass to navigate between checkpoints

Interpreting a Topographic Map

A hiker poised at the start of an unfamiliar mountain trail needs a special kind of map tucked into his or her backpack: a topographic, or contour, map. This kind of map shows the changes in elevation that lie ahead—and how quickly these changes take place. Does the trail climb steeply for the next mile, or is the grade a slow and steady rise? Will there be serious climbing involved, or can the hiker cover the distance at an easy, arm-swinging pace? How far can the hiker expect to go in a single afternoon? A good topographic map can be used to answer all these questions and help ensure the success and safety of a hike.

Introducing Topographic Maps

Topographic maps are useful tools with many applications. Backpackers take them along when they set out on hiking, rock climbing, and camping trips; however, they are not the only people who use topographic maps. Engineers use them when deciding where to build highways and dams. Police and emergency medical personnel often consult topographic maps during search-and-rescue operations for people who are lost in the woods.

The topographic map in Figure 1.8 shows the Pacific island of Tahiti. Use the following steps to study and analyze the map.

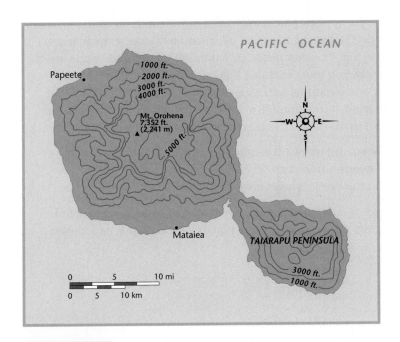

Figure 1.8   Topographic map of Tahiti
Courtesy of Geosystems Global Corporation

1. **Understand what contour lines measure.** The lines on a topographic map are called contour lines. A contour line connects all points where elevation is equal. If you were to hike along one of the contour lines shown on this topographic map, you would always be at the same height above sea level. Notice that the contour lines are labeled with numbers that tell the elevation in feet along that contour line. Now use the map to answer the following questions:

   - What elevation does the coastline represent?

   - What is the highest point on Tahiti?

   - Are Papeete and Mataiea at about the same or different elevations?

2. **Interpret the relationships among contour lines.** When a series of contour lines is close together, it means that the elevation of the land is changing rapidly—in other words, the terrain is steep. On the other hand, contour lines spread wide apart indicate that the elevation is changing slowly and the land is relatively flat. Answer the following questions:

   - Is the island generally steeper near the top of Mt. Orohena or near the coast?

   - Where is the steepest part of the Taiarapu Peninsula?

3. **Put the data you have collected to use.** After you understand how to read a topographic map, you can use this skill to help plan a hike or a camping trip. Use the map to answer the following questions:

   - If you and a friend wanted to climb to the top of Mt. Orohena, how would you plot the most gradual ascent possible?

   - How would you plot a steeper climb?

Marginal Information

The marginal information for topographic maps varies significantly from that of road maps. One major difference is that the marginal information on topographic maps is more standardized than that on other maps. However, all topographic maps are not the same. Consequently, you must examine this information carefully before using each map. This section identifies ten items of marginal information that you will need to know when using a topographic map in the remainder of this chapter. You will learn more about these items in subsequent sections in this chapter.

The topographic map shown in Figure 1.9 is only an extract of how one actually appears; there are three major differences. The mapped area and bar scales are drawn to scale, but the extract represents only a small portion of the actual map.

As you can see, this map has a detailed legend, which can be seen in more detail in Figure 1.10. The marginal information for this topographical map is as follows:

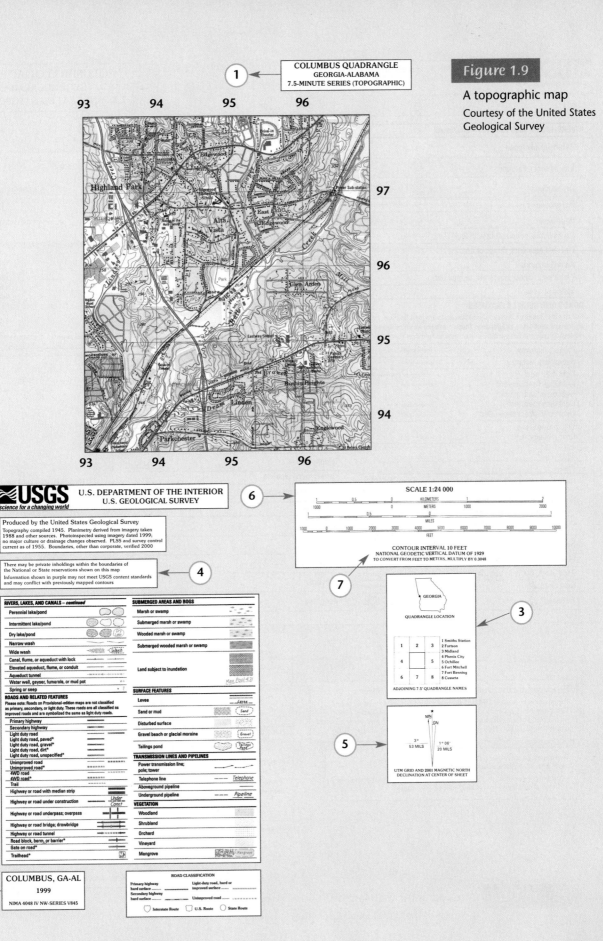

Figure 1.9

A topographic map
Courtesy of the United States
Geological Survey

383

1 → **COLUMBUS QUADRANGLE**
GEORGIA-ALABAMA
7.5-MINUTE SERIES (TOPOGRAPHIC)

3

GEORGIA

QUADRANGLE LOCATION

1	2	3
4		5
6	7	8

1 Smiths Station
2 Fortson
3 Midland
4 Phenix City
5 Ochillee
6 Fort Mitchell
7 Fort Benning
8 Cusseta

ADJOINING 7.5' QUADRANGLE NAMES

MN ★ GN

3°
53 MILS

1° 06'
20 MILS

UTM GRID AND 2001 MAGNETIC NORTH
DECLINATION AT CENTER OF SHEET

5

RIVERS, LAKES, AND CANALS – *continued*

Perennial lake/pond

Intermittent lake/pond

Dry lake/pond — Dry Lake

Narrow wash

Wide wash — Wash

Canal, flume, or aqueduct with lock

Elevated aqueduct, flume, or conduit

Aqueduct tunnel

Water well, geyser, fumarole, or mud pot

Spring or seep

ROADS AND RELATED FEATURES

Please note: Roads on Provisional-edition maps are not classified as primary, secondary, or light duty. These roads are all classified as improved roads and are symbolized the same as light duty roads.

Primary highway

Secondary highway

Light duty road
Light duty road, paved*
Light duty road, gravel*
Light duty road, dirt*
Light duty road, unspecified*

Unimproved road
Unimproved road*

4WD road
4WD road*

Trail

Highway or road with median strip

Highway or road under construction — Under Const

Highway or road underpass; overpass

Highway or road bridge; drawbridge

Highway or road tunnel

Road block, berm, or barrier*

Gate on road*

Trailhead*

SUBMERGED AREAS AND BOGS

Marsh or swamp

Submerged marsh or swamp

Wooded marsh or swamp

Submerged wooded marsh or swamp

Land subject to inundation — Max Pool 431

SURFACE FEATURES

Levee — Levee

Sand or mud — Sand

Disturbed surface

Gravel beach or glacial moraine — Gravel

Tailings pond — Tailings Pond

TRANSMISSION LINES AND PIPELINES

Power transmission line;
pole; tower

Telephone line — Telephone

Aboveground pipeline

Underground pipeline — Pipeline

VEGETATION

Woodland

Shrubland

Orchard

Vineyard

Mangrove — Mangrove

6

8

Produced by the United States Geological Survey

Topography compiled 1945. Planimetry derived from imagery taken 1988 and other sources. Photoinspected using imagery dated 1999; no major culture or drainage changes observed. PLSS and survey control current as of 1955. Boundaries, other than corporate, verified 2000

9

There may be private inholdings within the boundaries of the National or State reservations shown on this map

Information shown in purple may not meet USGS content standards and may conflict with previously mapped contours

4

SCALE 1:24 000

KILOMETERS

METERS

MILES

FEET

7 → CONTOUR INTERVAL 10 FEET
NATIONAL GEODETIC VERTICAL DATUM OF 1929
TO CONVERT FROM FEET TO METERS, MULTIPLY BY 0.3048

ROAD CLASSIFICATION

Primary highway
hard surface ....

Secondary highway
hard surface ....

Light-duty road, hard or
improved surface ......

Unimproved road ......

Interstate Route   U.S. Route   State Route

2 → **COLUMBUS, GA-AL**
1999
NIMA 4048 IV NW-SERIES V845

Figure 1.10   A topographic map legend
Courtesy of the United States Geological Survey

1. **Sheet Name.** You can locate the sheet name at the center of the top margin and in the lower left area of the map margin. As with road maps, mapmakers generally title a map after its prominent cultural or geographic feature.

2. **Sheet Number.** You can find the sheet number located in either the upper right or the lower left corners. Use it as a reference number for the map sheet.

3. **Adjoining Map Sheets Diagram.** Locate the adjoining (or adjacent) map sheets diagram in the right corner of the lower margin. This diagram contains nine squares; the center square is the map sheet at which you are looking. The remaining squares show the sheet numbers for those maps at the same scale that surround the area covered by the center square.

4. **Special Notes.** Special notes are statements of general information that relate to the mapped area; for example, the map is red-light readable (located in the lower right corner) or a lane is generally considered as being a minimum of 2.5 meters (located in the lower left corner).

5. **Declination Diagram.** Another item of information located in the lower right margin is the declination diagram. All you need to know at this time is that it indicates the direction and relationship of true, magnetic, and grid north.

6. **Scales.** Locate the graphic (bar) scales in the center of the lower margin of the map. Compare the differences between these scales and those found on road maps.

   Map scale is expressed as a representative fraction, which gives the ratio of map distance to ground distance. For example, the scale 1:50,000 indicates that one unit of measure on the map equals 50,000 units of the same measure on the ground.

   Most topographic maps have more than one scale, each using a different unit of measurement. The most common units of measurement are miles (statute and nautical), meters/kilometers, and yards.

   Mapmakers divide each scale into two parts: an extension scale and a primary scale. Use the primary scale, located to the right of the zero, to measure full units of measurement. Use the extension scale, located to the left of the zero, to measure tenths of a unit. Read the extension scale right to left from the zero and the primary scale left to right from the zero.

7. **Contour Interval Note.** The contour interval note also appears in the center of the lower margin. It represents the vertical distance between adjacent contour lines on the map.

8. **Unit Imprint.** You can find the unit imprint below the left corner of the mapped area. It identifies the agency that prepared and printed the map.

9. **Legend.** The legend appears below the unit imprint. It states the effective date of the road and other data and illustrates the symbols used on the map. Figure 1.3.3 shows another example of a legend.

10. **Grid Reference Box.** Some topographical maps also include a grid reference box. The grid reference box contains information for identifying the grid zone and the 100,000 meter square representing the area. It also provides instructions for giving grid references on the map. The next two sections present information on grid referencing systems and the usefulness of the grid reference box.

Key Terms

declination—
an angular difference between true north and either magnetic or grid north

true north—
a line from any position on the earth's surface to the geographic North Pole; symbolized by a line with a star at the apex

magnetic north—
the direction to the north magnetic pole, as indicated by the north-seeking needle of a magnetic instrument

grid north—
the direction of north that is established by using the vertical grid lines on a map

statute mile—
a unit of measurement that is approximately 5,280 feet

nautical mile—
a unit of measurement that is approximately 6,080 feet—which is one minute of latitude; it is slightly longer than a statute mile

grid zone—
one of the 60 north–south divisions of the earth's surface between 84 degrees north latitude and 80 degrees south latitude, each 6 degrees wide

UNIT VI

Map Symbols

As in the previous section on road maps, topographic maps use symbols to represent the position and shape of features as viewed from above. The legend explains the meanings for the symbols used on a topographic map.

Map symbols on topographic maps are generally more detailed than on other maps. For example, these maps include unimproved roads and trails, different gauges of railroad tracks, power lines, mines or quarries, bench marks, and spot elevations. However, the symbols are not always the same on every map. Always refer to the legend to avoid errors when reading a map.

Map Colors

The five colors (black, blue, brown, green, and red) used for road maps and the features they represent are also used on topographic maps. In addition, topographic maps use two colors that are usually not found on other maps. These two colors are white, which identifies an area void of vegetation, and reddish-brown, which identifies man-made and relief features and elevation such as contour lines on red-light readable maps. These can be seen in Figure 1.11.

> **Note:**
>
> Brown also identifies relief features and may indicate elevation, or contour lines, on older maps. Refer to Figure 1.11 to see these colors on an actual topographic map of Mt. Rainier in Washington.

If other colors appear on a topographic map, the marginal information must contain an explanation of their use.

Key Term

bench mark—
a surveyor's mark made on rocks or other permanent objects to indicate known elevations

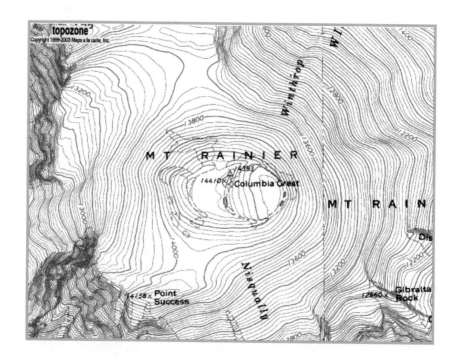

Figure 1.11

Topographic map of Mount Rainier

Courtesy of the United States Geological Survey

Grid Reference System

This section introduces you to the Universal Transverse Mercator Grid System and the military grid reference system. After you are familiar with these systems and how mapmakers divide the globe into north-south and east-west rings, you can better understand how to locate and identify points anywhere in the world. From this very broad perspective, this section will then show you how to locate a point on a map to within 100 meters using a six-digit grid coordinate.

To keep from getting lost, you must know how to find your location. Street addresses may not always be available to you. Learning to use the grid referencing system in conjunction with maps will help you to quickly and accurately pinpoint your location.

Lines of Latitude and Longitude

By drawing a set of east-west rings around the globe (parallel to the equator), and a set of north-south rings crossing the equator at right angles and converging at the poles, mapmakers can form a network of reference lines from which you can locate any point on the earth's surface (see Figure 1.12).

The distance of a point north or south of the equator is its latitude and the rings around the earth parallel to the equator are parallels of latitude, or simply parallels. Lines of latitude run east-west, but they are used to measure north-south distances. Starting with 0 degrees at the equator, mapmakers number parallels to 90 degrees both north and south.

The second set of rings around the globe, that are at right angles to the lines of latitude and that pass through the poles are called meridians of longitude, or simply meridians. One meridian is the prime meridian, which runs through Greenwich, England. The distance east or west of the prime meridian to a point is known as its longitude. Lines of longitude run north-south, but they are used to measure east-west distances. Starting with 0 degrees at the prime meridian, mapmakers number meridians to 180 degrees both east and west.

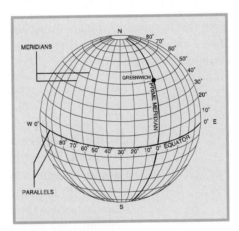

Figure 1.12

Meridians and parallels

UTM Grid System

The US military superimposed its grid reference system on the Universal Transverse Mercator Grid System, or UTM grid system. To better understand the military's grid reference system, you should have a basic knowledge of the UTM grid system.

The UTM grid system divides the surface of the earth into 60 north-south grid zones (each six degrees wide) like the one in Figure 1.13. Mapmakers number these zones from west to east, 1 through 60, starting at the 180 degree meridian. The grid zone in Figure 1.13 represents grid zone number 3.

Figure 1.14 is this same grid zone, but now further divided into 20 north-south segments. Each grid segment has a letter for identification. Mapmakers use the letters "C" through "X" (omitting the letters "I" and "O") to identify these 20 grid segments. They do not use "I" and "O" because those letters can easily be mistaken for the numbers "1" and "0," respectively. Nineteen of these grid segments are eight degrees high and the one row at the extreme north is 12 degrees high. This combination of zone number and row letter constitutes the grid zone designation.

With this designator, you are now able to identify specific grids. For example, if you wanted to locate the first segment north of the equator, its grid zone designation would be 3N.

However, if you were to cut out 60 shapes identical to those in Figures 1.13 or 1.14, your globe would not be complete at either end. Each of these 60 grid zones lay between the 84 degrees north and the 80 degrees south lines of latitude. The polar regions would be missing. Therefore, to complete your globe, extend these grid lines to 90 degrees in both directions: 90 degrees north latitude is the North Pole and 90 degrees south latitude is the South Pole. Mapmakers use the remaining four letters, "A," "B," "Y," and "Z," to identify the polar regions as shown in Figure 1.15.

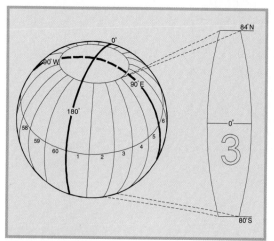

Figure 1.13

Grid zones of the UTM Grid System

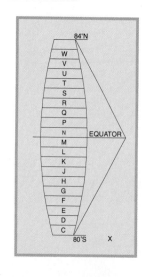

Figure 1.14

Grid segments of the UTM Grid System

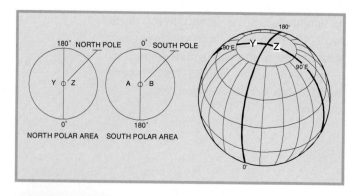

Figure 1.15

Polar regions of the UTM Grid System

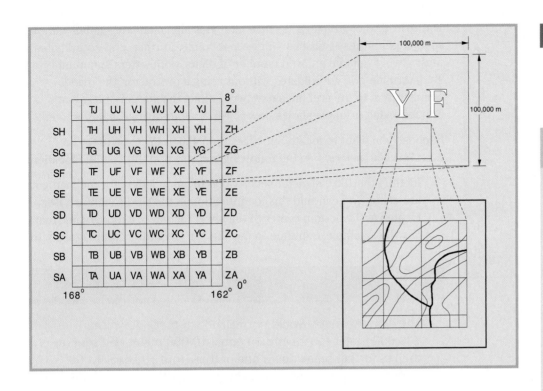

Figure 1.16

The Military Grid
Reference System

Key Terms

grid lines—
lines that are regularly spaced at 1,000 or 10,000 meter intervals that make up the grid on a map

grid square—
the intersecting of north–south and east–west grid lines at 90-degree angles to form a square

Military Grid Reference System

Superimposed on each grid zone segment are 100,000 meter squares. Each 100,000 meter square is assigned two identification letters (see Figure 1.16). The first letter is the column designation and the second letter is the row designation.

Each 100,000 meter square is then divided by parallel lines (or grid lines) that are 1,000 meters or 10,000 meters apart (depending on the scale of the map). These parallel lines come together at right angles to form 1,000 meter or 10,000 meter squares (called grid squares)— see Figure 1.17. These grid lines and grid squares are the lines that you see on a standard military topographic map. Mapmakers number grid lines along the outside edge of each topographic map for easy reference. Using the two 100,000 meter square identification letters in conjunction with these numbers, you can identify each grid square accurately, without any two grid squares having the same grid number (or grid coordinate).

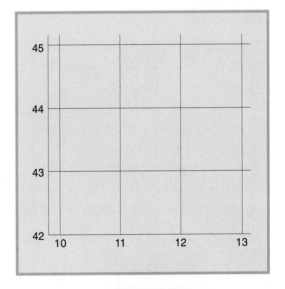

Figure 1.17

Grid squares

Locating a Point Using the Military Grid Reference System

Whenever you read a grid coordinate, you always read right first, then up. This is one of the cardinal rules in map reading. Based on this rule, you can determine locations on a map using grid coordinates. The number of digits in a grid coordinate represents the degree of precision to which you can locate and measure a point on a map—the more digits, the more precise the measurement. For example, a four-digit grid coordinate locates a point to within 1,000 meters, a six-digit grid coordinate to within 100 meters, and an eight-digit grid coordinate to within ten meters.

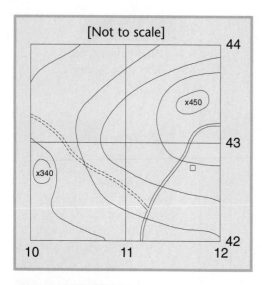

Figure 1.18

Determining a four-digit
grid coordinate

You write grid coordinates as one continuous alphanumeric symbol without spaces, parentheses, dashes, or decimal points. Further, grid coordinates must always contain an even number of digits, both letters and numbers. To determine grid coordinates without using a protractor, the reader simply refers to the grid lines numbered along the margin of any map. The following example shows how to form a four-digit grid coordinate.

Suppose you want to locate Spot Elevation 450 in Figure 1.18 to the nearest 1,000 meters. Use the following steps to find this specific location:

1. Identify the 100,000 meter square identification letters for the map you are using. You can find this identification in the Grid Reference Box located at the bottom center of the lower margin of a topographic map. For this example, continue to use the "YF" identifier from Figure 1.16.

Note:

The next two steps would normally be to break down the 100,000 meter square into 10 equal 10,000 meter grid squares, then to further break down one of those into 10 equal 1,000 meter grid squares. However, you can omit these steps because this example already has 1,000 meter grid squares.

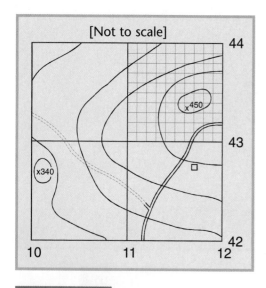

Figure 1.19

Determining a six-digit
grid coordinate

2. Identify the 1,000 meter grid square in which the spot elevation is located. To do this, remember the first cardinal rule of map reading: read right, then up. When reading a map right and up, each north-south grid line increases in value from west to east, and each east-west grid line increases in value from south to north.

3. Read right. You will see that the last north-south grid line before reaching the grid square containing Spot Elevation 450 is 11.

4. Read up. Note that the last east-west grid line before reaching the grid square containing Spot Elevation 450 is 43.

5. Combine these steps by writing the 100,000 meter square identifier (YF) and the coordinates of the 1,000 meter grid square (11 and 43) as one continuous symbol. Thus, you would write this grid coordinate as YF1143. You have now correctly located a point on the map (Spot Elevation 450) to the nearest 1,000 meters and written a four-digit coordinate.

Locating a Point Using Six-Digit Grid Coordinates

To locate a point to within 100 meters, follow the procedures in the previous section, and add one more step. In this step, you must divide the 1,000 meter grid square into tenths, or 100 meter increments. Figure 1.19 shows what a 1,000 meter grid square would look like if you divided it into 100 meter segments.

Suppose you now want to again locate Spot Elevation 450, but this time to within 100 meters. First, read right. Spot Elevation 450 is approximately six-tenths into the grid square. The right reading then is the value of the last north-south grid line before reaching this grid square, or 11, plus a 6 for the six-tenths. This value is read as 116.

By reading up, you can see that Spot Elevation 450 is approximately four-tenths of the way up into the grid square. Therefore, the up reading is the value of the last east-west grid line before reaching this grid square, or 43, and a 4 for the four-tenths. This value is read as 434.

Combining both of these numbers and the 100,000 meter square identifier labels the location as YF116434 for Spot Evaluation 450. You have now used one method to locate a point to the nearest 100 meters by using a six-digit grid coordinate.

Using a Coordinate Scale

Another way to locate a point to within 100 meters is to make use of a coordinate scale. The following is the correct way to use a coordinate scale. To explain this procedure, once again find the six-digit grid coordinate for Spot Elevation 450.

The coordinate scale used by the Army is the one shown in Figure 1.20. Note that in the center, it has three different scales: 1:100,000 meters, 1:50,000 meters, and 1:25,000 meters (or 1:250,000 meters).

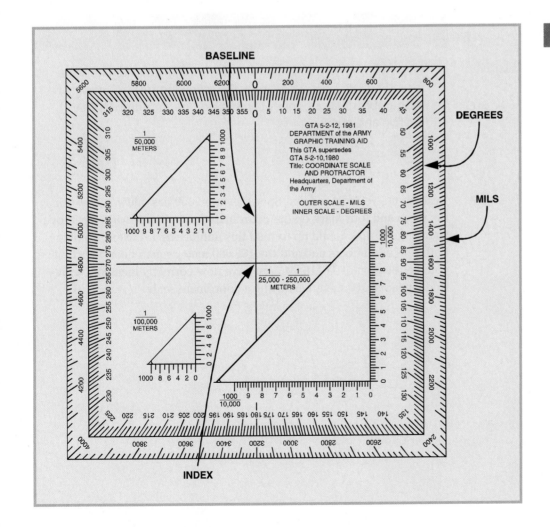

Figure 1.20

The Army coordinate scale

First, check to ensure that you are using the correct scale.

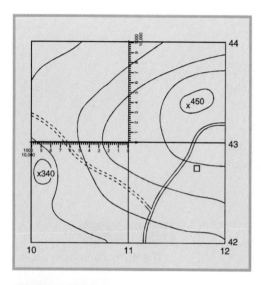

Figure 1.21

Using a coordinate scale

Place the horizontal scale parallel to and directly on top of grid line 43 with the "0 mark" at the lower left corner of grid square YF1143 (see Figure 1.20).

Keeping the horizontal scale on top of the 43 grid line, slide the scale to the right into the grid square until the vertical scale intersects the center of mass of Spot Elevation 450 (see Figure 1.21).

Now, reading left from the "0 mark," you can see that Spot Elevation 450 lies almost directly on the six-tenths indicator. Therefore, you would read this number as 116.

Note:

When you have to round off numbers using a coordinate scale for a six-digit coordinate, apply the following rule: round down for numbers that are four or less; round up for numbers that are five and above.

Reading up, you can see that Spot Elevation 450 lies midway between the three and four mark on the coordinate scale. By applying the above rounding-off rule, round up to read this number as 434. Next, combine both sets of numbers and add the 100,000 meter square identifier to give you the location of YF116434. You have now correctly located a point to the nearest 100 meters by using a coordinate scale.

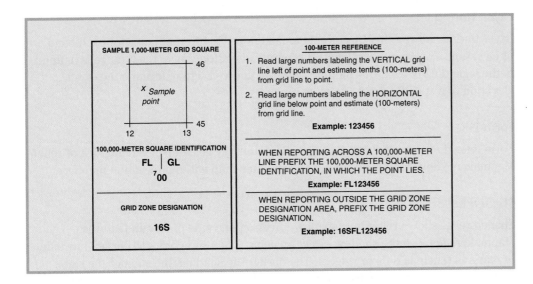

Figure 1.22

A grid reference box

Grid Reference Box

The grid reference box found on topographic map sheets contains step-by-step instructions for using the grid and military grid reference systems. Mapmakers divide the grid reference box into two parts (see Figure 1.22).

The left portion identifies the grid zone designation and the 100,000 meter square identifier. If the map sheet falls in more than one 100,000 meter square, the number of the grid line that separates these squares and the 100,000 meter square identifications are given. The right portion briefly explains how to find and write a six-digit coordinate.

Contours and Landforms

The next step to improving your map reading skills is to understand elevation and relief. This understanding includes your ability to recognize the different types of land formations.

This section introduces these two basic elements of map reading. It explains the concepts of contour lines and intervals. Mapmakers use them to show elevation and relief on a map as they would appear on the ground. It also explains and illustrates the 10 types of natural and manmade terrain features along with their corresponding contour lines.

Methods of Showing Relief

Knowing what the terrain looks like along your route before you start a trip may save you time and trouble in reaching your destination. Elevation is the height, or vertical distance, of a point on the earth's surface above or below mean sea level. Maps show elevation in feet, meters, or yards. Relief is the shape of landforms on the earth's surface.

Mapmakers use five methods to show elevation and relief on a map: layer tinting, form lines, shaded relief, hachures, and contour lines. This section defines all of these methods, but you will use only the contour lines in the remainder of your Map Reading instruction.

Layer Tinting

Layer tinting shows relief by color. Mapmakers use a different color for each band of elevation. Each band represents a separate elevation range. Each range is defined in the legend. However, this method does not allow you to determine the exact elevation of a specific point—only its range.

Form Lines

Form lines do not have a standard elevation and they give only a general idea of relief. Mapmakers show form lines as dashed lines on a map without elevation numbers.

Shaded Relief

Shaded relief shows relief by a shadow effect on one side of terrain features. Mapmakers achieve the shadow effect by using tones and colors to darken one side of features (such as hills or ridges). The darker the shading, the steeper the slope. This method is sometimes used with contour lines to emphasize those features.

Hachures

Hachures show relief using short broken lines. Mapmakers use them to show large, rocky outcrop areas and, on small-scale maps, to show mountain ranges, plateaus, and mountain peaks. As in the above methods, however, they do not represent exact elevations.

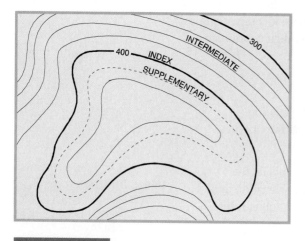

Figure 1.23

The three types of contour lines

Contour Lines

Contour lines show relief and elevation on a standard topographic map. A contour line represents an imaginary line on the ground. All points on a contour line are at the same elevation. Contour lines never cross one another. Standard colors for contour lines are brown, red, or black. The following are three types of contour lines (see Figure 1.23):

- **Index.** Starting at zero elevation, or mean sea level, every fifth contour line is always an index contour line, regardless of the contour interval. Mapmakers show index contour lines as a heavily drawn line with its elevation given somewhere along it, except where the contour interval is too small to print the elevation.

- **Intermediate.** The contour lines that fall between the index lines are the intermediate contour lines. These lines are more finely drawn and they do not show the elevation number. On US maps, there will always be four intermediate contour lines between indexed lines.

- **Supplementary.** These contour lines resemble dashes. They show sudden changes in elevation of at least one-half the contour interval for that map. If the map uses supplementary contour lines, do not count them as regular contour lines.

Contour Intervals

Printed below the bar scales in the middle of each map is the contour interval. This interval is the difference in height, or elevation, between one contour line and the one next to it.

You can estimate or determine the elevation of a point on a map by following these steps:

1. Determine the contour interval and the unit of measurement (feet, meters, or yards) from the marginal information.

2. Find the numbered index contour line nearest your point.

3. Count the number of intermediate contour lines to your point. If you are increasing elevation, add the contour interval to the nearest index contour line. If you are decreasing elevation, subtract the contour interval from the nearest index contour line.

For example, the point you want to locate is on the second intermediate contour line above the 300 meter index contour line (see Point A on Figure 1.24). Note the contour interval for this example is 20 meters. Since your point is closer to the 300 meter index contour line, start there and for each one of the intermediate contour lines that you cross or arrive at to reach your point, add 20 meters to the value of the 300-meter index line. Thus, the elevation of Point A is 340 meters. Notice that your elevation has increased.

However, let's say that your point (Point B) is now located on the intermediate contour line immediately below the 400 meter index contour line. Below means downhill, or at a lower elevation. Therefore, for the one intermediate contour line that you arrive at to reach this point, subtract 20 meters from the value of the 400 meter index line. The elevation of Point B is 380 meters.

To determine the elevation of the top of an unmarked hill, add one-half the contour interval to the elevation of the last (highest) contour line around the hill. In our example, the last contour line before the hilltop is an intermediate contour line at an elevation of 440 meters. Add one-half the contour interval, or 10 meters, to the value of this intermediate contour line. The elevation of the hilltop is 450 meters.

There may be times when you must estimate the elevation between contour lines. For example, for a point half-way between contour lines, estimate the elevation to one-half the contour interval. For points less than one-forth the distance between the lines, use the same elevation as the nearest line. Remember, if the desired point is on a contour line, its elevation is that of the contour line.

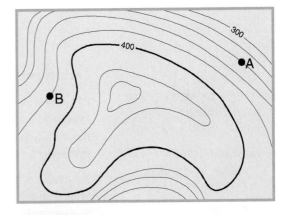

Figure 1.24

Using intermediate contour lines to calculate elevation

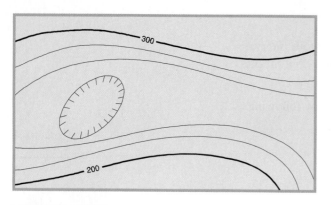

Figure 1.25

Estimating the elevation of a depression

To estimate the elevation to the bottom of a depression, subtract one-half the contour interval from the value of the lowest contour line before the depression. In Figure 1.25 (with the contour interval still at 20 meters), the lowest contour line before the depression is 240 meters, which is also the elevation at the edge of the depression. Because 10 meters is one-half the contour interval, the bottom of this depression is 230 meters. The tick marks on the contour line forming a depression always point to lower elevations.

In addition to contour lines, mapmakers use bench marks and spot elevations to indicate points of known elevation on a map. Bench marks (abbreviated BM) are the more accurate of the two. Mapmakers show a bench mark with a black "X" (such as BMx214) with the center of its elevation given in feet, meters, or yards above sea level. Mapmakers show spot elevations with a brown "X" to mark road junctions, hilltops, or other prominent terrain features.

Landforms

In addition to the map symbols introduced earlier in this chapter, mapmakers use symbols to represent natural land formations of the earth's surface. They position them on a map so that the center of the symbol remains in its true location. These symbols closely resemble the actual features when viewed from above.

No matter where you live, there are hills, valleys, streams, or other landforms in your area. The relief of an area is the illustration of these shapes as depicted on a map. For example, the relief of Denver would be different from that of Salt Lake City.

Most maps depict up to a total of 10 different natural or man-made landforms or terrain features. All terrain features result from landmasses known as mountains or ridgelines. A ridgeline is a line of high ground, usually with changes in elevation along its top and low ground on all sides, from which mapmakers classify the 10 terrain features (Figure 1.26).

Key Terms

depression—
a sunken or low place in the ground

ridgeline—
a line of high ground, usually with changes in elevation along its top

Figure 1.26

Ridgeline

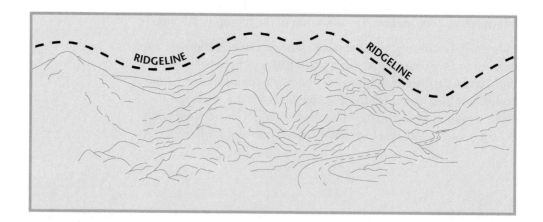

Figure 1.27

Hill

Terrain Features

The 10 natural or man-made terrain features fall into three categories: major features, minor features, and supplementary features. There are five major features, two minor features, and three supplementary features.

The five major terrain features are hill, saddle, valley, ridge, and depression.

Hill

A hill is an area of high ground (see Figure 1.27). When you are located on a hilltop, the ground slopes down in all directions. Maps will show a hill with a regular closed contour line, or a series of concentric closed contour lines. The inside of the smallest closed circle is the hilltop. The more contour lines, the higher the hill.

Saddle

A saddle is a dip or low point between two areas of higher ground (see Figure 1.28). It is not necessarily the lower ground between two hilltops; it may simply be a dip or break along a level ridge or crest. If you were in a saddle, there would be high ground in two opposite directions and lower ground in the other two directions. Maps will show a saddle with the contour lines forming an hourglass or a figure-eight-shaped feature.

Key Terms

concentric—
having a common center

saddle—
a low point between two areas of higher ground

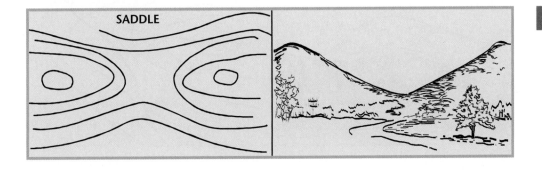

Figure 1.28

Saddle

CHAPTER 1 Geography, Map Skills, and Environmental Awareness

UNIT VI

Figure 1.29

Valley

Valley

A valley is a stretched-out groove in the land, usually formed by streams or rivers (see Figure 1.29). A valley begins with high ground on three sides, and usually has a course of running water through it, which always flows from higher to lower ground. If you were standing in a valley, there would be high ground in two opposite directions and a gradual slope in the other two directions. Contour lines forming a valley are either "U-shaped" or "V-shaped." To determine the direction water is flowing, look at the contour lines. The closed end of the "U" or "V" always points upstream or toward the high ground.

Ridge

A ridge is a sloping line of high ground (see Figure 1.30). If you were standing in the center of a ridge, you would normally have low ground in three directions and high ground in one direction.

If you cross a ridge at right angles, you climb steeply to the crest, and then descend steeply to the base. When you move along the path of the ridge, depending on your location, there may be either a barely noticeable slope or a very obvious incline. Contour lines forming a ridge tend to be "U-shaped" or "V-shaped." Notice that the closed end of the contour line points away from high ground.

Key Term

ridge—
*a sloping line
of high ground*

Figure 1.30

Ridge

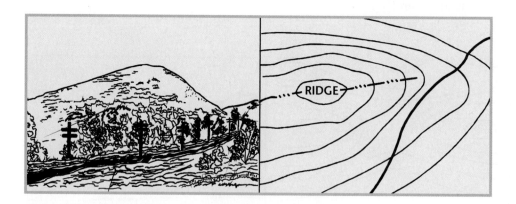

Figure 1.31

Depression

Depression

A depression is a low point in the ground, or a sinkhole, surrounded by higher ground in all directions (see Figure 1.31). Maps will show depressions by closed contour lines that have tick marks pointing toward the low ground. The closer the contour lines, the deeper the depression.

Minor Terrain Features

Along with the terrain features mentioned in the previous sections, there are three minor terrain features. These are draw, spur, and cliff.

Draw

A draw is a less developed stream course than a valley (see Figure 1.32). There is no level ground. If you were standing in a draw, the ground would slope up in three directions and down in the other. A draw is sometimes considered to be the initial formation of a valley. Maps will show a draw as a series of successive "U-shaped" or "V-shaped" contour lines that point uphill or upstream.

Figure 1.32

Draw

> ## Key Terms
>
> **sinkhole—**
> *a natural depression in a land surface communicating with a subterranean passage, generally occurring in limestone regions and formed by solution or by collapse of a cavern roof*
>
> **draw—**
> *a less developed stream course than a valley*

Figure 1.33

Spur

Spur

A spur is a short, continuous sloping line of high ground, normally jutting out from the side of a ridge (see Figure 1.33). It is often formed by two parallel streams cutting draws down the side of a ridge. The ground will slope down in three directions and up in one. Maps will show a spur as a series of successive "U-shaped" or "V-shaped" contour lines that point in a downhill direction.

Cliff

A cliff is a vertical or near vertical slope that is an abrupt change of the land formation (see Figure 1.34). Maps show the contour lines for cliffs as being very close together, and in some cases, touching each other.

Key Term

spur—
a sloping line of high ground projecting out from the side of a ridge

> ## Note:
>
> Although, as a general rule, a regular contour line is never broken, there are two exceptions when illustrating a cliff or a very steep slope. A contour line may be broken or may converge. Also, a contour line may be broken for the purpose of printing the elevation number.

Figure 1.34

Cliff

Supplementary Terrain Features

In the final category, the two supplementary terrain features are cut, and fill.

Cut and Fill

Cuts and fills are man-made features resulting from the cutting through of high areas and the filling in of low areas to form a level bed for a road or railroad track (see Figure 1.35). Maps will show cuts when they are at least 10 feet high. Mapmakers draw the contour lines along the length of the cut. They also use tick marks to extend from the cut line to the roadbed, if the map scale permits this level of detail.

As with cuts, maps will show fills when they are at least 10 feet high. Mapmakers draw the contour lines along the fill line for the length of the filled area and use tick marks to point toward the lower ground.

Your hand can help you visualize eight of the terrain features mentioned above (see Figure 1.36). You can demonstrate all but cuts and fills.

Key Terms

cut—
a man-made feature resulting from the removal of high ground, usually to form a level area for roads or railroad tracks

fill—
a man-made feature resulting from raising a low area, usually to form a level area for roads or railroad tracks

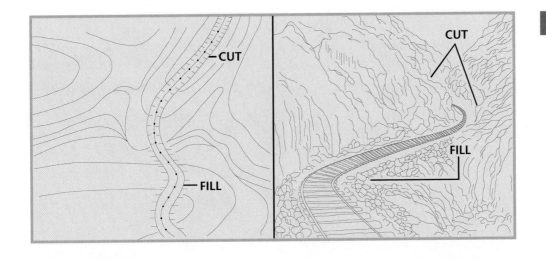

Figure 1.35

Cut and fill

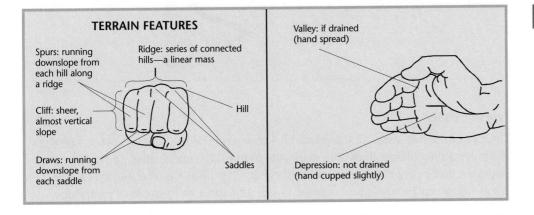

Figure 1.36

Using your hand to demonstrate terrain features

TERRAIN FEATURES

Spurs: running downslope from each hill along a ridge

Ridge: series of connected hills—a linear mass

Cliff: sheer, almost vertical slope

Hill

Draws: running downslope from each saddle

Saddles

Valley: if drained (hand spread)

Depression: not drained (hand cupped slightly)

Figure 1.37

The four types of slopes

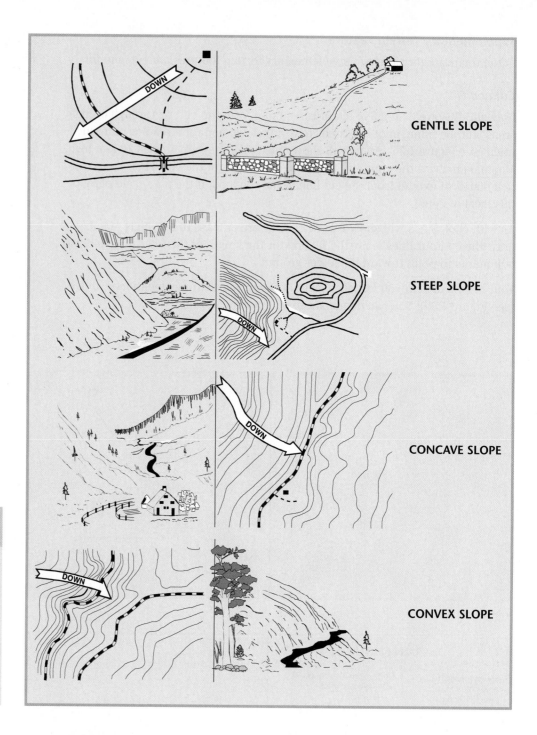

GENTLE SLOPE

STEEP SLOPE

CONCAVE SLOPE

CONVEX SLOPE

Key Terms

concave—
*curving inward,
as the inside of a bowl*

convex—
*curved outward,
as the outside of
a circle or sphere*

Types of Slopes

The rate of the rise or fall of the ground is known as its slope. You can determine slope by studying the contour lines on a map—the closer the contour lines, the steeper the slope; the farther apart the contour lines, the gentler the slope. The four types of slopes are gentle, steep, concave, and convex. Figure 1.37 gives an example of each slope.

Maps show the contour lines for concave slopes as being closely spaced at the top of the feature and widely spaced at the bottom. Contour lines for convex slopes are just the opposite.

Learning More About Contour Maps

For more information on contour maps, you can refer to the following websites:

Contour Maps Introduction:
http://academic.brooklyn.cuny.edu/geology/leveson/core/linksa/elevation.html

Contour Maps and Surface III:
http://www.kgs.ukans.edu/Tis/surf3/s3Cont1.html

Reading Contour Maps Interactive Games:
http://www.quia.com/jg/324701.html

Geography and Map Skills Handbook:
http://www.quia.com/jq/11269.html

America's Rooftops—West Virginia:
http://www.americasroof.com/highest/wv.shtml

Determining Distance

Navigating from one point to another with the use of a map and compass involves the ability to apply simple map-reading skills. Previous sections discussed how to plot locations on a map. In these next sections, you will learn how to determine distance and direction to those locations, both on the map and on the ground. You will also learn how to convert a grid azimuth on a map to a magnetic azimuth on the ground and vice versa. When you have successfully completed the next three sections, you will know "how to get there."

Determining Distance

As you know, a map is a scaled graphic drawing of a portion of the earth's surface. The scale of the map allows the user to convert distance on it to distance on the ground or vice versa. The ability to determine distance on a map, as well as on the earth's surface, is an important factor in plotting a distant location and determining how to get there.

There are two methods of determining distance on a map using the scales found in the marginal information.

- Mapmakers express a map scale as a representative fraction (RF), which gives the ratio of map distance to ground distance. For example, the scale 1:50,000 indicates that one unit of measure on the map equals 50,000 units of the same measure on the ground. The most common units of measurement are miles, meters, and yards.

Key Term

representative fraction (RF)— *the relationship of distance measured on a map to the corresponding distance on the ground; it is usually written as a fraction, such as if a map sheet is 1:50,000, RF is $^1/_{50,000}$*

Figure 1.38

The bar scale: primary scale and extension scale

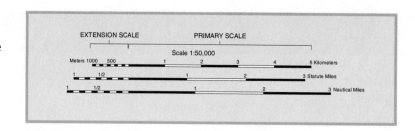

- Mapmakers divide the graphic (bar) scale into two parts: an extension scale and a primary scale. Use the primary scale, located to the right of the zero, to measure full units; use the extension scale, located to the left of the zero, to measure tenths of a unit. Read the extension scale right to left from the zero and the primary scale left to right from the zero (see Figure 1.38).

Most road maps indicate distance in miles along primary roads between towns, road junctions, or dots. However, this is not the case with topographic maps. When using a topographic map, you must determine the distance between two points because it is not given. To accomplish this, you must first measure the map distance, then convert that measurement to actual ground distance. Using the bar scale is the best way to perform this task.

Key Term

center of mass—
the point closest to the middle of an object

Measuring Straight-Line Distance

To determine a straight-line distance between two points on a map, lay a straight-edged piece of paper on the map so that the edge of the paper touches both points and extends past them. Make a mark on the edge of the paper at the center of mass for each point (see Figure 1.39).

Figure 1.39

Step 1: Measuring straight-line distance

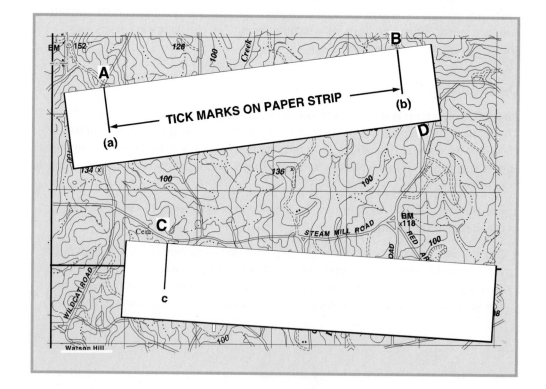

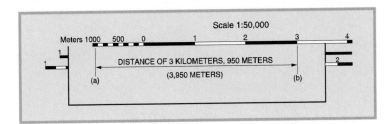

Scale 1:50,000

Figure 1.40

Step 2: Measuring straight-line distance

Figure 1.41

The extension scale magnified

To convert the map distance to ground distance, move the paper down to the graphic bar scale, and align the right mark (b) with a printed number on the primary scale so that the left mark (a) is in the extension scale (see Figure 1.40).

In this example, we aligned the right mark (b) with the 3,000-meter mark on the primary scale; thus, the distance is at least 3,000 meters.

Now, to determine the distance between those two points to the nearest 10 meters, look at the extension scale. Because mapmakers number the extension scale with zero at the right and increasing to the left, always read this scale from right to left. Notice that each alternating shaded and clear rectangle is equal to 100 meters. To determine the distance from the zero to mark (a):

1. Count the number of whole shaded and clear 100 meter rectangles. In our example, there are nine of them, representing 900 meters.

2. Mentally divide the distance inside the rectangle containing mark (a) into tenths (or 10-meter intervals)—see Figure 1.41. Since mark (a) is approximately half the distance of that rectangle, or five-tenths, you would add another 50 meters to the total in the first step.

Complete your calculations by adding the distance of 3,000 meters (determined using the primary scale) to the 950 meters (determined using the extension scale). The total distance between points (a) and (b) is 3,950 meters.

Measuring Curved Lines

To measure a distance along a winding road, stream, or any other curved line, you must first decide on which side of the feature to take your measurement. Never measure from side to side or down the middle. Start by making a mark on the straight-edged paper at the beginning point's center of mass. Move the edge of this paper along the curve, making marks at short straight distances on both the paper and the map as you proceed.

UNIT VI

Figure 1.42

Step 1: Measuring
curved lines

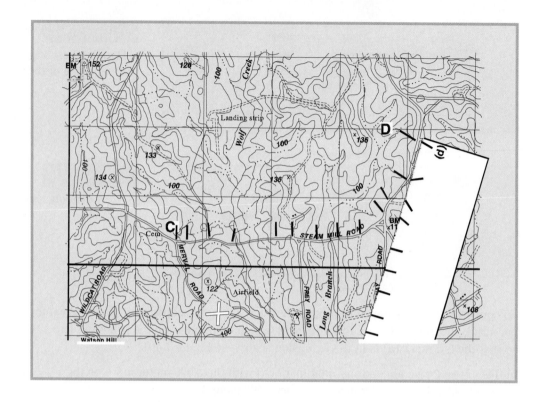

For accurate results, after placing a mark on both the paper and map, proceed to the next straight portion of this distance by pivoting the paper until the edge of the paper and area you are measuring are aligned. Use your pencil to hold the straight-edged paper in place while pivoting. Continue in this manner until you reach the center of mass at the ending point; then place the paper on the desired bar scale and read the distance between the beginning and ending marks.

In the next example, you measure the road distance between two points once again, by marking the beginning point (c) on the straight-edged paper (see Figure 1.6.2). Next, place marks on both the straight edge piece of paper and the map for each straight portion of road between points (c) and (d). Pivot the straight-edged paper as you make the marks on the paper and map until you reach point (d)—see Figure 1.42.

Place the straight-edged paper on the correct bar scale. Using only the beginning and ending marks (ignoring the ones in between), calculate the total distance. You can now use the same method as in the previous example. Notice in Figure 1.43 that point (d) falls on the 4,000 meter mark on the primary scale and point (c) is closest to the 550 meter reading on the extension scale. Thus, the road distance between points (c) and (d) is 4,550 meters.

Figure 1.43

Step 2: Measuring
curved lines

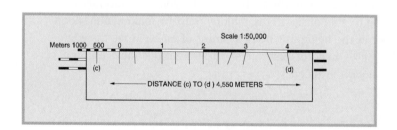

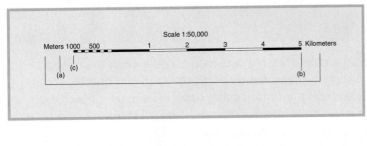

Figure 1.44

When the distance exceeds the scale

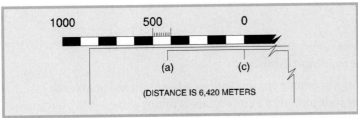

Figure 1.45

Measuring distance that exceeds the scale

Calculating Distance That Exceeds the Scale

There may be times when the distance you measure on the edge of the paper exceeds the graphic scale, as in Figure 1.44. When this happens, there is a procedure you can follow to measure this distance. The first step is to align the right mark (b) with the last printed number on the primary scale, in this case—5 kilometers.

When you include the 1000 meters in the extension scale, you can see that the distance from point (a) to (b) is more than 6,000 meters (or 6 kilometers). To determine the exact distance to the nearest 10 meters, place another mark (c) on the edge of the paper at the end of the extension scale. Remember that the distance from point (b) to (c) is 6,000 meters.

Slide the paper to the right to align mark (c) with zero, then measure the distance between marks (a) and (c). Because the distance between marks (a) and (c) is 420 meters, the total ground distance between start and finish points is 6,420 meters (see Figure 1.45).

Calculating Distance to a Point off the Map

To determine distance to a point off the map, measure the distance (straight-line or curved-line) from the start point to the edge of the map. Check to see if the marginal information gives the road distance from the edge of the map to the point you want. Oftentimes, maps will give distances to towns, highways, or junctions off the map. Then, add the distance measured on the map to the distance given in the marginal information. Ensure that the unit of measure is the same. When measuring distance in statute or nautical miles, round it off to the nearest one-tenth of a mile.

Note:

Distance measured on a map does not take into consideration the rise and fall of the land. All distances measured by using the map and graphic scales are flat distances. Therefore, the distance measured on a map will increase when actually measured on the ground. You must take this into consideration when navigating across country.

Other Methods of Determining Distance

When navigating, you may encounter circumstances where you are unable to determine distance using your map or where you are without a map. It is therefore essential to learn alternative methods by which you can accurately pace out or estimate distances on the ground.

Pace Count

One method used to measure ground distance is the pace count. A pace is equal to one natural step, about 30 inches long. To accurately use a pace count, you must know how many paces it takes you to walk 100 meters. To determine this, you must walk an accurately measured course and count the number of paces (steps) it takes. The pace course must be on terrain similar to that over which you will be walking. It will not help you very much to walk a course on flat terrain and then try to use that pace count on hilly terrain. Additionally, you may have to adjust your pace count because of the following conditions:

- **Slopes.** Your pace will lengthen on a down-slope and shorten on an upgrade.
- **Winds.** A head wind shortens the pace and a tail wind increases it.
- **Surfaces.** Sand, gravel, mud, snow, and similar surfaces tend to shorten your pace.
- **Elements.** Snow, rain, or ice may cause you to reduce the length of your pace.
- **Clothing.** Excess clothing and shoes with poor traction can also affect the pace length.
- **Visibility.** Poor visibility, such as fog, rain, or darkness, can shorten your pace.

There are several methods to keep track of the distance you travel when using a pace count. Some of the most common methods are:

- Put a pebble in your pocket every time you have walked 100 meters according to your pace count
- Tie knots in a string (one for every 100 meters)
- Put marks in a notebook (one for every 100 meters).

Never try to remember the count; always use one of these methods, or design your own.

Figure 1.46

Using estimation
to determine distance

Estimation

Another method is to use estimation. To effectively use this method, you must be able to visualize a distance of 100 meters on the ground. For distances up to 500 meters, determine the number of 100 meter increments between the two objects you wish to measure. Beyond 500 meters, select a point halfway to the objects and determine the number of 100 meter increments to the halfway point, then double it to find the distance to the objects (see Figure 1.46).

Determining Direction

In the last section, you learned how to determine the distance between two points. After you have determined this distance, you have part of the information you need to get where you are going. To reach your destination, however, you still need to know what direction to travel.

Directions play an important role in everyday life. People oftentimes express them as right, left, straight ahead, and so forth; but then the question arises, "to the right of what?" To answer that question, this section first defines different types of azimuths and three different types of north. It then explains how to determine grid and magnetic azimuths using a protractor and compass.

Expressing Directions

Direction is typically expressed as a unit of angular measure. The most common unit of measure is the degree. There are 360 degrees in a circle. Each degree is subdivided into 60 minutes and each minute into 60 seconds.

To express direction as a unit of angular measure, there must be a starting point (or zero measurement) and a point of reference. These two points designate the base direction or reference line. There are three base directions—true north, magnetic north, and grid north—but you will only be using magnetic and grid north in this section.

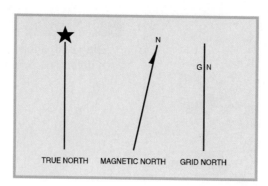

Figure 1.47

The three norths

- True north is a line from any point on the earth's surface to the north pole. All lines of longitude are true north lines. Mapmakers normally represent true north in the marginal information with a star, as shown in Figure 1.47.

- Magnetic north is the direction to the north magnetic pole, as shown by the north-seeking needle of a compass or other magnetic instrument. Mapmakers usually illustrate magnetic north in the marginal information by a line ending with a half arrow-head, as shown in Figure 1.47.

- Grid north is the north that mapmakers establish with the vertical grid lines on a map. They usually illustrate it by placing the letters "GN" on a vertical line in the marginal information, as shown in Figure 1.47.

Key Terms

azimuth—
a horizontal angle usually measured clockwise in degrees from a north base line (direction)

back azimuth—
the opposite direction of an azimuth obtained by adding 180 degrees to or subtracting 180 degrees from an azimuth

magnetic azimuth—
a direction that is expressed as the angular difference between magnetic north and a line of direction

grid azimuth—
the angle measured between grid north and a straight line plotted between two points on a map

Azimuths

An azimuth is defined as a horizontal angle measured clockwise from a base direction. The azimuth is the most common military method to express direction. When using an azimuth, the point from which the azimuth originates is the center of an imaginary circle (see Figure 1.48).

There are three distinct ways to express an azimuth: back azimuth, magnetic azimuth, and grid azimuth. Following the definition of these azimuths, the remainder of this section explains how to measure magnetic and grid azimuths.

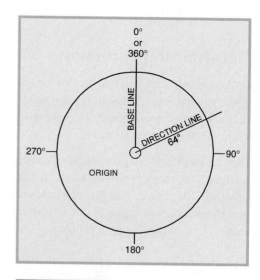

Figure 1.48

The circle used to determine an azimuth

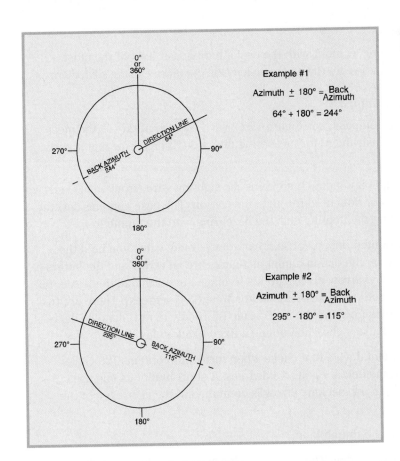

Figure 1.49

Calculating a back azimuth

Example #1

Azimuth ± 180° = Back Azimuth

64° + 180° = 244°

0° or 360°

270°

DIRECTION LINE 64°

BACK AZIMUTH 244°

90°

180°

Example #2

Azimuth ± 180° = Back Azimuth

295° - 180° = 115°

0° or 360°

DIRECTION LINE 295°

270°

BACK AZIMUTH 115°

90°

180°

A back azimuth is the opposite direction of an azimuth. It is just like doing an "about face." To obtain a back azimuth from an azimuth, *add* 180 degrees if the azimuth is 180 degrees or less; or *subtract* 180 degrees if the azimuth is 180 degrees or more (see Figure 1.49). The back azimuth of 180 degrees may be stated as 0 degrees or as 360 degrees.

A magnetic azimuth is a direction expressed as the angular difference between magnetic north and the direction line (see Figure 1.50). You can determine a magnetic azimuth using a compass or other magnetic instrument (such as surveying equipment).

A grid azimuth is the angle measured between grid north and a straight line plotted between two points on a map (see points "a" and "b" in Figure 1.50). You would use a protractor to measure this angle.

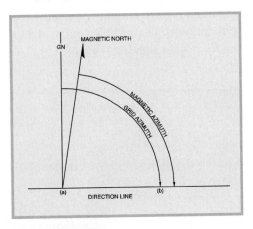

GN

MAGNETIC NORTH

MAGNETIC AZIMUTH

GRID AZIMUTH

(a) DIRECTION LINE (b)

Figure 1.50

Magnetic and grid azimuths

CHAPTER 1 Geography, Map Skills, and Environmental Awareness

Types of Compasses

You determine a magnetic azimuth with the use of a compass. Two of the most common types of compasses are the magnetic lensatic compass and the silva compass.

The Magnetic Lensatic Compass

The magnetic lensatic compass (see Figure 1.51), used by the military, is the most common and simplest instrument for measuring direction. It has three major parts: cover, base, and lens.

The cover protects the floating dial. It contains the sighting wire (front sight) and two luminous sighting slots or dots used for night navigation. The base contains several movable parts, including the floating dial, the bezel ring, and the thumb loop.

The floating dial is mounted on a pivot so it can rotate freely when you hold the compass level. Printed on the dial in luminous figures are an arrow and the letters E and W or E, W, and S. The arrow always points to magnetic north and the letters fall at East (90 degrees), South (180 degrees), and/or West (270 degrees). There are two scales. The outer denotes mils and the inner scale (normally in red) denotes degrees. Encasing the floating dial is a glass containing a fixed black index line.

The bezel ring is a ratchet device that clicks when turned. It contains 120 clicks when rotated fully. Each click is equal to 3 degrees. A short luminous line used in conjunction with the north-seeking arrow is contained in the glass face of the bezel ring.

The base also contains the thumb loop.

You use the lens to read the dial. The rear sight also serves as a lock and clamps the dial when closed. You must open the rear sight more than 45 degrees to allow the dial to float freely. There is also a rear-sight slot used for sighting on objects. Use this with the front sight sighting wire.

Key Term

mil—
a unit of angular measurement equal to $1/6400$ of a complete revolution

Figure 1.51

The magnetic lensatic compass

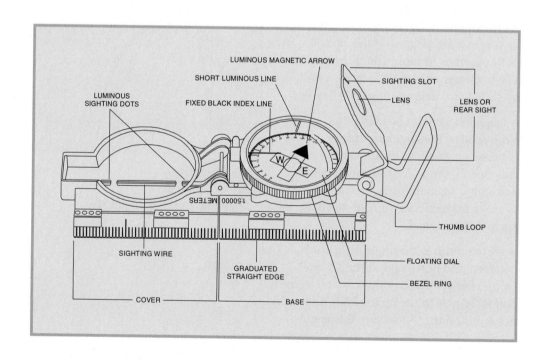

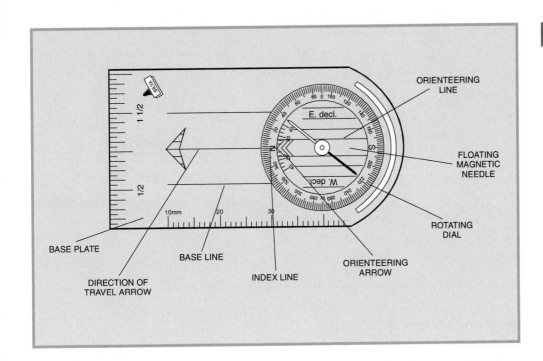

Figure 1.52

The Silva compass

The Silva Compass

The Silva Polaris (Type 7) precision compass (see Figure 1.52) is also one of the most accurate compasses on the market today. Some high schools prefer it over the military issued, magnetic lensatic compass due to the Silva's lower cost and higher availability. The Silva compass is easy to use, especially with its hand-contoured base plate. It is typically available at certain discount department stores for just under $10. Figure 1.52 shows the Silva Polaris (Type 7) compass along with its eight features.

The floating needle is mounted on a pivot so that it can rotate freely when you hold the compass level. It settles within four seconds, always pointing to magnetic north. Printed distinctly on the rotating dial are the letters N and S, to represent 0/360 degrees and 180 degrees, respectively. The dial is graduated at two degree intervals, marked at 20 degree intervals, and contains the letters E (at 90 degrees) and W (at 270 degrees).

The base plate contains two rulers (one measured in inches and the other in millimeters). It also has a 40-degree east and west declination scale inside the area of the floating dial.

Figure 1.53

The centerhold technique is used to determine a magnetic azimuth.

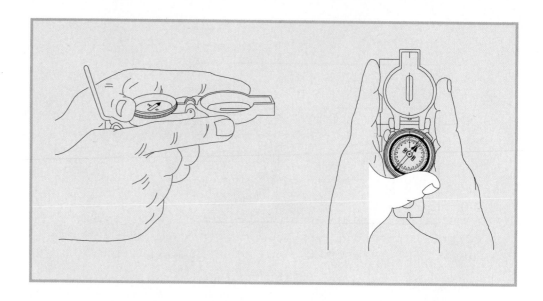

Measuring a Magnetic Azimuth

The following steps explain how to determine a magnetic azimuth using the center-hold technique (see Figure 1.53). This method is the fastest and easiest way to measure a magnetic azimuth. There is also a compass-to-cheek technique as well as ways for presetting a compass; however, those procedures will not be covered in this chapter.

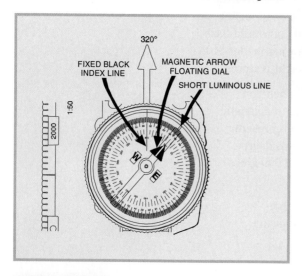

320°

FIXED BLACK INDEX LINE

MAGNETIC ARROW FLOATING DIAL

SHORT LUMINOUS LINE

1:50

2000

Figure 1.54

Using the centerhold technique to determine a magnetic azimuth of 320 degrees

These six steps are for the magnetic lensatic compass.

1. Open the compass to its fullest so that the cover forms a straightedge with the base.

2. Move the lens (rear sight) to the rearmost position, allowing the dial to float freely.

3. Place your thumb through the thumb loop, form a steady base with your third and fourth fingers, and extend your index finger along the side of the compass. Place the thumb of the other hand between the lens (rear sight) and the bezel ring. Extend the index finger along the remaining side of the compass, and the remaining fingers around the fingers of the other hand.

4. Pull your elbows firmly into your sides. This action places the compass between your chin and waist.

5. To measure an azimuth, simply turn your entire body toward the object, pointing the compass cover (zero or index mark) directly at the object.

6. After you are pointing at the object, look down and read the azimuth from beneath the fixed black index line. Figure 1.54 shows a magnetic azimuth of 320 degrees.

Note:

Ensure that you are away from power lines, vehicles, or other metal objects when using a compass because these objects will affect its accuracy.

Some compasses may have a 1:25,000 scale; you can still use this scale with a 1:50,000 scale map, but you must halve the values read.

For the Silva compass, modify step 3 to hold it either completely in one hand (with the curved end toward the back of the palm) or with both hands (as shown in Figure 1.53, but disregarding the information on thumb loop and rear sight).

Using Protractors

You determine a grid azimuth with the use of a protractor. There are several types of protractors: full circle, half circle, square, or rectangular. All of them divide the circle into units of angular measure, and each has a scale around the outer edge and an index mark. The index is the center of the protractor circle from which you measure all directions.

On the military protractor, you read the inner of two scales because it is graduated into degrees—from 0 to 360 degrees. Each tick mark on the degree scale represents one degree. The base line of this protractor is a line from 0 degrees to 180 degrees. Where the base line intersects the horizontal line, between 90 degrees and 270 degrees, is the index or center of the protractor.

When using the protractor, the base line is always oriented parallel to a north-south grid line. The 0- or 360-degree mark is toward the top or north on the map, and the 90-degree mark is to the right. Steps for determining and plotting grid azimuths are explained in the following section.

Figure 1.55

Using a protractor
to measure a grid azimuth

Courtesy of the United States
Geological Survey, modified by
Pearson Custom Publishing

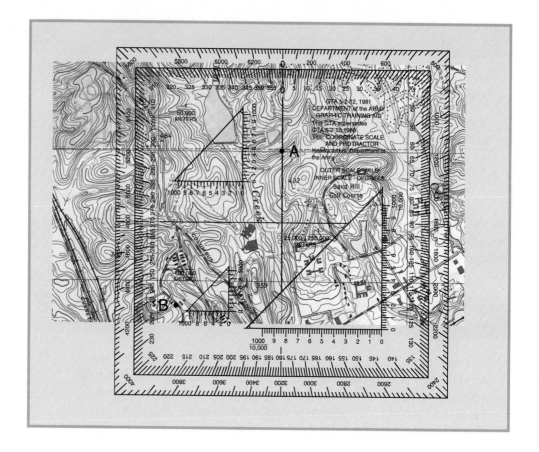

Measuring a Grid Azimuth

The following steps explain how to measure a grid azimuth using a map
and protractor (see Figure 1.55).

1. Draw a line connecting the two points (Points A and B on Figure 1.55).

2. Place the index of the protractor at the point where the drawn line crosses
   a vertical (north-south) grid line.

3. Keep the index at that point and align the 0–180 degree line of the protractor
   on the vertical grid line.

4. Read the value of the angle from the scale. This value is the grid azimuth
   from point A to point B, or 68 degrees in our example.

Note:

Distance has no effect on azimuths.

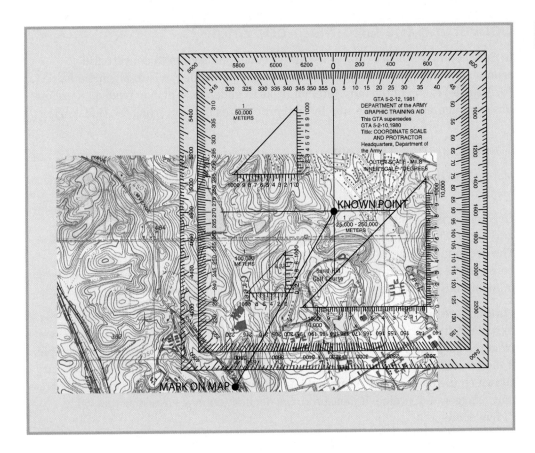

Figure 1.56

Using a protractor
to plot a grid azimuth

Courtesy of the United States
Geological Survey, modified by
Pearson Custom Publishing

Plotting a Grid Azimuth

Use the following steps to plot an azimuth from a known point on a map
(see Figure 1.56). For this example, you will *not* have to convert the azimuth
from magnetic to grid.

1. Place the protractor on the map with the index mark at the center of mass
   of the known point and the 0–180 degree base line parallel to a north-south
   grid line. (Use BM 145 on State Route 103.)

2. Make a mark on the map at the desired azimuth. (Use an azimuth of 210 degrees.)

3. Remove the protractor and draw a line connecting the known point and the
   mark on the map. This is the grid direction line or grid azimuth.

Proceed with Caution!

When measuring azimuths on a map, remember that you are measuring
from a starting point to an ending point. If you make a mistake and you
take the reading from the ending point, the grid azimuth will be opposite,
thus causing you to go in the wrong direction.

Converting the Grid-Magnetic Angle

In this section, you learn how to use the declination diagram to convert grid azimuths to magnetic azimuths and vice versa. Converting the Grid-Magnetic Angle (G-M Angle) is one of the most difficult tasks to understand in map reading; therefore, this section presents simple step-by-step procedures for converting the G-M Angle.

Key Term

Grid-Magnetic Angle (G-M Angle)— *angular difference in direction between grid north and magnetic north; it is measured east or west from grid north*

The Declination Diagram

Mapmakers place the declination diagram in the lower margin of most topographic maps.

Declination is the angular difference between true north and either magnetic or grid north. There are two declinations, a magnetic declination and a grid declination. The declination diagram shows the angular relationship, represented by prongs, between the three norths (see Figure 1.57). However, the position of the three prongs in relation to each other varies according to the declination data for each map.

Furthermore, mapmakers usually do not plot the angles between the prongs exactly to scale. Although you can obtain the position of the norths in relation to each other from the diagram, you should not measure the numerical value from it. For example, if the amount of declination from grid north to magnetic north is one degree, the arc shown on the diagram only represents the direction of the declination and the diagram may exaggerate its value. If measured, the declination may have an actual value of five degrees.

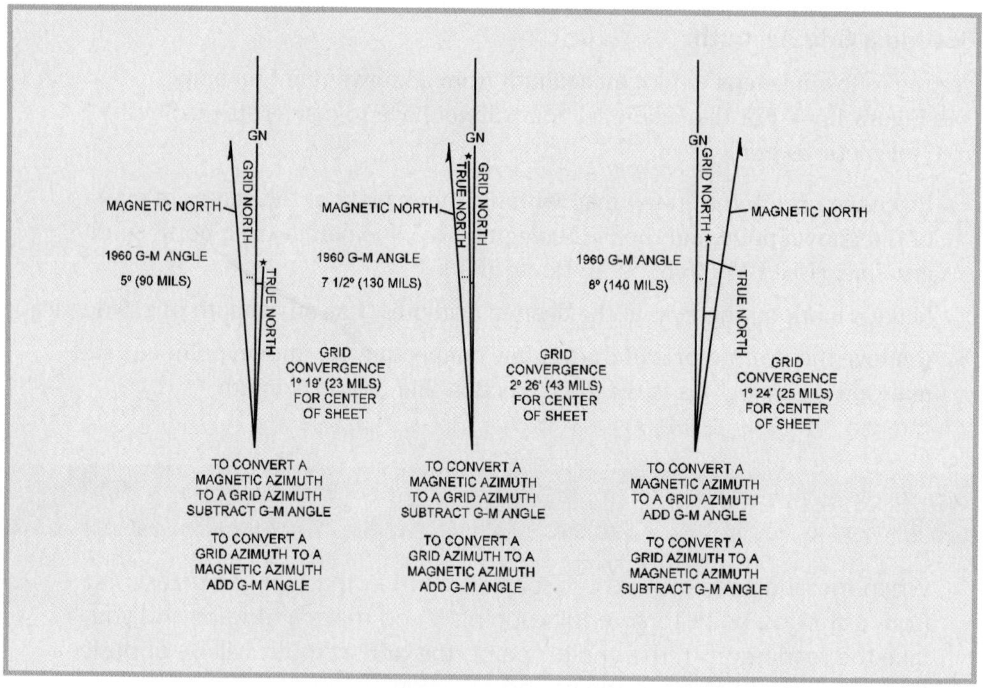

Figure 1.57

A declination diagram

The Grid-Magnetic (G-M) Angle

The Grid-Magnetic Angle, or the G-M Angle, is the angular size that exists between grid north and magnetic north in the year that mapmakers prepared the angular size. It is an arc, indicated by a dashed line, that connects the grid-north and magnetic-north prongs. Maps express this value to the nearest one-half ($1/2$) degree with mil equivalents shown to the nearest 10 mils. The G-M Angle is important in map reading because it helps a user to apply direction to an object that is on a map to its actual direction on the ground and vice versa.

Grid Convergence

The grid convergence is an arc indicated by a dashed line connecting the prongs for true north and grid north. The value of the angle for the center of the sheet is given to the nearest full minute (of degrees) with its equivalent to the nearest mil. Mapmakers show these data in the form of a grid-convergence note.

Conversion

There is an angular difference between the grid north and the magnetic north caused by the attraction of the earth's magnetic field (found in Northern Canada). Because all compasses point toward magnetic north, the location of this magnetic field does not match exactly with the grid-north lines on the maps; therefore, a conversion from magnetic to grid, or vice versa, is needed.

Conversion With Notes

If the declination diagram on a map provides conversion notes explaining the use of the G-M Angle, simply refer to them. One note gives instructions for converting a magnetic azimuth to a grid azimuth. The other shows how to convert a grid azimuth to a magnetic azimuth. The conversion (to add or subtract) depends on the direction of the magnetic-north prong relative to the grid-north prong.

Conversion Without Notes

Some maps, however, do not contain these declination conversion notes. Thus, it is necessary to convert from one type of declination to another. A magnetic compass gives a magnetic azimuth, but in order to plot this line on a map with grid lines, you must change the magnetic azimuth value to a grid azimuth value. Therefore, you must use the declination diagram for these conversions. A rule to follow when solving such problems is "starting from the reference line, *always* measure the angle to the azimuth line in a clockwise direction." With this rule in mind, you can now solve the problem using the following steps (see Figure 1.58).

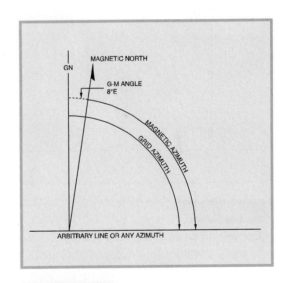

Figure 1.58

Converting without notes

1. Draw a vertical, or grid-north, line (prong). Always align this line with the vertical lines on the map.

2. From the base of the grid-north line, draw a direction line (or an azimuth line) at roughly a right angle from north, regardless of the actual value of the azimuth in degrees.

3. Examine the declination diagram on the map and determine the direction of the magnetic north (right-left or east-west) relative to that of the grid-north prong. Draw a magnetic prong from the base of the grid-north line in the desired direction.

4. Determine the value of the G-M Angle by drawing an arc from the grid prong to the magnetic prong and placing the value of the G-M Angle above the arc.

5. Complete the diagram by drawing an arc from each reference line to the vertical line you first drew. A glance at the completed diagram shows whether the given or desired azimuth is greater, and thus whether you must add or subtract the known difference between the two azimuths.

6. The inclusion of the true-north prong in relationship to the conversion is of little importance.

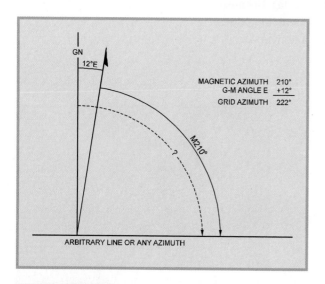

MAGNETIC AZIMUTH	210°
G-M ANGLE E	+12°
GRID AZIMUTH	222°

Figure 1.59

Converting an east magnetic azimuth to a grid azimuth

Applications of the G-M Angle Conversion

For the remainder of this section, you will learn how to apply this conversion technique when you have an east G-M Angle, a west G-M Angle, and when the G-M Angle is greater than the magnetic or grid azimuth.

The first application is to convert an east magnetic azimuth to a grid azimuth.

Working With an East G-M Angle

To plot a magnetic azimuth of 210 degrees on a map, you must convert it to a grid azimuth. To do so, follow these steps:

1. Determine the declination in degrees. In this example, it is 12 degrees east (see Figure 1.59).

2. Because the arc from magnetic north to the azimuth line is shorter than the arc from grid north to the azimuth line, you must add the G-M Angle. This yields a grid azimuth of 222 degrees.

To use a magnetic azimuth in the field with a compass when you have a grid azimuth of 303 degrees, you must convert it to a magnetic azimuth.

The second application is to convert an east grid azimuth to a magnetic azimuth.

1. Determine the declination in degrees. In this example, it is 10 degrees east (see Figure 1.60).

2. Because the arc from grid north to the azimuth line is longer than the arc from magnetic north to the azimuth line, you must subtract the G-M Angle. This yields a magnetic azimuth of 293 degrees.

The third application will be to convert to a magnetic azimuth when the G-M Angle is greater (see Figure 1.61).

In converting a grid azimuth to a magnetic azimuth, when the G-M Angle is greater than the grid azimuth, first do the following:

1. Add 360 degrees to the grid azimuth. In this example, the grid azimuth is 2 degrees (refer to Figure 1.61). You can now convert the grid azimuth to a magnetic azimuth because the grid azimuth is larger than the G-M Angle.

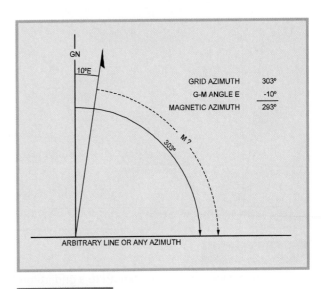

Figure 1.60

Converting an east grid azimuth to a magnetic azimuth

Note:

Because there are no negative azimuths on the azimuth circle, 0 degrees is the same as 360 degrees; therefore, 2 degrees (in this example) is the same as 362 degrees. This is because 2 degrees and 362 degrees are located at the same point on the azimuth circle.

2. This procedure is the same as Step 2 in the last example. Because the grid north arc of 362 degrees is longer than the arc from magnetic north to the azimuth line, you must subtract the G-M Angle. This yields a magnetic azimuth of 346 degrees.

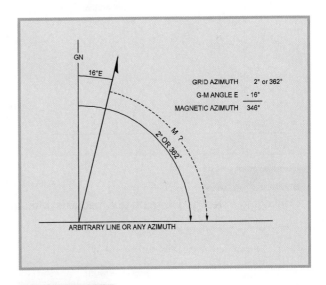

Figure 1.61

Converting to a magnetic azimuth when the G-M Angle is greater

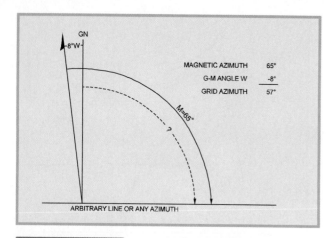

Figure 1.62

Converting a west magnetic azimuth to a grid azimuth

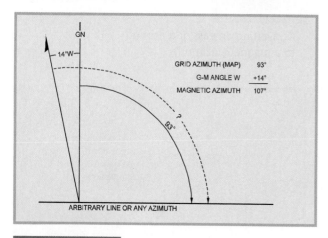

Figure 1.63

Converting a west grid azimuth to a magnetic azimuth

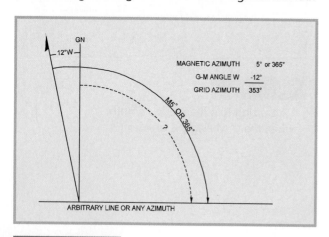

Figure 1.64

Converting to a grid azimuth
when the G-M Angle is greater

Working With a West G-M Angle

The fourth application is to convert a west magnetic azimuth to a grid azimuth. To plot a magnetic azimuth of 65 degrees on a map, you must convert it to a grid azimuth.

1. Determine the declination in degrees. In this example, it is 8 degrees west (see Figure 1.62).

2. Because the arc from magnetic north to the azimuth line is longer than the arc from grid north to the azimuth line, you must subtract the G-M Angle, giving you a grid azimuth of 57 degrees.

To use a magnetic azimuth in the field with a compass when you have a grid azimuth of 93 degrees, you must convert it to a magnetic azimuth.

The fifth application is to convert a west grid azimuth to a magnetic azimuth.

1. Determine the declination in degrees. In this example, it is 14 degrees west (see Figure 1.63).

2. Because the arc from grid north to the azimuth line is shorter than the arc from magnetic north to the azimuth line, you must add the G-M Angle. This yields a magnetic azimuth of 107 degrees.

The final application is to convert to a grid azimuth when the G-M Angle is greater. In converting a magnetic azimuth to a grid azimuth when the G-M Angle is greater than the magnetic azimuth, first do the following:

1. Add 360 degrees to the magnetic azimuth. In this example, the magnetic azimuth is 5 degrees (see Figure 1.64). You can now convert the magnetic azimuth to a grid azimuth because the magnetic azimuth is larger than the G-M Angle.

Note:

Because there are no negative azimuths on the azimuth circle, 0 degrees is the same as 360 degrees; therefore, 5 degrees (in this example) is the same as 365 degrees. This is because 5 degrees and 365 degrees are located at the same point on the azimuth circle.

2. Because the magnetic north arc of 365 degrees is longer than the arc from grid north to the azimuth line, you must subtract the G-M Angle. This yields a grid azimuth of 353 degrees.

Each time you convert a G-M Angle, construct a G-M Angle diagram that shows the required azimuths. The construction of a diagram takes the guesswork out of converting azimuths when the map does not give any conversion notes.

Converting the G-M Angle requires practice. Become familiar with the proper procedures to follow whether there is an east or west G-M Angle, or the G-M Angle is greater than your grid or magnetic azimuth.

Determining Location

Sometimes it is not enough to know how to locate a point to within 1,000 or 100 meters, or to estimate the location of a distant point on the ground. There may be times when you have to determine your location, or a distant point, even more accurately. Or, perhaps you will need to use certain known locations as reference points. This section will help you to accomplish these tasks.

In this chapter, you have encountered most of the basic map reading skills. However, skills such as determining an eight-digit grid coordinate and locating an unknown point using polar coordinates, intersection, and resection will help you to more accurately locate and plot points on a map. This section examines those skills and gives you an opportunity to practice them. You will also learn how to determine direction using a field-expedient method.

Key Term

field-expedient—
adapting to a particular situation by using available materials and/or resources

Determining an Eight-Digit Grid Coordinate

To determine an eight-digit coordinate, you must use a coordinate scale. Keep in mind that there are 100 meters between each 100-meter mark (number) on the coordinate scale, with a short tick mark to indicate 50 meters between each 100-meter mark. To locate spot elevation (SE) 450 in Figure 1.65 to within 10 meters, use the following procedures:

1. Recall that you must first identify the 1,000 meter grid square in which the spot elevation is located. To do this, remember the first cardinal rule of map reading: read right, then up. When reading a map right and up, each north-south grid line increases in value from west to east, and each east-west grid line increases in value from south to north.

   • By reading right, the last north-south grid line before reaching the grid square containing SE 450 is 11.

   • By reading up, the last east-west grid line before reaching the grid square containing SE 450 is 43.

   • By adding the 100,000 meter square identifier (YF), YF1143 locates SE 450 to the nearest 1,000 meters.

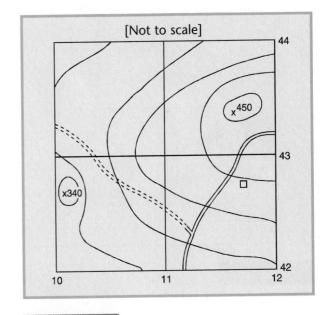

Figure 1.65

Determining an eight-digit grid coordinate

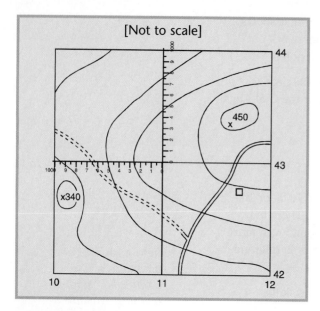

[Not to scale]

44

450
x

43

x340

42

10   11   12

Figure 1.66

Placing the coordinate scale

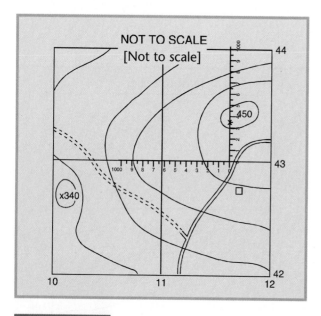

NOT TO SCALE
[Not to scale]

44

450
x

43

x340

42

10   11   12

Figure 1.67

Sliding the scale to the right

2. Place the coordinate scale parallel to and directly on top of grid line 43 with the "0 mark" at the lower left corner of grid square YF1143 (see Figure 1.66).

Note:

Ensure that you are using the correct scale.

3. Keeping the horizontal scale on top of the 43 grid line, slide the scale to the right into the grid square until the vertical scale intersects the center of mass of SE 450 (see Figure 1.67).

4. Reading from the "0 mark," the right reading shows that SE 450 lies between the 600 and 650 meter mark by approximately 30 meters.

Note:

You determine that it is approximately 30 meters by estimating how many tens SE 450 is beyond the 600-meter mark. In this case, there are three, which gives you the third and fourth digits of the coordinate. Thus, the center of mass of SE 450 is 630 meters into the grid square and you would read this number as 1163.

5. Reading up, you can see that SE 450 lies midway between the 300 and 400 meter marks, or 350 meters into the grid square; therefore, the up reading is 4335.

6. By combining both sets of numbers and adding the 100,000 meter square identifier, the location of SE 450 is YF11634335. You have now correctly located a point to the nearest 10 meters.

To trace the degree of accuracy of an eight-digit grid coordinate from 1,000 to 10 meters, you can break it down as follows:

1. The underlined numbers in YF11634335 represent the 1,000 meter grid square and they locate the point to within 1,000 meters.

2. The third and seventh digits of YF11634335 denote 600 and 300 meters and locate the point to within 100 meters.

3. The fourth and eighth digits of YF11634335 denote 30 and 50 meters and locate the point to within 10 meters.

Intersection

You can use intersection to locate an unknown point by determining where the azimuths from two (preferably three) known positions on the ground intersect. There are two ways to determine intersection—the map and compass method, and the straightedge method.

Map and Compass Method

The first way to find an unknown point by intersection is with a map and compass. Follow these steps and examine Figure 1.68.

1. Orient the map using the compass.

> ### Note:
>
> The best way to orient a map is to use a compass.

2. Determine the Grid-Magnetic Angle (G-M Angle) of the map you are using. In this example, the G-M Angle is 5 degrees east.

3. Locate and mark your first known position (Point A) on the map.

4. Measure the magnetic azimuth to the unknown point from Point A using a compass. In this example, the magnetic azimuth is 71 degrees.

5. Convert the magnetic azimuth to a grid azimuth. In this example, 71 degrees plus 5 degrees equals a 76-degree grid azimuth.

6. Place the coordinate scale on the map, ensuring that the zero-degree indicator is at the top and the index point is directly over the center of mass of Point A. Place a tick mark at 76 degrees on the map. Draw a line from Point A along this grid azimuth.

7. Move to Point B (the second known point) and locate it on the map; then, repeat steps 4, 5, and 6. For this example: 1) The magnetic azimuth in step 4 from Point B to the unknown point is 35 degrees; 2) Convert this to a grid azimuth using the formula 35 1 5 5 40; 3) Place a tick mark at 40 degrees on the map and draw a line along that grid azimuth.

8. The location of the unknown position is where the lines cross on the map. Determine the eight-digit grid coordinate for this position.

Key Term

intersection—
the method of locating an unknown point by determining where the azimuths from at least two known points meet (intersect)

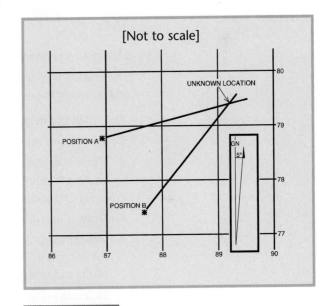

Figure 1.68

Using intersection: the map and compass method

Figure 1.69

Using intersection:
the straightedge method

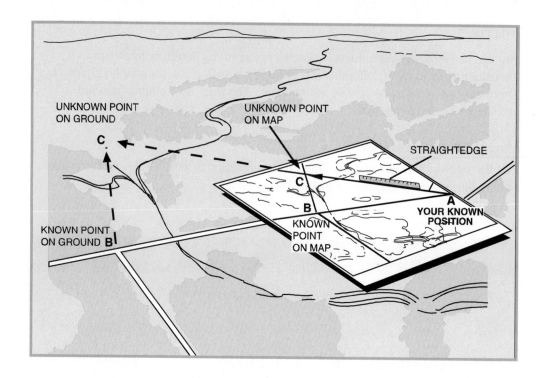

UNKNOWN POINT
ON GROUND

UNKNOWN POINT
ON MAP

STRAIGHTEDGE

C

C

B

A
YOUR KNOWN
POSITION

KNOWN
POINT
ON MAP

KNOWN POINT
ON GROUND B

Straightedge Method

The second way to locate an unknown point by intersection is by using a straight-edge. Follow these steps and examine Figure 1.69.

1. Orient the map (on a flat surface) to the ground by terrain association.

2. Locate and mark your known position on the map (Point A).

3. Place a straightedge on the map with one end at your position (Point A) as a pivot point. Rotate the straightedge until the unknown point (Point C) is sighted along the edge.

4. Draw a line along the straightedge.

5. Repeat steps 3 and 4 with the second known position (Point B) and check for accuracy. The intersection of these lines on the map is the location of the unknown point (Point C).

6. Determine the six- or eight-digit grid coordinate (depending upon the desired degree of accuracy) for the unknown point.

Resection

You can use resection to locate your unknown position on a map by determining the grid azimuth to at least two well-defined locations on the map. For greater accuracy, the desired method of resection would be to use three well-defined locations. There are three ways you can use resection: the map and compass method, modified resection, and the straightedge method.

Key Term

resection—
the method of locating your unknown position by determining where the back azimuths from two or three well-defined locations on a map meet

Map and Compass Method

The first way to find your unknown location by resection is with a map and compass. Follow these steps and examine Figure 1.70.

1. Orient the map using the compass.

2. Determine the Grid-Magnetic Angle (G-M Angle) of the map you are using. In this example, the G-M Angle is 3 degrees east.

3. Identify two or three known locations on the ground. Mark them on the map, such as Hilltop 408 and the control tower.

4. Measure the magnetic azimuth to one of the known positions from your location using a compass. In this example, the magnetic azimuth to Hilltop 408 is 312 degrees.

5. Convert the magnetic azimuth to a grid azimuth. In this example, 312 degrees plus 3 degrees equals a 315-degree grid azimuth.

6. Convert the grid azimuth to a back azimuth by adding or subtracting 180 degrees. In this example, 315 degrees minus 180 degrees equals a 135-degree back azimuth.

7. Place the coordinate scale on the map, ensuring that the zero-degree indicator is at the top and the index point is directly over the center of mass of the known point. Place a tick mark at 135 degrees. Draw a line on the map from the known position back toward your unknown location.

8. Repeat steps 4, 5, 6, and 7 for the second known position (the control tower). For this example:

   a. The magnetic azimuth to the control tower is 15 degrees.

   b. Convert this to a grid azimuth: 15 1 3 5 18.

   c. Convert this to a back azimuth: 18 1 180 5 198.

   d. Place a tick mark at 198 degrees on the map and draw a line back toward your unknown location.

9. The intersection of these two lines is your location. Determine the eight-digit grid coordinate for your position.

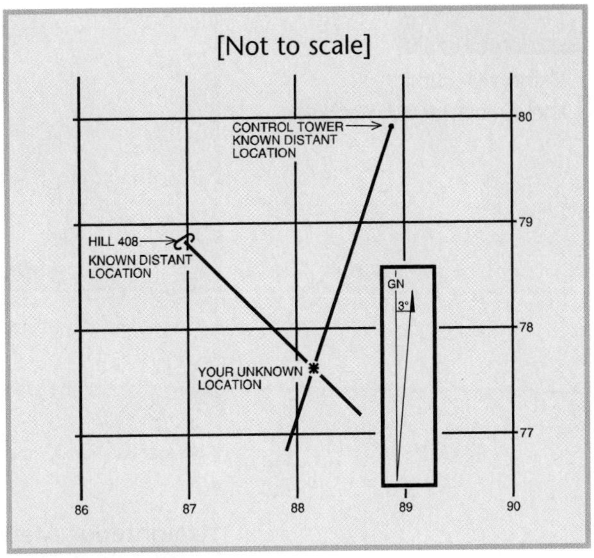

Figure 1.70

Using resection: the map and compass method

Note:

You can use modified resection to locate your position on the map when you are at a linear feature on the ground, such as a road, canal, stream, and so on. To do this, you need only one known location. Use the first seven steps; then where the drawn line (in step 7) crosses the linear feature is your location.

Figure 1.71

Using resection:
the straightedge method

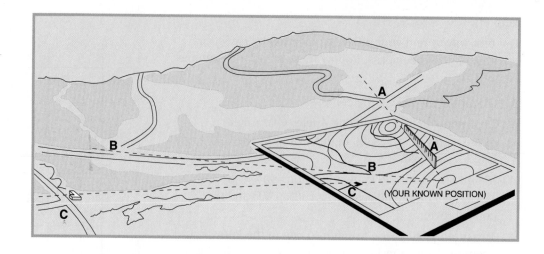

Straightedge Method

Another way to locate your unknown position by resection is by using a straightedge. Follow these steps and examine Figure 1.71.

1. Orient the map (on a flat surface) to the ground by terrain association.

2. Locate at least two known distant locations or prominent features on the ground and mark them on the map (Points A, B, and C).

3. Place a straightedge on the map pointing toward one of the known points (Point A). Rotate the straightedge until the known point on the map is aligned with the same known point on the ground.

4. Draw a line along the straightedge away from the known point on the ground toward your position.

5. Repeat steps 3 and 4 using the other known points (Points B and C).

6. The intersection of these lines on the map is your location.

7. Determine the six- or eight-digit grid coordinate (depending upon the desired degree of accuracy) for your location.

Figure 1.72

Using polar coordinates

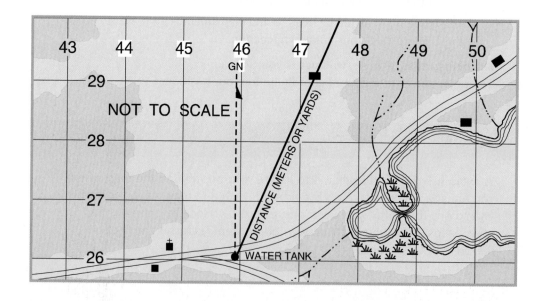

Polar Coordinates

You can use polar coordinates to locate or plot an unknown point from a known location by giving a direction and a distance along the direction line. Three elements must be present to use polar coordinates: a known location on the map, an azimuth (grid or magnetic), and a distance (normally in meters). There are two ways that you can use polar coordinates—the map and compass method, and the protractor method.

Key Term

polar coordinates— *a method of locating or plotting an unknown position from a known point by giving a direction and distance along that direction line*

Map and Compass Method

Use the following steps and examine Figure 1.72 for the map and compass method.

1. Orient the map using a compass.

2. Determine the Grid-Magnetic Angle (G-M Angle) of the map you are using. In this example, the G-M Angle is 0 degrees.

3. Identify the known location on the ground and mark it on the map. In this example, the known location is the water tank in grid square FL4526.

4. Measure the magnetic azimuth to the unknown point (a building in grid square FL4729) from the known location using a compass. In this example, the magnetic azimuth to the building is 24 degrees.

5. Convert the magnetic azimuth to a grid azimuth. In this example, 24 degrees plus 0 degrees equals a 24-degree grid azimuth.

6. Place a coordinate scale on the map, ensuring that the zero-degree indicator is at the top and the index point is directly over the center of mass of the known point.

7. Place a tick mark at 24 degrees.

8. Draw a line on the map from the known location along this grid azimuth until it intersects the building.

9. Determine the distance to the unknown position. Using a straightedge and the procedure for measuring straight line distance, you determine the distance to the building in grid square FL4729 to be 3,600 meters.

Protractor Method

The second way to locate or plot an unknown point from a known location using polar coordinates is the protractor method. Follow these steps and examine Figure 1.72.

1. Determine the location of a known point on the map to within 100 or 10 meters. In this example, the known location is the water tank at grid coordinates FL45952610.

2. Measure a grid azimuth to the desired location or destination (the building in grid square FL4729). By using your protractor, you determine the grid azimuth to be 24 degrees to the building.

3. Determine the distance as you did in step 9 of the map and compass method.

Determine Direction Using Field-Expedient Methods

Sometimes a compass is not available and you must determine your location by using the materials and resources available to you. There are several methods you can use to determine direction by using the sun and the stars. These include the shadow-tip method and the watch method.

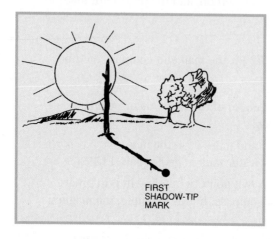
Shadow-Tip Method

The following steps show you how to use the shadow-tip method to determine direction and/or orient a map without a compass.

1. Place a stick or branch at least 12 inches long vertically into the ground at a fairly level spot where the sun will cast a distinct shadow. Mark the shadow tip on the ground with a small stone, twig, or other means. See Figure 1.73.

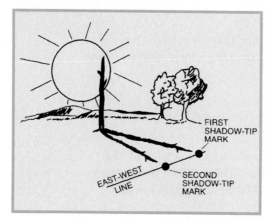
Note:

If the tip of the shadow is difficult to find, tap the end of the stick; the movement of the shadow will help you locate it.

2. Wait 10 to 15 minutes until the shadow moves a few inches. Mark the new position of the shadow tip in the same way as the first. See Figure 1.74.

3. Draw a straight line through the two marks to obtain an east-west line. Extend this line past the second mark (refer to Figure 1.74).

4. Determine which is the east end of the line and which is the west end using these tips: the sun rises in the east and sets in the west; the shadow tip moves in the opposite direction, and; the first shadow tip mark is always west, and the second mark is always east.

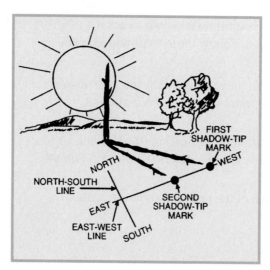
5. To find north and south, draw a line at a right angle to the east-west line at any point (see Figure 1.75). From this north-south line, you can now orient your map and determine the direction you want.

Watch Method

You can also use a watch to determine the approximate true north or true south; however, this method can result in errors, especially in the lower latitudes, and may cause circling.

In the northern hemisphere, point the hour hand toward the sun. Find a north-south line midway between the hour hand and 12:00 o'clock, standard time. If on daylight saving time, find the line between the hour hand and 1:00 p.m. If you have any doubt as to which end of the line is north, remember that the sun is in the east before noon and is in the west after noon (see #1, Figure 1.76).

In the southern hemisphere, point the 12:00 o'clock dial toward the sun, and halfway between 12:00 o'clock and the hour hand will be a north-south line. If on daylight saving time, the line will lie midway between the hour hand and 1:00 p.m. (see #2, Figure 1.76).

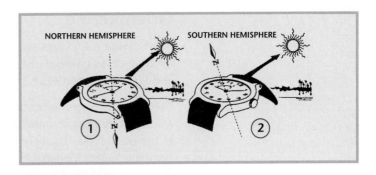

Figure 1.76 The watch method

Global Positioning System

The Global Positioning System (GPS) is a high-tech worldwide radio-navigation system formed from a network of 24 satellites and their ground stations. GPS is the first system to pinpoint a precise location for any point on the globe, during any kind of weather. This system utilizes these satellites to calculate positions down to a matter of meters. As a matter of fact, use of advanced forms of GPS can pinpoint locations down to a centimeter. GPS receivers have become more economical and, therefore, accessible in recent times. Uses of the GPS system include: air navigation, mapping, pinpointing locations, and navigating routes for cars and boats.

A GPS receiver uses the travel time of radio signals to measure distance. The satellites are closely monitored so that their exact location is always known. Any delays created by the radio signals traveling through the atmosphere are corrected.

A global positioning satellite
Courtesy of Photo Researchers

Orienteering

This section introduces you to orienteering, its techniques and terminology, as well as the various types of orienteering courses. In addition, many of the map reading and land navigation skills practiced in previous sections are applied.

Orienteering began in Scandinavia in the 1800s, primarily as a military event and as part of military training. By 1919 it had become a competitive sport in Sweden. In the early 1930s, the sport received a boost with the invention of an improved compass. Bjorn Kjellstrom, one of the inventors of that compass, introduced orienteering to the United States in 1946.

Orienteering is for all ages and degrees of fitness and skill. It provides the suspense and excitement of a treasure hunt. The object is to locate control points (see Figure 1.77) by using a map and compass to navigate the terrain.

Organizers of an orienteering event will give each participant a topographic map with various control points circled (see Figure 1.78). Each control point has a corresponding flag marker on the ground and a special punch which organizers use to mark the scorecard. Competitive orienteering involves running from point to point. It is more demanding than road running, not only because of the terrain, but because the participant must make decisions, and keep track of the distances covered. Courses may be as long as 10 kilometers.

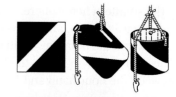

Figure 1.77

Orienteering control points

Key Term

control point—
a trapezoid-shaped marker (usually orange, red, or white) used to mark features on an orienteering course, usually with clipper or control punch attached to mark a control card as proof of arrival

Figure 1.78

Topographic orienteering map

Courtesy of Quantico Orienteering Club

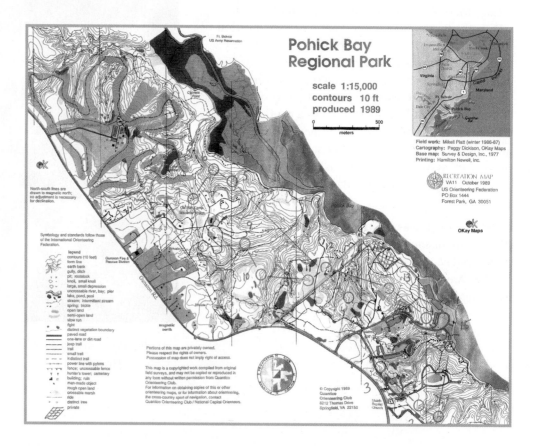

Although orienteering challenges both the mind and the body, the competitor's ability to think under pressure and make wise decisions is sometimes more important than speed or endurance. The person just starting out in orienteering should concentrate more on refining map reading and land navigation skills than on running between the control points.

Types of Orienteering Courses

There are different types of orienteering events that range from individual courses, to a relay event, to night competition. All types of orienteering courses are interesting and challenging, but they vary in their degree of difficulty. The best location for an orienteering course is one that is easily identifiable on both a map and the actual terrain. It should also be accessible from several routes. Listed below are some of the most common orienteering events/courses.

Route Orienteering

This form of orienteering can be used by beginners to the sport as well as for advanced competition. In route orienteering, a master (or advanced competitor) walks a route while beginners trace the actual route walked on the ground using their maps. Beginners circle the location of the different control points found along the walked route. When they finish, organizers analyze and compare the maps. For beginners, time is not a factor in this event.

Another variation of route orienteering involves a course laid out with markers for the competitor to follow. Because the route is indicated with flags or markers, there is no master map. The winner of the event is the competitor who successfully traces the route and accurately plots the most control points.

Line Orienteering

In line orienteering, competitors trace on their maps a pre-selected route from a master map that has at least five control points. The object is to walk the route shown on the map, circling the control points on the map as competitors locate them on the ground. See Figure 1.79.

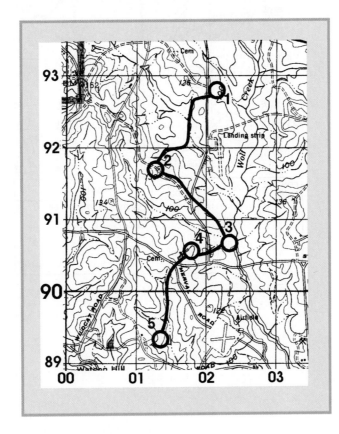

Figure 1.79

Line orienteering

Cross-Country Orienteering

Cross-country (or free-point orienteering) is the most common type of orienteering competition. It is considered to be the most competitive and intriguing form of orienteering. In this event, all competitors must visit the same control points in the same order. With the normal one-minute starting interval, it becomes a contest of route choice and physical skill. The competitor with the fastest time is the winner.

The length and difficulty of the course is determined by the skill of the competitors. There are usually six to 12 control markers on the course in varying degrees of difficulty and distances apart so that there are no easy, direct routes. The course may be closed-in with the start and finish located at the same position (see Figure 1.80) or the start and finish may be at different locations.

Organizers mark each point in order on a master map. They give competitors a clue list that describes each control point with an 8-digit grid coordinate, a two-letter control code, and a clue describing the terrain in the location of the marker. Competitors must indicate on their score cards proof of visiting each control marker. This is usually done with a special stamp or punch.

Figure 1.80

Cross-country orienteering

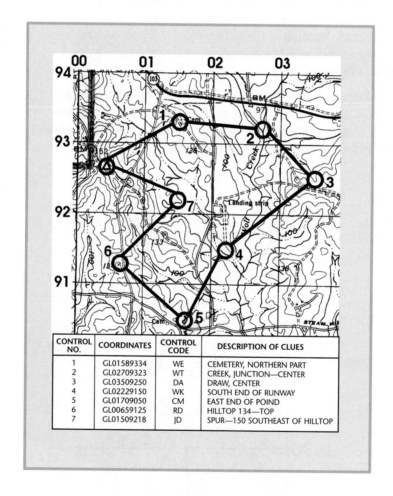

CONTROL NO.	COORDINATES	CONTROL CODE	DESCRIPTION OF CLUES
1	GL01589334	WE	CEMETERY, NORTHERN PART
2	GL02709323	WT	CREEK, JUNCTION—CENTER
3	GL03509250	DA	DRAW, CENTER
4	GL02229150	WK	SOUTH END OF RUNWAY
5	GL01709050	CM	EAST END OF POIND
6	GL00659125	RD	HILLTOP 134—TOP
7	GL01509218	JD	SPUR—150 SOUTHEAST OF HILLTOP

Figure 1.81

Score orienteering

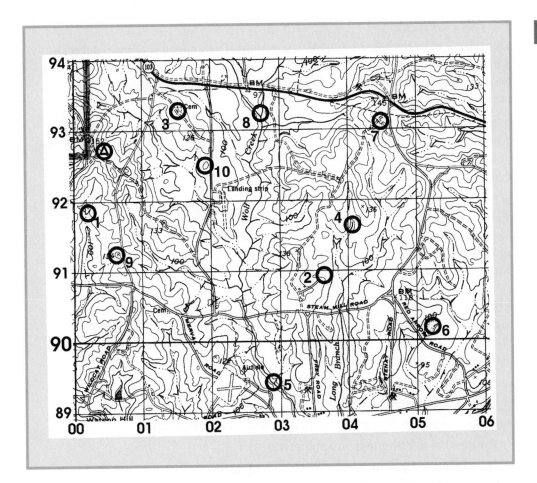

Score Orienteering

In this event, the area chosen for the competition has many control points.
The control points near the start/finish point (usually identical in this event) have
a low point value, while those more distant or more difficult to locate have a high
point value. The competitor must locate as many control markers as possible within
the specified time (usually 90 minutes).

As with a cross-country event, organizers give each competitor a map and an event
card. The card lists all the control points with their different values.

Organizers design the course (see Figure 1.81) so that there are more control points
than a competitor can possibly visit in the allotted time. Therefore, competitors must
plan and choose their route between control points carefully. Points are awarded
for each control point visited and deducted for exceeding the specified time; however,
there is no reward for returning early with time still available to find more points.
The good competitor must be able to coordinate time and distance with the ability
to land navigate while running the course. The competitor with the highest point
score is the winner.

Relay Orienteering

This type of orienteering is a popular team sport. Each member of the team runs a free-point or line orienteering leg of one to two miles. No person runs more than one leg. The competition may be held using a master map for the entire course or one for each leg.

In the case of a master map for the entire course, the first team member copies down all legs of the course. After completing the first leg, he or she hands the map to the next runner, who completes the next leg of the course. The team repeats this process until all members have run their portion of the course.

In the case of a master map for each leg, the first trainee goes to a master map that has only the first location on it. When that person completes the first leg, he or she gives the map to the next person, who goes to a different master map and copies the second portion of the course. This continues until all members of the team have completed their legs.

Night Orienteering

Night orienteering is a free-point or score event occurring in the evening. The main differences between a night conducted free-point or score and one conducted during the day are:

- Control points are marked by a light that is visible from 30 to 50 meters in all directions
- Control points are located no more than 400 to 800 meters apart
- The event is run over less difficult terrain
- The signal used to indicate the conclusion of the event or an emergency is a vehicle horn or a flare.

Controlling Your Movement

A sound knowledge of the basics of map reading will help you immensely as an orienteering event competitor. Additional skills such as accurate compass reading, good decision making, and using the terrain are critical as well. The beginner-level orienteer should learn the following techniques.

Determining Direction of Travel

After you have plotted the course's control points, you must determine how to get to the first and other control points. The basic compass technique used in orienteering to determine direction of travel consists of five steps:

1. Lay the map on a flat surface and orient it to magnetic north by placing the edge of the compass along a north-south grid line. Rotate the map and compass until the north arrow is under the black hairline.

2. Keeping the map oriented, move the compass in such a way that one side of the compass touches your location and your destination. The compass is now pointing in the direction of travel.

3. Rotate the bezel ring until the luminous line is pointing to grid north on the map. The luminous line should be over the north arrow (if the map is still oriented) and it should be parallel to the north-south grid line.

4. Lift the compass off the map and correct for magnetic declination. If the declination is west, rotate the bezel ring counterclockwise; if east, then rotate it clockwise.

5. Holding the compass in front of you, rotate your body until the north arrow lies under the luminous line. The direction of travel is now indicated by the black hairline.

Route Selection

As mentioned at the beginning of this section, orienteering develops many skills besides map reading. An important one is decision making. Route selection is where competitors must make decisions. Which is the fastest way from point A to point B? Is it over or around a hill? Is it going cross-country or using a road or trail? Except for those instances when organizers mark or specify the route in advance, wise route selection is important.

A good orienteering course will have some elevation obstacles. These obstacles will force you to decide if it is faster to go the most direct route over it or to take a longer detour around it. A simple formula to convert height into comparable flat distance is: 25 feet of elevation equals 100 meters on a flat surface. For example, suppose the straight line distance to point B is 500 meters with a 50 foot high hill en route. The energy you would expend would be equivalent to running 500 meters plus an additional 200 meters for going over the hill. If the detour around the hill equals a total of 680 meters, it may be easier to go around it, depending upon the type of terrain you encounter.

The type of terrain and vegetation that you encounter has a major impact on your pace. You must know your pace count through several types of terrain. In addition, you must know your pace when trotting and running, both when you are fresh and when you are tired. Although pacing will vary from individual to individual, Table 1.1 may be useful to a beginner. These figures apply during daylight, when the runner is fresh and on flat terrain. The numbers represent paces or each time the left foot strikes the ground.

Table 1.1	PACING CHART		
	SMALL (Less than 5'8")	MEDIUM	TALL (Over 6' tall)
Road/Path	42	40	37
Light Vegetation	45	43	40
Open Forest	50	46	43
Dense Forest	55	50	46

Movement Techniques

In addition to knowing where the control points are and where you are at all times, you must also know the best route for getting to the next control point. The shortest route may not be the fastest, and it may not pay to travel between two points as fast as possible if you tire yourself out in the process.

> **Note:**
>
> Remember, you can locate your position on a map using terrain features, a back azimuth, or resection.

There are several techniques available to aid you in moving from one control point to another. They include the following:

- **Direct line.** This method involves establishing a compass bearing between your location and the destination; then, follow the compass bearing until you reach the point. A variation of this technique is to establish a compass bearing that you will follow for a specific distance at which time you establish a new bearing. Repeat this process until you reach the final destination.

- **Steering marks.** A steering mark is a prominent object or terrain feature that you can see and that is in the general direction of travel. Such objects as a lone tree or building are good examples of steering marks. One of the advantages of this technique is that once you reach the steering mark, you can reorient yourself before continuing.

- **Aiming off.** The aiming off technique is valuable when your destination lies along a linear terrain feature such as a road or stream. Due to errors in compass or map reading, you may reach a linear feature and not know whether your objective lies to the right or the left. Furthermore, each degree that you are offset to the right or left will move the aim-off point from the destination 17 meters to the right or left for each 100 meters traveled. For example, if the number of degrees offset is 10 and the distance traveled is 100 meters, then your location is 170 meters to the left of the objective (10 degrees offset $\times$ 17 meters per 100 meters traveled = 170).

> **Note:**
>
> A proven technique to prevent this from occurring is to deliberately aim to one side of the destination; then, when you reach the linear feature, you will know in which direction to turn.

- **Attack points.** When using the attack points technique, you select a prominent terrain feature, such as a hilltop or road junction, near your destination. You may use any technique to arrive at this point. After arriving there, you can reorient yourself, and then make a final short approach to it. The purpose of this technique is to minimize the distance you have to travel on the final approach. This in turn limits any errors in compass work or pacing you might make in locating the destination. The difference between an attack point and a steering mark is that you select an attack point from a map.

- **Geographic orientation.** This technique involves keeping the map oriented as you travel and remembering what terrain features you will encounter en route to the next control point. For example, if you decide to follow a road to reach the next control point, you should orient the map as you stop and make turns along the road.

Using Figure 1.82, assume that you want to travel from your position at "A" to control point 4. One route that you could take would be to use the north-south intermittent stream bed. Pass the first two east-west intermittent stream junctions that you encounter and take the eastern fork at the third junction. Follow that intermittent stream and draw to the road junction (which you can call an attack point). From the road junction, shoot an azimuth of 77 degrees to the control point.

Clothing and Equipment

When planning to participate in an orienteering event, you should wear and take the proper clothing and equipment.

Choose the clothing to wear depending on the type of vegetation and terrain you will encounter on the course. For example, in bushy terrain, you should wear a long-sleeve shirt and long pants to protect against cuts and scratches. For those who want to pursue orienteering as a sport, consider purchasing light nylon racing suits. These are full-length suits (usually fluorescent) with long sleeves and pouches in the front to carry maps, compasses, and so on.

Hiking shoes or boots are excellent for orienteering because of their durability and the ankle support they provide. High-top sneakers also provide excellent ankle support. Cross-country running shoes are good because they are lightweight and have better traction in mud, but they do not normally support the ankles.

Although a standard military lensatic compass is very good for orienteering, its one disadvantage is the time required for the needle to stabilize prior to lining up an azimuth. Those who desire to pursue orienteering as a sport may want to acquire an induction dampened or liquid-filled compass.

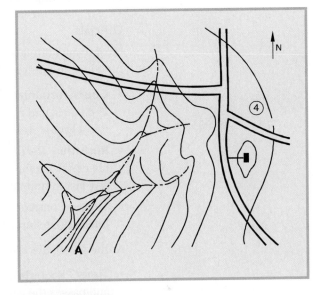

Figure 1.82 Using terrain features to plot a route

The map is probably the most important item the participant carries. The most common map used in orienteering is a topographic map with a 1:50,000 scale; however, competitors prefer a 1:25,000 scale because it is easier to read and it shows features in greater detail. Try to use multi-colored maps if they are available. After a competitor outlines the course details and copies the key terrain features from color-coded master maps, his or her own maps should be covered with a clear, plastic-like material such as a document protector to prevent these marks from smearing and/or becoming unreadable.

Organization of the Course

At every orienteering event, there are a few basic elements that you will encounter. These are essential to the efficient and safe operation of the event, and are covered in the following sections.

Officials

Most events often use the same officials at both the start and finish, although their functions are different at each end. At the start, these officials include:

- **Course organizer.** Briefs competitors in the assembly area, issues event cards and maps, and calls competitors forward to start individually (or in groups if it is a group event).
- **Recorder.** Records the competitor's name and start time on recorder's sheet, checks the competitor's name and start number on the event card, and issues any last-minute instructions.
- **Timer.** Controls the master clock and releases the competitors across the start line at their start time (usually at one-minute intervals) to the master map area.

At the finish, the officials include:

- **Timer.** Records the finish time of each competitor on his or her event card and passes the card to the recorder.
- **Recorder.** Records competitor's finish times on the recorder's sheet and tallies final score based on time and correctness of control points visited.
- **Course organizer.** Verifies correctness of names, finish times, and final score. Posts competitors' positions on a results board and accounts for all participants at the end of the event.

More officials and/or assistants may be used; however, the three listed here are the minimum required to run the competition.

Control Areas

In many orienteering events, there are at least three control areas. They are:

- **Assembly area.** Here participants register and receive instructions, maps, event cards, and start numbers. They may also change into their orienteering clothes if facilities are available, study their maps, and fill out their event cards. Sanitation facilities are normally available in this area.
- **Start (Start/Finish).** At the start, each competitor reports to the recorder and timer to be logged in and released. Oftentimes, the start and finish are at the same location.
- **Master map area.** There are three to five master maps 20 to 50 meters from the start. When the participants arrive at this area, they must mark all the course's control points on their maps. Having done this, competitors must decide on the route they will follow. Experienced competitors will take the time to orient their map and carefully plot the route before rushing off.

Control Cards

Organizers make the event card as small as possible so that competitors can easily carry it in a pocket. It contains the following items: name, start number, start time, finish time, total time, place, and spaces for marking the control points visited. It may also contain a listing of descriptive clues. Figure 1.83 is a sample event card for the most common type of an orienteering course.

Clue Description Cards

Organizers prepare these cards with the master maps after the course is set. They contain the descriptive clues for each control point, control code, grid coordinate references, returning time for competitors, removal times for each location, and panic azimuth. Organizers keep the clue description cards and the master maps confidential until the competitors start the event.

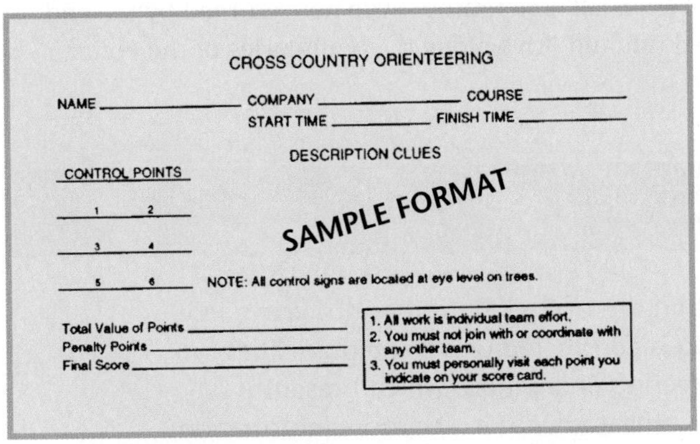
CROSS COUNTRY ORIENTEERING

NAME ______ COMPANY ______ COURSE ______
START TIME ______ FINISH TIME ______

DESCRIPTION CLUES

CONTROL POINTS
1 2
3 4
5 6

SAMPLE FORMAT

NOTE: All control signs are located at eye level on trees.

Total Value of Points ______
Penalty Points ______
Final Score ______

1. All work is individual team effort.
2. You must not join with or coordinate with any other team.
3. You must personally visit each point you indicate on your score card.

Figure 1.83

A typical control card

Scoring

Organizers score the cross-country or free event by the competitor's time alone. Competitors must visit all control points; failure to visit one results in a disqualification. In this event, the fastest time wins. A variation that organizers often use for beginners is to have a "not-later-than" return time at the finish and to add minutes onto their final time for the number of minutes late and for the number of control points not located.

The score event requires the participant to collect as many points as possible within the time limit. Organizers deduct points for extra time spent on the course—usually one point for every 10 seconds over the time limit.

Safety

The following items and provisions are required to ensure that an orienteering course runs as safely as possible. Furthermore, the course organizer should ensure that all participants receive a detailed safety briefing that covers the following key information.

- **First aid.** Ensure that a first aid kit is available at the start and finish. One of the officials should be trained in first aid, or a qualified medical person should be at the event.
- **Control points.** Locate all control points where the safety of the competitors is not endangered by hazardous terrain or other conditions.
- **Safety lane.** Designate a location, usually linear, on the course where competitors may go if injured, fatigued, or lost. A good course will usually have a well-defined boundary as a safety lane; then, competitors can set a panic azimuth on their compass and follow it until they reach the boundary.
- **Finish time.** All orienteering events must have a final return time. At this time, organizers should sound a loud siren or horn and all competitors must report to the finish line, even if they have not completed the course.
- **Search and rescue procedures.** If all competitors have not returned by the end of the competition, the officials should drive along the boundaries of the course to pick up the missing people.

Give Orienteering a Try!

Interest in orienteering within the United States has grown rapidly over the years. Orienteering is conducted under the guidelines of the United States Orienteering Federation, which presently has approximately 70 clubs affiliated with it. For more information, check out the International Orienteering Federation's website at http://www.orienteering.org/.

Conclusion

Maps permit you to see an area of the earth's surface with the key features of that area properly positioned. They can take the guesswork out of traveling to new locations, preventing wasted time and effort. The military most often uses the topographic map because of its detail in portraying terrain features, landforms, the horizontal positions of these features, and elevation and relief.

Successful map reading requires a thorough understanding of systems for finding locations. Your ability to use these systems and to locate four-, six-, and eight-digit grid coordinates can increase your confidence in identifying your location. But to navigate successfully, you also must also know how to determine distance. The most accurate method is to use a map scale and to convert the map distance (straight-line or curved-line) to ground distance.

You must also be able to express direction. The use of azimuths, compasses, protractors, and maps improves the accuracy of your directions. Using intersection, resection, and polar coordinates, you can locate an unknown point on a map.

Review Questions

1 What is the purpose of latitude and longitude lines on a globe?

2 How do you orient a map without using a compass?

3 What are three examples of symbols you might find on a topographic map that are not typically on standard road maps?

4 What do the six-digit coordinates on a map tell you, and how do you write them?

5 What are the 10 terrain features?

6 How do you measure curved-line distance on a topographic map using the map scale?

7 What are the differences among true north, magnetic north, and grid north?

8 What does the declination diagram on a map indicate?

9 How do you convert grid azimuths to magnetic azimuths?

10 How do you locate an unknown point on a topographic map by intersection? By resection?

11 What are the five movement techniques used in orienteering?

Fundamentals of Survival

Key Terms

- **mnemonic**
- **vanquish**
- **improvise**
- **turbid**
- **carbohydrates**
- **tinder**
- **ignite**
- **kindling**
- **combustible**
- **conifer**
- **plankton**

What You Will Learn to Do

Understand the basics of survival in several different environments

Skills and Knowledge You Will Gain Along the Way

✔ Explain the fundamentals of survival
✔ Describe how to survive in tropical areas
✔ Describe how to survive in cold areas
✔ Describe how to survive in water

Fundamentals of Survival

Have you ever thought of yourself as a "survivor"? Maybe not. Much of your daily routine, though, involves things you do to survive. Dressing appropriately for the weather; remembering your helmet when you go out on your bike; even eating, drinking, and sleeping are survival activities in the broadest sense.

But most of this is pretty tame stuff, isn't it? People who are out in extreme climates and conditions, including those serving in the armed forces, need survival skills of a much higher order. This chapter will introduce you to some of the skills those people have.

You may never be out at sea in an open boat or lost in a mangrove jungle. The closest you may ever come to a survival situation is a weekend camping trip. But you never know when these principles may come in handy. Many people get into situations they never thought would happen to them—because of severe weather, other natural disaster, or just getting lost during a hike in the woods.

Learning the fundamentals of survival will give you added confidence in all kinds of situations, and help you be more alert and aware of your environment wherever you are.

Severe weather and natural disaster can land you in survival mode, as happened to these refugees from Hurricane Katrina in New Orleans in September 2005.
Courtesy of Michael Ainsworth/Dallas Morning News/Corbis

CHAPTER 2 Fundamentals of Survival

S-U-R-V-I-V-A-L Spells 'Survival'

If you ever have to fend for yourself outside your usual support system, the word *survival* itself holds clues that may help you return safely home. You can use the letters that spell survival as a mnemonic device. A mnemonic device is a memory aid, like a sticky note on your bathroom mirror to remind you of a dental appointment, or the little jingle that helps you remember how long different months of the year are. ("Thirty days hath September . . . .")

The following little memory device will remind you of things you need to think about if you're ever in a survival situation—such as after a car breakdown or accident, an emergency aircraft landing, a mishap at sea, or getting lost in the wilderness or a desert.

1. **Size** up the situation, including:
   - Your surroundings. Are you in a forest, in a jungle, in a desert? Each of these kinds of places has its own features—and possible dangers.
   - Your physical condition: Have you been injured? If you have, give yourself first aid, and take care not to make your injuries worse.
   - Your equipment: Check to see what equipment you have and what its condition is.

2. **Use** all your senses, and remember that undue haste makes waste. In a survival situation, a false move can kill you. Don't do something just to be doing something. If you act in haste, you may forget or lose equipment. Pay attention to sights, sounds, even smells around you. Pay attention to changes in light, temperature, and weather.

3. **Remember** where you are. If you have a map, try to spot your location on it. Try to relate what you see on your map to what you see around you. If you see a mountain or a stream, for instance, can you find it on your map? Being able to do this is a basic survival skill. If there are others in your group, make sure they know where they are, too, but don't rely on them to keep track of your route. Pay attention to where you are and how you are moving. Orient yourself constantly; that is, keep locating yourself with respect to some clear reference point. Always keep an eye out for water resources—especially in the desert—and for areas that will provide good shelter.

4. **Vanquish** fear and panic. To vanquish is to conquer. In a survival situation you need to conquer fear and panic. They may leave you unable to think straight and will drain your energy. Formal survival training will build your confidence and enable you to stand up to these enemies of survival.

5. **Improvise.** You may not have much experience improvising. For instance, at home you have a bed you sleep in every night. In a survival situation, you may have to find shelter creatively. You'll have to improvise, in other words. It's good to learn to use your imagination to improvise. You can learn to use natural objects around you for different needs. You can use a rock as a hammer, for instance.

6. **Value** living. Your will to live can save your life. Most people are creatures of comfort in their day-to-day living. But in a life-or-death situation, you may have to cope with all kinds of stress and discomfort. Stubbornness, a refusal to let things get you down, will give you the mental and physical strength to endure.

S-U-R-V-I-V-A-L

1. **S**ize up the situation.
2. **U**se all your senses.
3. **R**emember where you are.
4. **V**anquish fear and panic.
5. **I**mprovise.
6. **V**alue living.
7. **A**ct only after thinking.
8. **L**ive by your wits.

7. **Act** only after thinking. Don't give up. If you see animals around you, watch them for clues about how to survive. After all, they also need food, water, and shelter. But remember that animals aren't an absolute guide. Many animals can eat plants that are poisonous to humans.

8. **Live** by your wits, but for now, learn basic skills. You need to know about the environment where you're going, and you must practice skills geared to that environment. In the desert, for instance, knowing how to find water is essential. You can use any training exercise—even a weekend hike with your friends—as an opportunity to practice basic survival skills. Survival training reduces fear of the unknown. It gives you self-confidence and teaches you to live by your wits.

A Survivor's Two Goals

If you're ever caught in a real survival situation, you will have two main goals: to stay alive, and to return—to your home, to your campground, to your base, to your ship. It's simple, maybe, but not necessarily easy.

To stay alive, you need to think about three things: personal protection, nutrition, and health.

Personal Protection

Personal protection involves:

- **Adequate clothing:** The human body can't tolerate much in the way of temperature extremes, but it has a wonderful ability to regulate heating and cooling. You must make the most of the clothing you have with you, especially in extreme hot or cold.

- **Survival equipment:** If you have it, it can be a great help. But you may find that what you have isn't helpful in the situation you're in, or that it is not in good repair. Be ready to improvise.

- **Shelter:** This provides a place to rest and protection from the elements. Where it's very cold or very hot, finding safe shelter from the elements will be your most important task. You may have only minutes to complete it.

- **Fire:** You can use fire to purify water, cook food, keep warm, and dry wet clothing. You can also use fire to send signals.

Nutrition

People always need food and water, of course. But in survival situations these normal needs become even more important because of the physical stresses you are under. In a survival situation, you must remember to keep drinking water. Your body needs it.

And although water comes first, you need to think about food, too. People caught in a survival situation may not think much about food for the first few hours, or maybe even the first couple of days. But lack of food will eventually lead to loss of energy, stamina, and strength. If you don't eat, you get irritable easily, too, and that won't help you get home.

A survival situation is no place for a picky eater, by the way. If you have an adequate supply of canned tuna and candy bars, you may do fine out in the woods waiting to be rescued. But if not, you may have to overcome prejudices about foods you don't like, and this goes way beyond broccoli. More on that later in the chapter.

Maintaining Your Health

If you're going to be a survivor, you may have to be your own doctor, nurse, psychologist, and cheerleader. You must protect your physical and mental health.

Where first aid supplies may be few or nonexistent, do everything you can to avoid injury in the first place. Take special care with knives and axes, especially if you're not used to using them.

Keeping your spirits up may be the best thing you can do to get yourself back home. Optimism, grit, and humor will all help.

Preparing a Survival Kit

If you're going to be out in a wilderness area where you might have to fend for yourself, it's a good idea to put together a survival kit. It should be in a case that is waterproof, durable, and easy to carry.

Items for a Survival Kit

Knife	Magnifying lens
Waterproof matches	Oxytetracycline tablets (an antibiotic)
Lighter	Water purification tablets
Snare wire	Solar blanket
Signaling mirror	Surgical blades
Compass	Butterfly sutures
Fishing line	Water container
Fish hooks	Needle and thread
Candle	Lip balm

Also good to include if possible: a small survival radio or beacon, and a length of rope.

Water

It bears repeating: In a survival situation, you have to be sure always to get enough water. The average adult needs two to three quarts of water daily in normal temperatures. Under the stresses of a survival situation, you could easily need much more than that. While you can live up to 30 days without food, you can only go one to three days without water.

If you notice yourself becoming inefficient as you try to perform even simple tasks, you may be in the early stages of dehydration. Weakness, dizziness, headache, and fever may follow. If you fail to get enough water to replace your body fluids, you will die. To prevent dehydration, drink small amounts of water throughout the day. Drink more water to keep from drying out if it gets hotter, or if you exert yourself more.

In tropical or temperate regions, you may find water in rivers, streams, or lakes. You may drink rainwater, too. In cold regions, you can get water by melting ice or snow.

You may need to purify the water you find before you drink it. Always treat water that has a strong odor, or foam or bubbles. Also treat water that is discolored or has a turbid appearance. Water that tastes salty or makes you gag also needs treatment. Healthy green vegetation growing around a water source is a good sign. If this is missing from the water source you've found, that's another indication that you need to treat the water before you drink it.

Among the ways to purify water are these:

- Boil it for at least 10 minutes
- Use your purification tablets
- Put eight drops of 2 percent iodine solution per quart.

Food

After water, your next most urgent need is normally food. Eating well, or at least adequately, can make the difference between surviving or not. You will need to pay attention to three types of foods—carbohydrates, fats, and proteins—plus vitamins and minerals. These latter are important in keeping certain bodily processes in good working order.

Carbohydrates are made up of simple molecules that are easily digested. They are good suppliers of energy. Nutrition experts say that in a survival situation, half your caloric intake should be carbohydrates. Starches and sugars are both carbohydrates. You find these in fruits, vegetables, and legumes, as well as in breads, cereals, and candy.

Fats are more complex than carbohydrates and release their energy more slowly. Butter, cheese, oils, nuts, egg yolks, margarine, and animal fats are sources of dietary fat.

Protein is the third type of food. The body breaks proteins down into amino acids and from these forms new body tissues such as muscles. Complete protein gives the body the exact amino acids it needs to rebuild itself. Protein lacking one or more of these amino acids is called *incomplete*. Fish, meat, and poultry are considered *complete* protein. Cheese, milk, grains, and legumes provide incomplete protein. You should have two to three ounces of complete protein daily.

Key Term

turbid—
cloudy, as with mud or sediment

Key Term

carbohydrates—
any of a group of organic compounds that includes sugars, starches, celluloses, and gums and serves as a major energy source in the diet

Table 2.1	CALORIC AND FAT VALUES OF SELECTED FOOD FOUND IN THE WILDS		
FOOD	QTY.	CALORIES	FAT (g)
Whole duck egg	1	177	12.0
Small- or large-mouth bass	3–4 oz.	109	3.6
Clams	4–5	88	.2
Freshwater crayfish	3–4 oz.	75	.6
Eel	3–5 oz.	240	20.0
Octopus	3–4 oz.	76	.9
Atlantic salmon	4 oz.	220	14.0
Rainbow trout	4 oz.	200	11.8
Banana	1 small	87	.3
Breadfruit	4 oz.	105	.5
Guava	1 medium	64	.7
Mango	1 small	68	.5
Wild duck	4 oz.	230	16.0
Baked opossum		235	10.6
Wild rabbit	4 oz.	124	4.0
Venison	4 oz.	128	3.1
Dandelion greens	1 cup	70	1.4
Potato	1 medium	78	.2
Prickly pear	4 oz.	43	.2

Source: *Cadet Field Manual*, p. 10-11

The average person needs 2,000 calories a day to function at a minimum level. In a survival situation, though, you need between 3,000 and 5,000 calories in warm weather, and between 4,000 and 6,000 in cold weather.

Eating in the Wilds

There is plenty to eat in the wilds, but it may take some getting used to. Along the seacoast, between the high and low tide marks, is one of the best places to find food. Marshes, mud flats, or mangrove swamps where a river flows into another river or the ocean are also good places to look for food. So are riverbanks, edges of forest meadows, protected mountain slopes, and abandoned farm fields.

Fish are a good source of protein and fat. They're relatively abundant and easy to catch, especially early in the morning or late in the afternoon. Light often attracts fish at night. Fish will gather in deep pools of water, under overhanging brush, and in and around logs and other things that provide shelter.

If you're going to go after animals, concentrate on the smaller ones. Those that inhabit a particular area and have regular feeding habits will be easier to stalk. Remember to move quietly.

Don't forget insects. They're easy to catch and full of protein—65 to 80 percent, as compared with 20 percent for beef. There are some insects you should avoid: all adults that sting or bite, all hairy or brightly colored insects, and any caterpillars or insects that have a sharp odor. Avoid spiders and disease carriers such as ticks, flies, and mosquitoes.

Shelter

A shelter can protect you from the elements and help you keep your spirits up and maintain your will to survive. Don't make your shelter too big. It needs to be large enough to protect you but small enough to contain your body heat. This is especially important in cold climates.

In choosing a shelter site, you want to consider weather, life forms (plant and animal), terrain, and time of day: How much time do you have to build before it gets dark? You want to get the maximum shelter for the minimum energy.

There are two general types of shelters—immediate-action shelters, for when you need protection right away, and improvised shelters, which you can build when you have some time and don't need immediate protection from the elements. You can find an immediate-action shelter in a natural formation such as a cave or a tree well. You can also make a shelter out of aircraft parts, parachutes, rafts, or tarpaulins.

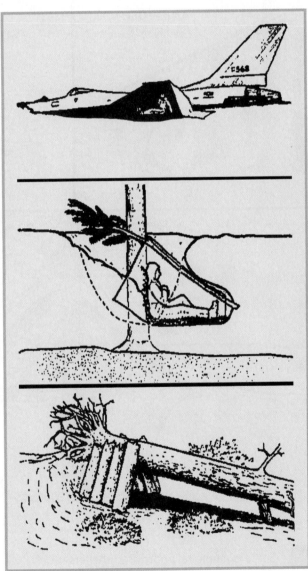

Figure 2.1

Some examples of immediate-action shelters
Courtesy of US Navy

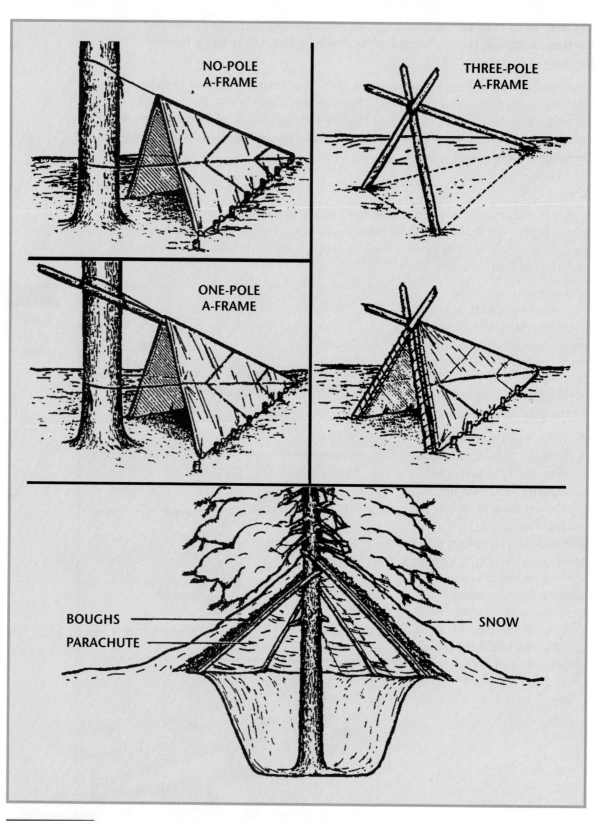

NO-POLE
A-FRAME

THREE-POLE
A-FRAME

ONE-POLE
A-FRAME

BOUGHS

PARACHUTE

SNOW

Figure 2.2 Some examples of improvised shelters
Courtesy of US Navy

Fire

Knowing how to start a fire is one of the many skills that, in a survival situation, can make the difference between life and death. Fire can provide warmth and comfort, can cook food and purify water, and can even provide a psychological boost.

Small is better than large when it comes to building a fire. Small fires require less fuel and are easier to control. Never leave a fire unattended unless it's "banked." To bank a fire, scrape cold ashes and dry earth onto the fire, leaving just enough air coming through the dirt at the top to keep the fuel smoldering.

A fire needs three things: air (oxygen), heat, and fuel. If you remove any of these, the fire goes out. With practice, you can learn to get these three elements into the right balance for the most efficient fire.

To build a fire, start with tinder. Tinder is any type of material that will ignite easily, even from just a spark: cedar or birch bark, dry wood shavings, straw, dry leaves, or paper. If you have matches or a lighter, they would be your best option for igniting your kindling. A magnifying lens can focus sunlight onto dry leaves to start them smoldering. Other methods of starting a fire involve friction, such as flint and steel, or a bow and drill.

After tinder comes kindling. Kindling will be larger pieces of combustible material that will ignite when you bring them into contact with the burning tinder. Take care not to let the bigger pieces of kindling smother the flame from the tinder. Twigs, plant fibers, small branches of trees, even pieces of split wood, should you have them, can all serve as kindling. Just make sure whatever you use is dry.

The next step is adding fuel to the fire. This is the point where you add bigger logs. They will burn slowly and steadily. They don't have to be completely dry, either, as long as the flames from the kindling raise the temperature high enough. Your first choice of firewood should be dry hardwood. Green wood is the next best, followed by pine and other conifers.

Once you have the flames started, you can add logs according to any of a number of different methods, each suited to a different purpose. Several examples are shown in Figure 2.3.

Key Terms

tinder—
material for starting a fire

ignite—
to start to burn or catch fire

kindling—
material larger than tinder used to ignite logs and other fuel in a fire

combustible—
capable of igniting and burning

conifer—
any tree or shrub that has cones and needles

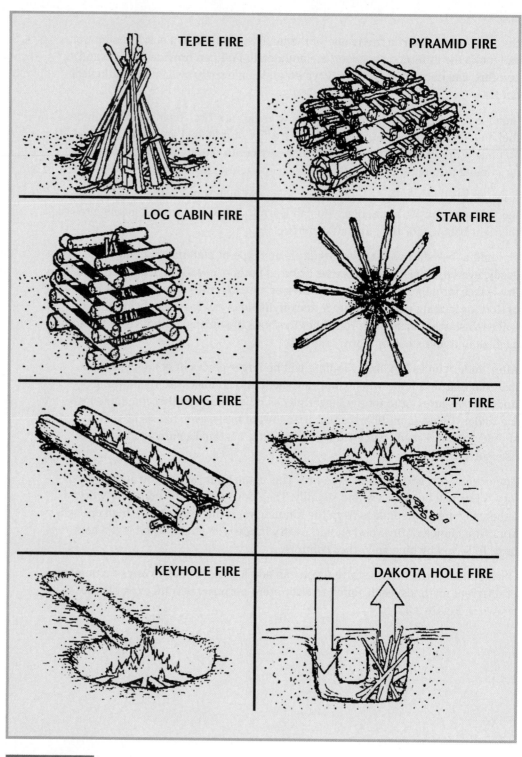

Figure 2.3   Several common types of fire lays, each best suited to a different purpose
Courtesy of US Navy

Traveling

In any survival situation you may find yourself in—for instance, the breakdown of your car in a remote area, or the emergency landing of your aircraft—you will have to decide whether to stay where you are or to try to return on your own. On land, you're generally better off staying with your vehicle or craft. You should strike out on your own only when: 1) you know where you are and know that you can reach water, shelter, food, and help by traveling; or 2) you've waited several days and rescue hasn't come. If weather conditions are uncertain, or if you're ill or injured, that would argue for staying put.

Signaling

One thing you can do while you await rescue is to try to signal those who may be looking for you. You can signal with a mirror, with fire, smoke, smoke grenades, flares, and even fireworks. On the water, a dye marker can help rescuers find you. It releases a quantity of fluorescent dye onto the surface of the water, where it is visible to pilots flying overhead. On the ground, you can spell out the letters SOS (an international distress signal) in rocks, with dye on snow, or with branches or brush in a clearing—anything that can be seen from the air.

Figure 2.4   Using a mirror to catch the sun's rays and signal to a rescue plane
Courtesy of US Navy

Take your time and watch your footing when moving through jungle areas.
Courtesy of Mary Beth Angelo/Photo Researchers, Inc.

How to Survive in Tropical Areas

A tropical jungle may be one of four types:

- *Mangrove jungle,* a swamp of tangled roots and branches along a tropical seashore
- *Primary jungle,* with large trees and a network of vines
- *Secondary jungle,* with very dense growth of vegetation at ground level
- *High mountain jungle,* probably the most difficult type of terrain in which to travel and find food. Problems here include rain and fog, as well as insects such as tree leeches, which often drop down onto passing travelers.

Food in Jungle Areas

Fish, crayfish, and mollusks are plentiful in jungle streams and in coastal areas alongside jungles. Oysters and fish abound in mangrove swamps. Water birds nest in mangrove swamps, and their eggs are good to eat. Monkeys and wild pigs are also common in these areas.

Travel in the Jungle

Be patient and plan carefully. Rivers, trails, and ridgelines often make the best routes, though these may all have dangers you must be alert to. Your machete, if you have one, is the best aid to survival in the jungle. But never cut brush if you can simply part it. If you must cut, use a down-and-out angle, to save effort, rather than a flat-and-level approach. Take your time. Watch your footing. Avoid grabbing at bushes or plants. Wear gloves and keep all your clothing buttoned for protection.

Quicksand can be a problem in the jungle. If you fall into it, don't panic, but assume a spread-eagle position and "swim" out of it.

How to Survive in Cold Areas

The key to survival in cold regions is preparation. You'll need adequate footgear, warm clothing, and an insulated sleeping bag. You'll need to know how to build emergency shelters to protect yourself against extreme cold, wind, and storms.

Clothing in Cold Areas

You may have already learned the principle of layering if you jog, bike, or hike. It's even more valid in extreme cold. Several shirts, a sweater, and a wind-resistant jacket will be more useful than one big heavy coat. And you'll have to keep adjusting your clothing—peeling off layers when you're active—to avoid heat buildup—and putting them back on when you're at rest.

Take care to avoid restricting circulation. The flow of blood through your body distributes heat and prevents frostbite. If this flow is restricted, you may get into trouble. Layering doesn't work right if you put on three pairs of socks and then try to get your feet into boots that give you room for only one pair.

Keep your head covered. When you're moving about, minimize perspiration by opening your clothing at the neck and wrists and loosening at the waist. If you're still feeling warm, take off an outer layer—but put it back on as soon as you're no longer exerting yourself.

If you have enough room in your boots, you can tuck dry grass or moss or similar material into them.

Travel in cold areas is dangerous; you're often better off staying put and waiting for rescue.
Courtesy of Photodisc/Getty Images

Keep your clothes as dry as possible. Brush snow off before you enter a shelter or get near a fire. If you take off clothes to warm them at a fire, beat the frost and snow out of them first.

Protection for your eyes is essential in the dazzling brightness of a snowy landscape. Some kind of sunglasses should be part of your equipment. But if not, you have to improvise. A strip of bark with a couple of slits for your eyes, for instance, might do the job.

Parachute material, if you have it, can be useful in improvising a shelter.

Sleeping

To make your bed in a cold-climate survival situation, you'll need a bottom layer under your sleeping bag. You can make this of tree boughs, seat cushions, a parachute, an inflated rubber life raft—whatever materials come to hand. Remember that you must fluff up your sleeping bag once it comes out of its carrying case. Otherwise it won't insulate you very well.

You'll want to keep your sleeping bag clean and dry, as well as fluffed. You can dry it by turning it inside out and warming it by your fire. But don't let it burn!

In a cold climate, your breath will condense and freeze. These little bits of ice can then get into your sleeping bag, where your bodily warmth will melt them and get the bag wet. To avoid all this, improvise a moisture cloth from a towel, a piece of clothing, or something similar (Warning: Don't use plastic!). Wrap this lightly around your head to trap the moisture from your breathing before it dampens your sleeping bag.

Food in Cold Areas

Plants in arctic regions are generally small and stunted, but you can eat many of them.

- *Dandelions*: Their leaves and roots are edible raw or cooked.
- *Black and white spruce*: Their buds, needles, and stems are a source of vitamin C if you chew them. In spring and summer the inner bark is edible as well.
- *Dwarf arctic birch*: You can eat its thin tooth-edged leaves, buds, and inner bark.
- *Lichens*: These are abundant; many species are edible as starch substitutes.

Water in Cold Areas

The physical exertion of surviving in extreme cold—including hauling firewood, building shelters, and shivering to keep warm—means that your body needs five to six quarts of water a day—two or three times normal water intake. If you're depending on dehydrated rations, you'll need even more water.

The good news here is that water is generally easy to find in cold climates because of an abundance of ice and snow. If possible, melt them first to avoid lowering your body temperature by ingesting something frozen.

Travel in Cold Areas

Travel in extreme cold can be so dangerous that you're better off waiting to be rescued. You should try to travel only if you need to move to escape danger or to reach an area of obviously better resources. You'll have to cope with intense cold and high winds, of course, and with a lack of landmarks. This makes it hard to judge distance. You may even face white-out conditions. And remember that your compass may act up in polar latitudes.

In the summer, cold regions offer another set of challenges: What was frozen solid in the winter may become a mass of bogs and swamps. You'll need protection against mosquitoes, midges, and black flies. If you're severely bitten, infections may develop.

In mountainous parts of extreme latitudes, travel along ridge lines to get a firmer footing freer of vegetation. If you're going over a glacier, be sure to have a probe pole with you, and test your footing at every step. A single slip through a crevasse can kill you.

How to Survive in Water

Water covers more than 70 percent of the earth's surface, and so if you ever find yourself in a survival situation, it may well be in the water—especially if you join the Navy.

All military ships and planes that operate over water are routinely equipped for emergencies at sea. Their lifeboats or life rafts include such supplies as fresh water, dry rations, first aid supplies, and signaling equipment.

In a survival situation in warm waters, one of your biggest challenges will be protecting yourself against the sun and getting adequate drinking water. Do everything you can to stay out of direct sun. Improvise a sun shade. Use sunscreen if you have it. Dampen clothing in sea water to get the cooling effect of evaporation.

In colder ocean areas, the challenge to survivors is staying dry and keeping warm. If you have an anti-exposure suit available, put it on at once. You should know that if you are wearing wet clothing, heat will leave your body much faster than if your clothing is dry. Survivors on the water in cold climates should put on any extra clothing that's available. Covering the floor of your raft or lifeboat with any material available will help insulate you against the cold.

Food on the Open Seas

If you're ever at sea in a lifeboat, remember that most seaweed is edible and a good source of carbohydrates or proteins. It can be washed and eaten raw or dried. You may also find small fish or crabs in bits of seaweed you find floating on the water.

You can also eat plankton—tiny plants and animals that float in the water. You can catch them with a net. But plankton is hard to digest, so if you are going to rely on it at sea, you'll want to start with small quantities until your system adjusts.

> **Key Term**
>
> **plankton—**
> *small organisms, including algae, that float or drift in great numbers in fresh or salt water, especially at or near the surface*

As noted earlier, fish are another food source. Almost any fish is edible; few are likely to be poisonous. Even if you lack fishing gear, you may be able to catch flying fish. You can attract them into your boat at night with a light. Seabirds are another source of food, though likely to be scarce in mid-ocean. You can use leftover bird bones to make lures and hooks. You can use feathers for insulation, too.

Drinking Water

Your biggest challenge on the open seas will be finding enough drinking water. Never drink seawater in its natural state. It will make you very sick in no time.

If you're fortunate, you'll have a solar still in your survival kit. Otherwise, wait for a rainstorm. When it comes, drink as much water as you can, and collect as much in small containers as you can. At night and in fog, you can use a sponge or cloth to collect dew from the outer surfaces of your boat. Don't worry if small amounts of seawater get into your fresh water supply; it will still be safe to drink.

There is no substitute for fresh water. Some substances like fish juices have only limited value in staving off dehydration, because they contain proteins. These, in turn, require more water to digest.

Don't ever drink urine. It contains waste material that will build up in your body and only require more water to eliminate.

Travel on the Open Seas

If you're ever adrift in a lifeboat, it will probably be after going down in an airplane or abandoning a sinking ship. Rescuers will know you're missing and will know where your vessel went down. Make it easier for them to find you by putting down an anchor if you can. If you have an emergency radar reflector in your survival kit, use it.

But if no help has arrived after a day or so, it may be best to strike out for the closest land available. If you have certain minimal equipment—a nautical chart, a compass, a protractor, a timepiece, a Nautical Almanac, perhaps even a handheld GPS receiver— and some knowledge of navigation, you may be able to set a course for land. Remember that it is better to "go with the flow." Even with a sail, you won't be able to make much progress against the prevailing current and wind. Better to aim for landfall at some distance downwind and down-current than for land that is closer but upwind.

Once you set your course, you can estimate your travel time. And once you know how long you'll be at sea, you can figure out how to make your supplies last. Keep checking your position. Make midcourse corrections as needed. When you start seeing more seabirds, land debris, and high cumulus clouds, you'll know you're getting close to land.

Stay calm, don't exert yourself, and take heart in the fact that you'll eventually reach either land or a major shipping lane.

Conclusion

The survival skills that help people make it back safely after experiences such as getting lost in the wilderness or having to bail out of an airplane rest on some basic concepts: Size up your situation. Use all your senses, and avoid undue haste. Remember where you are. Vanquish fear. Improvise. Value life. Act only after thinking. Live by your wits.

Most people never come close to a survival situation as we usually think of it. But learning the concepts behind these survival skills will give you more confidence and help you be more alert and aware of your environment wherever you are.

Review Questions

1 Why is it important to vanquish fear and panic in a survival situation?

2 What is improvising, and why is it important to a survivor?

3 What are a survivor's two goals?

4 What are some ways a survivor can signal for help?

The 24-Hour Clock

The military does not measure time by the standard 12-hour clock, which uses numbers from 1 to 12 followed by AM or PM to distinguish day from evening. Instead it uses the 24-hour clock, which utilizes the numbers 0000 through 2300. The number 0000 is used to designate midnight; 1200 designates noon. All other hours are designated by a separate number. Because each hour is designated by a unique number, there is no need to follow it by AM or PM. The table below illustrates the relationship of military to regular time.

Midnight	0000	Noon	1200
1:00 AM	0100	1:00 PM	1300
2:00 AM	0200	2:00 PM	1400
3:00 AM	0300	3:00 PM	1500
4:00 AM	0400	4:00 PM	1600
5:00 AM	0500	5:00 PM	1700
6:00 AM	0600	6:00 PM	1800
7:00 AM	0700	7:00 PM	1900
8:00 AM	0800	8:00 PM	2000
9:00 AM	0900	9:00 PM	2100
10:00 AM	1000	10:00 PM	2200
11:00 AM	1100	11:00 PM	2300

Minutes are measured the same way in military time as they are in regular time, using the numbers 01 to 59. The difference is that military time does not use colons between the hour and minutes, so 1:15 PM regular time would be written 1315 military time. If time is written to the second, there is a colon between the minutes and the seconds, so 47 seconds after 1:15 PM would be written 1315:47.

The Declaration of Independence

IN CONGRESS, July 4, 1776.

The unanimous Declaration of the thirteen united States of America,

When in the Course of human events, it becomes necessary for one people to dissolve the political bands which have connected them with another, and to assume among the powers of the earth, the separate and equal station to which the Laws of Nature and of Nature's God entitle them, a decent respect to the opinions of mankind requires that they should declare the causes which impel them to the separation.

We hold these truths to be self-evident, that all men are created equal, that they are endowed by their Creator with certain unalienable Rights, that among these are Life, Liberty and the pursuit of Happiness.—That to secure these rights, Governments are instituted among Men, deriving their just powers from the consent of the governed,— That whenever any Form of Government becomes destructive of these ends, it is the Right of the People to alter or to abolish it, and to institute new Government, laying its foundation on such principles and organizing its powers in such form, as to them shall seem most likely to effect their Safety and Happiness. Prudence, indeed, will dictate that Governments long established should not be changed for light and transient causes; and accordingly all experience hath shewn, that mankind are more disposed to suffer, while evils are sufferable, than to right themselves by abolishing the forms to which they are accustomed. But when a long train of abuses and usurpations, pursuing invariably the same Object evinces a design to reduce them under absolute Despotism, it is their right, it is their duty, to throw off such Government, and to provide new Guards for their future security.—Such has been the patient sufferance of these Colonies; and such is now the necessity which constrains them to alter their former Systems of Government. The history of the present King of Great Britain is a history of repeated injuries and usurpations, all having in direct object the establishment of an absolute Tyranny over these States. To prove this, let Facts be submitted to a candid world.

He has refused his Assent to Laws, the most wholesome and necessary for the public good.

He has forbidden his Governors to pass Laws of immediate and pressing importance, unless suspended in their operation till his Assent should be obtained; and when so suspended, he has utterly neglected to attend to them.

He has refused to pass other Laws for the accommodation of large districts of people, unless those people would relinquish the right of Representation in the Legislature, a right inestimable to them and formidable to tyrants only.

He has called together legislative bodies at places unusual, uncomfortable, and distant from the depository of their public Records, for the sole purpose of fatiguing them into compliance with his measures.

He has dissolved Representative Houses repeatedly, for opposing with manly firmness his invasions on the rights of the people.

He has refused for a long time, after such dissolutions, to cause others to be elected; whereby the Legislative powers, incapable of Annihilation, have returned to the People at large for their exercise; the State remaining in the mean time exposed to all the dangers of invasion from without, and convulsions within.

He has endeavoured to prevent the population of these States; for that purpose obstructing the Laws for Naturalization of Foreigners; refusing to pass others to encourage their migrations hither, and raising the conditions of new Appropriations of Lands.

He has obstructed the Administration of Justice, by refusing his Assent to Laws for establishing Judiciary powers.

He has made Judges dependent on his Will alone, for the tenure of their offices, and the amount and payment of their salaries.

He has erected a multitude of New Offices, and sent hither swarms of Officers to harrass our people, and eat out their substance.

He has kept among us, in times of peace, Standing Armies without the Consent of our legislatures.

He has affected to render the Military independent of and superior to the Civil power.

He has combined with others to subject us to a jurisdiction foreign to our constitution, and unacknowledged by our laws; giving his Assent to their Acts of pretended Legislation:

For Quartering large bodies of armed troops among us:

For protecting them, by a mock Trial, from punishment for any Murders which they should commit on the Inhabitants of these States:

For cutting off our Trade with all parts of the world:

For imposing Taxes on us without our Consent:

For depriving us in many cases, of the benefits of Trial by Jury:

For transporting us beyond Seas to be tried for pretended offences:

For abolishing the free System of English Laws in a neighbouring Province, establishing therein an Arbitrary government, and enlarging its Boundaries so as to render it at once an example and fit instrument for introducing the same absolute rule into these Colonies:

For taking away our Charters, abolishing our most valuable Laws, and altering fundamentally the Forms of our Governments:

For suspending our own Legislatures, and declaring themselves invested with power to legislate for us in all cases whatsoever.

He has abdicated Government here, by declaring us out of his Protection and waging War against us.

He has plundered our seas, ravaged our Coasts, burnt our towns, and destroyed the lives of our people.

He is at this time transporting large Armies of foreign Mercenaries to compleat the works of death, desolation and tyranny, already begun with circumstances of Cruelty & perfidy scarcely paralleled in the most barbarous ages, and totally unworthy the Head of a civilized nation.

He has constrained our fellow Citizens taken Captive on the high Seas to bear Arms against their Country, to become the executioners of their friends and Brethren, or to fall themselves by their Hands.

He has excited domestic insurrections amongst us, and has endeavoured to bring on the inhabitants of our frontiers, the merciless Indian Savages, whose known rule of warfare, is an undistinguished destruction of all ages, sexes and conditions.

In every stage of these Oppressions We have Petitioned for Redress in the most humble terms: Our repeated Petitions have been answered only by repeated injury. A Prince whose character is thus marked by every act which may define a Tyrant, is unfit to be the ruler of a free people.

Nor have We been wanting in attentions to our British brethren. We have warned them from time to time of attempts by their legislature to extend an unwarrantable jurisdiction over us. We have reminded them of the circumstances of our emigration and settlement here. We have appealed to their native justice and magnanimity, and we have conjured them by the ties of our common kindred to disavow these usurpations, which, would inevitably interrupt our connections and correspondence. They too have been deaf to the voice of justice and of consanguinity. We must, therefore, acquiesce in the necessity, which denounces our Separation, and hold them, as we hold the rest of mankind, Enemies in War, in Peace Friends.

We, therefore, the Representatives of the United States of America, in General Congress, Assembled, appealing to the Supreme Judge of the world for the rectitude of our intentions, do, in the Name, and by Authority of the good People of these Colonies, solemnly publish and declare, That these United Colonies are, and of Right ought to be Free and Independent States; that they are Absolved from all Allegiance to the British Crown, and that all political connection between them and the State of Great Britain, is and ought to be totally dissolved; and that as Free and Independent States, they have full Power to levy War, conclude Peace, contract Alliances, establish Commerce, and to do all other Acts and Things which Independent States may of right do. And for the support of this Declaration, with a firm reliance on the protection of divine Providence, we mutually pledge to each other our Lives, our Fortunes and our sacred Honor.

The Constitution of the United States

We the People of the United States, in Order to form a more perfect Union, establish Justice, insure domestic Tranquility, provide for the common defense, promote the general Welfare, and secure the Blessings of Liberty to ourselves and our Posterity, do ordain and establish this Constitution for the United States of America.

Article. I.

Section. 1.

All legislative Powers herein granted shall be vested in a Congress of the United States, which shall consist of a Senate and House of Representatives.

Section. 2.

The House of Representatives shall be composed of Members chosen every second Year by the People of the several States, and the Electors in each State shall have the Qualifications requisite for Electors of the most numerous Branch of the State Legislature.

No Person shall be a Representative who shall not have attained to the Age of twenty five Years, and been seven Years a Citizen of the United States, and who shall not, when elected, be an Inhabitant of that State in which he shall be chosen.

The actual Enumeration shall be made within three Years after the first Meeting of the Congress of the United States, and within every subsequent Term of ten Years, in such Manner as they shall by Law direct. The Number of Representatives shall not exceed one for every thirty Thousand, but each State shall have at Least one Representative; and until such enumeration shall be made, the State of New Hampshire shall be entitled to chuse three, Massachusetts eight, Rhode-Island and Providence Plantations one, Connecticut five, New-York six, New Jersey four, Pennsylvania eight, Delaware one, Maryland six, Virginia ten, North Carolina five, South Carolina five, and Georgia three.

When vacancies happen in the Representation from any State, the Executive Authority thereof shall issue Writs of Election to fill such Vacancies.

The House of Representatives shall chuse their Speaker and other Officers; and shall have the sole Power of Impeachment.

Section. 3.

The Senate of the United States shall be composed of two Senators from each State thereof for six Years; and each Senator shall have one Vote.

Immediately after they shall be assembled in Consequence of the first Election, they shall be divided as equally as may be into three Classes. The Seats of the Senators of the first Class shall be vacated at the Expiration of the second Year, of the second Class at the Expiration of the fourth Year, and of the third Class at the Expiration of the sixth Year, so that one third may be chosen every second.

No Person shall be a Senator who shall not have attained to the Age of thirty Years, and been nine Years a Citizen of the United States, and who shall not, when elected, be an Inhabitant of that State for which he shall be chosen.

The Vice President of the United States shall be President of the Senate, but shall have no Vote, unless they be equally divided.

The Senate shall chuse their other Officers, and also a President pro tempore, in the Absence of the Vice President, or when he shall exercise the Office of President of the United States.

The Senate shall have the sole Power to try all Impeachments. When sitting for that Purpose, they shall be on Oath or Affirmation. When the President of the United States is tried, the Chief Justice shall preside: And no Person shall be convicted without the Concurrence of two thirds of the Members present.

Judgment in Cases of Impeachment shall not extend further than to removal from Office, and disqualification to hold and enjoy any Office of honor, Trust or Profit under the United States: but the Party convicted shall nevertheless be liable and subject to Indictment, Trial, Judgment and Punishment, according to Law.

Section. 4.

The Times, Places and Manner of holding Elections for Senators and Representatives, shall be prescribed in each State by the Legislature thereof; but the Congress may at any time by Law make or alter such Regulations, except as to the Places of chusing Senators.

The Congress shall assemble at least once in every Year, and such Meeting shall be on the first Monday in December, unless they shall by Law appoint a different Day.

Section. 5.

Each House shall be the Judge of the Elections, Returns and Qualifications of its own Members, and a Majority of each shall constitute a Quorum to do Business; but a smaller Number may adjourn from day to day, and may be authorized to compel the Attendance of absent Members, in such Manner, and under such Penalties as each House may provide.

Each House may determine the Rules of its Proceedings, punish its Members for disorderly Behaviour, and, with the Concurrence of two thirds, expel a Member.

Each House shall keep a Journal of its Proceedings, and from time to time publish the same, excepting such Parts as may in their Judgment require Secrecy; and the Yeas and Nays of the Members of either House on any question shall, at the Desire of one fifth of those Present, be entered on the Journal.

Neither House, during the Session of Congress, shall, without the Consent of the other, adjourn for more than three days, nor to any other Place than that in which the two Houses shall be sitting.

Section. 6.

The Senators and Representatives shall receive a Compensation for their Services, to be ascertained by Law, and paid out of the Treasury of the United States. They shall in all Cases, except Treason, Felony and Breach of the Peace, be privileged from Arrest during their Attendance at the Session of their respective Houses, and in going to and returning from the same; and for any Speech or Debate in either House, they shall not be questioned in any other Place.

No Senator or Representative shall, during the Time for which he was elected, be appointed to any civil Office under the Authority of the United States, which shall have been created, or the Emoluments whereof shall have been encreased during such time; and no Person holding any Office under the United States, shall be a Member of either House during his Continuance in Office.

Section. 7.

All Bills for raising Revenue shall originate in the House of Representatives; but the Senate may propose or concur with Amendments as on other Bills.

Every Bill which shall have passed the House of Representatives and the Senate, shall, before it become a Law, be presented to the President of the United States: If he approve he shall sign it, but if not he shall return it, with his Objections to that House in which it shall have originated, who shall enter the Objections at large on their Journal, and proceed to reconsider it. If after such Reconsideration two thirds of that House shall agree to pass the Bill, it shall be sent, together with the Objections, to the other House, by which it shall likewise be reconsidered, and if approved by two thirds of that House, it shall become a Law. But in all such Cases the Votes of both Houses shall be determined by yeas and Nays, and the Names of the Persons voting for and against the Bill shall be entered on the Journal of each House respectively. If any Bill shall not be returned by the President within ten Days (Sundays excepted) after it shall have been presented to him, the Same shall be a Law, in like Manner as if he had signed it, unless the Congress by their Adjournment prevent its Return, in which Case it shall not be a Law.

Every Order, Resolution, or Vote to which the Concurrence of the Senate and House of Representatives may be necessary (except on a question of Adjournment) shall be presented to the President of the United States; and before the Same shall take Effect, shall be approved by him, or being disapproved by him, shall be repassed by two thirds of the Senate and House of Representatives, according to the Rules and Limitations prescribed in the Case of a Bill.

Section. 8.

The Congress shall have Power To lay and collect Taxes, Duties, Imposts and Excises, to pay the Debts and provide for the common Defence and general Welfare of the United States; but all Duties, Imposts and Excises shall be uniform throughout the United States;

To borrow Money on the credit of the United States;

To regulate Commerce with foreign Nations, and among the several States, and with the Indian Tribes;

To establish an uniform Rule of Naturalization, and uniform Laws on the subject of Bankruptcies throughout the United States;

To coin Money, regulate the Value thereof, and of foreign Coin, and fix the Standard of Weights and Measures;

To provide for the Punishment of counterfeiting the Securities and current Coin of the United States;

To establish Post Offices and post Roads;

To promote the Progress of Science and useful Arts, by securing for limited Times to Authors and Inventors the exclusive Right to their respective Writings and Discoveries;

To constitute Tribunals inferior to the supreme Court;

To define and punish Piracies and Felonies committed on the high Seas, and Offences against the Law of Nations;

To declare War, grant Letters of Marque and Reprisal, and make Rules concerning Captures on Land and Water;

To raise and support Armies, but no Appropriation of Money to that Use shall be for a longer Term than two Years;

To provide and maintain a Navy;

To make Rules for the Government and Regulation of the land and naval Forces;

To provide for calling forth the Militia to execute the Laws of the Union, suppress Insurrections and repel Invasions;

To provide for organizing, arming, and disciplining, the Militia, and for governing such Part of them as may be employed in the Service of the United States, reserving to the States respectively, the Appointment of the Officers, and the Authority of training the Militia according to the discipline prescribed by Congress;

To exercise exclusive Legislation in all Cases whatsoever, over such District (not exceeding ten Miles square) as may, by Cession of particular States, and the Acceptance of Congress, become the Seat of the Government of the United States, and to exercise like Authority over all Places purchased by the Consent of the Legislature of the State in which the Same shall be, for the Erection of Forts, Magazines, Arsenals, dock-Yards, and other needful Buildings;—And

To make all Laws which shall be necessary and proper for carrying into Execution the foregoing Powers, and all other Powers vested by this Constitution in the Government of the United States, or in any Department or Officer thereof.

Section. 9.

The Migration or Importation of such Persons as any of the States now existing shall think proper to admit, shall not be prohibited by the Congress prior to the Year one thousand eight hundred and eight, but a Tax or duty may be imposed on such Importation, not exceeding ten dollars for each Person.

The Privilege of the Writ of Habeas Corpus shall not be suspended, unless when in Cases of Rebellion or Invasion the public Safety may require it.

No Bill of Attainder or ex post facto Law shall be passed.

No Capitation, or other direct, Tax shall be laid.

No Tax or Duty shall be laid on Articles exported from any State.

No Preference shall be given by any Regulation of Commerce or Revenue to the Ports of one State over those of another; nor shall Vessels bound to, or from, one State, be obliged to enter, clear, or pay Duties in another.

No Money shall be drawn from the Treasury, but in Consequence of Appropriations made by Law; and a regular Statement and Account of the Receipts and Expenditures of all public Money shall be published from time to time.

No Title of Nobility shall be granted by the United States: And no Person holding any Office of Profit or Trust under them, shall, without the Consent of the Congress, accept of any present, Emolument, Office, or Title, of any kind whatever, from any King, Prince, or foreign State.

Section. 10.

No State shall enter into any Treaty, Alliance, or Confederation; grant Letters of Marque and Reprisal; coin Money; emit Bills of Credit; make any Thing but gold and silver Coin a Tender in Payment of Debts; pass any Bill of Attainder, ex post facto Law, or Law impairing the Obligation of Contracts, or grant any Title of Nobility.

No State shall, without the Consent of the Congress, lay any Imposts or Duties on Imports or Exports, except what may be absolutely necessary for executing it's inspection Laws: and the net Produce of all Duties and Imposts, laid by any State on Imports or Exports, shall be for the Use of the Treasury of the United States; and all such Laws shall be subject to the Revision and Controul of the Congress.

No State shall, without the Consent of Congress, lay any Duty of Tonnage, keep Troops, or Ships of War in time of Peace, enter into any Agreement or Compact with another State, or with a foreign Power, or engage in War, unless actually invaded, or in such imminent Danger as will not admit of delay.

Article. II.

Section. 1.

The executive Power shall be vested in a President of the United States of America. He shall hold his Office during the Term of four Years, and, together with the Vice President, chosen for the same Term, be elected, as follows:

Each State shall appoint, in such Manner as the Legislature thereof may direct, a Number of Electors, equal to the whole Number of Senators and Representatives to which the State may be entitled in the Congress: but no Senator or Representative, or Person holding an Office of Trust or Profit under the United States, shall be appointed an Elector.

The Congress may determine the Time of chusing the Electors, and the Day on which they shall give their Votes; which Day shall be the same throughout the United States.

No Person except a natural born Citizen, or a Citizen of the United States, at the time of the Adoption of this Constitution, shall be eligible to the Office of President; neither shall any Person be eligible to that Office who shall not have attained to the Age of thirty five Years, and been fourteen Years a Resident within the United States.

In Case of the Removal of the President from Office, or of his Death, Resignation, or Inability to discharge the Powers and Duties of the said Office, the Same shall devolve on the Vice President, and the Congress may by Law provide for the Case of Removal, Death, Resignation or Inability, both of the President and Vice President, declaring what Officer shall then act as President, and such Officer shall act accordingly, until the Disability be removed, or a President shall be elected.

The President shall, at stated Times, receive for his Services, a Compensation, which shall neither be increased nor diminished during the Period for which he shall have been elected, and he shall not receive within that Period any other Emolument from the United States, or any of them.

Before he enter on the Execution of his Office, he shall take the following Oath or Affirmation:—"I do solemnly swear (or affirm) that I will faithfully execute the Office of President of the United States, and will to the best of my Ability, preserve, protect and defend the Constitution of the United States."

Section. 2.

The President shall be Commander in Chief of the Army and Navy of the United States, and of the Militia of the several States, when called into the actual Service of the United States; he may require the Opinion, in writing, of the principal Officer in each of the executive Departments, upon any Subject relating to the Duties of their respective Offices, and he shall have Power to grant Reprieves and Pardons for Offences against the United States, except in Cases of Impeachment.

He shall have Power, by and with the Advice and Consent of the Senate, to make Treaties, provided two thirds of the Senators present concur; and he shall nominate, and by and with the Advice and Consent of the Senate, shall appoint Ambassadors, other public Ministers and Consuls, Judges of the supreme Court, and all other Officers of the United States, whose Appointments are not herein otherwise provided for, and which shall be established by Law: but the Congress may by Law vest the Appointment of such inferior Officers, as they think proper, in the President alone, in the Courts of Law, or in the Heads of Departments.

The President shall have Power to fill up all Vacancies that may happen during the Recess of the Senate, by granting Commissions which shall expire at the End of their next Session.

Section. 3.

He shall from time to time give to the Congress Information of the State of the Union, and recommend to their Consideration such Measures as he shall judge necessary and expedient; he may, on extraordinary Occasions, convene both Houses, or either of them, and in Case of Disagreement between them, with Respect to the Time of Adjournment, he may adjourn them to such Time as he shall think proper; he shall receive Ambassadors and other public Ministers; he shall take Care that the Laws be faithfully executed, and shall Commission all the Officers of the United States.

Section. 4.

The President, Vice President and all civil Officers of the United States, shall be removed from Office on Impeachment for, and Conviction of, Treason, Bribery, or other high Crimes and Misdemeanors.

Article. III.

Section. 1.

The judicial Power of the United States shall be vested in one supreme Court, and in such inferior Courts as the Congress may from time to time ordain and establish. The Judges, both of the supreme and inferior Courts, shall hold their Offices during good Behaviour, and shall, at stated Times, receive for their Services a Compensation, which shall not be diminished during their Continuance in Office.

Section. 2.

The judicial Power shall extend to all Cases, in Law and Equity, arising under this Constitution, the Laws of the United States, and Treaties made, or which shall be made, under their Authority;—to all Cases affecting Ambassadors, other public Ministers and Consuls;—to all Cases of admiralty and maritime Jurisdiction;—to Controversies to which the United States shall be a Party;—to Controversies between two or more States;—between Citizens of different States;—between Citizens of the same State claiming Lands under Grants of different States, and between a State, or the Citizens thereof, and foreign States, Citizens or Subjects.

In all Cases affecting Ambassadors, other public Ministers and Consuls, and those in which a State shall be Party, the supreme Court shall have original Jurisdiction. In all the other Cases before mentioned, the supreme Court shall have appellate Jurisdiction, both as to Law and Fact, with such Exceptions, and under such Regulations as the Congress shall make.

The Trial of all Crimes, except in Cases of Impeachment, shall be by Jury; and such Trial shall be held in the State where the said Crimes shall have been committed; but when not committed within any State, the Trial shall be at such Place or Places as the Congress may by Law have directed.

Section. 3.

Treason against the United States, shall consist only in levying War against them, or in adhering to their Enemies, giving them Aid and Comfort. No Person shall be convicted of Treason unless on the Testimony of two Witnesses to the same overt Act, or on Confession in open Court.

The Congress shall have Power to declare the Punishment of Treason, but no Attainder of Treason shall work Corruption of Blood, or Forfeiture except during the Life of the Person attainted.

Article. IV.

Section. 1.

Full Faith and Credit shall be given in each State to the public Acts, Records, and judicial Proceedings of every other State. And the Congress may by general Laws prescribe the Manner in which such Acts, Records and Proceedings shall be proved, and the Effect thereof.

Section. 2.

The Citizens of each State shall be entitled to all Privileges and Immunities of Citizens in the several States.

A Person charged in any State with Treason, Felony, or other Crime, who shall flee from Justice, and be found in another State, shall on Demand of the executive Authority of the State from which he fled, be delivered up, to be removed to the State having Jurisdiction of the Crime.

Section. 3.

New States may be admitted by the Congress into this Union; but no new State shall be formed or erected within the Jurisdiction of any other State; nor any State be formed by the Junction of two or more States, or Parts of States, without the Consent of the Legislatures of the States concerned as well as of the Congress.

The Congress shall have Power to dispose of and make all needful Rules and Regulations respecting the Territory or other Property belonging to the United States; and nothing in this Constitution shall be so construed as to Prejudice any Claims of the United States, or of any particular State.

Section. 4.

The United States shall guarantee to every State in this Union a Republican Form of Government, and shall protect each of them against Invasion; and on Application of the Legislature, or of the Executive (when the Legislature cannot be convened), against domestic Violence.

Article. V.

The Congress, whenever two thirds of both Houses shall deem it necessary, shall propose Amendments to this Constitution, or, on the Application of the Legislatures of two thirds of the several States, shall call a Convention for proposing Amendments, which, in either Case, shall be valid to all Intents and Purposes, as Part of this Constitution, when ratified by the Legislatures of three fourths of the several States, or by Conventions in three fourths thereof, as the one or the other Mode of Ratification may be proposed by the Congress; Provided that no Amendment which may be made prior to the Year One thousand eight hundred and eight shall in any Manner affect the first and fourth Clauses in the Ninth Section of the first Article; and that no State, without its Consent, shall be deprived of its equal Suffrage in the Senate.

Article. VI.

All Debts contracted and Engagements entered into, before the Adoption of this Constitution, shall be as valid against the United States under this Constitution, as under the Confederation.

This Constitution, and the Laws of the United States which shall be made in Pursuance thereof; and all Treaties made, or which shall be made, under the Authority of the United States, shall be the supreme Law of the Land; and the Judges in every State shall be bound thereby, any Thing in the Constitution or Laws of any State to the Contrary notwithstanding.

The Senators and Representatives before mentioned, and the Members of the several State Legislatures, and all executive and judicial Officers, both of the United States and of the several States, shall be bound by Oath or Affirmation, to support this Constitution; but no religious Test shall ever be required as a Qualification to any Office or public Trust under the United States.

Article. VII.

The Ratification of the Conventions of nine States, shall be sufficient for the Establishment of this Constitution between the States so ratifying the Same.

The Word, "the," being interlined between the seventh and eighth Lines of the first Page, the Word "Thirty" being partly written on an Erazure in the fifteenth Line of the first Page, The Words "is tried" being interlined between the thirty second and thirty third Lines of the first Page and the Word "the" being interlined between the forty third and forty fourth Lines of the second Page.

Attest William Jackson Secretary

Done in Convention by the Unanimous Consent of the States present the Seventeenth Day of September in the Year of our Lord one thousand seven hundred and Eighty seven and of the Independence of the United States of America the Twelfth In witness whereof We have hereunto subscribed our Names,

G. Washington
President and deputy from Virginia

Delaware
Geo: Read
Gunning Bedford jun
John Dickinson
Richard Bassett
Jaco: Broom

Maryland
James McHenry
Dan of St Thos. Jenifer
Danl. Carroll

Virginia
John Blair
James Madison Jr.

North Carolina
Wm. Blount
Richd. Dobbs Spaight
Hu Williamson

South Carolina
J. Rutledge
Charles Cotesworth Pinckney
Charles Pinckney
Pierce Butler

Georgia
William Few
Abr Baldwin

New Hampshire
John Langdon
Nicholas Gilman

Massachusetts
Nathaniel Gorham
Rufus King

Connecticut
Wm. Saml. Johnson
Roger Sherman

New York
Alexander Hamilton

New Jersey
Wil: Livingston
David Brearley
Wm. Paterson
Jona: Dayton

Pennsylvania
B. Franklin
Thomas Mifflin
Robt. Morris
Geo. Clymer
Thos. FitzSimons
Jared Ingersoll
James Wilson
Gouv Morris

McREL Standards

Correlated to McREL Standards for Life Skills, Behavioral Studies, Language Arts, History, Health, Civics, and Science

McREL STANDARDS	UNIT I: NJROTC AND YOUR FUTURE
LIFE SKILLS	
Life Work	
LW 1.Makes effective use of basic tools	Practicing the Navy Core Values, 8 The Naval Science Curriculum, 10–13 Career Direction—Getting to Know Yourself, 24–25 Developing Good Study Habits, 32–38
LW 2. Uses various information sources, including those of a technical nature, to accomplish specific tasks	Developing Good Study Habits, 32–38
LW 3. Manages money effectively	Career Choices, 25–26
LW 4. Studies or pursues specific job interests	The NJROTC's Mission, Goals, and Policies, 4–6 Careers Versus Jobs, 23–24 Career Direction—Getting to Know Yourself, 24–25 Career Choices, 25–26 The US Navy as a Career Option, 27–31 Developing Good Study Habits, 32–38

LW 5. Makes general preparation for entering the work force	The NJROTC's Mission, Goals, and Policies, 4–6 Careers Versus Jobs, 23–24 Career Direction—Getting to Know Yourself, 24–25 Career Choices, 25–26 The US Navy as a Career Option, 27–31 Developing Good Study Habits, 32–38
LW 6. Makes effective use of basic life skills	Practicing the Navy Core Values, 8 Naval Skills, 13 Career Direction—Getting to Know Yourself, 24–25
LW 7. Displays reliability and a basic work ethic	Career Choices, 25–26 Developing Good Study Habits, 32–38
LW 8. Operates effectively within organizations	The NJROTC's Mission, Goals, and Policies, 4–6 NJROTC Unit Activities, 14–18

Self-Regulation

SR 1. Sets and manages goals	The NJROTC's Mission, Goals, and Policies, 4–6 The Naval Science Curriculum, 10–13 Military Career Assistance, 20 Careers Versus Jobs, 23–24 Career Direction—Getting to Know Yourself, 24–25 Career Choices, 25–26 The US Navy as a Career Option, 27–31 Developing Good Study Habits, 32–38
SR 2. Performs self-appraisal	Practicing the Navy Core Values, 8 Career Direction—Getting to Know Yourself, 24–25 Developing Good Study Habits, 32–38
SR 3. Considers risks	Career Direction—Getting to Know Yourself, 24–25 Career Choices, 25–26
SR 4. Demonstrates perseverance	Careers Versus Jobs, 23–24 Developing Good Study Habits, 32–38
SR 5. Maintains a healthy self-concept	Career Direction—Getting to Know Yourself, 24–25
SR 6. Restrains impulsivity	Practicing the Navy Core Values, 8

Thinking and Reasoning

TR 1. Understands and applies the basic principles of presenting an argument	Essay Tests, 36
TR 2. Understands and applies basic principles of logic and reasoning	Essay Tests, 36
TR 3. Effectively uses mental processes that are based on identifying similarities and differences	Developing Good Study Habits, 32–38

Listening and Speaking

LA 8. Uses listening and speaking strategies for different purposes	Listening and Note-Taking Skills, 36–37

Viewing

LA 9. Uses viewing skills and strategies to understand and interpret visual media	Photos, 2, 3, 4, 5, 9, 11, 12, 13, 15, 16, 20, 22, 25, 28, 30, 33, 35 Paintings, 11 Tables, 10 Graphics, 31 Developing Good Study Habits, 32–38

HISTORY

Historical Understanding

HU 2. Understands the historical perspective	History and Background of the NJROTC Program, 3–4 Maritime History, 12 Naval Knowledge, 12

HEALTH

H 4. Knows how to maintain mental and emotional health	The NJROTC's Mission, Goals, and Policies, 4–6 Physical Fitness, 15
H 10. Understands the fundamental concepts of growth and development	The NJROTC Program's Benefits, 18 What's in It for Me?, 19 Military Career Assistance, 20–21 Selecting and Charting a Good Career Path, 22 Career Direction—Getting to Know Yourself, 24 Career Choices, 25 The US Navy as a Career Option, 27–31 Developing Good Study Habits, 32–38

CIVICS

What Is Government and What Should It Do?

C 1. Understands ideas about civic life, politics, and government	The NJROTC's Mission, Goals, and Policies, 4–6 Introduction to the NJROTC Program, 11
C 3. Understands the sources, purposes, and functions of law, and the importance of the rule of law for the protection of individual rights and the common good	The NJROTC's Mission, Goals, and Policies, 4–6 Introduction to the NJROTC Program, 11

What Are the Basic Values and Principles of American Democracy?

C 10. Understands the roles of voluntarism and organized groups in American social and political life	The NJROTC's Mission, Goals, and Policies, 4–6 Community Activities, 1

What Are the Roles of the Citizen in American Democracy?

C 22. Understands how the world is organized politically into nation-states, how nation-states interact with one another, and issues surrounding U.S. foreign policy	Navy Core Values, 6
C 27. Understands how certain character traits enhance citizens' ability to fulfill personal and civic responsibilities	The NJROTC's Mission, Goals, and Policies, 4–6
C 28. Understands how participation in civic and political life can help citizens attain individual and public goals	The NJROTC's Mission, Goals, and Policies, 4–6

SCIENCE

Earth and Space Sciences

S 1. Understands atmospheric processes and the water cycle	Nautical Sciences, 12
S 2. Understands Earth's composition and structure	Nautical Sciences, 12
S 3. Understands the composition and structure of the universe and the Earth's place in it	Nautical Sciences, 12

Nature of Science

S 11. Understands the nature of scientific knowledge	Nautical Sciences, 12

Unit II — Leadership Skills

Correlated to McREL Standards for Life Skills, Behavioral Studies, Language Arts, and Health

McREL STANDARDS	UNIT II: LEADERSHIP SKILLS
LIFE SKILLS	
Life Work	
LW 1. Makes effective use of basic tools	Leadership Etiquette, 53 The Hierarchy of Human Needs, 65–67 Key Elements of Coaching and Mentoring, 70–72 Improving Group Effectiveness, 82–84 Conflict in Groups, 84–87

BEHAVIORAL STUDIES

BS 1. Understands that group and cultural influences contribute to human development, identity, and behavior

BS 2. Understands various meanings of social group, general implications of group membership, and different ways that groups function

BS 3. Understands that interactions among learning, inheritance, and physical development affect human behavior

LANGUAGE ARTS

Reading

Viewing

HEALTH

Correlated to McREL Standards for Behavioral Studies, Language Arts, History, Business Education, and Civics

McREL STANDARDS	UNIT III: CITIZENSHIP AND AMERICAN GOVERNMENT
BEHAVIORAL STUDIES	
BS 1. Understands that group and cultural influences contribute to human development, identity, and behavior	The Judeo-Christian Heritage, 109 Contemporary Influences, 109–110 "Ordinary" Citizens Defend the Capital on 9/11, 111
BS 2. Understands various meanings of social groups, general implications of group membership, and different ways that groups function	The Judeo-Christian Heritage, 109 Contemporary Influences, 109–110 "Ordinary" Citizens Defend the Capital on 9/11, 111
BS 3. Understands that interactions among learning, inheritance, and physical development affect human behavior	The Judeo-Christian Heritage, 109 Contemporary Influences, 109–110 "Ordinary" Citizens Defend the Capital on 9/11, 111
BS 4. Understands conflict, cooperation, and interdependence among individuals, groups, and institutions	The Great Compromise, 118 Other Constitutional Balancing Acts, 119 "Ordinary" Citizens Defend the Capital on 9/11, 111
LANGUAGE ARTS	
Reading	
LA 5. Uses the general skills and strategies of the reading process	Key Terms, 102, 103, 104, 107, 108, 109, 110, 113, 114, 117, 118, 120, 121, 122, 123, 124, 128, 129, 130, 135 Review Questions, 112, 127, 137
LA 7. Uses reading skills and strategies to understand and interpret a variety of informational texts	Key Terms, 102, 103, 104, 107, 108, 109, 110, 113, 114, 117, 118, 120, 121, 122, 123, 124, 128, 129, 130, 135 Review Questions, 112, 127, 137
Viewing	
LA 9. Uses viewing skills and strategies to understand and interpret visual media	Photos, 100, 101, 107, 108, 109, 110, 113, 116, 117, 118, 119, 120, 128, 129, 130, 131, 136 Tables, 136 Figures, 132, 133, 134 Graphics, 134, 135, 136

HISTORY

Historical Understanding

US History

Era 3—Revolution and the New Nation (1754–1820s)

BUSINESS EDUCATION

Management

CIVICS

What Is Government and What Should It Do?

What Are the Basic Values and Principles of American Democracy?

C 17. Understands issues concerning the relationship between state and local governments and the national government and issues pertaining to representation at all three levels of government	The Tenth Amendment: Powers Reserved to the States, 124
C 18. Understands the role and importance of law in the American constitutional system and issues regarding the judicial protection of individual rights	The Bill of Rights, 121 The First Amendment: Religious and Political Freedom, 121–122 The Second Amendment: the Right to Bear Arms, 122 The Third Amendment: Quartering of Soldiers, 122 The Fourth Amendment: Search and Seizure, 122 The Fifth Amendment: Criminal Proceedings and Due Process, 123 The Sixth Amendment: the Right to a Jury Trial, 123 The Seventh Amendment: the Right to a Civil Trial, 124 The Eighth Amendment: Punishment for Crimes, 124 The Ninth Amendment: Unenumerated Rights, 124 The Tenth Amendment: Powers Reserved to the States, 124 Other Constitutional Amendments, 125–126

What Are the Roles of the Citizen in American Democracy?

C 24. Understands the meaning of citizenship in the United States, and knows the requirements for citizenship and naturalization	The Citizen's Role—Rights and Responsibilities, 104–105 Characteristics of a Good Citizen (bulleted list), 105 The Bill of Responsibilities (list), 106
C 25. Understands issues regarding personal, political, and economic rights	The Citizen's Role—Rights and Responsibilities, 104–105 The Bill of Rights, 121 Amendments, 121–126
C 26. Understands issues regarding the proper scope and limits of rights and the relationships among personal, political, and economic rights	The Citizen's Role—Rights and Responsibilities, 104–105 Characteristics of a Good Citizen (bulleted list), 105 The Bill of Responsibilities (list), 106 The Bill of Rights, 121 Amendments, 121–126

C 27. Understands how certain character traits enhance citizens' ability to fulfill personal and civic responsibilities	Characteristics of a Good Citizen (bulleted list), 105 "Ordinary" Citizens Defend the Capital on 9/11, 111
C 28. Understands how participation in civic and political life can help citizens attain individual and public goals	Characteristics of a Good Citizen (bulleted list), 105
C 29. Understands the importance of political leadership, public service, and a knowledgeable citizenry in American constitutional democracy	The Judeo-Christian Heritage, 109 Contemporary Influences, 109–110 James Madison and Constitutional Republicanism, 110 "Ordinary" Citizens Defend the Capital on 9/11, 111

Unit IV   The US Navy

Correlated to McREL Standards for History, Language Arts, Business Education, Technology, and Civics

McREL STANDARDS	UNIT IV: THE US NAVY
HISTORY	
Historical Understanding	
HU 2. Understands the historical perspective	Background of Naval Aviation, 161–163
US History	
Era 8—The Great Depression and World War II (1929–1945)	
US 25. Understands the causes and course of World War II, the character of the war at home and abroad, and its reshaping of the US role in world affairs	Background of Naval Aviation, 161–163
Era 10—Contemporary United States (1968 to the present)	
US 31. Understands economic, social, and cultural developments in the contemporary United States	The Mission of Navy Ships, 141–142 Types of Navy Ships, 146–155 Background of Naval Aviation, 161–163 Naval Aircraft and Missions, 164–170

World History

WH 44. Understands the search for community, stability, and peace in an interdependent world	The Mission of Navy Ships, 141–142 Types of Navy Ships, 146–155 Background of Naval Aviation, 161–163 Naval Aircraft and Missions, 164–170
WH 45. Understands major global trends since World War II	The Mission of Navy Ships, 141–142 Types of Navy Ships, 146–155 Background of Naval Aviation, 161–163 Naval Aircraft and Missions, 164–170

LANGUAGE ARTS

Reading

LA 5. Uses the general skills and strategies of the reading process	Key Terms, 140, 141, 142, 145, 160, 161, 163, 167, 170, Review Questions, 159, 170
LA 7. Uses reading skills and strategies to understand and interpret a variety of informational texts	Key Terms, 140, 141, 142, 145, 160, 161, 163, 167, 170, Review Questions, 159, 170

Viewing

LA 9. Uses viewing skills and strategies to understand and interpret visual media	Photos, 139, 140, 146, 147, 148, 149, 150, 151, 152, 153, 154, 155, 157, 164, 165, 166, 167, 168, 169, 170, Figures, 162, 163 Graphics, 143, 144

BUSINESS EDUCATION

Management

BE 39. Understands various organizational structures and the advantages and disadvantages of each	Ship Terminology, 142–145 Types of Navy Ships, 146–155 Shipboard Customs and Courtesies, 156–158 Aircraft, 162 Aircraft Model Designations, 163
BE 42. Understands operations management principles and procedures	Ship Terminology, 142–145 Types of Navy Ships, 146–155 Shipboard Customs and Courtesies, 156–158 Aircraft, 162 Aircraft Model Designations, 163 Naval Aircraft and Missions, 164–170

TECHNOLOGY

CIVICS

How Does the Government Established by the Constitution Embody the Purposes, Values, and Principles of American Democracy?

Unit V   Wellness, Fitness, and First Aid

Correlated to McREL Standards for Health, Life Skills, Behavioral Studies, and Language Arts

McREL STANDARDS	UNIT V: WELLNESS, FITNESS, AND FIRST AID
HEALTH	

H 7. Knows how to maintain and promote personal health	
H 8. Knows essential concepts about the prevention and control of disease	
H 9. Understands aspects of substance use and abuse	

LIFE SKILLS

Life Work

SR 5. Maintains a healthy self-concept	The Benefits of Exercise, 178–180 Sticking with an Exercise Program, 194 Fitness Throughout Life, 197–198 More Than Healthy Rewards, 203 The Importance of a Proper Diet to Your Health, 209 Personal Hygiene, 260–262 Stress Strategies, 274–277
SR 6. Restrains impulsivity	Eating in Moderation, 210 Eating Disorders, 225–226 Step 1: Restricting Your Fat Intake, 237–238 Step 3: Food Control and Choice, 239–240 Managing Your Weight, 246–250 Learn to Reduce Stress, 263–264 Why Do People Abuse Drugs?, 284

BEHAVIORAL STUDIES

BS 3. Understands that interactions among learning, inheritance, and physical development affect human behavior	Defining Your Goals, 182 Fitness Throughout Life, 197–198 Building Health Skills, 200–202 The New American Diet—Step by Step, 225 Stress and Leadership, 278 Drug Use, Misuse, and Abuse, 283–284

LANGUAGE ARTS

Reading

LA 5. Uses the general skills and strategies of the reading process	Key Terms, 174, 180, 193, 199, 203, 205, 206, 209, 210, 212, 213, 214, 216, 224, 225, 226, 236, 259, 260, 264, 265, 269, 271, 272, 275, 282, 283, 285, 308, 309, 310, 321, 322, 326, 328, 336, 343, 345, 347, 349, 357 Review Questions, 198, 204, 223, 235, 258, 281, 307, 362
LA 7. Uses reading skills and strategies to understand and interpret a variety of informational texts	Key Terms, 174, 180, 193, 199, 203, 205, 206, 209, 210, 212, 213, 214, 216, 224, 225, 226, 236, 259, 260, 264, 265, 269, 271, 272, 275, 282, 283, 285, 308, 309, 310, 321, 322, 326, 328, 336, 343, 345, 347, 349, 357 Review Questions, 198, 204, 223, 235, 258, 281, 307, 362

Viewing

LA 9. Uses viewing skills and strategies to understand and interpret visual media	Photos, 173, 174, 175, 176, 180, 182, 184, 185, 187, 190, 194, 199, 205, 212, 214, 218, 221, 224, 229, 236, 243, 252, 254, 255, 259, 261, 263, 264, 266, 269, 270, 277, 278, 282, 284, 286, 291, 293, 295, 302, 308, 310, 311, 314, 329, 340, 346, 350, 355, 361
	Tables, Charts, and Graphs, 178, 179, 186, 188, 190, 193, 195, 207, 208, 217, 219, 220, 227, 234, 243, 245, 290, 304, 348
	Graphics, 196, 200, 201, 208, 209, 210, 228, 232, 240, 241, 248, 250, 271, 272, 275, 276, 279, 280, 288, 305, 316, 317, 318, 322, 323, 326, 327, 335, 338, 341, 344, 350, 355, 356, 357, 359

Unit VI Geography and Survival Skills

Correlated to McREL Standards for Geography, Life Skills, and Language Arts

McREL STANDARDS	UNIT VI: GEOGRAPHY AND SURVIVAL SKILLS
GEOGRAPHY	
The World in Spatial Terms	
G 1. Understands the characteristics and uses of maps, globes, and other geographic tools and technologies	The Globe: An Overview, 366–373 Introduction to Maps, 373–380 Introduction to Topographic Maps, 380–386 Grid Reference System, 387–393 Contours and Landforms, 393–403 Determining Distance, 403–409 Determining Direction, 409–417 Converting the Grid-Magnetic Angle, 418–422 Determining Location, 423–431 Orienteering, 432–442
G 2. Knows the location of places, geographic features, and patterns of the environment	The Globe: An Overview, 366–373 Introduction to Maps, 373–380 Introduction to Topographic Maps, 380–386 Grid Reference System, 387–393 Contours and Landforms, 393–403 Determining Distance, 403–409 Determining Direction, 409–417 Converting the Grid-Magnetic Angle, 418–422 Determining Location, 423–431 Orienteering, 432–442

LANGUAGE ARTS

Reading

LA 5. Uses the general skills and strategies of the reading process

Key Terms, 364, 365, 373, 385, 386, 387, 388, 393, 396, 397, 398, 399, 400, 401, 402, 403, 404, 410, 412, 419, 429, 430, 432, 438, 439, 444, 446, 449, 453, 459
Review Questions, 443, 461

LA 7. Uses reading skills and strategies to understand and interpret a variety of informational texts

Key Terms, 364, 365, 373, 385, 386, 387, 388, 393, 396, 397, 398, 399, 400, 401, 402, 403, 404, 410, 412, 419, 429, 430, 432, 438, 439, 444, 446, 449, 453, 459
Review Questions, 443, 461

Viewing

LA 9. Uses viewing skills and strategies to understand and interpret visual media

Photos, 364, 367, 368, 369, 370, 375, 376, 379, 380, 431, 444, 445, 456, 457
Tables, 384, 437, 448, 450
Graphics, 376, 384, 389, 390, 391, 392, 393, 394, 395, 396, 397, 398, 399, 400, 401, 402, 404, 405, 406, 407, 409, 410, 411, 412, 413, 414, 417, 418, 419, 420, 421, 422, 423, 424, 425, 426, 427, 428, 431, 441, 447, 451, 452, 454, 455
Maps and Globes, 366, 372, 373, 374, 375, 376, 381, 383, 386, 387, 388, 406, 416, 432, 433, 434, 435

References

Active Duty Military Personnel, 1940–2006. Information Please Database. Pearson Education, Inc. Retrieved 21 August 2007 from http://www.infoplease.com/ipa/A0004598.html

Cadet Field Manual. (2005). US Navy Junior Reserve Officers Training Corps. Pensacola, FL: Naval Education and Training Command.

Citizenship in American History and Government: Introduction. (2005). Boston, MA: Pearson Custom Publishing.

Defense Industry Daily. (1 March 2007). *CEC Combined Fleet Defense Program: FY 2006*. Retrieved 26 August 2007 from http://www.defenseindustrydaily.com/cec-combined-fleet-defense-program-fy-2006-01869/

Ellenson, A. (1982). *Human Relations*. 2nd ed. Upper Saddle River, NJ: Prentice-Hall, Inc.

Eugene B. Ely. (n.d.). First Flight Society. Retrieved 28 August 2007 from http://www.firstflight.org/shrine/eugene_ely.cfm

Hersey, P., Blanchard, K. H., & Johnson, D. E. (2001). *Management of Organizational Behavior: Leading Human Resources*. 8th ed. Upper Saddle River, NJ: Prentice-Hall, Inc.

Johnson, J. L. (1997). Remarks at the US Naval Academy, 31 July 1997. Retrieved 29 June 2007 from http://www.navy.mil/navydata/people/flags/johnson_j/speeches/usna0731.txt

Kline, J. A. (2003). *Listening Effectively: Achieving High Standards in Communication*. Upper Saddle River, NJ: Prentice Hall.

Lavin, L. M. (n.d.). *Naval Junior Reserve Officers Training Corps: Introduction*. Pensacola, FL: Naval Education and Training Command.

Leadership Education II: Communication, Awareness, and Leadership. (2006). Boston, MA: Pearson Custom Publishing.

Leadership Education III: Life Skills and Career Opportunities. (2006). Boston, MA: Pearson Custom Publishing.

The National Security Council. (n.d.). Washington, DC: The White House. Retrieved 16 August 2007 from http://www.whitehouse.gov/nsc

Navy Organization: A Look at the US Navy—Operating Forces. (n.d.). US Navy. Retrieved 16 August 2007 from http://www.navy.mil/navydata/organization/orgopfor.asp

Roberson, P., ed. (1998). *Leadership Education II: Intercommunication Skills.* Maxwell AFB, AL: Air Force Reserve Officer Training Corps.

Ships of the US Navy. (n.d.). US Navy. Retrieved 21 August 2007 from http://www.navy.mil/navydata/our_ships.asp

United States Navy Fact File. (n.d.). US Navy. Retrieved 5 September 2007 from http://www.navy.mil/navydata/fact.asp

Glossary

ability—the mental or physical power to do certain things; the knowledge, experience, and skill a team member or a team brings to a task

abrasion—a part of the skin that has been lightly torn or scraped

abuse—improper or excessive use or treatment

acids—chemical compounds with a sour taste that have a pH value of less than 7, react with metals to form hydrogen gas, and have the capability to eat away or dissolve metals and other materials

addiction—physical or psychological dependence on a substance, habit, or behavior that can lead to health, social, or economic problems; dependence on a drug

advancement—promotion, as in rank

aerobic—allowing sufficient amounts of oxygen to be delivered to the muscles

affiliation need—a desire to be and feel a part of a group

aiming off—an orienteering method by which the navigator aims to one side of a destination point instead of directly at it; this produces certainty that after the distance is covered the target point can only be in one possible direction

alkalis—any base, such as soda or potash, that is soluble in water, combines with fats to form soap, neutralizes acids, and forms salts with them

allergic reaction—a physical reaction, often marked by sneezing, breathing difficulties, itching, rash, or swelling, that some people have when they come in contact with certain substances

amendment—a formal alteration to a document such as a constitution or a law

amenorrhea—an abnormal absence or suppression of the menstrual period

amino acids—the basic units of proteins, produced by living cells or obtained as an essential component of a diet

ampule—a small, sealed glass container that holds one dose of a solution, usually a medicine, to be administered by injection

amputation—the removal of an external part of the body, most often a limb or part of it, when it has been severely crushed or following the death of the extremity due to impaired blood circulation

anaerobic—working in the absence of adequate amounts of oxygen being delivered to the muscles

anorexia nervosa—an aversion to food syndrome; an eating disorder characterized by an extreme (prolonged) loss of appetite and very decreased food intake

antivenin—an antitoxin used to counteract venom

anxiety—eager, often agitated desire; one's anxiety to make a good impression, for example

apathy—a lack of feeling or emotion; a lack of interest or concern

appointment—the designation of someone to an honor or a position, such as a place at the Naval Academy

appropriate—to decide to spend money for a specific use

aptitude—an inherent ability or talent

arteries—blood vessels that carry blood away from the heart to all parts of the body

attack point—an easy-to-find landscape feature shown on the map from which the final approach to a control may be made

attitude—a person's feelings or state of mind

automated external defibrillator (AED)—a device used to treat a patient with cardiac arrest whose heart is beating irregularly

autonomy—the quality or state of being self-governing

avulsion—the tearing away of a body part accidentally or surgically

azimuth—a horizontal angle usually measured clockwise in degrees from a north base line (direction)

back azimuth—the opposite direction of an azimuth obtained by adding 180 degrees to or subtracting 180 degrees from an azimuth

bar scale—a ruler used to measure actual ground distances by converting distances on a map

basal metabolic rate (BMR)—the number of calories burned at complete rest; measurement of it indicates an individual's general metabolism or state of health

bases—chemical compounds with a slippery or soapy feel that react with acids to form salt, have a pH value above 7, and are used as cleaning materials

bench mark—a surveyor's mark made on rocks or other permanent objects to indicate known elevations

bivouac—a temporary camp or shelter

bulimia—a disease (or eating disorder) with symptoms of binging and purging or overeating and vomiting

buoyancy—a tendency or ability to stay afloat in water

calisthenics—light gymnastic exercise designed to promote good health by developing strength and grace

calories—the amount of energy it takes to raise the temperature of one kilogram of water one degree Celsius; a measurement of energy

carbohydrates—one of the various neutral organic compounds composed of carbon, hydrogen, and oxygen (including starches and sugars) produced by plants and used to provide energy necessary for growth and other functions cardiac arrest—the sudden stoppage of the heart

cardiopulmonary resuscitation (CPR)—an emergency method to keep blood and oxygen flowing through a person whose heart and breathing have stopped

cardiorespiratory—of or relating to the heart and the respiratory system

career—the general course or progression of one's working life

caustic—capable of destroying or eating away by chemical action; corrosive

center of mass—the point closest to the middle of an object

certified—officially approved

chain of command—the system by which authority passes down through the military ranks, with each level accountable to a superior

chlorine—a gaseous greenish-yellow element used as a bleach and disinfectant in water purification

citizen—a member of a political community

citizenship—the status of a citizen with its attendant duties, rights, and privileges

civic virtue—the dedication of citizens to the common good, even at the cost of their individual interests

clammy—damp, soft, sticky, and unusually cool

classical republicanism—a theory that holds that the best kind of government is one that promotes the common welfare instead of the interests of one class of citizens

closed (simple) fracture—a fracture in which the broken bone does not push through the skin's surface

color guard—the ceremonial escort for the flag

combustible—capable of igniting and burning

commitment—a state of being bound, emotionally or intellectually, to a course of action, or to a person or persons

complex carbohydrates—a carbohydrate that is formed by the body or by plants after the conversion of simple carbohydrates, which supplies the body with long-term energy

compresses—folded cloths or pads applied to press on a body part to stop bleeding or cool a burn

concave—curving inward, as the inside of a bowl

concentric—having a common center

confidence—faith or belief that a person will act in a right, proper, or effective way; self-assurance

conifer—any tree or shrub that has cones and needles

consent—approval for what is to be done or proposed by another

constituted authority—power to influence or command thought, opinion, or behavior, exercised by one lawfully elected or appointed

constitutional convention—a special meeting held to draw up a new constitution

control point—a trapezoid-shaped marker (usually orange, red, or white) used to mark features on an orienteering course, usually with clipper or control punch attached to mark a control card as proof of arrival

controlled substance—a substance whose manufacture, possession, or sale is controlled by the law

convex—curved outward, as the outside of a circle or sphere

courage—mental or moral strength to venture, persevere, and withstand danger, fear, or difficulty

cramming—preparing for an exam at the last minute

curl-ups—one of the four events in the PFT consisting of a sit-up movement from a lying position up to the point where your elbows touch your thighs

curriculum—a course of study

cut—a man-made feature resulting from the removal of high ground, usually to form a level area for roads or railroad tracks

declination—an angular difference between true north and either magnetic or grid north

defense mechanisms—behaviors a person uses to deal with anxiety, stress, or pressure

deficient—having too little of something, such as a nutrient in the body

degree—a unit of latitude or longitude, equal to $1/360$ of the globe

dehydration—the condition that results when fluids are lost from the body and are not replaced; symptoms can include thirst, weakness, exhaustion, and confusion, and may result in death

dependency—addiction to a substance

depression—1. *psychol.* psychiatric disorder characterized by an inability to concentrate; insomnia; loss of appetite; anhedonia; feelings of extreme sadness, guilt, helplessness, and hopelessness; and thoughts of death; 2. *geog.* a sunken or low place in the ground

deterrence—prevention of war by instilling fear in potential enemies

diabetes—a disease in which the body is unable to use sugars properly

dilated—having been widened; expanded

discrimination—unfair treatment based on prejudice against a certain group

disinfect—to destroy harmful germs; to purify

dislocation—the separation of a bone from its joint

displacement—the weight of the volume of water that a ship displaces when afloat; in other words, the weight of a ship by itself

distilled—heated and condensed to purify, form a new substance, or concentrate

diuretics—food, medication, etc., that promotes or tends to increase the excretion of urine

diversity—variation or difference

divine right—a right or responsibility given by a divine being or deity that is therefore beyond question by humanity

draw—a less developed stream course than a valley

dressing—ointment and bandages applied to a wound

drone—an unmanned aircraft or ship guided by remote control

drugs—chemicals that cause a change in a person's body or behavior

dysentery—any of several intestinal disorders usually caused by infection and characterized by stomach pain and diarrhea with passage of mucous and blood

electrolyte—substance that, when dissociated into ions in solution or fused, becomes electrically conducting; obtained from minerals in the diet

empathetic—having the ability to understand; being aware of, and sensitive to, the feelings, thoughts, and experiences of another

enumerate—to list, or to specify individually

episodic—occurring, appearing, or changing at irregular intervals; incidental

esophageal—of or relating to the esophagus (a muscular tube through which food passes from the mouth to the stomach)

essential fat—fat that the body needs in certain amounts to maintain bodily functions

established religion—a religion supported by the state through tax money

evaluate—to determine if an act, process, or method has been attained; to assess; to determine the significance by careful appraisal and study

exploit—employ to the greatest possible advantage

fat soluble vitamin—a vitamin that is absorbed through the intestinal tract with the help of fats and is stored in the body

fats—nutrients made up of fatty acids that are insoluble in water and provide energy to the body

ferment—to produce a chemical change in a carbohydrate material, resulting in alcohol

fiber—coarse food made mostly of carbohydrates, such as bran or broccoli, that serves to stimulate and aid the movement of food through the digestive tract

field-expedient—adapting to a particular situation by using available materials and/or resources

fight-or-flight response—an involuntary reaction to an immediate danger or threat, which prepares a person physically either to respond to the danger or run away

fill—a man-made feature resulting from raising a low area, usually to form a level area for roads or railroad tracks

first aid—the immediate care given to a victim of injury or sudden illness before professional medical help arrives

flexed-arm hang—an alternative event for the pull-up in the Presidential Physical Fitness Test

followership—displaying the attitudes, behaviors, and actions that help a leader succeed at leading

frostbite—an injury caused to body tissue by frost or extreme cold

galvanized—coated with zinc

gateway—a term attached to alcohol and tobacco due to the fact that their use often leads to further drug abuse

gender stereotyping—the practice of thinking about people in limited ways on the basis of whether they are male or female

generalized—generally prevalent

goal—an external aim, or end, to which one directs one's effort

Good Samaritan Law—a law enacted in most states that protects people from lawsuits if medical complications arise after they have administered first aid correctly

grid azimuth—the angle measured between grid north and a straight line plotted between two points on a map

grid convergence—the horizontal angle at a point between true north and grid north

grid coordinate—a set of letters and numbers specifying the location of a point to the desired position within a 100,000 meter square

grid lines—lines that are regularly spaced at 1,000 or 10,000 meter intervals that make up the grid on a map

grid north—the direction of north that is established by using the vertical grid lines on a map

grid square—the intersecting of north–south and east–west grid lines at 90-degree angles to form a square

grid zone—one of the 60 north–south divisions of the earth's surface between 84 degrees north latitude and 80 degrees south latitude, each 6 degrees wide

Grid-Magnetic Angle (G-M Angle)—angular difference in direction between grid north and magnetic north; it is measured east or west from grid north

hachure—a short, broken line used for showing relief on a map

hallucinogen—a drug that causes hallucinations

heat cramps—a condition that is marked by the sudden development of cramps in the skeletal muscles and that results from prolonged work in high temperatures accompanied by profuse perspiration with loss of sodium chloride from the body

heat exhaustion—a condition that occurs when a person is exposed to excessive heat over a period of time, caused by the loss of water and salt from the body through excessive perspiration

heatstroke—a life-threatening condition caused by prolonged exposure to high heat

Heimlich maneuver—an upward push to the abdomen given to clear the airway of a person with a complete airway obstruction; procedure used to expel an object lodged in the airway of a choking victim

hemorrhage—heavy, uncontrollable bleeding

hierarchy—a ranking or series of steps that follows a specific order; for example, largest to smallest, oldest to newest, most important to least important

honor—a keen sense of ethical conduct

humanitarian—referring to help given to individuals in need, such as assistance to disaster victims, without regard to military or political concerns

hygiene—practices or conditions that aid in good health; the science that deals with maintenance of good health and the prevention of infection and disease

hypothermia—too little body heat with abnormally low internal body temperature

ignite—to start to burn or catch fire

ignorance—lack of knowledge, education, or awareness

improvise—to make do with what you have on hand or make it up as you go along

incentive—something that incites or has a tendency to incite to determination or action incision—a wound that is made by cutting into the body

indictment—a written statement charging someone with a crime or other offense, drawn up by a prosecuting attorney, and found and presented by a grand jury

inhalants—medications or chemicals that are inhaled

insight—the ability to grasp a hidden or inward truth

instill—to introduce by gradual persistent efforts

insulate—to use materials to protect or isolate from the elements of weather

interdiction—blocking, intercepting, or preventing the passage of something

interest—a subject or an activity that captures a person's attention, curiosity, or concern

intersection—the method of locating an unknown point by determining where the azimuths from at least two known points meet (intersect)

intoxicated—drunk; affected by alcohol to the point that physical and mental control are significantly impaired

iodine—a nonmetallic element having important medical uses

isokinetic—building muscle strength using special machinery to provide the resistance

isometric—building muscle strength using resistance without joint movement

isotonic—building muscle strength using resistance with joint movement

job—the work someone does to make a living

Joint Chiefs of Staff—a committee made up of the senior officer from each branch of the armed services; it gives the president and the National Security Council professional military advice

Judeo-Christian—relating to beliefs and practices that have their historical roots in Judaism and Christianity

justice—the fair and equal treatment of everyone under the law

kindling—material larger than tinder used to ignite logs and other fuel in a fire

knot—one nautical mile per hour, or about 1.15 statute (land) miles per hour

laceration—a wound that is torn and ragged

latitude—the angular distance north or south of the earth's equator, measured in degrees along a meridian, as on a map or globe

law—a rule of conduct or procedure established by custom, agreement, or authority

legend—an explanatory description on a chart, map, or other illustration

levy—to impose or collect (a tax)

lice—small, wingless, parasitic insects that live on warm-blooded animals, especially in hair, and suck the animal's blood

ligament—a fibrous band of tissue that holds bones together at a joint

logistics—the aspect of military or naval operations that deals with the procurement, distribution, maintenance, and replacement of materiel and personnel

longitude—lines that run from the North Pole to the South Pole and are equal in length on a map or globe

magnetic azimuth—a direction that is expressed as the angular difference between magnetic north and a line of direction

magnetic north—the direction to the north magnetic pole, as indicated by the north-seeking needle of a magnetic instrument

man of war—a general term for an armed naval vessel

manic-depressive illness—bipolar disorder

marginal information—instructions placed around the outer edge of a map

maritime—relating to the sea

marksmanship—skill in shooting at a target

maturity—the state of being fully grown or developed

mean sea level—the position of the level of the surface of the sea midway between high and low water

meditation—a contemplative discourse, usually on a religious or philosophical subject

mentor—an individual with advanced experience and knowledge who is committed to giving support and career advice to a less experienced person

meridian—an imaginary circle on the earth's surface passing through the North and South Poles; a line or parallel of longitude

metabolism—the chemical process by which the body produces energy and maintains vital functions

meticulous—extremely careful and precise, especially with regard to detail

midshipman—a student at the Naval Academy or in NROTC studying to be an officer in the Naval Service

migraine—a severe, recurring headache, usually affecting only one side of the head, characterized by sharp pain and often accompanied by nausea, vomiting, and visual disturbances

mil—a unit of angular measurement equal to $\frac{1}{6400}$ of a complete revolution

minerals—natural chemical elements of the earth used by the body to supply necessary nutrition

misuse—the incorrect or improper use of a substance

mnemonic—(nee-MAH-nik) a word, abbreviation, or rhyme that helps you remember something

modification—an alteration or adjustment, as of an aircraft or other vehicle

monounsaturated fats—oil or fat that is liquid at room temperature and is low in hydrogen, which can lower the level of blood cholesterol

motivation—the inner force that drives people to act

mottled—marked with irregular spots or splotches of different colors or shades of color

nacelle—a separate, streamlined enclosure on an aircraft for sheltering the crew or cargo or housing an engine

narcotic—a drug used medically to relieve pain, produce sleep, and dull the senses

National Security Council—the president's committee for considering national security and foreign policy matters with advisers and cabinet officials; the president, vice president, Secretary of State, Secretary of the Treasury, and Secretary of Defense are members

nautical mile—a unit of measurement that is approximately 6,080 feet—which is one minute of latitude; it is slightly longer than a statute mile

navigational aid—a general term for lighthouses, buoys, beacons, lanterns, and radio signals; the Coast Guard maintains these to help mariners of all kinds find their way on the water

neutralize—to counteract the activity or effect of; to make chemically neutral

nicotine—the drug in tobacco that may act as a stimulant and cause addiction

nomination—the naming, or submitting the name, of someone for an appointment; to the Naval Academy, for instance

nutrients—substances found in food that allow the body to function properly

obesity—overweight to the point of injuring health

occupation—an activity that serves as one's regular source of livelihood

open (compound) fracture—a fracture in which the broken end of a bone pierces the skin

operating forces—those forces whose primary mission involves combat, plus their integral supporting elements

orderliness—neatness, freedom from disorder

orient—to align or position oneself (or a map) in relationship to one's surroundings

orienteering—a competitive form of land navigation in which each participant uses a map and compass to navigate between checkpoints

osteoporosis—a condition characterized by a calcium deficiency in the bone mass; the body pulls calcium from the bones, causing them to lose their density and possibly leading to fractures

parallel—lines that do not intersect

personal dignity—the internal strength that helps people feel connected, worthwhile, and valued

personal hygiene—an individual's practice of taking care of him- or herself in order to maintain good health

personality—what an individual is inside and what he or she shows to others; it includes actions, opinions, beliefs, biases, desires, and ambitions

perspective—an individual's way of seeing the world

plankton—small organisms, including algae, that float or drift in great numbers in fresh or salt water, especially at or near the surface

polar coordinates—a method of locating or plotting an unknown position from a known point by giving a direction and distance along that direction line

polyunsaturated fats—an oil or fatty acid containing more than one double or triple bond and is, therefore, cholesterol defensive

pontoon—a floating structure, such as the float on a seaplane

port security—measures taken to protect a harbor or other marine facility against crime, espionage, or sabotage

posterity—future generations

potential—what an individual is capable of doing or becoming

preamble—an introduction to a document such as a constitution, explaining its purpose

precision—exactness

prejudice—an unfair opinion or judgment of a person or a group of people

Presidential Physical Fitness Award (PPFA)—an award earned by achieving a standard of 85 percent or higher on the Presidential Physical Fitness Test

pressure bandage—a snug bandage used to control bleeding

pressure point—a point on the body where a major artery lies near the skin surface and passes over a bone

prime meridian—the line of longitude that passes through Greenwich, England, designated as zero degrees longitude, and from which longitude east and west are measured

private morality—the principles of virtue as expressed in Judeo-Christian teachings

proactive—taking the initiative and assuming part of the responsibility to make things happen

profession—an occupation or career, especially one such as the law, medicine, or engineering, that requires considerable training and specialized study

projection—the act of falsely attributing to others one's own unacceptable feelings, impulses, or thoughts

protégé—a less experienced person who benefits from a mentor's guidance and advice

protein—nutrients that are made of amino acids and that maintain body tissues and supply energy to the body

protocol—a special form of ceremony and etiquette

providence—the care, guardianship, and control exercised by a deity

pull-ups—an exercise that consists of pulling the body up from a dead-weight hanging position on a bar to having the chin clear of the bar

purified—free from undesirable elements or impurities; cleaned

quartering—providing living quarters for soldiers

rabies—a viral disease affecting the central nervous system of mammals that is transmitted by a bite from an infected animal; it can result in paralysis and death if left untreated

ratify—to formally confirm or approve, as of a treaty or a constitutional amendment

rationalization—concealing the true motivation for one's thoughts, actions, or feelings by offering reassuring, but incorrect, explanations

readiness—how prepared a team member is to carry out a particular task or tasks

Referenced Daily Intake (RDI)—standards developed by the US government for the regulation of vitamin and mineral requirements

relationship behavior—a leader's engagement in supportive, two-way communication with his or her team members

relief—the shape of land formations on the earth's surface

religious respect—honor for the right of other people to hold their own personal religious beliefs

representative fraction (RF)—the relationship of distance measured on a map to the corresponding distance on the ground; it is usually written as a fraction, such as if a map sheet is 1:50,000, RF is $\frac{1}{50,000}$

rescue breathing—the act of forcing air into and out of the lungs of a person by another person

resection—the method of locating your unknown position by determining where the back azimuths from two or three well-defined locations on a map meet

respect—the attention, regard, and consideration given to people and their rights, property, and ideas

ridge—a sloping line of high ground

ridgeline—a line of high ground, usually with changes in elevation along its top

rotor—an assembly of rotating horizontal airfoils (wings), such as on a helicopter

saddle—a low point between two areas of higher ground

sanitation—the promotion of hygiene and prevention of disease by working to keep a clean and healthy environment

saturated fats—a fat that does not melt at room temperature and can raise the blood cholesterol level

seamanship—skill in sailing, navigating, or managing a boat or ship

self-actualization—the process of becoming what you are capable of becoming

separation of powers—the division of the government into executive, legislative, and judicial branches

shore establishment—the land-based facilities that support the fleet

shuttle run—one of the five events of the Presidential Physical Fitness Test that consists of a run back and forth between two points 30 feet apart

simple carbohydrates—a sugar that is found in food and the body in its simple state, which supplies the body with short-term energy

sinkhole—a natural depression in a land surface communicating with a subterranean passage, generally occurring in limestone regions and formed by solution or by collapse of a cavern roof

situational leadership—a leadership model based on the concept that there is no single best way to influence and lead people

solvents—liquid substances capable of dissolving or eliminating something unwanted

spirit of association—the fondness American citizens have for banding together in organizations to address problems of common interest

splint—to support and immobilize a body part with a stiff material

sprain—an injury caused by twisting a ligament or tendon around a joint

spur—a sloping line of high ground projecting out from the side of a ridge

stability—steadiness or order in the international or political realm

statute mile—a unit of measurement that is approximately 5,280 feet

steering mark—an easily identifiable feature in the landscape not shown on the map; used by the orienteer to follow a bearing

stereotype—an idea or a concept that is based on oversimplified assumptions or opinions, rather than on facts

stimulant—an ingredient found in beverages, food, or drugs that speeds up the activity of the mind or body; a drug that speeds up the activities of the central nervous system, the heart, and other organs; for example, caffeine in tea or chocolate

storage fat—fat that the body keeps in reserve which can lead to over-fat problems or obesity

strain—an injury caused when a muscle or tendon is overstretched

strategic—referring to a country's long-range weapons or plans; the "big picture"

strategy—a country's top-level political and military plan

stroke—a reduction of blood flow to a part of the brain

subcutaneous—beneath the top layer of skin

substance—something, such as a drug or alcohol, deemed harmful and usually subject to legal restrictions

superficial—not serious; on the surface; shallow

superimpose—to place over or on top of something else

surveillance—close observation of the enemy

systemic—affecting the body in general; acting throughout the body after absorption or ingestion

tactical—referring to short-range weapons, or to assets used in support of ground forces

task behavior—the leader's involvement in defining the duties and responsibilities of an individual or a group

temperament—a person's typical way of thinking, behaving, or reacting

terrain—a region or tract of land; the character (or topography) of a tract of land

tetanus (lockjaw)—an acute infectious disease caused by the poison of a certain bacterium that enters the body through a wound, resulting in muscle contractions, rigidity, and death; it is preventable by immunization

tinder—material for starting a fire

tolerance—respect for people's differences and values

tone—a degree of tension or firmness, as of muscle

topographic map—a map that shows relief and the position of natural and man-made features

trauma—a behavioral state resulting from mental or emotional stress or physical injury that has a lasting effect on the mind; a physical wound or injury

true north—a line from any position on the earth's surface to the geographic North Pole; symbolized by a line with a star at the apex

turbid—cloudy, as with mud or sediment

unalienable—incapable of being taken away or transferred to another

Universal Transverse Mercator Grid System—a grid system that has been designed to cover the part of the world between latitude 84 degrees north and latitude 80 degrees south, and, as its name implies, is imposed on the transverse Mercator projection

values—principles, standards, or qualities considered worthwhile or desirable vanquish—to conquer

veins—blood vessels that carry blood from all parts of the body to the heart

venom—a poison produced by animals such as snakes and spiders that is transmitted by a bite or sting

ventilation—circulation of air; a system or means of providing fresh air

veto—the right (of a president) to reject a piece of legislation

visualization—to make visible

vitamins—nutrients that occur naturally in plant and animal tissue and are required for proper function of the body

v-sit reach—one of the five events of the Presidential Physical Fitness Test that consists of stretching a number of inches past an established baseline

VTOL—vertical takeoff or landing; refers to either the capability or to the aircraft that has it

water soluble vitamin—a vitamin that is dissolved in the water of tissues

willingness—the degree to which a team member or a team shows confidence, commitment, and motivation to accomplish a task

Index

Presidential Physical Fitness Award, 203
Pressure bandage, 322
Pressure point, 322
Prevention of cold injuries, 354
Prevention of electrical burns, 335–336
Prevention of exposure to poisonous
    plants, 361
Prevention of heat burns, 333
Prevention of heat injuries, 347
Prevention of insect bites and
    stings, 360
Prevention of snakebites, 358
Price, of food, 257
Primary factors of the leadership
    situation, 54
Primary training, 30
Prime meridian, defined, 372
Private morality, 109
Proactive, defined, 47
Profession, 23. *See also* Career
Projection, as defense mechanism, 86, 97
Projection of power ashore, 142
Prominent features on maps, 375
Proper diet, 209
Protégé, 70–72
Protein, 209, 215–216, 242
Protocol, defined, 16
Protractor method, 415–417, 429
Providence, defined, 107
Prowler electronic aircraft, 164–165
Psychological benefits of exercise, 180
Psychological effects of stress, 272
Psychological factors to injury, 349
Pull-ups, 203
Purified water, 264

Q

Quarterdeck, in ship terminology, 145
Quartering, of soldiers, 122

R

Rabies, 358
Ratify, defined, 120
Rationalization, as defense mechanism, 86, 97
Readiness, of followers, 43
Reasons for prejudice, 78–79
Receiving line, 16
Reconnaissance, 162, 164
Reducing weight safely, 248
Referenced Daily Intake (RDI), 216
Reflective listening, 37
Regulating your body, 216
Relationship behavior, 50
Relationship with the Marine Corps, 134
Relationships, 75–87
Relaxation techniques, 276

Relay orienteering, 436
Relief, in maps, 375, 393–394.
    See also Contour lines
Religion, 108–109
Religious respect, 80
Remember the Titans, 83
Replenishment at sea, 155
Representative fraction, 403
Repression, as defense mechanism, 97
Republicanism, classical, 108
Rescue breathing, 317–318
Rescue ships, 155
Resection, 426–428
Reserve, Naval, 132
Respect, 76–77
Responsibility, 59
Responsibilities as citizens, 104–107
Restoring breathing, 317–318
Restricting fat intake, 237–238
Retreating, as method of handling conflict, 86
Rewards system, 69
RICE, 328
Ridge, as terrain feature, 398
Ridgeline, as terrain feature, 396
Right angle push-ups, 202–203
Rights, 104, 109.
    See also Bill of Rights
Road maps, 375–379
Role of government, 107–110
Roman Republic, 108
Rotary-wing aircraft, 162, 169–170
Rotor, defined, 170
Route orienteering, 433
Route selection, 437
RQ-2A Pioneer, 168
Rules of exercise, 202
Rules of the road, 13

S

S-3B Viking, 166
Saddle, as terrain feature, 397
Safe workout, 190–192
Salutes, 156
Salvage ships, 155
Sanitation, 260–262, 264–265
SAT, 27
Saturated fats, 214
S-B3, 163
Score orienteering, 435
Scoring, in orienteering, 442
Sea control, 141
Sea Dragon rotary-wing aircraft, 169
Sea power, 12
Sea Ranger training helicopter, 170
SEALS, 132
Search and rescue, 135
Seawolf-class submarines, 150